14.99

RISING IN TH

The Regeneration o

RISING IN THE EAST?

The Regeneration of East London

Edited by

Tim Butler and Michael Rustin

Lawrence & Wishart
LONDON

Lawrence & Wishart Limited
99a Wallis Road
London E9 5LN

First published 1996 by Lawrence & Wishart

ISBN 0 85315 844 4

British Library Cataloguing in Publication Data.
A catalogue record for this book is available from the British Library.

Cover design by Jan Brown Designs
Photoset in North Wales by
Derek Doyle & Associates, Mold, Clwyd.
Printed and bound in Great Britain by
Redwood Books, Trowbridge.

Contents

CONTENTS

Culture and Space

Preface

This collection is the outcome of work currently being undertaken by members of staff at the University of East London, mainly in the Faculty of Social Sciences.

This work is in the best traditions of the University – and of the Polytechnic of East London before it – in bringing together rigorous academic research and policy-oriented analysis. It marks our commitment to the study and development of the East London area to which we belong. The University, in association with Queen Mary and Westfield College and London City Guildhall University, is committed to developing a new Campus on the site of the old Royal Docks, which has now received sufficient funding to ensure that it becomes a reality. The Faculty of Social Sciences is currently setting up a Centre for East London Studies and has plans to continue the momentum which, hopefully, this book has started with a series of publications, conferences and courses at graduate and undergraduate level in order to further our understanding of the culture, economy and history of the area. We want to see this understanding lead to an improvement in the quality of life for those working and living in East London and the Thames Gateway area. We believe that there is now a unique window of opportunity to halt and turn around the deprivation which has marked the area since its development in the mid-nineteenth century. Our aim is to work for that regeneration in partnership with local, national and European agencies.

All the authors of the individual chapters that follow work at UEL, apart from David Albury who is now a Fellow of the Office of Public Management. A version of Andrew Blake's chapter 'The Echoing Corridor' appeared in the first edition of *Soundings* and we thank the editors for agreeing to allow us to publish it here. The editors would like to thank Prue Chamberlayne for her invaluable contribution to the conception of this book, and Ruth Borthwick for bringing it to publication.

Tim Butler
Michael Rustin

Dagenham
December 1995

Perspectives on East London

Introduction

Michael Rustin

East London is changing. This area, whose traditional working-class essence is still represented each week in *EastEnders*, is now measured by the volume of public and private investment taking place there, in what is the largest urban development zone in the United Kingdom. Government has defined 'the East Thames Gateway' (formerly the East Thames Corridor) as a major site for regional urban regeneration. East London's population is now one of the most ethnically diverse in Britain. It is also becoming significantly, though still in the minority, more 'middle-class', by criteria of occupation, education, and property-ownership. Its industrial base has been shifting, as the financial sector and communications industries have moved east from the City into the Isle of Dogs. The downside of these changes is the close-down of former economic assets, like the London Docks, a loss of population to the outer south-east region, and the emergence of high levels of long-term unemployment and economic inactivity.

The purpose of this book, which presents initial reports of a number of research programmes currently being undertaken at the University of East London, is to explore the meaning of these changes. Our aim is to see if it is possible to construct, from the social changes and interventions now taking place in East London, a vision of regeneration of this deprived region which could serve the interests of all of its people.

Some History

London has always been an uneven city, with its wealth, prosperity, and more salubrious districts concentrated in the west, and its poverty, deprivation, and environmental pollution located in large measure to the east. The boundary line marking the beginning of the east still lies more or less where it always did, at Aldgate. On one side, lie populous, industrial, rather run down and cosmopolitan neighbourhoods, which mostly do not aim to impress with appearances. On the other side, as one enters the City of London, are a variety of gleaming high-tech and postmodern office blocks, part of a vigorous renovation of London's financial district. Enclaves of expensive development have been spreading eastwards, but in stark contrast, very often, to the run-down municipal housing nearby.

In this book, what we mean by East London is chiefly the six London boroughs of Hackney, Tower Hamlets, Newham, Barking and Dagenham, Redbridge and Havering. This boundary is artificial, as neither the inner city nor the suburbs confine themselves neatly within these political boundaries. Nevertheless, East London, or 'the East End', as it used often to be called, is a distinctive region. It has had, over two centuries, a concentration of the poor, of newcomers and immigrants, often from overseas, and of polluting industries which were unwelcome in more privileged districts. It has been widely regarded as a source of social problems and dangers, and has attracted its reformers and missionaries because of that reputation. And it has its particular subcultures of surviving, resistance, and making-out, for example the 'ducking and diving' way of life described in Dick Hobbs's vivid book.[1]

Explanations of London's tilted social geography are not hard to find. The most basic is the prevailing wind, which made it most desirable to live on the westward side of the accumulated smoke and pollution of an early industrial city. Another is the flow of the Thames, which became more polluted downstream, or eastwards, and whose docks, with their bustle of trading and industrial activity, were located east of London Bridge, in the Upper Pool to the west of the Tower and in the Lower Pool to the east. There was no river crossing downstream of this, and the land was flatter and marshier too. As Daniel Defoe put it in 1724, referring to south Essex:

> This side of the county is rather rich in land, than in inhabitants, occasioned chiefly by the unhealthiness of the air; for these low marsh

> grounds, which, with all the south-side of the county, have been saved out of the River Thames, and out of the sea, where the river is wide enough to be call'd so, begin here, or rather begin at West-Ham, by Stratford, and continue to extend themselves. From hence eastward, growing wider and wider, till we come beyond Tilbury, when the flat country lyes six, seven, or eight miles broad, and is justly said to be both unhealthy, and unpleasant.[2]

Once the royal palaces, the Parliament and the trading houses of the City were in place, the pattern of unbalanced development was set, as it was, in not dissimilar ways in Paris. Such spatial patterns, once established, become self-sustaining, since new activities locate themselves in proximity to those to which they have most affinity. In the case of the City of London, close proximity was an advantage in maintaining trading networks which depended on face-to-face contact. With regard to residential accommodation, areas once laid out in spacious or architecturally impressive ways establish site-values which exclude other users. Central shopping districts likewise benefit from the concentration of consumers of similar incomes and tastes, and rental values reflect these levels of affluence. It takes a major change in some significant circumstance or other to alter the balance of advantage and disadvantage between different zones of a city.

Nevertheless, East London has already seen one major change in this century, and may be now experiencing a second one. The first such change was the impact of industrialism and popular democracy on urban life. The disorganised, exploited region of urban poverty investigated by Charles Booth in 1902[3] and described in Gareth Stedman Jones's historical study *Outcast London*,[4] was to a degree transformed in the period from the 1930s to the 1960s into an area of rising living standards and relative economic security. Modern industrial labour, initially in the gas, dock and railway industries, and subsequently in many forms of manufacturing from chemicals to cars, gave a measure of security and stability, and also a power of collective organisation, to the working class of East London, which a casualised and divided labour force had not possessed. (The implications of these differences are discussed in John Marriott's chapter on East London Labourism.) This led to the working class acquiring some political power, as part of a movement among whose heroic moments were the Bryant and May matchgirls' strike in 1888, and when reaction asserted itself in the 1930s, Lansbury's 'Poplarism' and the resistance on the streets to Mosley's Blackshirts in 'The Battle of Cable Street' in 1936. This popular advance led to a kind of municipal social democracy, in which the Labour-controlled London County Council, and the local boroughs, with the support of national government, were able significantly to improve the quality of popular life. The bombing of the East End in the Second World War brought a reparative response in post-war reconstruction. Decent quality housing, health services, and at least basic education came within the reach of nearly all, in the post-war period, with near-full employment also bringing rising living standards and a measure of economic security. Barking and Dagenham, with its still-large Ford Motor plant, its huge Becontree Estate, and its spacious if rather featureless public parks, remains the archetype of this social democratic compact of private manufacturing and public infrastructure.

On a national scale, this has been described as the social formation of 'Fordism',[5] in which the functional requirements of mass manufacture (pioneered by the Ford Motor Company of Detroit and Dagenham) for mass markets gave rise to a 'regime of accumulation' characterised by rising living standards, industrial discipline, and a State-supported infrastructure of regulative social services intended to give stability to both labour and consumer markets. The effect of this system on East London was to change it from a zone predominantly of overcrowding, poverty and social disorganisation, into one of ordered and respectable working-class life. As Booth's study of urban poverty was the epitaph of the earlier epoch, so *Family and Kinship in East London*[6] and other publications of the Institute of Community Studies in Bethnal Green provided the classic descriptions of the later period. Whilst these changes did not much alter the positions of East and West London in the hierarchy of relative well-being, since living standards were improving in all areas they did remove much absolute deprivation.

In the past twenty years, a second major process of change has been taking place in East London. 'Fordism', as the embodiment of a truce between working class and capital, with the 'welfare state' and the 'mixed economy' as its compromise outcomes, broke down in severe conflicts in the 1970s, and was then comprehensively destroyed by the Thatcher governments. At the same time, an economy based earlier on trade with the Empire (the names of the East India and West India Docks, and of East London streets like Mafeking and Ladysmith commemorate this history) shifted its focus. As international restrictions on flows of capital, labour and goods were lifted, with global reductions of tariff barriers, and increased European integration, whole sectors of British manufacturing industry collapsed, or were relocated abroad. The East London economy which had *always* been integrated into a global system (via the London Docks, in particular) now found itself being affected by global 'restructuring' in new ways.

Some of these effects have been mainly negative for the region. High technology manufacturing and information-based industries have grown more strongly on the western side of London, in the M4 Corridor, and on green field sites in the outer south-east region, though manufacturing has survived better in East London than in inner London as a whole. But the growth of the financial sector has brought investment to East London through the Docklands development and has brought high-income 'gentrifiers' to Hackney and Tower Hamlets. Economic integration of the United Kingdom with Europe is also bringing strong pressures for development – signified by the concept of East London as a 'gateway' for traffic to and from the Continent.

Theorists of 'globalisation' have described the ways that the international division of labour advantages and disadvantages different kinds of city. Capital cities have always enjoyed certain relative benefits, as a consequence of their concentration of political power, luxury consumption, and heritage resources. London is, like Paris, a prominent example of the pre-eminence of a capital city, and some of East London's long-standing trades and industries (for example, clothing) derive their market advantage from this status. 'Global cities'[7] achieve another kind of comparative advantage, according to contemporary theorists, through their concentration of 'command and control' functions, of which the financial sector, various other producer services and the communications industries are the most prominent examples in London. A third overlapping category which is central to these discussions, and which has an obvious application to London, though somewhat less so to East London, is the 'Post-Industrial City', dominated, it is argued, by services and consumption.[8]

An academic debate is in progress about whether or not these 'high-level' economic functions in 'global cities' have as their obverse a growing underclass of people condemned to menial service occupations or to long-term unemployment.[9] There may be locational advantages for command and control functions in global cities, and for the infrastructures to support these and their associated forms of consumption (including tourism), but, in an open international economy, there may be no such advantages in locating many forms of manufacturing in centres which have generally high costs of labour, land and congestion.

These changes can be seen to be impacting powerfully on East London, in de-industrialisation and in the rise of the service sector of the economy, especially financial services, to a dominant economic position. The largest and most visible sign of this transition has been the closure of the London Docks, the inner docks on the Isle of Dogs, the Surrey Docks across the river, and the Royals downstream. As these have closed, so many of the industries of ship-repairing, warehousing, and raw material processing which surrounded them have been shut down or relocated too. Only a few of these former port-related industries survive. One example is the Tate and Lyle sugar refinery, next to the former Royal Docks, destination for some of the last remaining seagoing ships which still sail this far upstream, beneath the planes taking off and landing at London City Airport.

Literally taking the place of docks and their associated industrial activities has been the rise, in the Isle of Dogs, of a new mini-city of modernist and postmodernist office blocks, in an astonishingly rapid time scale – the body responsible for this, the London Docklands Development Corporation, was established only in 1981.[10] This office complex on the Isle of Dogs employs thousands of professional and white-collar workers, nearly all commuting in from outside the area, but it provides work for very few of the manual workers who were the mainstay of the docks and their associated industries' labour force. In Wapping and the districts closer to Tower Bridge, warehouses and wharfs have been converted into professional offices, studios, and apartments. All over docklands, new housing, in bright postmodern legoland colours, has been constructed to house the middle- and upper-income employees expected to work in the new service industries.

Generally, East London has done less well than West London in attracting the technologically-advanced and science-based industries of the 'post-Fordist' type. What it has seen, in the former Docklands areas closest to the City, is the development of communications industries (the national press has largely transferred to Docklands from Fleet Street) and of the financial sector. In East London there is now a very diverse economy, with traditional mass manufacturing, sweatshops and outworking (especially in the clothing trade), financial and professional services, and a large sector still employed in the utilities and in the welfare sector. And, as I have said, a significant population is in a marginal relationship to any labour market. Different segments of the population – men and women, whites and ethnic minorities, those with more and less formal education, manual and non-manual workers – are differently distributed between these sectors, although data on the precise distributions are difficult to come by. It is, however, clear that ethnic minority and unskilled white working people are disproportionately excluded from the labour market.

How can we explain the effects of these large changes, often summarised in the term 'restructuring', on East London in particular? How has at least part of East London, formerly the preferred location only of sweated, polluting, or land- and water-greedy industries, and of the working class who laboured in them, now become an attractive location for banks, newspapers, and corporate head offices? What implications will this have for the future of the region? How have locational disadvantages which in the past led to a concentration of activities that no-one wanted anywhere else, now turned into a demand for comprehensive regional regeneration, and to the construction of the highest building in Europe, at 1 Canada Square, Canary Wharf?

Much can still be explained by natural geographical resources and their changing uses and meanings. Peter Willmott and Michael Young once explained the historical distribution of activities in London by comparative topographical advantage.[11] Low-lying land, which was formerly less healthy and liable to flooding, in London forms the rough shape of a cross, and it is here that docks, industry, main road and rail routes were concentrated. East London had the largest area of low-lying land, and thus of working-class settlement and of 'undesirable' industrial activities.

It is on the higher ground in the segments between the arms of this cross (and in the exceptionally favoured central districts) that richer people have always lived. 'All the old villages established on relatively high ground in such places as Highgate, Hampstead, Harrow on the Hill, Campden Hill, Richmond Hill, Kingston Hill, Sydenham Hill, Blackheath and Buckhurst Hill, became nuclei for surrounding middle-class settlement when the population of London expanded.' This argument led to a bold prediction, centring on the changing role of the Thames. They pointed out that a river can sharply polarise land-use. For the rich, it is a repellent if it is used as a port, but a magnet if its edge is unencumbered by commerce. The Thames east of the Pool (except for Greenwich) was such a repellent, lined with docks and industry for fifteen miles. But above Westminster, it has been a magnet for high-income residence. 'Chelsea, Barnes, Chiswick, Kew, Twickenham, Richmond, are on the route that the Royal Barges used to take between the palaces of St James, Hampton Court and Windsor;

they are all desirable places for people who have the money to make their desires effective.'

Willmott and Young's forecast, in 1973, was that as commercial uses of the river moved downstream, the role of the Thames as an industrial and commercial river would 'give way to a new role as an amenity and residential river.' They predicted also that the industrial uses and relative deprivation of areas further downstream might even be reinforced in this process. (This throws doubt on the more inclusive hopes of development throughout the 'East Thames Gateway'.) In other words, once industrial activities left the Thameside areas, the natural geographical advantages of the river were likely to be seized by more affluent and powerful users.

This forecast has proved accurate, both for London and for many other former port cities. Postmodern developers have discovered and exploited the attractions, for residence, market-places and commerce, of disused river-fronts, and harbours, initially in the United States, in Baltimore, Boston, and Manhattan, later in East London.[12] Postmodernism in urban design has developed as a more consumer- and tourist-friendly idiom, in contrast with the sometimes elitist and authoritarian symbolic language of high modernism. It was realised that the proximity of large areas of water, especially with the preservation of tokens of the former port heritage (cranes, bollards, the occasional ship, seafaring names), would increase the commercial value and attractiveness of a place. The central issue is whether the 'amenity and residential river' will be for the benefit of the many or the few.

Back Regions

There has been a neglect, in the urban sociological and political literature, of the existence and problems of the large 'back regions' of cities, even though they are mostly far more populous than the city centres which most visitors come to see. Discussion of inner city problems, and strategies for remedying them, have tended to be more localised, as for example in the small-scale urban regeneration programmes which are discussed later in this book.

This conceptual blight both derives from and reinforces the political subordination and fragmentation of the poorer regions of cities. To see an area such as the East End merely as a locus of social problems, is to marginalise its potential value for the city and its legitimate claims on it. Structures of government in London in particular have failed to represent the common interests of large, relatively deprived areas such as East London, and indeed most of South London with its appalling transport networks, too. Whilst the abolition of the Greater London Council in 1986 was a blow to the idea of planned development, the earlier removal in 1965 of the London County Council (which had presided over mid-century social democracy in London) had been an even greater one, since the new GLC had few substantive powers, and the separate boroughs were often fiercely territorial and unwilling to co-operate with one another. The fact that in the end major economic development only took place in Docklands over the heads of the various elected authorities says a great deal about the weakness of local self-government in East London.

But in the last few years, planners and policy-makers have begun to consider the problems and potentialities of East London on a larger regional scale. There have been several components to this new thinking. The first is the opportunity perceived in the closure of the London Docks, and the vast amounts of vacant land in potentially desirable locations made available by this. The second is the recognition that the permanent imbalance between the east and west of the city represents a loss of economic potential for London as a whole. The isolation and under-qualification of the labour force of the east, and the large amounts of under-utilised land, were seen, by academic planners like Peter Hall,[13] and by the then Secretary of State for the Environment, Michael Heseltine, as economic opportunities missed. Hall was highly aware too of the contrast between the far-sighted regional dimension of the planning being undertaken in Paris (with the new RER express rail network, for example), and the piecemeal and short-sighted approaches being followed in London. The third major factor in this recognition of the potential of the east was the increasing integration of the British economy with that of western Europe, of which the belated decision to construct the Channel Tunnel, though without a high-speed rail link, remains a potent if ambivalent symbol. The concept of the East Thames Corridor, subsequently renamed 'Gateway', depended on the importance of this anticipated throughput of trade and visitors to London as a whole. The idea is that the east side of London needs to be comprehensively upgraded if it is both to attract and take advantage of this increased traffic. This change of thinking has already brought large new investments in infrastructure – the Docklands Light Railway, the Limehouse Link road, the M11 extension, and the Jubilee Line extension from Green Park to Stratford due to open in 1998. More are likely to follow, including a new road crossing, rail crossings for the DLR and the North London Link, a

Channel Tunnel passenger terminal at Stratford, and Crossrail, the proposed new east-west London rail link. In much of the Royal Docks there is virtually nothing *but* new infrastructure, waiting for something to happen to justify its expensive existence. (This is the exact reverse of what happened at Canary Wharf.) Later in this book (notably in Anna Whyatt's and in David Albury and Carole Snee's chapters), we describe some projected initiatives which might make something more of these large investments.

A Development Strategy for East London

East London thus seems to have acquired some new locational advantages. But a serious problem for the whole region remains the legacy of past pollution and of environmental degradation, which threatens to confine development only to the more desirable waterside areas, and to the Kentish hinterland. East London's population is becoming more socially balanced than hitherto, both in class and ethnic terms. The new ethnic communities, to judge from the high take-up of educational opportunity by Asian children, should provide a considerable new economic input before long.

There is need to develop a comprehensive vision of the prospects of the East London region, to help this potential to be realised. Modern industrial and post-industrial investment seems to be particularly sensitive to environmental quality. So city centre renovations (such as that being undertaken through Stratford City Challenge), improving the quality of and access to natural environments such as the Lea Valley, making the most of the Thames frontages, and cleaning up the legacy of pollution (waste-sites, contaminated land, overhead cables) recognised as a major obstacle to development, now become crucial.[14] Education and training are fundamental too, since otherwise the greatest potential asset of the region, its large working population, will not be able to take advantage of opportunities provided by new investments and improved transport access.

East London needs to seek some benefit from the huge world-wide growth of tourism and leisure activities. Although London currently attracts the majority of visitors to Britain (some arriving from the east, via Harwich, Stansted, Dover or London City Airport), few of them presently venture to the east once they have arrived. Such developments will require imagination, as well as planning and investment. Twenty years ago, the Afro-Caribbean community in

West London created the Notting Hill Carnival, which has since become the largest annual street festival in Europe. The ethnic diversity of East London should be thought of as a similar potential resource and its own forms of cultural self-expression encouraged. The highest buildings in Manhattan, the World Trade Centre and the Empire State Building, have viewing platforms which are visited by millions, yet what must be a comparable view from the Canary Wharf Tower is accessible to invited guests only. The old foot tunnel under the Thames between Greenwich and the Isle of Dogs is not an inviting link between two major tourist attractions.

The development of the East London region must be a balanced one, if it is to serve the interests of all its citizens. The different sectors of the East London economy – finance and banking, the cultural industries (music, measured by net income earned, is now the third largest net export from the UK), public services including higher education, utilities, manufacturing of different kinds, tourism and leisure – can provide employment, meaning and incomes for different elements of its population, whether defined by class, educational qualification, gender or ethnicity. This is why a comprehensive approach to development is needed.

The idea of the 'East Thames Gateway' has been useful in focusing attention on the regional scale of both problems and potentials. Although there are possible dangers in setting the claims of East and West London against one another, there are also benefits to the whole city in recognising the necessary scale of any development that is going to make a difference and the interdependencies which are involved. Merely piecemeal developments will not work.

For this reason the emergence of the concept of partnership (between local authorities, national government, business and voluntary sector agencies) has been positive in transcending narrower forms of territorial and sectoral self-interest. It must be acknowledged that even an institution which has suffered from a huge democratic deficit, like the London Docklands Development Corporation, has nevertheless been an extremely dynamic force for development. In its final years, working outside the planning-free Enterprise Zone, and as local authorities within the former Zone, such as the London Borough of Newham, have resumed their powers, it has also moved closer to a partnership model.

At this point, it is not possible to set out an institutional blueprint for development in East London. We are, however, certain that development cannot be achieved through the agency of elected local authorities by themselves, or even by elected authorities acting in concert with central Government. The private sector is too important to be left out, and in any case, the diversity of interests that needs to be included in any development process requires a more pluralist model. Democracy itself requires this, since the electoral mandate given to a political majority in local or national government is only one of several forms of representation that needs to be recognised as valid, though it carries the greatest legitimacy. So the new models of partnership of interests, at the level of London as a whole, of East London as a sub-region, and for more local developments within East London, need to be further developed. The role of researchers and academics in this process is to inform the planning process, and to try to represent the experience and interests of the community within it. This book is intended as an initial contribution to this debate.

The following chapters of *Rising in the East* elaborate some of these issues. 'Social and Demographic Change in East London', by Vikki Rix, gives an up-to-date demographic account of the population of six East London boroughs, based mainly on detailed analysis of the 1981 and 1991 Census returns. It reveals a tide of social change lapping through the region, more profound in its effects in some areas (Tower Hamlets, Hackney) than in others (Barking and Dagenham, or Redbridge), but visible in all. There is evidence of a simultaneous upward and downward drift in opportunities and life-chances. Higher proportions of the population, in each borough, have become owner-occupiers, are staying longer in education and are in white collar and professional occupations. But there are also larger numbers who are unemployed and economically inactive, suggesting a pattern of economic polarisation. East London is also now markedly diverse in its ethnic as well as its class composition, and it is evident that ethnic minorities for the most part occupy the lower positions in the economic hierarchy of the region. Rix's chapter thus describes a situation both of opportunity, and of social risk.

The second section of the book explores issues related to changing class structures, and their wider implications. In 'Family Life in Barking and Dagenham', Margaret O'Brien and Deborah Jones are able to compare findings from their current research on this district with the study of Dagenham which Peter Willmott conducted in 1959.[15] Their work reveals a remarkable continuity in family life in this still largely white, working-class borough. Nearly half of their sample of parents had maternal grandparents living in Barking and Dagenham, a proportion which has scarcely changed over thirty-five years. More than half of the school children studied were in daily or weekly contact with their maternal grandmother. The kinship ties shown in the 1950s to be characteristic of East London by the Institute of Community Studies remain strong, in Barking and Dagenham at least. There are some changes, with higher levels of marital breakdown, and more dual earner and single parent households, reflecting in part greater economic opportunities for women. But changes, whether in the dimensions of class, gender, or ethnicity, have been much less marked than elsewhere in East London; Barking and Dagenham continues to be a remarkably stable working-class community.

Tim Butler's ' "People Like Us": the Gentrification of Hackney in the 1980s', describes the opposite end of the spectrum of continuity and change. Butler describes the settlement in one of the poorest boroughs in London of an unusually well-educated and affluent segment of the 'service class'. These are mainly young professionals, attracted to two particular neighbourhoods of Hackney by the high quality of housing and amenities available there, by their proximity to the City of London and the West End, and even, given the cosmopolitan orientations of this group, by the mixed social character of the area. The other side of this picture is the displacement or migration, mainly to outer London, of many former working-class inhabitants, in part as a result of the substitution of crowded privately rented housing, by more spacious owner occupation. These new service class inhabitants of Hackney were, at the time of Butler's survey, left-leaning in their political attitudes. Although there are risks in East London that different social groups will have incompatible aims and interests, one could also envisage that such newcomers could become a positive resource for the regeneration of the area.

John Marriott's 'The Political Modernism of East London', explores the diversity of East London through one aspect of its political history. Whilst the Labour Party is often thought to have dominated East London politics during this century, Marriott shows that the reality has been more complicated. He relates the particular strength of the Labour Party in West Ham (since 1965 part of the London Borough of Newham) to the strength of modern industrial labour – especially in the railway, dock, and gas industries, and also to a corresponding organisation of women through the Women's Co-operative Guild. This contrasts, from the Labour Party's origins to the present, with its more precarious position in Stepney, Bethnal Green and Poplar (now Tower Hamlets), where casual labour was more significant, and where divisions of interest between organised labour and the unemployed seriously weakened Labourism as a political force. A different kind of political resistance, which Marriott describes as 'the carnivalesque', characterises populations which are excluded from the modern industrial regime. Marriott points out that these distinctions are not of merely historical interest. Whereas in Newham Labour's rule has remained unbroken, Tower Hamlets has recently seen both a Liberal majority on its council, and the election of a British National Party candidate.

The third section of the book focuses on the ethnic diversity of East London. Greg Smith's chapter, 'The Unsecular City: the Revival of Religion in East London', provides evidence to refute the idea that modern cities are increasingly secular places. His findings, based mainly on research in Newham, reveal a high level of religious involvement, especially among the African and Asian populations. Even the white UK population, the least religious of all according to the data available, has over a third reporting attendance or membership of a religious group. Smith suggests that religion in East London expresses a need for ties of community amidst rapid social change. Although the ethnic basis of much Newham religious activity might give grounds for concern about potential conflict, Greg Smith's perspective is a hopeful one. He reports co-operation between religious groups in Newham, and notes that the vast majority of those surveyed believe 'that different religions should work together to help people in need.' This chapter shows that the ethnic and cultural diversity of East London should be seen as one of its positive resources.

'Refugees in Newham', by Alice Bloch examines the problems of some of the most vulnerable new communities in the area, those which have formed as a result of political exile. Newham has large ethnic minority populations, with distinct patterns of location of each of the main groups in particular neighbourhoods. There are also significant numbers of refugees (about 9,000), especially Tamils from Sri Lanka and Somalis, but others too, widely dispersed across the borough. Bloch describes refugees' considerable difficulties in gaining access to basic services, such as housing, health, employment and education. Although there are a variety of statutory and voluntary sector initiatives being taken to respond to their needs, Alice Bloch suggests many areas where improvements could be made and argues for a co-ordinated national approach to these problems. East London has long been an area of settlement for newcomers of all kinds, and Bloch shows how ambivalent national policy remains even though humanitarian considerations and the awareness of the potential contribution of newcomers to Britain, should lead to more positive attitudes.

Phil Cohen's chapter, 'All White on the Night?', is based on an ethnographic study undertaken by himself, Tareq Quereshi and Ian Toon on the Isle of Dogs in Tower Hamlets, examining the ideas of 'home' and territoriality found among members of different ethnic communities. Cohen contrasts traditional representations of the East End as on the one hand a place of disorder and danger, on the other of resilient and cheerful survival against the odds, with the current perceptions of East Enders, and especially 'Islanders', themselves. Their idealisation of the old way of life of the Isle of Dogs, and their belief that it is under acute threat from Asian newcomers, seems to Cohen to be a reflection of the difficulties of coping with the transformation of this area, where male working-class employment has been largely undermined.

Andrew Blake's 'The Echoing Corridor: music in the postmodern East End' draws attention, like Greg Smith's chapter, to the positive consequences of ethnic diversity for cultural life in East London. He describes the astonishing variety of popular music which has emerged in the East Thames region, from the East End to Southend, linking the development of mixed musical genres such as ragga, jungle and bhangra to the more abstract ideas of globalisation. 'What we have here in microcosm, from the late 1950s on,' Blake says, 'is an important aural history of British post-coloniality.' The development of popular musical forms is the prism through which Blake is able to trace the interactions of indigenous white East London, Afro-American, and now Asian subcultures. His remarks on the 'commanding place of Afro-American music in British popular culture ... continuously available as a marker of the black presence', shows the importance of this cultural register of social affinities and conflicts. Whilst, Blake says, the battle for multicultural musical education in schools has been largely won in East London, much remains to be done in providing support for popular musical education at more advanced levels. A cultural opportunity is being missed by the paucity of public provision, for example of performance venues.

The next section of the book is concerned with issues of culture and space in East London. Areas of popular settlement are normally deemed to be of little cultural interest, this usually being directed more to the historic centres of cities, or their expensive modern developments.

Bill Risebero's 'Architecture in East London', looks at the region through its built environment. He sees the post-war redevelopment of Poplar, in its time the largest Comprehensive Development Area in Britain, as a symbol of a hopeful post-war modernism, but also sees a split between the utopian architects' vision and the more brutal realities imposed first by government bureaucracy and the market, and then by economic decline. He contrasts this with Canary Wharf, the dominating architectural moment of 'enterprise culture'. Here, modern building structures were wrapped in historicist architectural styles, as a means by which their occupants can lay claim to social status. 'There is a sense,' says Risebero, 'in which the implanted Canary Wharf is colonial'. Finally, some recent developments and projects in East London are described, as instances of the kinds of friendly architecture that a more democratic and pluralistic society would encourage. Risebero's is a useful glimpse of the contribution which design and representation could make to the regeneration of the region.

'Hints of Open Country', by Martin Hoyles, looks at the history of public parks and open space in East London. People with few material resources have found pleasure in the open spaces made available by popular demand, from the creation of Victoria Park in 1841 onwards. Hoyles explores the many different uses made of green spaces, which range from gardening and allotments, public entertainments, and political demonstrations, to ecologically-oriented natural parks and city farms in modern times. Yet many of these amenities now face a crisis, of dangerousness and neglect. He argues that parks and open spaces should be integrated into any development plan for the East Thames region. Popular culture has almost by definition been self-made, with few material resources, and this explains the neglected importance of open space.

Finally, Bruce Jerram and Richard Wells outline a conception of what might be done to enrich the leisure of East Londoners and to attract visitors to East London from elsewhere, by the development of the North London Line. This long-established railway, once one of the most successful in England, runs overground from North Woolwich to Richmond, joining the Thames in the East to the Thames in the West. Jerram and Wells argue that this railway, if lifted out of its present semi-neglect, has the potential to be a major leisure resource for the whole of London north of the Thames.

The last section of the book is concerned with prospects for future development. Anna Whyatt in 'London East: Gateway to Regeneration', provides an overview of a feasible economic strategy for the East Thames region. She points to the 'schizophrenic' quality of contemporary thinking about the area, which 'is hailed as the geographic opportunity *par excellence* for London if not the South East', whilst having many districts on the list of the most severely deprived in western Europe. Whyatt points to the need for a detailed analysis of economic potential, both in traditionally strong sectors of activity, such as manufacturing, and in new sectors which are still scarcely developed in East London, such as tourism. She draws attention to the organisational problems of achieving such development. Only improved forms of partnership between between business, central and local government can meet the development needs of the region.

Gavin Poynter's 'Manufacturing in East London', describes the development of manufacturing in the latter half of the last century and the first half of the twentieth. He reports a substantial decline in manufacturing employment in recent years – estimated at one in five jobs between 1990 and 1994 – although East London still retains a higher proportion of manufacturing employment than London as a whole. The decline has been uneven in its spatial location and human impact, some areas like Canning Town having suffered severely, whilst close by new service industries have a quite different catchment of white collar and professional employees. Poynter reports a first stage of current research, the findings of a LETEC survey into East London manufacturing firms, which examines how far East London conforms to the widely-discussed paradigms of post-fordist industrial strategies. The evidence is mixed. The majority of firms remain small, and continue to employ mainly male, full-time workers. There are few signs here of the growth of high-technology industries. On the other hand, the sector shows considerable resilience and there is evidence that new methods of organisation are having a widespread impact. Whilst the manufacturing sector in East London does not have the dynamism found to the west of London, it has survived, and is in a position to benefit from wider economic improvements in the region.

Greg Clark's 'East London and Europe' examines the opportunities for East London to benefit from European Union resources available for urban regeneration. He explains that until recently, East London's problems and needs were obscured, by the relative prosperity of London as a whole, and by a political reluctance to acknowledge the evidence of severe deprivation in Britain's capital city. But thanks to the initiatives of the London boroughs acting together (now as the Association for London Government), this situation is changing. Areas of urban deprivation, such as East London, have been separately recognised, and parts of the region have gained 'Objective Two' (industrial regeneration) status. This, says Clark, 'has put London on the map, and provided for qualification for a broader tranche of European Union programmes'. Whilst problems of co-ordination and long-term strategy remain, Clark makes clear the importance of these European links to a regeneration strategy for East London.

John Pratt's and Rebecca Fearnley's chapter, 'Stratford City Challenge', examines the process of urban redevelopment as it operates at a more local level. They describe this area-based programme in the larger context of post-war urban development initiatives by central government.[16] They explain the key features of City Challenge programmes (there are three in the six East London boroughs). They were awarded from among competitive bids by local authorities, have a fixed life-span, are driven by specific monitored objectives and require partnerships between elected local authorities, business and other agencies. The aim is that limited public funding should generate 'leverage' funding from the private sector. Pratt and Fearnley describe this 'partnership model' as a step forward from the property-led model of development practised in Docklands. They point out, however, that it is difficult to assess the long-term effects on urban regeneration, even of a closely monitored programme such as this one.

In the concluding chapter of the book, 'Higher Education and East London: A Case for Social Renewal', David Albury and Carole Snee set out the vital role of post-school education. They argue the case for a new concept of a mass, popular university, based on flexible access programmes, decentralised modes of study in home, community and workplace as well as on campuses, and of relevance to economic, social and political needs. In earlier debates about development strategies for East London, both sides – those advocating a market-led development of tertiary industries, and those who wished to preserve the old industrial and port economy – neglected the needs of the majority population, who need new skills and flexibilities if they are to survive in a modern economy. The project for the Royal Docks Campus, which has recently been awarded government funds, embodies the ideal of a popular university as set out by Albury and Snee. The co-ordinating role of the University of East London in the consortium of four universities responsible for this project (City University, the University of East London, London Guildhall University, and Queen Mary and Westfield College) makes this chapter a fitting end to the volume.

Notes

[1] Dick Hobbs, *Doing the Business: Entrepreneurship, the Working Class and Detectives in East London*, Oxford University Press, Oxford 1988.
[2] Daniel Defoe, *A Tour through England and Wales*, Everyman Edition, 1927, Volume 1, p9.
[3] Charles Booth, *Lives and Labour of the People of London*, (seventeen volumes), 1902.
[4] Gareth Stedman Jones, *Outcast London: A Study in the Relationship Between Classes in Victorian Society*, Oxford University Press, Oxford 1971.
[5] See Ash Amin (ed), *Post-Fordism: a Reader*, Blackwell, Oxford 1994.
[6] Michael Young and Peter Willmott, *Family and Kinship in East London*, Routledge and Kegan Paul, London 1957.
[7] Saskia Sassen, *The Global City: New York, London, Tokyo*, Princeton University Press, Princeton 1991.
[8] H.V. Savitch, *Post-Industrial Cities: Politics and Planning in New York, Paris and London*, Princeton University Press, Princeton 1988.
[9] See Sassen, *op. cit.*, and Susan Fainstein, and Michael Harlow (eds), *Divided Cities: New York and London in the Contemporary World*, Blackwell, Oxford 1992.
[10] A good account of this development is in Fainstein, *op cit.*, 1994.
[11] P. Willmott and M. Young, 'Social Class and Geography', in *London: Urban Patterns, Problems and Policies*, Heinemann, London 1973.
[12] For an admiring account of these harbourside developments, see Peter Hall, and for a more critical one, David Harvey, 'Flexible Accumulation through Urbanisation: Reflections on Post-modernism' in the American City', in A. Amin (ed), *Post-Fordism: a Reader*, Blackwell, Oxford 1994.
[13] Peter Hall, 'A new strategy for the South East,' *The Planner*, 22.3.91.
[14] In the Llewellyn-Davies Report.
[15] Peter Willmott, *The Evolution of a Community: A Study of Dagenham after Forty Years*, Routledge and Kegan Paul, London 1963.
[16] This history is described in Rob Atkinson and Graham Moon, *Urban Policy in Britain*, Macmillan, London 1994.

Social and Demographic Change in East London

Vikki Rix

Introduction

The six main boroughs selected to represent East London are Tower Hamlets, Newham, Hackney, Redbridge, Waltham Forest and Barking and Dagenham (see Figure 1).

Figure 1: Main East London Boroughs

The chapter will review the major social and economic changes that have occurred within these boroughs over the past fifteen years. Social change within the family, education, housing, and the economic spheres have been widespread in Britain and in many western European nations since the 1970s. All have, on some level, experienced a decline in fertility, a decline in marriage, an increase in cohabitation, higher rates of divorce and a large increase in one-parent families. A plurality of family types and a more diverse set of household structures now exist, occurring as a result of cultural change and the growth in women's employment. Other key changes have been the increased participation in higher education, as well as an increase in the number of children staying on at school after sixteen. Economic change has been widespread, especially within London. The decline of manufacturing industry, the closure of the London Docks and the increase in service sector employment have hit the region of East London hard. Certain localities within East London now have high levels of unemployment, an increasing proportion of economically inactive men, and a decline in full time employment. With regards to housing, key trends throughout the 1980s have been the growth in owner occupation, a decline in social housing and a return to the problem of homelessness, now widespread in London. This chapter will assess how far such national trends are being reflected at the local level in East London, illustrating areas of change and continuity within the region. A number of different sources will be drawn upon, primarily data from the 1981 and 1991 Censuses.

Section One: Demography of East London

Population Trends

East London, like London as a whole, has been losing population since the late 1950s, largely as a result of high rates of net out-migration. Between 1971 and 1981, 10 per cent of London's population moved out, amounting to three quarters of a million people. In the following decade, London lost 321,000 residents, a population decline of 5 per cent. In fact every year it is estimated that around 350,000 people leave the metropolis of London, while only 250,000 move in.[1] East London boroughs have similarly experienced population decline due to out-migration, a decline far greater between 1971 and 1981 compared to the following decade. Between 1971 and 1981, the inner East London boroughs experienced higher rates of population decline compared to Redbridge, Waltham Forest and Barking and Dagenham. The loss of residents has been particularly high in the borough of Hackney, which has experienced an overall population decline of 28 per cent since 1971, amounting to a loss of 57,000 residents. Nearly a fifth moved out of Hackney during the ten years after 1971, while between 1981 and 1991 10 per cent, a total of 18,000 residents, left this inner city area.

*Table 1 Population Change in East London, 1981–1991**

	1971	1981	1991	% Change 71–81	% Change 81–91
Greater London	7,368,693	6,608,767	6,287,426	−10.3	−4.9
Inner London	2,959,315	2,425,630	2,265,815	−18.0	−6.6
Outer London	4,409,378	4,183,137	4,021,611	−5.1	−3.9
East London Region					
Redbridge	238,383	224,731	219,925	−5.7	−2.1
Waltham Forest	235,929	214,595	201,823	−9.0	−6.0
Barking & Dag.	161,849	148,979	140,039	−8.0	−6.0
Tower Hamlets	164,349	139,996	150,533	−14.8	+7.5
Newham	233,699	209,128	199,346	−10.5	−4.7
Hackney	218,594	179,529	161,590	−17.9	−10.0

Source: 1981 Census and 1991 Census, Crown Copyright.

* The 1991 Census imputed data for missing households. Population change has been calculated using 1981 population base. Other aspects of change have been calculated using 1991 population base. Differences in percentage points therefore are affected by the exclusion of absent households in 1981 population base.

Newham and Tower Hamlets have also experienced large population losses since the 1970s. Newham's population in 1971 was 233,699. By 1981 this had dropped to 209,128, declining further to 199,346 in 1991, an overall population decline of 15 per cent. Although 15 per cent of the population left Tower Hamlets between 1971 and 1981, the population of this inner London borough increased in the following decade. The resident population of Tower Hamlets rose from 139,996 in 1981 to 150,533 by 1991, an increase of 7.5 per cent. This increase was entirely due to a high rate of natural change in that there were more births than deaths in Tower Hamlets. The outer East London boroughs, although similarly populated, had lower rates of population decline between 1971 and 1981, all below the London average of 10 per cent. Although population loss also slowed down in outer East London between 1981 and 1991, Barking and Dagenham and Waltham Forest were still losing residents at a faster rate than London and Outer London as a whole.

Population loss took place in all East London boroughs, apart from Tower Hamlets, throughout the 1980s. Where have East London residents moved to? The more affluent white working class, able to enter the owner occupied sector, have moved out of East London areas and settled in many neighbouring Essex boroughs, such as Brentwood, Chelmsford, Epping Forest, Thurrock and Basildon. Cockney Essex, as Hobbs[2] argues, is living proof of this out-migration which has largely occurred because of a search for a better quality of life; the greener Essex suburbs being perceived as more attractive localities because of less population density and more open space. Essex's population density in 1991 was a mere 4.2 compared with London's and Inner London's density of 42.3 and 78.1 respectively.[3] The fact that Essex remains overwhelmingly white and British-born has and continues to be another reason for the out-migration of the white working class of East London; for example 97 per cent of all those residents who had moved into Essex boroughs in 1990 were white.[4] As a result of out-migration, Essex gained around 145,000 new residents between 1981 and 1991, a population increase of 10 per cent.

Since the early 1970s, many local East London residents who have been able to move have done so, and have set up home in various parts of Essex. Which and how many new residents have actually moved into East London? Using the data from the Census question regarding address one year before the Census, the nature and extent of population mobility within East London can be highlighted. The proportion of residents with a different address one year before the 1991 Census was lower than the London average of 11 per cent in all East London boroughs. Also, although every borough, apart from Tower Hamlets, experienced an increase in the proportion of migrants since 1981, the increase was again low compared to other London boroughs. Table 2 provides data on East London migration.

The proportion of residents moving between 1990 and 1991 was slightly higher in the three inner East London boroughs, which had just over 10 per cent of migrants. The outer East London boroughs, Barking and Dagenham, Redbridge and Waltham Forest had just

Table 2 Population Mobility in East London

	Total Migrants	As a % of all residents	81–91 % Change
Barking & Dagenham	11,790	8.2	0.9
Redbridge	19,674	8.7	1.3
Waltham Forest	20,286	9.6	1.6
Tower Hamlets	16,501	10.2	−1.5
Newham	22,464	10.6	1.4
Hackney	20,154	11.1	0.8
Greater London	758,206	11.4	0.8

Source: 1981 and 1991 Census, Crown Copyright.

under 10 per cent. The largest increase in migration was found in Waltham Forest, with a 2 per cent rise between 1981 and 1991. Surprisingly, Tower Hamlets had the second highest decrease in the proportion of migrants in the whole of London, despite the Dockland redevelopment. East London migrants, however, like London as a whole, had only moved short distances between 1990 and 1991. For example, over half of all migrants in Hackney, Newham, Tower Hamlets and Waltham Forest were already local residents, moving within their usual borough of residence. Barking and Dagenham, having a more stable population, had nearly two thirds of moves occurring within the same borough, compared with under half in London and Outer London as a whole. Movement into Barking and Dagenham from outside Great Britain was three times lower than the London average of 14 per cent, whilst Newham had the highest proportion of new residents having moved from outside the UK. 51 per cent of all migrants in Newham were non-white in 1991, double the figure of London and Inner London. Hackney, Tower Hamlets, Redbridge and Waltham Forest were fairly similar, having on average 10 to 12 per cent of new residents from outside the UK, of which a high percentage were non-white; 32 per cent in Hackney, 34 per cent in Tower Hamlets, 27 per cent in Redbridge and 31 per cent in Waltham Forest. Longer distance moves from outside London were more common in outer East London boroughs. Barking and Dagenham had over a fifth of residents who had moved into the borough from outside of London, while in Waltham Forest and Redbridge it was nearly one third.

Summing up, since the early 1970s population decline and out-migration have been the dominant trend in both London and East London. The proportion of people moving into East London boroughs throughout the 1980s has remained low when compared to other London boroughs.

Age Structure

Nationally, as a result of fertility decline and increased life expectancy, the numbers of young children have declined and the population of older people has increased. In 1991 a fifth of the UK population was aged fifteen and under, and another fifth was aged sixty and over. Britain's population has remained predominantly white and UK born, as only 5 per cent of residents were non-white and 9 per cent non-UK born in 1991.[5] The East London region, however, is much more diverse and complex as shown in the next two sections.

East London boroughs all have large populations of young people. The proportion of children aged fifteen and under exceeded the London average of 19 per cent and the national average of 20 per cent in all East London boroughs. This was especially the case in Tower Hamlets, having the highest proportion in the whole of London (26 per cent) in 1991. Larger numbers of very young children are living in the inner East London boroughs, which are also more racially diverse. The proportion of under fives in Tower Hamlets was the highest in London, 9.1 per cent, this being double the national average. Newham similarly had 9 per cent of children aged under five, while Hackney's figure was 8.4 per cent. Between 1981 and 1991, both Tower Hamlets and Newham experienced particularly large increases in the under five population, having absolute rises of 35 per cent and 21 per cent respectively. The proportion of under fives in Barking and Dagenham and Waltham Forest also increased, rising to around 7.5 per cent by 1991, both above the London and Outer London average. Redbridge had slightly fewer young children, 6.6 per cent, compared with its East London neighbours.

East London, therefore, still has a preponderance of large families. Alongside large numbers of young people, the outer East London boroughs have a higher proportion of older residents compared with inner East London boroughs. Both Barking and Dagenham and

Redbridge, due to lower out-migration of the traditional population, had an above average population of older people in 1991, as 21 per cent and 18 per cent of residents were aged sixty and over. Hackney, Tower Hamlets and Newham, however, due to the settlement of new, younger ethnic communities and the exodus of many local residents, had a much smaller population of older people of around 14 per cent.

Table 3 1991 Age Structure of Residents in East London

	0–4	5–15	16–29	30–44	45 to PA	PA & over
Redbridge	6.5	13.3	21.4	21.9	18.5	18.4
Waltham Forest	7.5	12.8	24.6	21.6	16.7	16.8
Barking & Dagenham	7.6	13.4	21.7	19.8	17.0	20.6
Hackney	8.4	14.6	25.2	22.2	15.3	14.3
Newham	8.9	15.5	24.7	21.2	15.5	14.2
Tower Hamlets	9.1	16.5	23.9	19.3	160	15.3
Greater London	6.9	12.6	23.8	22.2	17.7	16.8
Inner London	7.1	12.0	26.2	22.4	16.6	15.6
Outer London	6.8	12.9	22.3	22.1	18.4	17.5

PA = Pensionable Age
Source: 1991 Census, Crown Copyright.

A key aspect of change within the age structure of East London residents therefore lies within the younger population. Throughout the 1980s, every borough had an increase in the proportion of young people, resulting in East London boroughs now having a higher proportion of children aged fifteen and under than London as a whole. With regards to the presence of older people, those aged 75 and over increased in the three outer East London boroughs and Newham, while Hackney and Tower Hamlets had small decreases in those aged 75–84, but slight increases in those aged 85 and over. East London boroughs therefore slightly diverge with regards to the elderly. The outer East London boroughs of Redbridge, Waltham Forest and Barking and Dagenham have older communities, as a result of having more stable populations.

Ethnicity and Racial Diversity in East London

East London has always been an area of racial and cultural diversity. It has had, like London as a whole, a long history of immigration, particularly after the 1850s with Jewish and Irish settlement in the 'old' East End. More recently, since the 1950s, immigration from the New Commonwealth has added to the mixed communities of East London. Many of these newcomers settled in London, with large numbers of Asians and Afro-Caribbeans moving into inner London areas such as Tower Hamlets, Newham, Hackney, Lambeth, as well as Brent and Southall. By 1981, London's New Commonwealth immigrant population had risen to 634,000, subsequently increasing to just over 691,000 in 1991, 11 per cent of London's total population.[6]

The immigrant population in London has continued to increase throughout the 1980s, a trend also experienced by East London boroughs. In 1981, 18 per cent of London's population were born outside the UK, amounting to over one million people. This had increased to 22 per cent by 1991. Within Inner London, 28 per cent of all residents were non-UK born, while Outer London had nearly a fifth of non-British born residents. The neighbouring county of Essex however, reveals the spatial diversity of immigration where in 1991 only two per cent of Essex residents were non-white and only five per cent were born outside the UK. London, therefore, has remained the most popular location for new immigrants, with double the number of immigrants settling in London compared with Great Britain as a whole.

East London, particularly inner East London, has been a major area of settlement for different ethnic minorities. Hackney, Newham and Tower Hamlets now have large immigrant populations, with over a quarter of residents born outside the UK in 1991; 29 per cent, 28 per cent and 27 per cent respectively. Throughout the 1980s, both Newham and Tower Hamlets continued to attract new ethnic communities, with the arrival of Bangladeshi, Somali, Vietnamese and Ethiopian residents. As a result, Tower Hamlet's immigrant population rose from 26,599 in 1981 to 40,643 in 1991, while Newham had an increase of 13,999.

Waltham Forest and Redbridge have had quite high increases in the proportion of residents born outside the UK, 4.6 per cent and 5.6 per cent. By 1991, in both these outer East London suburban boroughs nearly a fifth of the resident population were born outside the UK. East London boroughs therefore, apart from Barking and Dagenham,

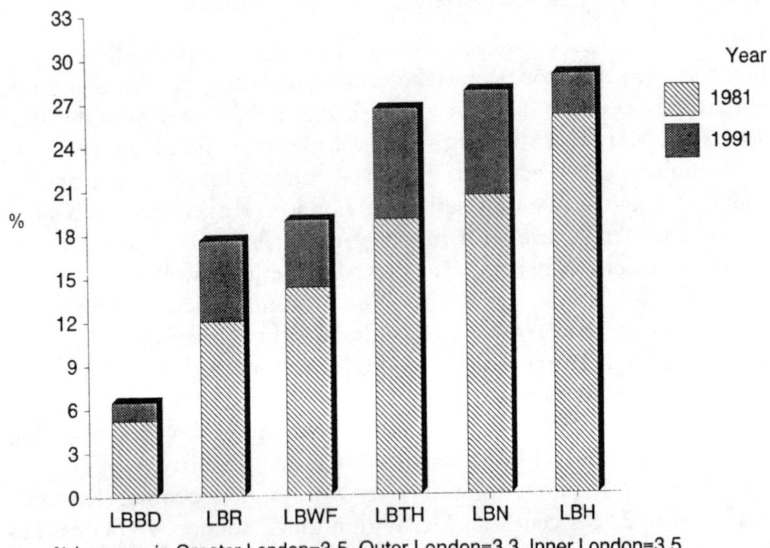

Graph 1: Percentage of Residents Born Outside the UK, East London 1981–1991

have fairly large immigrant populations. Barking and Dagenham, however, is an exception and has remained a predominantly white, British-born community. An overwhelming 93.5 per cent of its residents were born in the UK, a decline of only 1.3 per cent, while nine out of ten people were white in 1991,[7] with one of the smallest ethnic minority populations in London.

On the other hand, Newham has one of the most racially and culturally diverse populations of any London borough.[8] In 1991, 42 per cent of the borough's population were of African, Caribbean, Asian or other ethnic origin. The Asian community is particularly large, having over a fifth of residents who are Indian, Pakistani or Bangladeshi. Newham is a locality which is still attracting new communities with the more recent settlement of Bangladeshis and Somalian refugees.[9] Both Hackney and Tower Hamlets also have over a third of residents from ethnic groups other than white. In Tower Hamlets, around a quarter (24.7 per cent) of residents were of Indian, Pakistani or Bangladeshi origin. The black community is more predominant in Hackney, which had over a fifth of residents being black Caribbean, black African or black Other in 1991. In Redbridge and Waltham Forest, 21.4 per cent and 25.6 per cent of residents were non-white. In Redbridge, the largest ethnic community was also Asian (14 per cent), whilst Waltham Forest had similar proportions of both Asian and Black ethnic groups, 10.5 per cent and 11 per cent respectively.

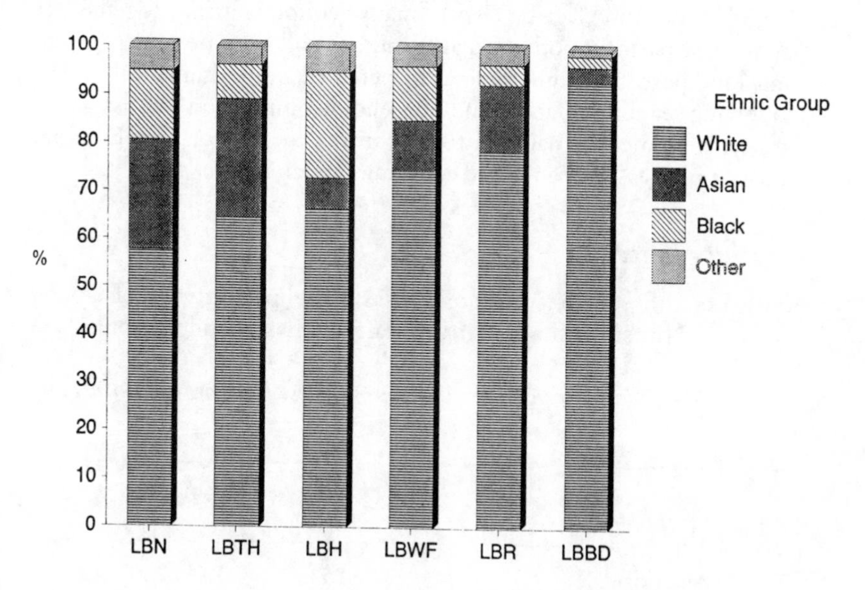

Graph 2: Ethnic composition of East London Boroughs, 1991

In summary, the three inner East London boroughs are much more racially and culturally diverse than the outer East London boroughs. Hackney, Newham and Tower Hamlets, although predominantly white back in the 1960s, now have non-white populations above both the London and Inner London average. In contrast, the populations of the outer East London boroughs are still largely white and British-born, although Waltham Forest and Redbridge have experienced some change in the ethnicity of their population over the past ten years. Barking and Dagenham, however, has remained overwhelming white.

Section Two: Family and Household Composition – Change and Continuity

Marital decline, divorce, cohabitation and the rise in individuals living alone are demographic trends which have greatly influenced family and household structure in Britain since the early 1970s. A plurality of family types now exists, with many couples living together as unmarried partners both with and without children. Both step-parent and lone parent families have also increased quite dramatically. The following section on family and household composition will assess the impact of some key national trends on the locality of East London, illustrating areas of change and continuity in family life.

Fertility Patterns

East London, as already shown, has large proportions of young children. Not surprisingly, fertility rates of East London women are

Table 4 Total Period Fertility Rates, East London 1983–1991*

	1983	1991
Redbridge	1.71	1.84
Barking & Dagenham	1.76	2.05
Waltham Forest	1.95	2.00
Hackney	2.10	2.20
Newham	2.17	2.36
Tower Hamlets	2.54	2.32
Greater London	1.71	1.76
Inner London	1.69	1.72
Outer London	1.73	1.81
England & Wales	1.76	1.83

Source: Annual Abstract of Greater London Statistics, 1983–84 and 1991–92, London: HMSO.

* Total Period Fertility Rate measures the average number of children a woman would be expected to have if she experienced the age-specific rates of the year in question throughout her child-bearing life.

high and above average when compared with London and Britain as a whole. Table 4 provides female fertility rates for East London boroughs in 1983 and 1991. In 1991, women living in East London, apart from Redbridge (fertility rate of 1.8), had on average two children compared with 1.8 both nationally and in London. Only one other London borough, Greenwich, had a fertility rate above 2.0 in 1991. Female fertility rates in East London were similarly high in 1983, again all above the London average apart from Redbridge. Newham, Hackney and Tower Hamlets had the highest number of children per woman in East London in both years. East London boroughs, apart from Tower Hamlets, have, like England and Wales and London as a whole, experienced a rise in fertility since 1983.

East London boroughs therefore have a large proportion of households with dependent children, particularly those containing children aged under five. Why do women in East London have more children? Changes within the age structure of the female population, the age at which women have children, ethnicity and social class are all contributory factors. Between 1981 and 1991, the number of women of childbearing age (16-44) increased across all East London boroughs. By 1991 nearly half of all women were of childbearing age in Hackney, Waltham Forest, Newham and Tower Hamlets, whose increases were 6 and 5 per cent respectively. Within Barking and Dagenham and Redbridge the increase in women of childbearing age was slightly lower, rising from 36 to 40 per cent and 39 to 42 per cent. Immigration and the presence of different ethnic groups in inner East London has also influenced the rise in the young population. The proportion of births born to women from outside the UK, particularly those from the New Commonwealth are much higher in inner East London boroughs compared to London as a whole. In Hackney, Tower Hamlets and Newham, 44 and 54 per cent of all births were born to non-British women in both 1983 and 1991. In Tower Hamlets nearly half of all births were born to women from the New Commonwealth in 1991, a figure double that of London as a whole.[10]

Nationally, women's participation in education and employment has grown dramatically since the late 1960s. As a result, marriage and parenthood have been postponed, with women generally having children later in life. Throughout the 1980s, marital decline and the postponement of parenthood have occurred in East London boroughs to varying degrees. The proportion of births to young women has remained above the London average of 61 per cent in all East London boroughs apart from the more affluent suburb of Redbridge, where

Table 5 Total Live Births by mother's age in 1991, and % change since 1983, East London

	1991 Total Live Births	% under 20	% 20–29	% 30 & over	1983 Total Live Births	% <20	% 20–29	% 30 & over
Redbridge	3,335	4.5	55.9	39.5	2,741	+0.5	−6.5	+6.0
Barking & Dagenham	2,367	8.4	66.5	24.5	1,896	−1.6	−3.0	+4.0
Waltham Forest	3,856	6.1	58.8	35.1	3,173	−1.8	−5.8	+7.6
Newham	4,558	7.1	62.5	30.4	3,784	−3.3	−4.9	+8.3
Hackney	3,798	7.0	55.9	37.1	3,223	−4.2	−4.7	+8.9
Tower Hamlets	3,228	9.5	59.6	30.9	2,808	−4.5	−3.4	+7.9
Greater London	105,813	5.3	55.3	39.4	91,567	−2.4	−4.7	+7.2

Source: Annual Abstract of Greater London Statistics, 1983–1991, HMSO, London.

women tend to have children in their late twenties and older. Young mothers were particularly common in the traditional white working-class community of Barking and Dagenham and in the racially and culturally diverse boroughs of Newham and Tower Hamlets, where over two thirds of all births were born to women aged 16-29.

The prevalence of teenage parenthood in East London is particularly significant. Although teenage parenthood declined between 1983 and 1991, the inner East London boroughs, along with Barking and Dagenham and Waltham Forest still had above average teenage births, nearly double the London average 5.3 per cent. Only Redbridge was just below average in 1991. Recent research into teenage parenthood found that low educational achievement and low socio-economic status were significant factors on whether teenagers became young parents.[11] As we shall see in section four, East London has remained a predominantly working-class locality with low educational performance. In the next section patterns of marriage, cohabitation and divorce will be examined.

Marriage and Alternative Living Arrangements

Since the mid-1970s, the popularity of marriage in Britain and in many European countries, particularly for young individuals, has declined rapidly with an increase in cohabitation and living alone. London and East London reflect these trends. Between 1981 and 1991, the decline in marriage amongst young people was particularly high in Waltham Forest and Newham (see table 6). The proportion of young people married in Waltham Forest dropped from over a third to less than a quarter, and from 38 per cent to around a quarter in Newham. Although the proportion of married residents aged 16-29 declined in Barking and Dagenham by 10 per cent, over a quarter were still married in 1991, the highest proportion of all London boroughs. Despite the general trend of marital decline, young people living in East London were still more likely to be married compared with young people in London, Inner London and Outer London as a whole. Hackney was the only East London borough to diverge from this marital pattern, having a much higher proportion of residents remaining single. In 1991, under a fifth of Hackney residents aged 16–29 were married, whilst nearly a third of those aged thirty up to retirement age had not married. This compared with only 13 per cent in Barking and Dagenham and Redbridge.

Table 6 Marital decline by age groups, 1981–1991

	1991 16–29 % M	81–91 % change	1991 30–64/59 % M	81–91 % change	1991 60–65 & over % M	81–91 % change
Hackney	19.2	−7.0	54.5	−15.0	44.5	−3.0
Waltham Forest	22.2	−13.0	68.8	−11.0	50.1	−4.0
Redbridge	22.7	−9.0	76.5	−6.0	52.4	−2.0
Tower Hamlets	22.8	−9.0	61.9	−10.0	42.4	−4.0
Newham	25.7	−12.0	68.9	−9.0	48.1	−3.0
Barking & Dagenham	29.1	−10.0	73.4	−8.0	46.9	−9.0
Greater London	20.1	−9.0	67.7	−9.0	49.8	−2.0
Inner London	17.3	−8.0	57.2	−11.0	44.5	−2.0
Outer London	22.1	−10.0	73.8	−7.0	52.7	−2.0

M = Married
Source: 1981 Census and 1991 Census, Crown Copyright.

Marital decline also occurred in the older age groups between 1981 and 1991, largely as a result of divorce where both borough and age variations are apparent. Divorce was particularly common for young people in Barking and Dagenham, with around three per cent of residents aged 16-29 divorced in 1991, nearly double the London average of 1.5 per cent. This is most likely as a result of early marriage, as in 1991 Barking and Dagenham had the highest proportion of young people married of all London boroughs. The three inner East London boroughs similarly had an above-average proportion of young people divorced in 1991.

Following marital decline and the rise in divorce, family forms have changed. The trend of having children outside of marriage has been particularly dramatic. In the 1950s, only five per cent of children were born outside of marriage in Britain, rising to 31 per cent in 1991.[12] Within London, the proportion of births born outside of marriage between 1974 and 1991 nearly trebled, rising from 12 per cent to 32 per cent. East London boroughs have experienced equally high increases. This has been particularly pronounced in Hackney, which had over a fifth of births outside of marriage in 1974 increasing to 41 per cent by 1991. Newham and Tower Hamlets have experienced a similar rise from

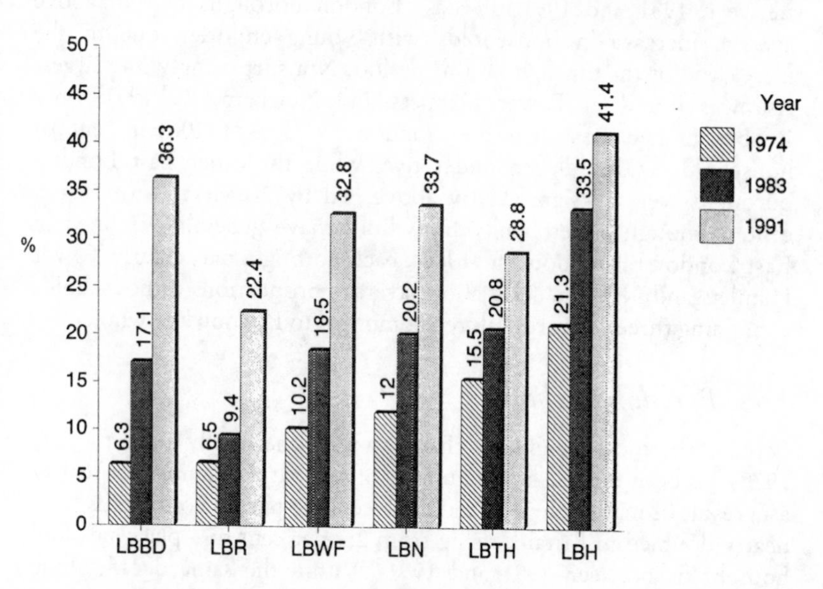

Graph 3: Increase of births born outside of marriage, East London, 1974–1991

12 per cent to 34 per cent, and from 15 per cent to 29 per cent respectively.

Interestingly, the increase has been even greater in the outer East London boroughs. In 1974, Barking and Dagenham and Redbridge had only 6 per cent of births to unmarried mothers, compared with 10 per cent in Waltham Forest, both below the London average. By 1991 this had risen to 36 per cent in Barking and Dagenham, 22 per cent in Redbridge and 33 per cent in Waltham Forest. The 1991 Census included a question on cohabitation for the first time: of those births born outside marriage in 1991, over half were jointly registered to both parents living at the same address in Barking and Dagenham, Tower Hamlets and Waltham Forest.[13] In Redbridge the figure reached nearly two thirds, 61 per cent, whilst in Hackney and Newham the percentages were slightly lower but still above 40 per cent. On the other hand, births registered only to one parent were particularly high in Newham and Hackney, boroughs which have a higher proportion of lone parents.

Household Composition

Between 1981 and 1991, all East London boroughs had an above average increase in households with young children, due to the increase in births throughout this period. Not surprisingly, the largest rise was found in Tower Hamlets and Newham. By 1991, only Redbridge had less than the London average of 10 per cent of households with children under five, while the other East London boroughs were all significantly above, led by Newham with 18 per cent. Although larger family households have generally declined in East London throughout the 1980s, each borough, particularly Tower Hamlets and Newham, had above average proportions of households containing three or more children compared to London as a whole.

Lone Parent households

Perhaps the most significant change within the family since the late 1970s has been the rise in the number of one parent families. Primarily as a result of marital decline and divorce, lone parent households have nearly doubled in Britain, rising from 2.1 per cent to 4 per cent of all households between 1981 and 1991. Within the same decade, lone parent households similarly increased both within London and East London. Throughout the 1980s, the number of lone parent households doubled in Barking and Dagenham, Waltham Forest and Newham,

Table 7 Change in households with child(ren) under five and households with three or more dependent children, East London, 1981–1991

	1991 % Hhlds with child(ren) under 5	% change 81–91	1991 % Hhlds with 3 or more children	% change 81–91
Redbridge	13.0	1.2	4.9	−1.2
Waltham Forest	14.1	1.4	5.2	−2.0
Barking & Dagenham	14.3	2.0	5.3	−1.0
Hackney	15.0	1.5	6.5	−1.9
Tower Hamlets	16.3	3.3	9.6	+2.1
Newham	17.7	2.7	8.1	−1.0
London	12.9	1.1	4.7	−1.7
I. London	12.5	1.4	4.6	−1.6
O. London	13.1	0.8	4.7	−1.8

Hhlds = Households
I. London = Inner London, O. London = Outer London.
Source: 1981 and 1991 Census, Crown Copyright.

rising to 5 per cent and 7 per cent of all households in 1991. Newham had the second highest increase in lone parent households in London of 3.8 per cent. Hackney however continued to have the highest proportion of lone parent households in London, 8.4 per cent, well above the London average of 4.8 per cent. By contrast, lone parenthood was less common in Redbridge. Here three per cent of households contained lone parents (2,644 households), a proportion similar to many other Outer London boroughs.

Although attitudes towards parenthood are slowly changing, especially with regard to men's roles, this has yet to impact on the gender of lone parents. In 1991, 93 per cent of all lone parents were female in the UK, 94 per cent in London, and in each East London borough over 90 per cent were women.[14]

Another key trend contributing to the diversity of household structure has been the rise in single person households over the past

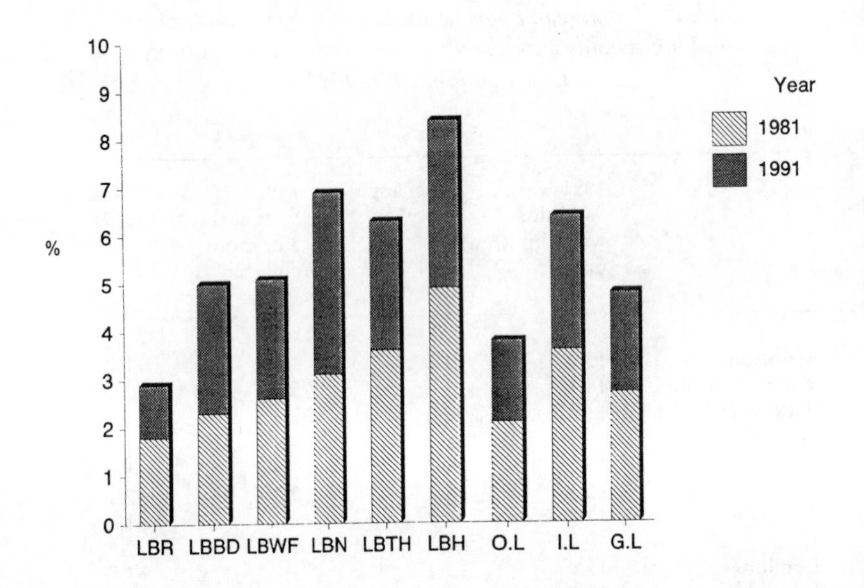

Graph 4: Increase in Lone Parent households, East London, 1981–1991

twenty years. Many young adults today are remaining single for longer and living alone, while increased life expectancy has resulted in many pensioners also living alone. A quarter of all households in Britain today contain one person only and a third have no more than two people.[15] Throughout the 1980s, single person households have increased in all East London boroughs. By 1991, Hackney and Tower Hamlets had over a third of single person households, possibly due to middle-class gentrification in certain parts of these boroughs. In the other East London boroughs, over a quarter of all households contained one adult only in 1991 compared to over a fifth in 1981. In the outer East London boroughs a high proportion of single person households consisted of an older person living alone. In 1991 around half of all single person households in Barking and Dagenham, Redbridge and Waltham Forest were single pensioner households. The inner East London boroughs, however, had a higher proportion of adults under pensionable age living alone, illustrating again the heterogeneity of East London. Throughout the 1980s, people living alone has continued to be a significant trend across East London.

The pace of change in family life and household structure has been more pronounced in inner East London boroughs than elsewhere.

Fertility rates have risen, marriage has declined, children born outside marriage have increased, as has lone parenthood. The consequence has been a diversity of household structures, notably an increase in households with young children, a decline in larger households and a rise in single people living alone.

Section Three: Housing

Tenure Change and Homelessness in East London

The growth in owner occupation has been overwhelming in Britain since the Second World War, particularly throughout the 1980s when the property market took off in an unprecedented way. During this period, the Thatcher government actively promoted owner occupation with the implementation of the 'Right to Buy' scheme. Many council properties have subsequently been sold through Right to Buy, but the imposition of severe restrictions on local authorities on using capital receipts from those sales meant that profits have not been reinvested in new housing programmes. This market-led ideology has brought about striking changes between tenures, especially in London and East London.

In London as a whole, owner occupied accommodation rose from 48 per cent in 1981 to 57 per cent in 1991. During that decade, around 363,000 more households moved into or set up home in owner occupied accommodation. The largest decline was found in households rented from local authorities, which declined from 30 to 23 per cent between 1981 and 1991. The private rented sector, despite the Government's attempt to expand, it fell from 15 to 12 per cent, while those households renting from housing associations increased by over a half, from 3 per cent to 6 per cent.[16] East London experienced similar changes with regards to housing tenure. The greatest changes within owner occupation since 1981 have taken place in two East London boroughs, Barking and Dagenham and Tower Hamlets. In 1981, Tower Hamlets had a mere 2,440 owner occupied households and had by far the largest proportion of council housing in the country. As a result of the redevelopment of London's docklands and the impact of Right to Buy, the proportion of owner occupied households rose from 4.6 per cent to 23.3 per cent between 1981 and 1991. Despite this increase, home ownership is still very low in Tower Hamlets compared with the national owner occupation average of 66 per cent, the London average of 57.2 per cent and the Inner London average of 38.6 per cent.

The white working-class area of Barking and Dagenham has also experienced a dramatic shift in its tenurial distribution. The Becontree Estate built up in the 1930s in Dagenham used to be the largest council estate in Europe. The Right to Buy policy, however, which allowed existing council tenants to fulfil their aspiration of being home owners, has radically changed the tenure of housing stock. Between 1981 and 1991, owner occupied households rose from 17,498 to 30,059, and by 1991 52 per cent of all households had become owner occupied compared with under a third ten years earlier.

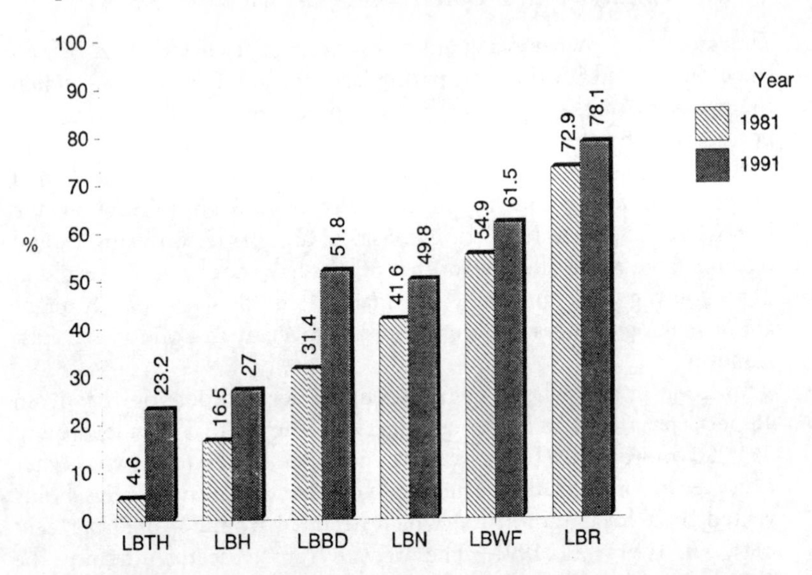

Graph 5: Increase in owner occupation, East London, 1981–1991

Hackney has also shared the trend of increasing owner occupation. Between 1981 and 1991, owner occupied households nearly doubled, rising from 16 to 27 per cent. By contrast, Newham had a smaller increase in home ownership. By 1991, 50 per cent of all households were owner occupied compared with 42 per cent in 1981. Waltham Forest and Redbridge differ as they have always been largely owner occupied boroughs, experiencing very little change in housing tenure throughout the 1980s.

Decline in Social Housing

Since 1979 the availability of council housing has declined dramatically, largely as a result of central government policy. Selling council housing to existing tenants was not new, but it took off rapidly in the 1980s, and although much more widespread in outer suburban areas than in inner city estates, all East London boroughs have experienced a decline in the proportions of council housing. In 1981, Tower Hamlets had 82 per cent of households in local authority accommodation; by 1991 this proportion had dropped to 58 per cent. Barking and Dagenham had a similar decrease (22 per cent) in council housing between 1981 and 1991, an absolute loss of around 11,000 households. Since 1980, Barking and Dagenham has lost a third of its council stock through right to buy sales alone. Why was the Right to Buy scheme so successful in Barking and Dagenham? Over two thirds of Dagenham's council properties were terraced houses built in the 1930s. Owning a house was obviously much more attractive for existing tenants than buying a flat, especially given the reduced rates at which many such houses were offered for sale since the early 1980s. Barking and Dagenham has a very stable population. Many residents therefore, having been council tenants for a long period of time, were given large concessions as part of the Government's aim to promote the private sector and perhaps to win back some support in a traditionally Labour controlled borough. These electoral considerations certainly played their part in Conservative-ruled boroughs like Westminster and Wandsworth. However, despite this rapid decline in social housing, local authority rented accommodation was still twice that of the London average of 23 per cent in 1991. Both Redbridge and Waltham Forest have much lower proportions of social housing, 15 per cent and 25 per cent respectively. In Hackney and Newham the proportion of local authority rented accommodation dropped by nine per cent and eight per cent respectively, although the proportion of council housing was still above the London average in 1991.

Recent government housing policy, therefore, has not promoted new supply, but has brought about a major change of tenure in already existing properties. Also as a result of government policy, London as a whole and East London in particular have experienced a dramatic shift in the tenure of new buildings. In 1980, 70 per cent of new building in London was completed by local authorities. By 1991 this had been reduced to a mere 5 per cent. The number of new dwellings completed by local authorities in East London has similarly declined. Between

1986 and 1991 only 90 new local authority dwellings were built in Tower Hamlets, while Redbridge had no new completions at all during those years. 468 new council dwellings were completed in Hackney between 1981 and 1985. This had dropped to 337 in the second half of the decade, an absolute decline of 27 per cent. Newham similarly had a large decline in new local authority dwellings between 1981 and 1991 of 34 per cent. Barking and Dagenham experienced little change in new completions, dropping from 335 to 246 between the two time periods, unlike Waltham Forest which had an absolute decline of 48 per cent.[17]

Table 8 New dwellings completed by local authorities, 1981–1991

	1981–85	1986–91
Redbridge	201	0
Barking & Dagenham	335	246
Tower Hamlets	442	90
Hackney	468	337
Waltham Forest	1,069	553
Newham	1,376	910
Greater London	32,076	9,098

Source: London Housing Statistics, 1991.

With the growth in owner occupation, and with access to housing having become more dependent on ability to pay, housing polarisation has increased throughout the 1980s and early 1990s. Those on low incomes and in insecure employment, the unemployed, ethnic minorities, older people and lone parents are now increasingly dependent on a declining council stock, with home ownership being beyond their means in London and East London (average house prices in East London were around £72,000 in 1991 – the lowest (£60,000) was in Barking and Dagenham, the highest (£88,000) in Tower Hamlets).

This had led to a housing crisis in London and a return to the pre-war problem of homelessness. With the rapid decline in social housing, the Government attempted to bridge the gap by promoting the private rented sector and housing associations throughout the 1980s. London's private rented sector has however continued to decline by about 40 per cent between 1981 and 1988, whilst housing association stock increased by 27 per cent during the same time period.[18] The private rented sector declined in all East London boroughs apart from Barking and Dagenham where the increase was minimal. However, the London trend of increasing numbers of housing association households has been apparent within East London throughout the 1980s. Housing association households are more frequent in inner East London boroughs, where co-operative schemes, especially in Newham, are widespread. Since 1981, the proportion of housing association households has doubled in both Newham and Tower Hamlets and nearly trebled in Hackney, rising to 6.4, 9.3 and 11.3 per cent respectively. These proportions were all above the London average of 6 per cent, an indication that the Government's scheme of funding housing association households within local authorities is having an effect, especially in inner East London.

Housing Crisis – Increase in Homelessness in East London

With the reduction in council stock and despite the slight increases in housing association stock, London overall and certain East London boroughs now face a housing crisis. The number of homeless people, both street homeless and those in temporary accommodation (or bed and breakfast), has increased dramatically within the London region since the early 1980s. Exact figures of the homeless are not known – the estimated figure of the street homeless in London was 3,000 in 1990, but is suspected to be much higher in reality. Latest DoE statistics found that 28,040 households were placed in temporary accommodation by local authorities in 1990, a 29 per cent increase since 1989.[19] The number of households accepted as homeless (households which have applied to local authorities and have been subsequently defined as homeless and in priority need) has steadily increased in both London and throughout England since 1978. Not surprisingly, the problem of homelessness has spread to East London and today is a problem particularly in the East London boroughs of Hackney, Newham and Tower Hamlets. Table 9 shows that the number of households accepted as homeless nearly trebled in Hackney, rising from 732 to 2,134 homeless households between 1978 and 1991. Similarly in Newham, homeless households more than doubled between the same period, rising from 539 to 1,467. The inner East and outer East London divergence is again illustrated, as the number of households homeless in Barking and Dagenham and

Redbridge was significantly lower; only 309 and 438 in 1991 respectively compared with 950 in Tower Hamlets, 1,467 in Newham and 2,134 in Hackney. Waltham Forest, however, did have a higher number of homeless households in 1991, having had a fairly large increase of 535 households since 1978.[20]

*Table 9 Homeless acceptances in East London, 1978–1991 and homelessness rate for 1990–91**

	1978	1986–87	1990–91	1990–91 Rate (%)
Barking & Dagenham	184	218	309	5.3
Redbridge	268	314	438	4.6
Waltham Forest	369	411	904	10.6
Newham	539	1,853	1,467	18.3
Tower Hamlets	701	782	950	13.8
Hackney	732	1,521	2,134	25.1

Source: London Housing Statistics, 1991.

* Rates of homelessness calculated as the number of households accepted as homeless in relation to the number of households within the local authority district.

Having analysed tenure change throughout the 1980s, it is apparent that East London still largely consists of two dominant tenures, owner occupation and council housing. Borough variations however, have remained. Barking and Dagenham, Tower Hamlets, Newham and Hackney still have an above average proportion of local authority accommodation, while Waltham Forest and Redbridge were the only two East London districts with owner occupation levels above the London-wide average in 1991. Tenure change has been particularly evident in Barking and Dagenham and Tower Hamlets, which experienced rapid increases in owner occupation. The transitional tenures of the private rented sector and housing associations are much more common in Newham, Hackney and Waltham Forest, which, along with Tower Hamlets, also have an increasing homeless problem.

Section Four: The Local Economy of East London: Educational and Employment Change Throughout the 1980s

East London is a region well known for its low academic achievement in schools and its low participation in higher education. Over the past fifteen years however, this has begun to change. Between 1981 and 1991, the percentage of 17-year-old residents in further education increased in all East London boroughs, particularly in Tower Hamlets, Newham and Hackney. In Tower Hamlets, nearly half of 17-year-old residents remained in further education in 1991 compared with a quarter in 1981. Barking and Dagenham, although experiencing a fairly large increase, still had the lowest proportion of 17-year-olds staying on in education in East London, rising from just over a fifth in 1981 to a third in 1991. Despite the general increase in participation in further education, only Redbridge had an above average proportion of 17-year-old students in 1991.

Table 10 Percentage of 17-year-old residents in further education in East London, 1981–1991

	1981	1991	% Change
Barking & Dagenham	21.7	33.7	12.0
Waltham Forest	34.8	47.4	12.6
Redbridge	41.9	56.7	14.8
Newham	30.6	47.0	16.4
Tower Hamlets	25.7	48.9	23.2
Hackney	38.1	53.8	15.7
Greater London	41.2	56.2	15.0

Source: 1981 Census and 1991 Census, Crown Copyright.

Qualifications

The proportion of year eleven pupils achieving five or more GCSEs at high grades (A–C) was still below the national average in all East London boroughs in 1993.[21] In Barking and Dagenham less than a fifth of pupils aged 15 obtained five or more A-C grade GCSEs, well below the national average of 41 per cent. Just over 20 per cent of year eleven students achieved five or more high grades in Newham and Hackney, while the best results were found in Waltham Forest and Redbridge, whose respective figures were 31.1 per cent and 40.5 per cent. The number of pupils at year eleven obtaining five or more GCSEs at all grades was also below the national average in all East London boroughs, apart from Redbridge. School performance at GCSE therefore has remained below average, particularly in the three inner East London boroughs and Barking and Dagenham.

Table 11 Percentage of pupils aged 15 achieving GCSE, East London, 1993

	5+ (A–C) GCSEs	5+ (A–G) GCSEs
Barking & Dagenham	19.3	78.3
Newham	22.0	70.5
Redbridge	40.5	85.2
Tower Hamlets	18.9	64.0
Waltham Forest	31.1	82.7
Hackney*	22.7	71.2
National average	41.1	84.3

Source: Department of Education.

* 1994 figure for Hackney.

Despite the general rise in higher qualifications between 1981 and 1991, the proportion of East London residents aged eighteen and over with a diploma, degree or higher degree was below the London average of 17.5 per cent.[22] This was particularly evident in Barking and Dagenham, which had a mere 3.5 per cent of residents highly qualified in 1991: the lowest of any district in Great Britain. The uniqueness of Barking and Dagenham is again illustrated, having decreased by 0.1 per cent in ten years. Despite poor school performances, pockets of severe deprivation and high unemployment, Hackney and Tower Hamlets had the largest increase in higher qualifications within East London, rising from 11.8 per cent to 16.3 per cent and 6.9 per cent to 11.3 per cent of the population respectively. This increase has occurred due to the settlement of new middle-class residents, and may be the outcome of the increasing student population. Newham and Waltham Forest however experienced little change, having only 8.7 per cent and 12.9 per cent of the resident population highly qualified in 1991. Highly qualified East London residents therefore have remained very much a minority group.

Employment – Economic Characteristics of the Male Population in East London

Since 1981, a key aspect of employment change in East London has been the decline of economically active men, a London-wide trend. This was particularly marked in Tower Hamlets and Newham, which along with Hackney had the lowest proportion of economically active men in East London and all London boroughs in 1991. Although the proportion of men in the labour force declined in Barking and Dagenham, Waltham Forest and Redbridge, they still had higher proportions of economically active men compared with London as a whole.

After 1981, East London boroughs, like the rest of London, also experienced a dramatic decline in the proportion of full-time male employees.[23] Full-time male employment dropped by over a fifth in all East London boroughs, apart from Barking and Dagenham, the only borough below the London average rate of decline. By 1991, less than half of all men in Hackney and Tower Hamlets were working full-time, compared with 52 per cent in Newham, 58 per cent in Redbridge and 59 per cent in Waltham Forest. By contrast, Barking and Dagenham had the highest proportion of full-time male employees in 1991, 61.7 per cent.

The London-wide trend of men who are increasingly economically inactive is also manifest in East London and particularly in the inner East London boroughs. By 1991, nearly a fifth of men aged 16-64 were economically inactive in Hackney, Tower Hamlets and Newham, compared with between 10 per cent and 12 per cent ten years earlier. By contrast, the outer East London boroughs had much lower proportions of economically inactive men in 1991, around 12 per cent. It is quite striking that men in Barking and Dagenham appear to have been more successful in coping with the overall decline in manufacturing and manual industries. In 1991, Barking and Dagenham had the highest economic activity rates for men, the highest proportion of men in full time employment, the lowest proportion of

Table 12 *Proportion of economically active men and women in East London, 1981–1991*

	Total Males	1991 % EA	81–91 % change	Total Females	1991 % EA	81–91 Change
Hackney	56,525	82.5	–5.5	57,068	63.7	–0.1
Tower Hamlets	49,315	82.8	–7.9	46,088	57.0	–5.7
Newham	66,714	83.6	–7.1	63,532	58.9	–1.9
Redbridge	71,884	87.4	–3.3	67,947	67.1	+4.0
Waltham Forest	67,679	87.9	–3.8	65,596	68.2	+3.8
Barking & Dagenham	43,236	88.3	–4.7	40,713	64.4	+4.4
Greater London	2,157,837	86.3	–3.5	2,096,257	67.7	+2.9

EA = Economically Active.*
Source: 1981 and 1991 Census, Crown Copyright.
* Difference in percentage points will have been affected by change in definitions. 1991 Census included students who were also in employment or seeking work in the week before the Census as economically active. 1981 base counts however categorised all students as economically inactive.

Table 13 *Main employment characteristics of men aged 16–64 in East London, 1981–1991*

	1991				1981–1991 % Change		
	F–T	P–T	Self Employed	E. Inactive	F–T	P–T	E. Inactive
Hackney	45.4	3.7	10.1	17.5	–24.8	2.0	5.5
Tower Hamlets	48.5	2.0	9.2	17.2	–23.4	0.6	7.9
Newham	52.3	2.1	9.0	16.4	–24.3	1.3	7.1
Redbridge	57.9	2.0	17.6	12.6	–24.9	1.0	3.4
Waltham Forest	59.1	2.1	12.3	12.1	–22.0	1.0	3.9
Barking & Dagenham	61.7	1.5	11.6	11.7	–19.7	0.9	4.7
Greater London	57.8	1.9	13.7	13.7	–21.9	0.3	4.1

F–T = Full Time, P–T = Part Time, E. Inactive = Economically Inactive.
Source: 1981 and 1991 Census, Crown Copyright.

economically inactive men and the second lowest unemployment rate in East London. Economic restructuring and industrial change however appears to have had a more widespread, damaging effect on men living in the inner East London boroughs.

Economic Characteristics of the Female Population in East London

The inner East and outer East London divergence is similarly apparent with regard to women and employment. Between 1981 and 1991, Barking and Dagenham, Waltham Forest and Redbridge all had an increase in the proportion of economically active women, an increase in full-time female employees and a decline in female economic inactivity. By contrast, women's participation in the labour force declined in Newham, Hackney and Tower Hamlets. The proportion of women in full-time employment also declined, whilst those economically inactive actually increased. All East London boroughs however shared an overall decline in part-time female employment.

In 1991 over two-thirds of all women aged 16–59 in Waltham Forest and Redbridge were economically active compared with 64 per cent in Barking and Dagenham. Tower Hamlets, Newham and Hackney, however, had lower proportions of economically active women. Despite the Docklands development and the creation of many new non-manual jobs, by 1991 Tower Hamlets had the lowest proportion of women in the labour force of all London boroughs (57 per cent), followed by Newham and Hackney.

A major aspect of economic change for women living in the inner East London boroughs has been the widespread decline in their participation in full-time employment and an increase in those who are economically inactive. In Hackney and Tower Hamlets, for example, the decline in female full-time employees was nearly six times greater than that of London as a whole. A significant proportion of women aged 16-59 in inner East London boroughs was economically inactive in 1991: 43 per cent in Tower Hamlets, 41 per cent in Newham and just over a third in Hackney. By contrast, the outer East London boroughs had an increase in the proportion of women working full-time and a decline in those economically inactive. Part-time female employment was much more common in Barking and Dagenham which had around a fifth of women working part-time compared with 17 per cent and 15 per cent in Redbridge and Waltham Forest respectively. Interestingly, the decline in female part-time employ-

Table 14 Main economic characteristics of women aged 16–59 in East London, 1981–1991

	1991				1981–1991 % Change		
	F–T	P–T	Self Employed	E. Inactive	F–T	P–T	E. Inactive
Tower Hamlets	34.2	10.3	2.3	43.0	–5.8	–5.5	5.7
Hackney	36.1	10.9	3.5	36.3	–5.9	–3.0	0.1
Newham	36.2	10.6	1.9	41.1	–3.4	–4.4	1.9
Barking & Dagenham	37.6	19.5	1.3	35.6	2.1	–0.8	–4.4
Redbridge	41.0	16.8	3.8	32.9	0.3	–2.1	–4.0
Waltham Forest	43.3	15.0	2.7	31.8	3.0	–4.5	–3.8
Greater London	42.4	14.2	4.0	32.3	–0.9	–3.3	–2.3

F–T = Full Time, P–T = Part Time, E. Inactive = Economically Inactive.
Source: 1981 and 1991 Census, Crown Copyright.

ment, and the increase in women who were economically inactive was again particularly high in Tower Hamlets between 1981 and 1991. The economic regeneration of the Dockland area, therefore, has not benefited all sections of the community, as the numbers of economically inactive and unemployed people have risen for both men and women in this inner East London borough.

Throughout the 1980s, unemployment increased for both men and women living in East London. The proportion of economically active men unemployed in Hackney and Tower Hamlets rose to over a quarter (26 per cent) in 1991, and to 22 per cent in Newham, well above the London male rate of 13.8 per cent. However, the outer East London boroughs had lower proportions of economically active men out of work. Male unemployment in Redbridge rose to 10.4 per cent in 1991, compared with 14.4 per cent in Barking and Dagenham and 15.2 per cent in Waltham Forest. The inner East London boroughs similarly had much higher female unemployment rates. In 1991, under 10 per cent of economically active women were unemployed in outer East London boroughs, compared with around 15 per cent in Newham and Tower Hamlets, and nearly a fifth in Hackney. Only Redbridge and Barking and Dagenham had female unemployment levels below the London average of 9.4 per cent.

Table 15 Unemployment levels of economically active men and women in East London, 1981–1991 (%)

	1991 M	% increase 81–91	1991 F	% increase 81–91
Redbridge	10.4	2.7	7.3	1.8
Barking & Dagenham	14.4	2.6	8.4	1.4
Waltham Forest	15.2	4.7	9.6	2.6
Newham	22.3	7.6	15.5	5.2
Tower Hamlets	26.3	7.1	15.8	4.8
Hackney	26.4	8.1	18.5	6.1
Greater London	13.8	3.4	9.4	2.4
Inner London	19.0	4.5	12.9	3.6
Outer London	10.7	2.7	7.2	1.6

Source: 1981 and 1991 Census, Crown Copyright.

Table 16 Unemployment by ethnic group, 1991, East London*

		Black					
	White	Caribbean	African	Other	Indian	Pakistani	Bangladeshi
Redbridge	7.7	11.3	26.5	15.5	11.5	20.6	17.6
Waltham Forest	10.2	15.6	28.2	20.0	15.2	29.1	33.3
Barking & Dagenham	11.4	14.0	22.6	22.5	12.0	27.8	21.9
Newham	15.5	18.2	39.6	22.9	18.9	35.4	42.8
Tower Hamlets	17.1	23.1	32.6	28.3	18.7	31.6	47.3
Hackney	19.4	26.2	32.2	33.7	25.1	29.2	39.1
Greater London	10.0	19.0	29.6	24.1	11.8	23.8	35.8

Source: 1991 Census, Crown Copyright.
* The percentage unemployed is the number of unemployed aged 16 and over expressed as a percentage of the number of economically active people aged 16 and over by ethnic group.

Economic change, therefore, for both men and women has been more pronounced in Hackney, Newham and Tower Hamlets, largely, it seems, as a result of racial and cultural diversity. Looking at unemployment by ethnicity, an East London pattern emerges, particularly in inner East London where unemployment is exceptionally high for both Bangladeshi and Pakistani, and black residents. In Newham and Tower Hamlets, for example, over 40 per cent of economically active Bangladeshis were unemployed in 1991 compared with 39 per cent in Hackney. Similarly, over 30 per cent of economically active black Africans were unemployed in the inner East London boroughs in 1991, all above the London average.

Earnings

East London has remained a region with generally low gross weekly earnings for both men and women. Wage levels, however, vary considerably across East London boroughs, illustrating social polarisation both between and within the local East London communities. Results from the latest New Earnings Survey show that employees in London still earned significantly more than employees elsewhere in the UK, with average gross weekly earnings of £467 for full-time males and £336 for full-time females. Despite high unemployment and low economic activity rates, full- time males in Tower Hamlets earned above London average wages in both 1991 and 1994. With regard to full-time female wages, women in Hackney and Tower Hamlets had above average earnings in the early 1990s, a gap which has widened since 1991. It is quite clear that economic change has benefited certain sections of the community in Tower Hamlets and Hackney, with the better educated middle-class residents displacing the less skilled, uneducated residents. By contrast, Waltham Forest, Redbridge and Newham had the lowest weekly gross earnings for men and women. What stands out is that local economies within East London are both diverse and complex. For example, although Barking and Dagenham has an extremely poor educational profile and below average proportions of professional and managerial workers, unemployment there is low and earnings are high compared with East London generally. Male full-time earnings in Barking and Dagenham were the second highest in East London in both 1991 and 1994, and although below the London average, they were above the national average. This may well be due to the presence of a large proportion of skilled manual workers, who tend to work more hours and more overtime. In 1994, for example, full-time males in Barking and Dagenham had the highest number of hours worked and the highest number of overtime hours of all London boroughs.[24]

Table 17 Average gross weekly full-time earnings by gender in East London, 1991 and 1994 (£) (rounded up to nearest pound)

	April 1991		April 1994	
	M	F	M	F
Waltham Forest	309	241	360	267
Redbridge	322	247	385	298
Newham	343	255	374	308
Barking & Dagenham	350	*	401	*
Tower Hamlets	422	288	556	372
Hackney	*	294	*	361
Greater London	409	285	467	336
Great Britain	319	222	362	261

Source: *New Earnings Survey*, 1991 and 1994.

* Due to small sample earnings data not published, as standard error was above 5 per cent for full-time males in Hackney and full-time females in Barking and Dagenham.

Industry and Social Class in East London

Since the 1970s, industrial change has been widespread, particularly in London. Manufacturing and heavy industrial employment has declined and has been largely replaced by service sector occupations or economic inactivity. These trends have impacted on East London as, throughout the 1980s, manufacturing employment continued to decline. By 1991 the main sectors of employment in East London had become banking and finance, as well as government and services. Borough variations however have persisted. Table 18 shows that although East London boroughs experienced overall decline in manufacturing, they still had above average proportions of employees working in manufacturing industries in 1991. Barking and Dagenham and Newham have remained predominantly working-class communities, exceeding the London average in both manufacturing,

Table 18 Main industries of employment in East London boroughs, 1991, and key aspects of industrial change since 1981

	Percentage of residents working in					% change between 1981 and 1991		
	Manu-facturing	Construc-tion	Distr. & Catering	Banking & Finance	Gov't & Services	Manu-facturing	Banking & Finance	Gov't & Services
East London Region								
Hackney	11.4	4.8	16.2	16.7	38.4	−10.4	7.9	7.9
Redbridge	11.4	6.9	19.1	23.1	26.7	−7.7	6.1	1.7
Tower Hamlets	11.8	6.1	18.0	19.2	32.8	−12.1	7.0	7.0
Waltham Forest	13.5	6.4	17.3	18.1	31.8	−10.7	6.5	6.3
Newham	14.5	7.5	19.7	14.9	27.8	−10.9	3.4	6.0
Barking & Dagenham	14.9	9.9	19.8	16.4	22.8	−14.6	4.3	3.9
Greater London	10.6	6.5	19.2	20.4	30.7	−8.5	6.7	1.8
Inner London	8.7	5.0	18.0	21.8	34.9	−7.5	8.2	2.6
Outer London	11.5	7.3	19.7	19.7	28.6	−9.1	5.9	1.6

10 per cent sample.
Source: 1981 and 1991 Census, Crown Copyright.

construction and distribution and catering sectors. They both experienced a rise in service sector employment, but still had a below average proportion of employees working within those industries. By contrast, over half of residents in Hackney and Tower Hamlets were employed in service sector employment, which had above average increases throughout the 1980s. Redbridge and Waltham Forest have rather complex industrial profiles. Over a third of residents in 1991 were working in manufacturing, construction, and distribution and catering industries, whilst 50 per cent were employed in professional and managerial sectors. It is clear that with regard to industrial employment East London boroughs are also heterogeneous.

Following the growth in professional and managerial employment, the proportion of residents in service class occupations increased in all boroughs apart from Redbridge and Barking and Dagenham.[25] Due to the Docklands development, the proportion of professional and managerial workers doubled in Tower Hamlets, rising from 8.5 per cent to 17 per cent between 1981 and 1991. In Hackney, the proportion of service class residents rose from 14.5 per cent to 20.1 per cent between the same period. Barking and Dagenham and Newham have the lowest proportion of professional and managerial employees, with only 10.6 per cent and 14.7 per cent of residents in the service class compared with the London average of 27.2 per cent. Throughout the 1980s therefore, there has been a relative professionalisation of East London's workforce, a phenomenon particularly widespread in Hackney and Tower Hamlets. A major aspect of change within the social class composition of East London localities has been the dramatic decline in the proportion of residents in the lower working-class manual occupations and skilled manual groups. The decline in skilled manual workers was greater than the London average in all East London boroughs, apart from Redbridge. Interestingly, the decline in manual workers was particularly high in Tower Hamlets, which also had the largest rise in economic inactivity for men and women. The decline in lower working-class occupations was also particularly high in East London, above the London average in all boroughs apart from Redbridge. Industrial and economic change therefore have resulted in an overall decline in working-class occupations in East London. Barking and Dagenham and Newham, however, have remained predominantly working-class localities, with 34 per cent and 30 per cent of residents employed in skilled manual, partly skilled and unskilled groups in 1991. By contrast, the respective proportions for the other East London boroughs were around a quarter.

*Table 19 Decline in skilled manual, partly skilled and unskilled occupations, East London 1981–1991**

	Skilled Manual (IIIM) 1991 %	81–91 % change	Partly skilled and unskilled (IV & V) 1991 %	81–91 % change
Hackney	10.9	−11.5	12.9	−9.4
Tower Hamlets	11.5	−14.0	14.5	−13.3
Redbridge	14.7	−7.5	8.4	−3.4
Waltham Forest	15.0	−12.1	10.5	−6.0
Newham	15.3	−10.9	14.4	−10.5
Barking & Dagenham	19.6	−11.1	14.0	−7.1
Greater London	13.0	−9.2	9.6	−5.1

* Data refers to social class by occupation of Household Head.
10 per cent sample.
Source: 1981 and 1991 Census, Crown Copyright.

Conclusion

Throughout the 1980s both social and economic change has been widespread in the region of East London. However, the pace of change has been more pronounced in the inner East London boroughs. This has contributed to the inner and outer East London divergence, apparent in many spheres of social and economic life. Hackney, Newham and Tower Hamlets have large immigrant populations, and are now racially and culturally diverse communities. These boroughs also have higher female fertility rates and a higher proportion of young children. Furthermore, there is a higher prevalence of lone parenthood and single person households. Economically, the inner East London boroughs had the lowest economic activity rates, the highest proportion of economically inactive men and women and very high unemployment levels, particularly for non-white residents. However, the middle-class infiltration of Hackney and Tower Hamlets has brought about a fairly large increase in owner occupation and a large increase in professional and managerial employees and in those with higher qualifications.

By contrast, the impact of immigration and ethnicity has not been so marked in the outer East London boroughs. Although Redbridge and

Waltham Forest have experienced some change in ethnicity, Barking and Dagenham is an interesting exception. This borough has remained relatively homogenous, as it is still predominantly white, British born and working-class. It has remained economically quite successful despite below average educational attainment. Unemployment is lower in the outer East London boroughs, which also have a larger proportion of men and women in the labour force.

It is quite clear from this research that social change has been highly variable. Throughout the 1980s, East London has remained a heterogeneous locality and continues to be a 'back region' of complexity and diversity.

Notes

[1] R. Porter, *A Social History of London*, Hamish Hamilton, London 1994.
[2] D. Hobbs, *Doing the Business: Entrepreneurship, the Working Class and Detectives in East London*, Oxford University Press, Oxford 1989.
[3] Population density defined as persons per acre.
[4] *1991 Census*, HMSO, London.
[5] 1991 Census, HMSO, London.
[6] R. Porter, *op.cit.*
[7] *1991 Census*, HMSO, London.
[8] Newham had the second highest proportion of non-white residents in London in 1991. Brent had the highest with 45 per cent.
[9] These matters are discussed in subsequent chapters by Greg Smith and Alice Bloch.
[10] *Birth Statistics*, OPCS, HMSO, London 1991.
[11] Social Policy Research 80, *Social backgrounds and post-birth experiences of young parents*, Joseph Rowntree Foundation, July 1995.
[12] J. Obelkvich and P. Catterall, *Understanding Post-War British Society*, Routledge, London 1994.
[13] *Key Local Authority Statistics*, HMSO, London 1991.
[14] *1991 Census*, *op.cit.*
[15] J. Obelkvich and P. Catterall, *op.cit.*
[16] London Research Centre, *Population Change in London 1981–1991*, HMSO, London 1993.
[17] London Research Centre, *London Housing Statistics*, HMSO, London 1992.
[18] S. Brownhill and C. Sharp in Andy Thornley (ed), *The Crisis of London*, Routledge, London 1992.
[19] *Ibid.*
[20] London Research Centre, 1992, *op.cit.*
[21] Department of Education, *Performance School League Table*, 1993.
[22] *1991 Census*, *op.cit.*
[23] Economic characteristics of all men aged 16–64.
[24] Overtime hours for full-time males in Barking and Dagenham were 5.4

compared with the London average of 2.4. The average number of hours worked a week were 44 compared with the London figure of 40. *New Earnings Survey*, London 1994.

[25] Service class includes residents in social class I and social class II. In the 1991 Census, persons with a paid job are assigned to a social class by reference to their occupation in the week preceding the census. Unemployed persons are assigned on the basis of their last job. Comparisons with the 1981 Census have been made with reference to the social class of the head of household.

Social Class: Continuity and Change

Family Life in Barking and Dagenham

Margaret O'Brien and Deborah Jones

East London has been well mined by social scientists interested in exploring links between locality and family life.[1] From the 1950s onwards sociologists and policy-makers, notably Peter Willmott and Michael Young, have carefully examined the state of family networks in Inner and Outer East London.[2] Their work has highlighted the janus-like nature of family relationships in modern societies – close but distant, resilient yet fragile, rigid as well as flexible – and has shown how community, economy and family are intimately interwoven.

This chapter reports on a study in which we returned to one of the localities investigated by Peter Willmott in the 1950s – Barking and Dagenham.[3] We were interested in re-visiting the locality and exploring family life in the context of the 1990s, particularly from the vantage point of young people. Fears about a decline in family solidarity, commitment, and obligation have been growing during the latter part of the twentieth century.[4] International and national demographic patterns show that family life is undergoing radical change and, as will be shown in this chapter, Barking and Dagenham has not been immune to these global changes.[5] Cohabitation, divorce, remarriage, and the growth of maternal employment have created a range of new family types. Whilst it is still unclear whether these structural shifts have resulted in any straightforward changes in individual lifestyles and values, some writers have suggested that family life is increasingly organised much more by negotiation rather than prescription.[6] Released from the traditional dictates of community, kin, church and gender it is argued that individuals are free to choose lifestyles based on their own wishes and desires. Other writers have cautioned against the wholesale adoption of an individualisation thesis, pointing to the constraints on change caused by continuing inequalities which stem from differences in economic status, ethnicity, location and gender.[7]

Barking and Dagenham is well-placed to explore traditional and new family forms and their links with the economy and community. It has an interesting age structure with a significant proportion of older residents yet a higher than average level of households with young children (see Rix, this volume). Like many urban localities, the area has been subject to economic restructuring in the 1980s but has maintained a relatively low level of unemployment. It lies just ten miles away from an international finance centre – the City of London – and houses a New University, but we shall show Barking and Dagenham has one of the poorest educational profiles in the UK. Sandwiched between the more affluent outer East London boroughs of Havering and Redbridge and the more deprived inner East London borough of Newham, Barking and Dagenham is border, inbetween territory.[8]

Our investigation is a study of inter-generational perceptions of family life. The overall aim of the study is to examine contemporary constructions and meanings of family life across generation. This chapter will draw on data from the first phase which has consisted of a survey of young people in the borough and a longitudinal Census analysis. Phase two will be a qualitative interview study of a sample of adults and children drawn from the survey sample.

This first stage began the examination of the experiences of the child generation and was designed to give a profile of young people's views on and constructions of contemporary family life, as well as to capture accounts of their daily lives at home, at school, at work and in leisure. For younger generations, an individualisation thesis would predict a rejection or at least a questioning of traditional values such as belief in the importance of marriage, children within marriage, 'commitment', self-sacrifice or belief in the value of kin. In this study, perceptions and experiences of family life were examined in the context of young people's socio-economic conditions and educational and occupational aspirations.[9] Six hundred young people, drawn from class groups in six of the eight state schools in Barking and Dagenham have been surveyed (there are no private secondary schools in the borough).[10] Whilst the sample of 600 young people resided in all the (nineteen) wards, there were three predominant wards from which the sample was drawn: Chadwell Heath to the north of the borough and Goresbrook and Village in the south-east of the borough, where the Ford Motor Company is based.

Barking and Dagenham: Socio-historical developments

In order to understand why different localities come to be as they are, we need to look at how social processes interact with the unique spatial organisation of a place over time. With this perspective in mind, we have used Peter Willmott's observations to help us begin to understand the making of contemporary Barking and Dagenham.[11]

The profile of the borough at the time of Willmott's study was one of uniformity in class and visual character. In fact the re-development of Barking and Dagenham began with the building of the Dagenham Estate in 1921, created to house families displaced by slum clearance in London's East End, an impoverished and densely overcrowded area. The original plan was to build 29,000 council homes in five years. This target was reached in 1935 and by 1963 the total population of Dagenham (including the estate) was greater than 90,000, twice the population size of Bethnal Green and physically larger than places such as Bath, Doncaster or Burnley.[12] Willmott described the area as 'the biggest housing estate in the world' (we are not sure if it actually was), with an atmosphere of vast flatness, openness and uniformity, a uniform spatial structure, with a 'monotone air', lacking in visual contrast.

The area experienced collective migration of entire families from inner East London. This collective migration can be described as the movement of a community from the slum tenements of inner East London out into the leafy suburbs of Essex. The cockney, mainly white, East End families, highly organised by kin, often relocated together or sometimes the younger generation would migrate first, soon to be followed by their parents. As children of the first generation to migrate grew up and married themselves, families still remained geographically close to one another. By the late 1950s Peter Willmott found that four-fifths of married couples who grew up on the estate and whose parents were still alive had them living close by. There were, however, a significant proportion of more recent newcomers to the area who were spatially isolated from kin, similar to Willmott and Young's Greenleigh sample.

Barking and Dagenham's spatial uniformity was matched by its social uniformity – overwhelmingly working-class in character, described by Willmott as a 'one class colony'.[13] His sample of 877 Dagenham residents consisted of 89 per cent employed in skilled manual, semi-skilled manual and unskilled manual occupations; and only 4 per cent were employed in professional and managerial occupations. Research at the time showed that over 50 per cent of the population of Barking and Dagenham were locally employed (in either Barking, Dagenham or Ilford). One-fifth of all men and 6 per cent of all employed women on the estate were employed at Ford's or worked in its associated industries. Willmott felt that education suffered as a consequence of the estate's uniformity: there was little intellectual/cultural cross-fertilization of ideas between children and adults from different backgrounds. He quoted a national study carried out by Moser and Scott which showed Dagenham to have the third highest proportion of children leaving school under the age of fifteen (84 per cent) and the lowest proportion of people between fifteen and twenty-four in full-time education. Willmott's data pointed to low parental expectations of children's educational and occupational futures.

On other indicators of family life, his data showed that traditional family forms prevailed: 78 per cent of Willmott's sample were married, less than one per cent divorced and 13 per cent single (mainly unmarried and living with parents). Two-thirds of the second generation were married to people they met locally, that is, inter-marriage was common between those in the second generation. There was a clear tendency towards 'matrilocality' in the community, with couples living with or near wives' parents more often than husbands' parents. Among the women who had mothers living on the estate, over half had seen them during the previous twenty-four hours and nine-tenths had seen them at least once during the previous week.[14]

We shall now examine continuity and change in the borough, using data from the 1991 National Census and from our own empirical investigation to uncover to what extent the social fabric of Barking and Dagenham has changed since the time of Peter Willmott's classic study and to explore the interplay between locality and family life. To what extent has the area withstood global change and still maintained its local 'flavour'? We were particularly interested to uncover whether social and spatial homogeneity still captured the essence of the place and to what degree this manifested itself in young people's consciousness and experiences.

Barking and Dagenham – 1990s

The 1991 Census indicates that, on the whole, the population is stable and is still predominantly white and working-class in character. The borough is however experiencing some of the changes which are occurring across Great Britain, Europe and other westernised countries. For example, one is beginning to see a pluralisation of family forms within Barking and Dagenham, reflected, for example, in an increase in lone parent households.

Geographical Mobility

Overall Barking and Dagenham still has a relatively stable population. It has experienced little outward migration, mainly movement within the borough. It has the smallest number of out-migrants when compared with all other East London boroughs (1991 Census).[15] If one considers residents' movements one year before the census was collected, a majority (66 per cent of those who had moved) had moved *within* the borough. This figure is higher than for all East London boroughs, perhaps indicating that identification with place is still strong. Indeed we do find some evidence for this, at least from the point of view of the children from our study, with 77 per cent being satisfied with their neighbourhood; 46 per cent of these because it is a 'pleasant environment' and 30 per cent because they have 'nice neighbours'.

Even though Barking and Dagenham is still predominantly white, there has been a considerable growth of the Asian population since the 1960s and, to a lesser extent, of the Afro-Caribbean population. However, Barking and Dagenham still has one of the smallest ethnic group populations in London, well below most of its neighbouring East London boroughs: 93.2 per cent of the population is white, 3.3 per cent Asian, 1.9 per cent black Caribbean/black African, with 1.6 per cent categorised as other (*Barking & Dagenham Borough Profile*, 1993). These trends are reflected in the increase in Asian restaurants and places of worship, more or less absent at the time of Willmott's investigation. Nine per cent of the children from our study came from the Asian community (predominantly Muslim and Hindu in religion although a significant minority were Christian), and 3 per cent were Afro-Caribbean/black British, but the majority (83 per cent) were white British (with 5 per cent categorized as other).

Overall, 59 per cent of the children said they lived in owner occupied housing and 30 per cent in rented council accommodation. The remainder lived in other forms of rented accommodation such as those owned by housing associations (2 per cent) or were unsure of their type of accommodation (9 per cent)). Barking and Dagenham has seen a decline in local authority rented accommodation from 65.3 per cent in 1981 to 43.3 per cent in 1991. In parallel, the borough has experienced an increase in owner occupation of 20.4 per cent, this being the largest increase in owner occupation when compared with all other East London boroughs in the period from 1981 to 1991. It must be noted, however, that the borough still has the highest proportion of households renting from the local authority when compared with the whole of Outer London and the second lowest proportion of owner occupiers in Outer London.

One can only speculate whether this trend in owner occupation, initiated by the Conservative Party's 1980s Right To Buy policy, will hasten social diversification and mobility. As we have seen, the population is geographically very stable. People are buying their council properties but on the whole they appear to remain in the borough rather than selling up and moving on.

Economy, Social Class and Education

Changes in the economy of Barking and Dagenham reflect national economic changes since the 1950s: manufacturing in general has experienced a decline whilst service industries have grown. Between 1981 and 1991 the proportion employed in manufacturing declined from 29.6 per cent to 8.5 per cent of the total population. Those employed in service industries, construction, distribution and catering have increased. However, the borough also referred to by David Widgery as 'that vast factory suburb to our east'[16] still has greater proportions employed in manufacturing and fewer in services, including banking and finance, than the Greater London average.[17] Generally speaking the borough is not an area associated with high unemployment; the unemployment rate for the borough as a whole is 11.8 per cent, less than the inner London average (16.4 per cent), but more than the outer London average (9.1 per cent).[18]

Whilst Barking and Dagenham has experienced an increase in non-manual social classes since the 1950s, particularly for women, the majority of the male population are still employed in the skilled manual occupations (Table 1). This occupational pattern was also reflected in our study, where over half of the men were employed in the manual trades. Typical occupations for men included: plumbers, electricians, car mechanics, builders and decorators. Although manufacturing employment has declined, skilled manual occupations retain their predominance outside of the manufacturing context and, significantly, within the realms of self-employment.[19] However, this is not to overlook the significant change that has occurred in the numbers of people employed in the professional and managerial occupations which now account for 18.7 per cent of the total male population (Table 1) and 18.1 per cent of the total female population (Table 2).

Put in the broader context, however, when one compares the 1991 census data on social class for Barking and Dagenham with East London as a whole, Barking and Dagenham still has the lowest proportion of men and women in professional and managerial occupations.[20] Occupational homogeneity, the 'one-class community',

Table 1 Occupational Class of Men, in Dagenham (1958), England and Wales (1951, 1991) and Barking and Dagenham (1991,1994)

	Dag 1958	E&W 1951	B&D 1991	E&W 1991	B&D 1994
Professional & Managerial	4	18	18.7	35.6	22.8
Skilled non manual	7	8	12.9	11.0	7.2
Skilled manual	49	44	40.5	31.1	53.8
Semi-skilled manual	22	16	18.5	14.2	12.6
Unskilled manual	18	14	6.8	4.4	3.8

Sources: Dagenham (1958) and England and Wales (1951) P. Willmott, (1963) *The Evolution of A Community*, p14.; Barking and Dagenham (1991) and England and Wales (1991) *Census* (10 % LBS) (as a percentage of all men in employment, aged over 16 yrs); *Barking and Dagenham Study* (1994), Margaret O'Brien and Deborah Jones (as a percentage of all fathers in employment from a sample of 600).

Table 2 Occupational Class of Women in Barking and Dagenham (1991, 1994) and England and Wales (1991).

	B&D 1991	E&W 1991	B&D 1994
Professional Managerial	18.1	29.4	17.8
Skilled non manual	52.1	38.5	42.0
Skilled manual	5.8	6.8	7.8
Semi-skilled manual	16.1	16.2	22.4
Unskilled manual	6.1	6.9	9.9

Sources: Barking and Dagenham (1991) and England and Wales (1991) *Census* (10 % LBS) (as a percentage of all women in employment, aged over 16 yrs) *Barking and Dagenham Study* (1994), Margaret O'Brien and Deborah Jones (as a percentage of all mothers in employment from sample of 600).

is still a characteristic feature of the borough. Similarly there is still educational underachievement. In 1991 only 3.5 per cent of those over eighteen years had a degree or diploma, compared to 3.6 per cent in 1981. In fact, Barking and Dagenham has the lowest proportion of people with such qualifications in London, the London-wide average being 18.5 per cent. The data from our own study shows similar trends although parents had slightly more experience of post-school education: 17 per cent of mothers and 22 per cent of fathers were reported as having some form of further education after leaving school. But significant proportions of children did not know about their parents' education histories (39 per cent for mothers, 41 per cent for fathers). It appears that cultural capital resources generated from formal educational and professional occupational experiences are still relatively low in the locality and that this has not changed substantially, in the adult generation, since 1950s. There are however signs of change in younger cohorts which will be discussed below.

Where there has been significant change it has been in the proportion of households containing dual worker couples. In our study 79 per cent of fathers and 62 per cent of mothers were in paid employment with the majority working full-time (74 per cent of men, 36 per cent of women) and 26 per cent of women worked part-time. Typical occupations for women included: sales assistant, administrative and clerical work, child-minder or care assistant for older people. It seems that contemporary women in Barking and Dagenham have more occupational opportunities than the women of Willmott's study only 17 per cent of whom worked full-time (and 17 per cent part-time) and mainly in the local neighbourhood. He gives no direct data on the type of work that they did, but implies that much of it was semi-skilled or unskilled.

Household Structures and Childbearing Patterns

So far the patterns of social life examined have shown more continuity than change between the past and the present but this is not the case for household structure. Census data shows an increasing diversity of household structures. For example, between 1981 and 1991, Barking and Dagenham experienced a two-fold increase in one-parent households (2.3 per cent in 1981), so that one-parent households now account for 5.4 per cent of all households in the borough (Table 3), slightly less than the national average, but more one suspects than during the 1950s when Willmott was conducting his investigation.

Table 3 Barking & Dagenham Household Composition

	Dependent Children	%
1 Adult Pensioner	0	17.4
1 Adult Non-Pensioner	0	10.0
Lone Parent	1+	5.4
2 Adults (M + F)	0	28.1
2 Adults (M + F)	1+	18.6
2 Adults (same sex)	0 or 1+	3.6
3 or more Adults	0 or 1+	16.9

Source: 1991 Census.

The national increases in divorce and remarriage are reflected in our own sample. Many of the children had personally experienced changes in household and family structures in their first fourteen years of life.

Whilst a majority currently lived with both natural parents (68 per cent), 14 per cent lived in step-family households (12 per cent with their mothers and stepfathers, 2 per cent with their fathers and stepmothers) and 14 per cent in lone parent households (10 per cent lone mothers, 4 per cent lone fathers). In some wards of the borough over a quarter of children live in one parent households.[21]

Fertility rates (live births per 1,000 women aged 15-44 years) are generally high in Barking and Dagenham irrespective of age (75.7 as against 64.9 London average).[22] Overall 13 wards (out of the 19) have fertility rates which exceed the London average.[23] As in other localities the portion of births outside marriage has increased over the period. In 1991 36.5 per cent of all the live births occurred outside marriage in Barking and Dagenham (higher than the national average of 31 per cent and second highest of all East London boroughs).[24] There are in addition extremely high levels of teenage fertility in the borough. Barking and Dagenham has both the second highest rate of teenage births and the second highest rate of teenage births outside marriage when compared with other inner and outer East London boroughs.[25] In 1993 the local teenage fertility rate (46.0 live births per 1,000 females aged 15–19 years) exceeded both the England and Wales average (31.0) and the Greater London average (28.6).[26] These trends suggest a movement away from traditional family lifestyles, and for a minority of young women, an early transition into motherhood. National research indicates that whilst a growing proportion of teenage mothers cohabit with the child's father (about 38 per cent) these relationships may not be long-lasting.[27]

The 1991 Census included a specific question about cohabitation for the first time and it was found that cohabitation was generally much more common in London in comparison with other areas in the country. Whilst Barking and Dagenham had a low rate of cohabitation for couples without children (4.9 per cent of families as against 8.4 per cent in Inner London and 6.2 per cent in Outer London), the rates were higher when couples with children were considered (3.4 per cent of families as against 3.0 per cent in Inner London and 2.4 per cent in Outer London). Further demographic analysis is needed to uncover to what extent this pattern of non-marital childrearing is a rejection or postponement of marriage. The highest proportion of families cohabiting with dependent children is in the Gascoigne ward, which also has the highest rate of unemployment and one parent family households in the borough.

Kinship

So far we have charted the structural context to the lives of the young people in our study. We wish now to examine the interplay of locality and family life by exploring the place of kinship. We were interested in whether the sample of young people of Barking and Dagenham in the 1990s were surrounded by relatives, in much the same manner as Willmott described in *The Evolution of A Community.* Although Willmott noted some variations in the community, he concluded that: 'In part, Dagenham is the East End reborn',[28] particularly for those families that had grown up in the area. 'In all sorts of ways relationships with kin follow familiar patterns. Women see their mothers, and their fathers, more than men do ... The mother's home, again, is the most common centre for her daughters.'[29] His vantage point was from an adult sample of married couples, whereas we were looking at kinship through the accounts of fourteen year olds, the majority of whom had lived in the area since birth. For the young people of our investigation the 'mum' figure of community studies is, of course, the grandmother.

We wished to explore the link between kinship and social mobility as part of our examination of inter-generational patterns in family life. The survey material has generated some interesting findings which will be fleshed out by the qualitative stage of the study. We have been influenced by the work of Paul Thompson whose argument that strong family cultures, far from promoting upward mobility, are normally 'conservative and protective', seemed to resonate with the intergenerational patterns we observed.[30]

The Salience of Kin

Like Willmott, our findings show that there is still a pattern of 'matrilocality', with 47 per cent of the sample having their maternal grandparents living in Barking and Dagenham, compared with 38 per cent of paternal grandparents (these proportions include co-residential grandparents). This proximity is similar to that found by Willmott in 1959: 44 per cent of grandparents co-resided or lived locally (see Table 4). Fewer grandparents co-resided when compared with Willmott's sample (2 per cent as against 17 per cent), however a further 2 per cent of contemporary households contained great-grandparents.

Table 5 shows the frequency of contact with paternal and maternal grandparents. Overall, contact with maternal grandparents is highest: 35 per cent see her weekly, 16 per cent daily and 49 per cent

Table 4 Proximity of Kin (%)

	Dagenham 1959	B&D 1994*
Same Dwelling	17	10
Local	27	51
Further away	56	49

Source: Willmott (1963), p25. Willmott's data on co-resident parents only.

* The data in this column does not total 100 per cent as data derived from two questions (co-residence and proximity of non-co-resident kin). *Barking and Dagenham Study* 1994.

Table 5 Contact with Grandparents (%)

	Maternal		Paternal	
	GdM N = 412	GdF N = 292	GdM N = 370	GdF N = 254
Daily	16	13	7	6
Weekly	35	31	24	18
Occasionally	49	56	69	76

N = Total number of alive grandparents in each category.

occasionally. In general, frequency of contact with paternal grandparents is less than half that of maternal grandparental contact. The maternal grandmother was also the most popular grandparent.[31] She is talked to more frequently by grandchildren and the most frequently mentioned topic of conversation is school and educational matters, 'how I'm getting on at school' (44 per cent of the sample cited this), followed by the topic of leisure (24 per cent). Although she is the favourite for both boys and girls, girls are slightly more likely to favour her than boys, 60 per cent of the girls compared with 47 per cent of the boys.[32]

The special place of 'mum's mum', particularly for conversations about educational progress and school, is clear for this childhood generation and the relative absence of dad's dad and other male relatives suggests that the male line for inter-generational transmission of masculinities and work identities is weak in this locality. Neither did we find much evidence for the importance of uncles as a replacement role model for grandfathers and fathers. This pattern was suggested by Willmott in his 1960s study of adolescent boys in East London:

> Grandfathers will no longer do as models; boys prefer someone closer to their own age, more in touch with their lives. An uncle can offer a relationship something like that between father and son but without the inhibitions.[33]

There was, however, a stronger connection with the male line for the Asian children. Twenty per cent had daily contact with their paternal grandmother and 22 per cent with their paternal grandfather (and this pattern could not be explained by co-residence). Although frequency of contact with the paternal grandparent is greatest amongst the Asian sample, an overwhelming 76 per cent of Asians chose their maternal grandmother as their favourite grandparent, greater than for all other ethnic groups (52 per cent of white British, 57 per cent black British). Matricentredness, in the sense of emotional ties rather than matrilocality, prevailed for these Asian children. In phase two it will be interesting to uncover what influence, if any, the higher degree of contact with paternal kin has for the aspirations of Asian children.

Seventy-two per cent of the sample had a relative visit their home within the last week, 15 per cent within the month, and only 10 per cent 'not for a long time'. Whilst half of the sample reported having no kin living in their neighbourhood, of the remainder a significant minority had five or more relatives living close by (see Table 6). Indeed 20 per cent with nearby kin had a network of over ten relatives living locally.

Daily and weekly contact with the maternal grandmother was most frequent for those children having five or more kin living locally. These kin relationships need further exploration, but the pattern is suggestive of an extended family network with a high level of interdependence and cohesiveness for a significant minority of Barking

Table 6 Numbers of Kin in Neighbourhood (%)

1–4 relatives	63
5–9 relatives	21
10–19 relatives	10
20–29 relatives	4
30+ relatives	2

(N = 276, excluding those with no kin in neighbourhood (N = 271) and missing value cases)

and Dagenham families. We found lone parents and Asian families were consistently more likely to have greater numbers of kin who lived nearby (however, significant numbers of Asian children also had little or no contact with key relatives, such as grandparents who lived outside of the UK).

High contact was notable for children living in stepparent households (82 per cent of whom reported a relative visiting within the last week). Since stepfamilies were no more likely than other families to have local kin, it is possible that the increased size of the kin network of children living in stepparent households must account for this finding.

Kinship and Social Mobility

As we noted above, Thompson has argued that in communities with strong kin ties social mobility is low and that the loosening of ties may be an important precursor for upward social mobility. This model seems to explain partially the pattern of social homogeneity and low educational achievement in Barking and Dagenham since the 1950s, at least for the white, working-class community. However, educational opportunities and encouragement are important too. Indeed, Roy Greenslade, returning to his Dagenham grammar school in the 1970s some ten years after he left it and interviewing his old classmates, concluded that streaming in the school helped create 'a domesticated class', a generation who took 'the path to apathy and complacency'.[34] Only those children in the higher streams were socially mobile and often went on to leave the locality.

However, there appears to be the beginnings of change in the aspirations of young people in Barking and Dagenham, at least from the perspective of this study's sample. The findings indicate that the majority have occupational and educational aspirations way beyond their parents' experiences. For instance, 67 per cent of the sample had ambitions towards a professional/managerial job whilst only 23 per cent of fathers and 18 per cent of mothers currently worked in these occupations. Similarly, the vast majority, 80 per cent of the sample, wished to pursue some form of further education after year eleven, mostly staying on to the sixth form or going to sixth form college or having some other form of education. Only 13 per cent were expecting to go to work at sixteen years. On the familial front, young people had a clear idea about what they expected for their future. Often these expectations are centred around marriage, childbearing and family solidarity, but with a view to more equality between the sexes than in their parents' generation, and a companionate relationship (88 per cent envisaged getting married at about 24 years of age and 26 years was the average anticipated age for the start of childbearing). These beliefs contained characteristics of 'old' and 'new' cultural models. There seems to be little evidence of uncertainty about their future or for the postponement or rejection of marriage and childbearing as suggested by Oeşchle and Zoll in their study of German youth. However, it must be said that the German respondents were older (20–25 years) and in employment. Similarly there was no evidence that the girls planned to have children in their teenage years, a minority but significant pattern identified in the Census.

Moreover, an overwhelming majority of young people did not wish to pursue a career along the lines of their mother and father. 91 per cent of the sample did not identify with their mother's job. 59 per cent of these felt that their mother's job was 'boring' or they had 'other ambitions'. Similarly, a majority (83 per cent) did not identify with their father's job, for the same main reason 'boring/other ambitions' (55 per cent). Within this mass repudiation of parental occupation there was some same-gender identification and cross-gender rejection (for instance, daughters were more likely to reject paternal jobs than were sons, who were in turn more often rejecting of maternal jobs than daughters).

The tendency not to identify with a father's job was slightly less strong amongst the Asian children, although still the majority response – 73 per cent of the Asian sample rejected their fathers' job in contrast to 93 per cent of the black British sample and 83 per cent of the white British sample. These Asian children were more likely to mention a good salary as the reason for their positive identification.

Whilst historical precedent suggests that the opportunities for this generation to achieve their aspirations may be limited, it is apparent that more young people are beginning to stay on at school. Recent destination data for Barking and Dagenham's 16 year olds shows that in fact the proportion, albeit of different cohorts, pursuing some form of further education after year eleven was 63 per cent, not as high as our sample's expectation but still higher than previous years.[35] Examination participation rates have generally increased with more girls than boys being entered into GCSE examinations and achieving higher grades.[36] However, whilst new opportunities may emerge from the experience and credentials earned by further education there is still a clear reproduction of disadvantage in the locality. In 1993 Barking and Dagenham still had the third lowest rate of young people staying on for further education in the thirty-two London boroughs. Moreover, Beynon's study of Ford car workers (in Liverpool) has shown how idealism is replaced by realism when the responsibilities of breadwinning take young men over:

> People, living their lives, develop a pretty accurate idea of their own life chances, of the odds they face and the hopes they can realistically entertain ... Working-class people are faced with a limited number of employment prospects all of which are dreary. If you are young, with family responsibilities ... you attempt to get as much money as you can ... In a hard world you become a hard man ... If you work at Ford's, on the line, you let your mind go blank and look forward to pay day and the weekend.[37]

It is clear though that many of the assembly line jobs such as these have now disappeared and radical changes are occurring in the labour market for boys and girls alike. In the future, the move to new technologies may indeed serve to shake the cohesive kin cultures embedded in Barking and Dagenham. But in communities such as this with many people surrounded by strong family bonds and friends of similar social standing, individuals lack the bridges to other social networks that control access to new sets of opportunities and meanings. Increasingly, individuals may have access to new perspectives though television and the global electronic media, but it may well be that young people will relate to that which is around them, which they see as available, rather than the abstract. It is possible that the lack of tangible, concrete alternatives combined with low educational opportunities and residual educational underachievement will continue to constrain change in this locality despite shifts in personal aspirations.

Conclusion

The Census and study data show that kin contact and association do not appear to have changed significantly since Willmott's study of the borough in the 1950s: 72 per cent of the households had a relative visit their home within the last week; about half the sample had kin living nearby with 20 per cent of these having a local kin network of over 10 relatives; and 51 per cent had daily or weekly contact with their maternal grandmother. In some ways the community has stayed static through the period we have surveyed. However, the types of families and households created by Barking and Dagenham inhabitants is changing. There is a clear pluralisation of lifestyles – for instance, more dual earner households and one parent households than in the 1950s. Barking and Dagenham has witnessed an increase in marital breakdown but the pace of change appears slower than in other inner East London boroughs. This lag may be explained by the continuing strength of kinship structures and cultural support for family life, particularly for having children either within or outside of marriage. Barking and Dagenham has a generally high fertility rate which is also reflected at early ages: the borough has one of the highest teenage fertility rates in the country. Young women's pathways in adulthood in this locality are complex. Whilst a majority appear to be staying on at school, taking examinations and doing well in them, at least up to 16 years, the Census data shows that a significant minority of young women are opting for early motherhood. The fourteen year olds in our sample did not anticipate this early transition to parenthood identified in the wider Census findings. They had relatively high educational and occupational aspirations which may be explained by the slightly higher than average educational and socio-economic status of the sample when compared to the borough.

The decline of the manufacturing base and rise of the service sector has clearly opened up new employment opportunities, but in many ways Barking and Dagenham remains a stable enclave of working-class life. Renewal and regeneration, for instance through the influences of ethnic groups, has been marginal to date although this is beginning to change. Similarly, increases in the professional and managerial sector may shift the one-class cultural profile. The relatively low levels of unemployment in the borough may explain why some of its people end up being 'conservative' in regard to education and mobility. Similarly the strong local economy may be more able to support young mothers both at a formal and informal level. The study affirms the important point that social change is not linear but checkered and often contradictory; and that throughout this investigation we will need to examine the specificity of social processes through the lens of time, generation and place.

We would like to thank the following for their assistance: Justin Donovan, Alistair McGechie, all from the secondary schools who participated; and Peter Willmott and Michael Young.

Notes

[1] For example, Cornwell, 1984; Holme, 1985; Wilmott, 1963; Willmott and Young, 1967; Young and Willmott, 1957.
[2] Willmott and Young, *op.cit*.
[3]There is not an exact matching however. Willmott's survey in *The Evolution of a Community* was of households in the Dagenham estate which is now located partly in Barking as well as Dagenham. The present sample was accessed via schools throughout the whole of the present borough of Barking and Dagenham.
[4] See for example U. Bjornberg, 1992.
[5] U. Bjornberg, *op.cit.*; J. Haskey, 'Patterns of Marriage, Divorce and Cohabitation in the Different Countries of Europe', *Population Trends 69*, OPCS, HMSO, London 1992.
[6] For example, U. Beck, *Risk Society*, 1992.
[7] For example, G. Jones and C. Wallace, Youth, Family and Citizenship, publisher, place, 1992.
[8] Also noted by D. Widgery, 1991.
[9] There has been some German research to support this prediction, Oechsle and Zoll (1992), in Bjornberg, *op.cit*.
[10] At least four classes from each school were selected by head teachers on the basis of age (13–15 years) and timetable availability (the questionnaire had been piloted at one of the schools). We asked heads to select typical class groups (and not 'high' or 'low' ability groups). The response rate was nearly 100 per cent with only two refusers. However, absentee pupils were not included. Questionnaires were completed in the classroom. The average age was 14 years 9 months and the sample consisted of 45 per cent of girls and 55 per cent of boys. Other characteristics of the sample will be outlined in the chapter. All respondents were given a weekly confidential diary to complete. These were returned (to school secretary/teacher in a sealed envelope) by 26 per cent of the sample. When compared with the main sample the diary sub-sample contained slightly more boys than girls (60 per cent as against 55 per cent) and more Asian children (13 per cent as against 9 per cent). There were no differences by household type.

[11] P. Willmott, *op.cit.*
[12] P. Willmott, *ibid.*, pp3–4.
[13] P. Willmott, *ibid.*, p57.
[14] P. Willmott, *ibid*,. p29.
[15] Less than 12,000 compared with Newham which had nearly 225,000 (highest). Where reference is made to East London boroughs these include: Hackney, Newham, Tower Hamlets (inner East London); Havering, Barking and Dagenham, Redbridge and Waltham Forest (outer East London).
[16] D. Widgery, *op.cit.*, p154.
[17] *Barking and Dagenham Borough profile*, Policy Review Unit, London Borough of Barking and Dagenham, 1993.
[18] There are, however, pockets of high unemployment in the borough. Gascoigne ward, for example, has an unemployment rate which stands at 19.6 per cent (highest). Conversely, some wards have unemployment rates less than half the borough average, e.g. Longbridge, where the university is located, has an unemployment rate of 5.4 per cent. Department of Employment (April 1995) personal communication.
[19] The number of self-employed individuals has increased by a quarter since 1981 (*Barking and Dagenham Borough Profile*, 1993). Local informants have described Barking and Dagenham small businesses as commonly servicing the more affluent households of Havering and Redbridge.
[20] Percentage of employed women/men in professional and managerial occupations: Hackney (38.0, 34.3), Newham (25.8, 24.3), Tower Hamlets (30.9, 29.8), Havering (24.2, 32.9), Barking and Dagenham (18.1, 18.7), Redbridge (32.5, 40.9), Waltham Forest (32.7, 33.3), 1991 Census.
[21] *Barking and Dagenham Borough Profile*, 1993.
[22] *Vital Statistical Rates for London Wards*, OPCS, 1991.
[23] *Ibid.*
[24] *Social Trends*, HMSO 1994; Key Local Authority Statistics, HMSO 1993.
[25] *Annual Abstracts of Greater London Statistics*, No 130, HMSO 1994.
[26] Population and Statistics Division, OPCS, Commission Analysis.
[27] P. Selman and C. Glendinning, 'Teenage Pregnancies: Do Social Policies Make a Difference?' in J. Brannen and M. O'Brien (eds), *Children in Families: Research and Policy*, Falmer Press, London 1996.
[28] P. Willmott, *op.cit.*, p109.
[29] *Ibid.*, p32.
[30] P. Thompson, 'Family Myths, Models andDenials in the Shaping of Individual Life Paths', in D. Bertaux and P. Thompson (eds), *Between generations: Family Models, Myths and Memories*, Oxford University Press, 1993.
[31] Fifty-three per cent of the sample chose their maternal grandmother as their favourite grandparent, 21 per cent their paternal grandmother, 17 per cent their maternal grandfather and 9 per cent their paternal grandfather.
[32] Girls' second favourite is the maternal grandfather; boys' second favourite is the paternal grandmother.
[33] P. Willmott, *Adolescent Boys in East London*, London 1966.
[34] R. Greenslade, *Goodbye to the Working Class*, London 1976.
[35] *London School Leaver's Destinations Survey*, The Careers Service in London, 1994.

[36] Raw data from Education Office, London Borough of Barking and Dagenham.

GCSE Exam

	1992		1994	
	Entered 5+	passed 5+ A–C	Entered 5+	passed 5+
Boys	79.3	13.7	84.5	24.1
Girls	84.7	18.1	89.0	32.1

[37] H. Beynon, *Working for Fords*, 1973.

'People like us': the Gentrification of Hackney in the 1980s

Tim Butler

Introduction

It is perhaps not an unreasonable hypothesis, on the basis of the research which is reported in this chapter, to predict that a significant number of the people who read this will either be living in Hackney or will have done so in the relatively recent past. Thus to talk about Hackney is perhaps to talk about very familiar territory!

In this chapter, I draw upon research that I undertook in the 1980s on gentrification in two areas of Hackney (Figure 1): De Beauvoir Town and Stoke Newington (Figure 3). Face to face interviews with 250 middle-class recent homebuyers equally divided between the two areas revealed a very distinctive 'type': highly educated, likely to have come from a middle-class background and committed to Labour Party (or a more radical) politics. These findings and the reasons for them are discussed in more detail below; first however, both 'gentrification' and 'Hackney' need some definition and discussion.

Gentrification

Gentrification refers to the process whereby some working-class inner-city areas have become regenerated by the influx of middle-class homeowners. Although its usage has been mainly North American, at least in the academic literature, the term's origin lies in the changes that the British urban sociologist Ruth Glass noted in London in the 1960s:

> One by one, many of the working-class quarters of London have been

> invaded by the middle-classes – upper and lower. Shabby, modest mews and cottages ... have been taken over when their leases expired and have become elegant expensive residences. Larger Victorian houses, downgraded in an earlier or recent period – which were used as lodging houses or were otherwise in multiple occupation – have been upgraded again. Once this process of 'gentrification' starts in a district it goes on rapidly until all or most of the original working-class occupiers are displaced and the whole social character of the districts is changed.[1]

The phenomenon is however more complex and wide-ranging than housing differences with, for example, the suburban middle classes, as Sharon Zukin argues:

> From the moment the English sociologist invented the term 'gentrification' to describe the residential movement of middle-class people into low-income areas of London , the word evoked more than a simple change of scene. It suggested a new attachment to old buildings and a heightened sensibility to space and time. It also indicated a radical break with the suburbs, a movement away from child-centred households toward the social diversity and aesthetic promiscuity of city life. In the public view, at least, gentrifiers were different from other middle-class people thus gentrification may be described as a process of spatial and social differentiation.[2]

Whilst the idea has created a lot of academic research data and debate,[3] it has had a rather bad press,[4] being seen as responsible for the displacement of existing lower-class residents and for the abandonment of parts of the inner city with houses lying empty often for years whilst they await redevelopment as either single family dwellings or flat conversions. This process has been more dramatic in New York[5] than London but I can certainly remember whole streets of mainly empty houses in Stoke Newington in the late 1970s and early 1980s – usually full of squatters! To blame inner city poverty, displacement and abandonment on gentrification is, to some extent at least, to treat the manifestation of a problem as its cause; on the other hand, it is not clear that the housing redevelopment of much of inner London over the last twenty years has done much for those who, unable to afford inner city owner occupation, have found themselves displaced into the increasingly deprived public rented sector.

The literature shows that gentrification is not a 'return to the city' movement but rather a process whereby young singles and childless couples have remained in the city rather than playing the game of

Figure 1: the London Borough of Hackney, showing ward boundaries

'urban leapfrog' out to the distant suburbs. There is considerable disagreement about its causes and whether it is 'a back to the city movement by capital not people'[6] or whether it is the consequence of new lifestyles and occupational divisions within the middle classes.[7] There has been a reversal of the suburbanisation of capital back to devalued inner city locations (Docklands being the prime example) but there have also been changes within the middle classes socially, occupationally and culturally.[8] Gender has also emerged as an important influence on gentrification.[9]

> A female population increasing faster than the male population; an unusually high proportion of young and single women; very high

> proportions of women in the professional and technical occupations; high levels of academic credentials; a high proportion of dual earner households but few families, presence of young single professional women; and the postponement of marriage and childbearing ... [A]n inner city location minimises journey to work costs for households containing more than one earner, enhances the efficiency of household production, and facilitates the substitution of marketed services for domestic ones.[10]

As Glass above has indicated, the gentrification of inner London has its origins in the 1960s. It was initially 'sighted' in North London and particularly in Islington;[11] by the early 1980s most of inner London was undergoing gentrification.[12] By the 1980s, however, the rise in house prices in many of these areas had put them beyond the range of many young middle-class households and the gentrification of Hackney can be traced back to this period. The gentrification process is begun by 'pioneers' who, as it were, push back the 'frontiers' of (middle-class) 'civilisation' into areas previously thought out of bounds and 'redlined' by the building societies.[13] Damaris Rose has argued that many of these people are what she terms 'marginal gentrifiers' (often women and others needing to live in the inner city but unable to afford the prices of existing gentrified areas) and they take the initial risks, often living in unconventional households and improving the property primarily through the use of 'sweat equity'.[14] This was the reason for my initial interest in the subject, having bought a large run-down terraced house in Stamford Hill with six other people shortly after leaving university in 1971! It seemed to me that many of the other people I got to know living in the area had similar backgrounds; my subsequent research has shown that this concept of 'people like us' continued to be a feature of the gentrification of Hackney through the 1980s. In the next section, I outline the demographic changes that preceeded and accompanied the gentrification of Hackney and in the following section I present the findings of my own survey research.[15]

The Gentrification of Hackney

It was really only during the 1980s that gentrification in Hackney 'took off' and the reason for this is simply that it had some of the last remaining housing stock suitable for conversion to middle-class use which was near to the centre and particularly to the City. During the 1980s the City expanded rapidly and many of the gentrified areas of

Table 1: Occupational Structure of the Resident Hackney Population 1971–91

Description and SEG	1971	1981	1991[17]	1971 %	1981 %	1991 %	71–81 ppc	81–91 ppc
Prof, empl & man 1,2,3,4,13	8,006	8,198	15,220	7.2	9.5	22.6	+2.3	+13.1
Other non-manual 5,6	30,358	26,321	24,190	27.3	30.5	35.8	+3.2	+5.3
Skilled manual 8,9,12,14	32,359	18,813	8,080	29.1	21.8	12.0	−7.3	−9.8
Semi-skilled manual 7,10,15	24,797	18,727	11,910	22.3	21.7	17.6	−0.6	−4.1
Unskilled manual 11	10,230	6,731	4,700	9.2	7.8	7.0	−1.4	−0.8
Other 16,17 & Govt schemes	5,449	7,508	3,380	4.9	8.7	5.0	+3.8	−3.7
Total Economically Active	111,200	86,300	67,480	100	100	100	0	0
Total Population	218,594	179,529	161,590					

Source: Census Tables 1971, 1981, 1991.

Hackney were within a half hour cycling distance of City desks. The timing and scale of the demographic changes that took place in Hackney between the 1971 and 1991 Censuses point to important changes in the demographic structure of the borough's population.

The most dramatic change that took place between 1971 and 1991 was the loss of population, which declined by 57,000 or 26 per cent; most of this took place between 1971 and 1981. There is nothing particularly unique to Hackney here, all inner London boroughs lost population during this decade mainly to the outer London boroughs and the rest of the south east. Vikki Rix (this volume) discusses the extent to which East London as a whole followed and departed from this pattern. However, within the context of an overall loss of population, the occupational structure of Hackney changed significantly over these years (see Table 1). Broadly this shows that the middle-class group (i.e. professionals, employers and managers)[16] doubled in size between 1971 and 1991. The pattern of this growth is quite complex in that it occurred within the context of a steep decline in both the overall population and in the economically active population. Thus between 1971 and 1981 the actual number of economically active middle class remained more or less stable although it increased its 'share' of the economically active population (from 7.2 per cent to 9.5 per cent). In the period 1981-91 however, it doubled in size (from 8,198 to 15,220) and constituted nearly 23 per cent of the borough's economically active population. It is this population loss that provides the basis for the gentrification of Hackney in the 1980s. In the 1980s, however, the overall population loss slowed (although the number of economically active people continued to decline significantly) but the actual number of middle class more or less doubled thus increasing their visibility considerably.

Other non-manual (i.e. routine white collar workers) have declined in actual numbers, although the decline in the total population has been such to mean that relatively their share of the population has grown. The mirror image of the increase in the middle classes is the decline in the proportion and numbers of skilled manual workers which, as the table shows, has accelerated over the two intercensal periods. From constituting nearly a third of those economically active in 1971, this was down by 1991 to less than one in eight. Both the other manual groups show a similar, if not so dramatic, trend downwards both in actual and percentage terms over the period. The reasons for this are not hard to guess and are broadly in line with the points made by Michael Rustin in his introductory chapter: the restructuring of

Table 2: Changes in Household Tenure Hackney 1971–9

	1971		1981		1991		1971–81		1981–91	
HH Tenure[20]	HH	HH%	HH	HH%	HH	HH%	71–81	71–81 ppc	81–91	81–91 ppc
OO	9290	11.6	11,302	16.5	20358	26.9	+012	+4.9	+9056	+10.4
CR	34,020	42.6	39,317	57.4	36,242	47.9	+5297	+14.8	−3057	−9.5
RU	26,380	33.1	6781	9.9	3,735	4.9	−19,599	−23.2	−3046	−5.0
RF	9010	11.3	5411	7.9	5631	7.4	−599	−3.4	−220	−0.5
Other	1110	1.4	5617	8.2	9665	12.8	+4507	+6.8	+4048	+4.6
Total	79,810	100	68,445	100	75,631[21]	100	−11,382	0	+6781	0

Source: Census, 1971, 1981, 1991.

manufacturing employment, the increasing importance of producer services and the rise in professional employment. The increase in the proportion of the population who are economically inactive is another clear and important trend – whilst some of this can be accounted for by a rising population of under 16 year olds much of it is is caused by permanent displacement from the labour market.

In general social terms one might argue that this points to an increasingly polarised social structure, given that the other large increase is in the economically inactive population, between a small but growing affluent group and a large group dependent on state benefits, albeit in the context of a shrinking total population. It is, of course, possible to argue that, far from demonstrating a process of occupational polarisation, this points to an upgrading of skills and professionalisation.[18] The problem here is that most of this upgrading appears to be the result of inward migration of young university graduates whilst much of the decline in the skilled manual category can be accounted for by the migration out of Hackney and into owner occupation elsewhere.[19]

The implications of these occupational changes for the changing social structure of Hackney over the last two decades can be seen by looking at the changes that have taken place in household tenure (Table 2) which shows a doubling of owner occupation from just over 9,000 households in 1971 to over 20,000 households in 1991 – from ten per cent to about a quarter of all households which compares to a national figure, for owner occupation, of about two thirds of all households in 1991.

Most of this growth took place between 1981 and 1991. In terms of council housing, there was an increase of 15 per cent between 1971 and 1981 and then a decline of 10 per cent between 1981 and 1991 – presumably through the sale of council houses and the transfer of property to housing associations. The most dramatic change that has taken place in the Hackney housing market was the decline in the private rented sector between 1971 and 1981 which lost nearly 20,000 households and shrank by approximately a quarter. This released housing stock which in many cases was developed either by individuals as single family dwellings or by small-scale developers into flat conversions for the incoming middle classes. This 'displacement data' should be kept in proportion because there were something like 6,000 new persons living in owner occupation and 51,000 fewer private tenants, so direct displacement was low. The main losses from the private rented sector took place 1971–81, whereas the growth in owner occupation occurred in the period 1981–91. Separate analysis shows that whilst some of those displaced from the private sector went into public sector housing in Hackney, more left the borough and many if not most of them went into owner occupation in outer London or the Rest of the South East (ROSE).[22] The conclusion from all of this however does point to a clear social polarisation between those in owner occupation and those in public sector housing.

We can therefore point to occupational and housing tenure changes over the past twenty years in Hackney which have resulted in a bimodal population distribution between those in middle-class employment and enjoying (pre-negative equity at least!) the benefits of owner occupation and the rest who are concentrated at the 'lower' end of the occupational structure and in public sector housing. It would be tempting to argue that this has led to a growth in social polarisation but the picture is probably more complicated, compounded as it is by family structure, ethnicity, age and above all, space. It would certainly be a mistake to talk of Hackney (and indeed most other gentrified boroughs in London) in one breath: it is precisely the juxtaposition of affluence and poverty that is so striking even within the gentrified areas which are, for the most part, concentrated to the west of the borough. This is visually represented by the contrast, often in the same street,[23] between the owner occupied housing, on the one hand, and the council blocks and other forms of rented housing on the other. The other contrast is between those wards in the north-west of the borough, in which a relative affluence is concentrated, and the rest. The figures are, however, somewhat misleading in that the total ward figures often subsume the extremes; for example, my study area of De Beauvoir Town is in a ward which is split between highly affluent owner occupiers and a massively deprived council estate which has the statistical effect of masking the affluence. Equally in the gentrified wards to the north-west, there are still high levels of deprivation: for instance, nowhere in Hackney does owner occupation exceed 50 per cent.

It is generally accepted that possession of higher educational qualifications is the best empirical indicator we have of gentrification.[24] When this is applied to Hackney we can see a clear pattern emerging in the wards to the north-west of Hackney. These wards also tend to have the lowest proportions of elderly people and also to be where there are more than 25 per cent of residents in social classes 1 and 2 – the so-called service class of higher and lower professionals, managers and employers. The same patterns emerge for levels of owner

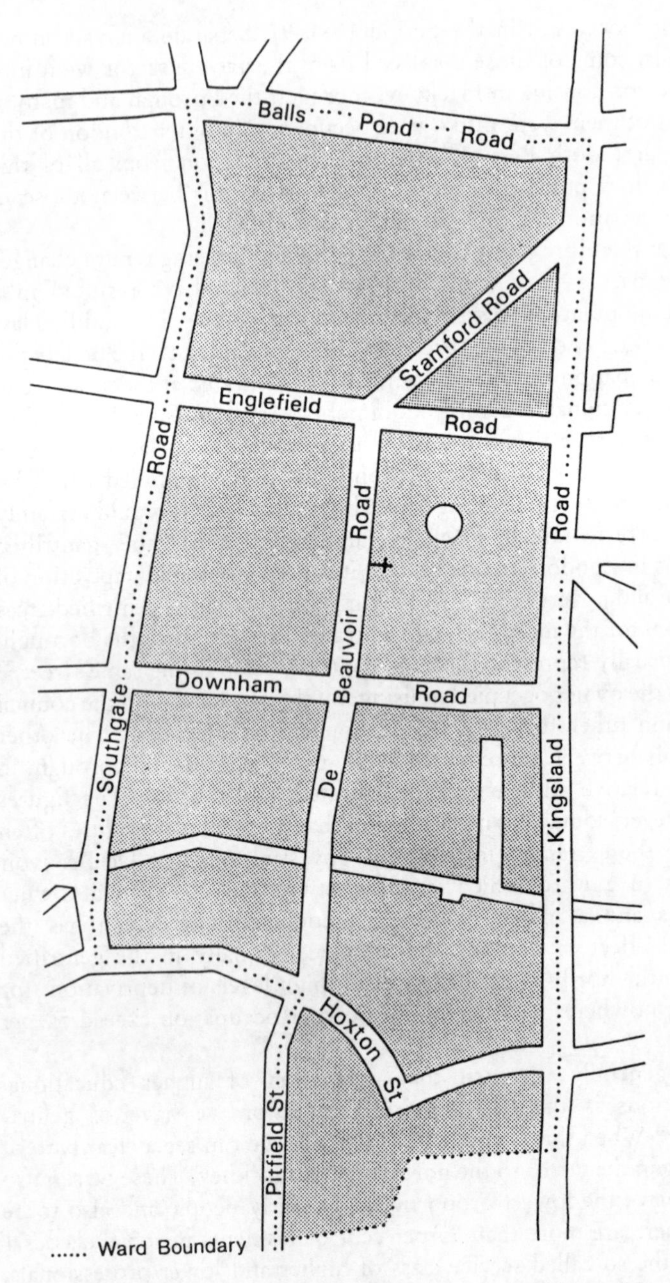

Figure 2: De Beauvoir ward, showing the main thoroughfares

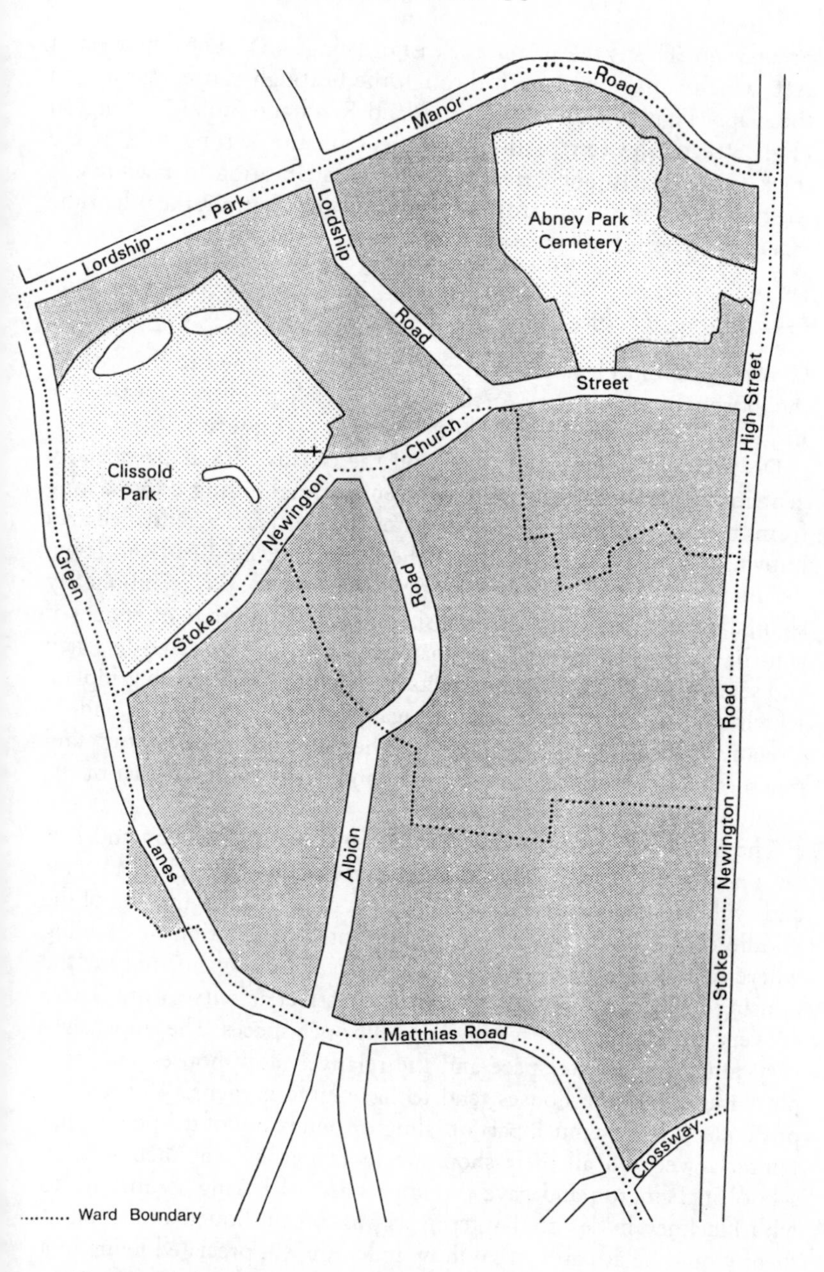

Figure 3: Stoke Newington wards (Clissold, North Defoe, South Defoe), showing the main thoroughfares

occupation. This is the area to the east of Islington[25] and to the west of A10 which runs north-south through the borough and is marked on the maps (Figures 2 and 3) as Kingsland Road and Stoke Newington High Street. The rest of the borough is on the 'wrong side of the tracks' and largely uncharted territory. Gentrification in Hackney is westward looking – towards Islington and the centre rather than the Hackney Marshes and the east

Gentrified Hackney

Gentrification in Hackney is therefore largely confined to the west of the borough and my research was undertaken in two areas: De Beauvoir (see Figure 2) and Stoke Newington (see figure 3)

De Beauvoir does not show up on the census data as particularly gentrified because it is divided between a large housing estate dating from the early 1970s to the south end of the ward and a gentrified area known as De Beauvoir *Town*[26] at the north end. De Beauvoir Town neighbours Islington geographically and shares the symbolically significant N1 postcode. Its housing differs from that of much of gentrified north London in that many of its houses are semi-detached and set in quite large plots; its streets form a most un-English gridplan, which again sets it apart. It was, atypically for much of North London, a relatively large scale development in the mid-nineteenth century and much of the property is still leasehold and is owned by a trust of the family that originally developed it.[27]

The houses are cheaper than those elsewhere in Islington and it is very near to the City – many offices can be walked to in half an hour and cycled to in considerably less – which, given the lengthening of the middle-class working day, is an important consideration in deciding where to live. De Beauvoir Town is a strange place: not only is the housing atypical but there is very little on-street activity or life. There are very few shops, and even fewer public open spaces. The emphasis is very much on private space and the relatively low houses and large plots mean that the houses tend to have large gardens. With its N1 postcode, it is very much part of Islington and many of the people that I interviewed did all their shopping in Islington, sent their kids to school in Islington and gave the impression of having as little to do with Hackney in day to day terms as possible, although almost all of them would be at pains to say how much they appreciated living in a 'place like Hackney'.

Stoke Newington differs from De Beauvoir Town in many respects.

Architecturally, it is 'North London terrace' with an almost postmodern mixture of styles as a result of its piecemeal development in the late-nineteenth century. Whereas in De Beauvoir Town there is little public space and relatively generous private space, in Stoke Newington the private houses seem more cramped but there is a lot of public space and plenty of shops. It is centred around Stoke Newington Church Street and estate agents market it as Stoke Newington 'Village' stressing the park, Church Street and the general conviviality. The number of restaurants in Church Street seems to rise each time I go there it seems and now one is confronted by a wide range of choice of food and prices.[28] The research was undertaken in the North Defoe ward which has the highest proportion of 'service class' residents of all the wards in Hackney, with 35 per cent of the heads of household in social classes 1 or 2, according to the 1991 Census. Apart from Church Street, much of the attractiveness of Stoke Newington can be explained by its closeness to Clissold Park which provides much of the open space which is lost in the long, narrow and often sunless gardens of many of the houses. Particularly for the large number of people who I talked to with children, 'the park' was a major asset and a place of considerable conviviality where 'people like us' or 'our' nannies could meet and the children could play.[29] 'The' school which most middle-class parents had identified as the best primary school was also located in this area.

The findings of my research can be summarised briefly as pointing to a group who (in comparison with the middle class as a whole) tend to come from middle-class backgrounds, to have been educated in the private sector or at selective secondary schools, to have gone to Oxbridge or Redbrick universities and studied non-scientific or technical subjects and are now found to be working in professional as opposed to managerial or technical occupations. Where they are living in non-single person households, both partners almost always have full-time professional jobs and the household income is considerably higher than for a similar national group. Finally, and perhaps most tellingly, party political identification is biased towards the Labour Party and support for the Conservative Party is under-represented. What I found, therefore, was a group of people in their 30s and 40s, who could be characterised as forming a post-1968 generation whose political and cultural identifications had remained very much to the left as compared with the middle-class population nationally. Perhaps the single clearest indicator of 'who' these people are is given by the daily paper they read: 70 per cent of those who read a daily paper in Stoke

Newington, and 49 per cent in De Beauvoir Town, took *The Guardian*. In the remainder of this section, I discuss some of the most salient findings from my research which support the argument that the Hackney middle class are different.[30]

Two thirds of those that I interviewed came from service-class backgrounds. Almost all the rest came from the self-employed or other non manual groups – only 11 per cent came from the manual working class. Two thirds of those *not* from a service-class background came from a home-owning one. Few of the studies on gentrification tell us much about the social and spatial origins of those who gentrify the inner city, although Williams[31] asserts that they tend to be drawn from suburban childhoods and Warde[32] makes reference to the suggestion that they are upwardly socially mobile. The data from Hackney tends to confirm the first claim but to deny the second. Goldthorpe[33] indicates that two thirds of the service class have been upwardly mobile into it. It would seem that those living in gentrified Hackney are different from other members of the middle class in that they were born into it. This sense of difference is reinforced by looking at their experience of education and higher education which in Britain has a distinct class bias. In the post-war period approximately 5 per cent of all children had a private education but as the following table (Table 3) shows nearly a third of the Hackney respondents were educated

Table 3: Type of secondary school attended

	De Beauvoir Town		Stoke Newington		Total	
	n	%	n	%	%	n
Grammar	47	37	37	32	34	84
Independent	40	32	28	24	28	68
Comprehensive	13	10	28	24	17	41
Direct Grant	14	11	12	10	11	26
Secondary Modern	5	4	4	3	4	9
Other	8	6	8	7	7	16
Total	127	100	117	100	100	244

Missing Data = 1.
Source: Butler 1992.

privately. Of course, given the high proportion from middle-class backgrounds, we would expect the percentage receiving private education to be higher than the national average but nevertheless this is a very high figure. In addition, about another third went to grammar school and a further 11 per cent to direct grant schools, many of which were 'public schools' (i.e. private) in all but name and have mostly now become totally feepaying.

Perhaps not unsurprisingly given this privileged background, over 80 per cent went to university and of these 20 per cent went to Oxbridge which continues to represent the élite end of the higher education system; of the rest 34 per cent went to the older Redbrick universities and 15 per cent to newer ('plateglass') universities founded in the 1960s. In other words, over two thirds went to what are now seen as the established universities. What is probably more interesting for their subsequent lives is what they studied when they got there: nearly 60 per cent of respondents studied humanities or social sciences and only 12 per cent followed science and technology courses. The figures are given in Table 4:

Respondents were therefore highly educated but in a particularly narrowly defined set of disciplines which Gouldner has referred to as a

Table 4: Discipline Studied

Discipline Studied	De Beauvoir Town		Stoke Newington		Total	
	%	n	%	n	n	%
Arts & Humanities	34	38	37	32	70	35
Social Sciences	31	18	17	29	47	24
Science & Tech.	11	14	14	10	24	12
Business	1	3	3	1	4	2
Law & Accountancy	2	12	12	2	14	7
Art & Design	7	10	10	7	17	9
Other/failed to complete	14	9	9	11	23	12
Total	100	104	100	95	199	100

Missing data = 46.
Source: Butler 1992.

'speech community', whose communality was acquired during many years of higher education:

> They speak a special linguistic variant, [which] is characterized by an orientation to a qualitatively special culture of speech: the culture of a careful and critical discourse (CCD).[34]

David Ley has also noted this tendency amongst gentrifiers to be:

> ... tertiary educated professionals in the arts, media, teaching and academic positions as well as public sector managers in regulatory and welfare activities – a subgroup I shall identify as the *cultural new class*.[35]

Given this, it is perhaps not surprising how difficult it is to summarise the occupational characteristics of respondents, except in the most general of terms, largely because most of the categories devised by social science (as opposed to marketing) seem to address working-class occupations. Nevertheless, nearly twice as many (59 per cent) worked in what might be broadly termed 'professional' or 'administrative' as opposed to 'managerial' occupations (34 per cent). Erik Olin Wright[36] looks at the 'assets' that people draw upon in their employment: these are based upon the capital, skill and organisational position possessed by the individual. Crudely one might argue that professionals draw primarily upon skills or credentials (largely gained through the education system), managers draw upon organisational assets (i.e. having worked their way up through the organisational hierarchy) and the petit bourgeoisie on the possession of capital. There are many problems with this approach but it does allow us to draw distinctions between sections of the middle classes.[37] Using this typology (table 5) we can immediately see, not surprisingly given what we know about respondents' educational history, that almost all respondents depend on their credentials for their position in the occupational structure.[38] This applies equally to the self-employed group who are almost exclusively professionals of one kind or another. Of those who are employed, 30 per cent work in the public sector, 39 per cent in the private sector and 3 per cent in the voluntary sector. Over half of those to whom I talked had worked for the same employer for more than five years whilst less than 8 per cent had swopped jobs in the previous twelve months.

All of this contrasts dramatically with research conducted by Savage *et*

Table 5 Respondents' Wright Classification

	De Beauvoir		North Defoe		Total	
	%	n	%	n	n	%
Self-employed	21	43	35	24	67	29
Credentialed Managers	13	27	22	15	42	18
Credentialed Supervisors	4	8	7	4	12	5
Credentialed Employees	57	42	34	64	106	45
Uncredentialed Managers	4	0	0	4	4	2
Workers	1	2	2	1	3	1
Total	100	122	100	112	234	100

Source: Butler 1992.

al on the service class in Berkshire in the same period.[39] Their respondents were almost exclusively working in high tech industry, either in technical or managerial capacities and there was a high rate of labour turnover (50 per cent had changed jobs in the last year); they found very few people working in professional occupations.

Hackney respondents were better paid than the middle class nationally (this is illustrated in Table 6 by comparison with the 1987 General Household Survey data for people with degrees). Those living in De Beauvoir were better paid than those in living in Stoke Newington and men were better paid than women. Whilst women may benefit from gentrification in terms of occupational status and salary, this is only in relation to women in general; compared with middle-class men there appears to be a consisent gender disadvantage in terms of status and salary. High salaries are restricted to the private sector and, to a lesser extent, the self-employed. Nobody working in the public or voluntary sector earned more than £30,000 per annum.

Compared with the middle class nationally, respondents generally were better educated, better paid and more likely to be in professional or administrative sections of it. They were also more likely to have come from a similar social background to their current one than the

Table 6: Salary Comparisons for Respondents

Category	De Beauvoir Town		Stoke Newington		General Household Survey (1987)[40]	
	male	female	male	female	male	female
Average salary	£30,625	£19,768	£19,956	£14,915	NA	NA
% earning over £20,000	68%	34%	32%	14%	18%	4%
% earning over £40,000	29%	8%	9%	4%	NA	NA
Household income over £50,000	28%		6%		NA	

Source: Butler 1992.

class as a whole. Their expressed sympathy for the Labour Party,[41] shown in Table 7, might therefore, on the face of it, seem surprising. Particularly in Stoke Newington there was massive support for the Labour Party (70 per cent of respondents) and almost none for the Conservatives; this was less so in De Beauvoir Town but even there only 26 per cent supported the Conservatives. To give these figures some context, Marshall *et al* found that 52 per cent of their national sample supported the Conservatives and 22 per cent supported Labour;[42] in his analysis of voting trends in the 1987 General Election Ivor Crewe reported 59 per cent supporting the Conservatives and 14 per cent Labour.[43]

Table 7: Voting Intention

Voting intention	De Beauvoir Town %	Stoke Newington %	All %
Labour	33	70	51
Conservative	26	9	18
Liberal/SDP	18	7	13
Other	22	14	19

Source: Butler 1992.

Crewe also looked at the effect of higher education by looking at the voting intentions of university graduates which is the nearest category to the Hackney respondents (Table 8).[44] Although support for the Conservatives declined compared with the middle class as a whole, Hackney respondents remained far less inclined to vote Conservative and much more likely to vote Labour than university graduates as a whole. Graduates in Hackney were more than twice as likely to vote for the Labour Party once the votes for other parties had been eliminated.

Table 8: Voting Intentions of Graduates (share of three party vote)

Voting intention	Hackney %	Crewe %
Conservative	16	34
Labour	68	29
Liberal/SDP	27	36
n	163	4,886

Source: Butler 1992.

There are many ways we could explain away these differences;[45] nevertheless, I remain convinced that the middle class in Hackney *is* different and this difference is associated with where they live. Whether this is a consequence of living where they do or is associated with the same sort of reasons for choosing to live there is difficult to tell. As one respondent, who owned a flourishing business and had a second home in the country put it:

> It's very easy to live around here and state socialist views, there's some areas of London where I've lived where one could never state those views because you would either be regarded as mad or needing conversion whereas around here people accept your opinion and that's fine. There's no doors closed in your face because of it.

In fact much of the support for the Labour party is 'without illusions' and the following comment by another respondent is far from atypical:

> We would both have no doubt that we would still vote Labour, we don't particularly like Neil Kinnock, we don't like the Labour Party but we would still vote Labour rather than anything else. There doesn't seem any alternative ... I am sure that I used to know why, but now it would just feel like the only thing that I could do. I have never voted anything but Labour in my whole life; I just don't see how I could change unless there was a more radical alternative that seemed pragmatically possible in a way that I don't see any of the alternative left parties seem possible ... if you lived in another country there are socialist parties ... that I would find much more appealing than the socialist party in this country.

Things though have changed since she first came to Stoke Newington when

> No-one other than Labour supporters declared their politics; whereas now it is socially acceptable to put an SDP sticker in your window.

Discussion

These findings raise three questions which I would like to address in this concluding section. First, why might this be, second, how permanent is it likely to be and, third, what implications might this have for urban change particularly in the wider context of East London?

Sociologists have perhaps tended to dismiss such findings as being 'location effects' as if these are of little or no consequence. I would not wish to claim that location has a causal influence on the manner in which people vote and express themselves, nevertheless there appears to be an increasing tendency towards spatial segmentation within the middle class both occupationally and residentially.[46] Bagguley[47] has argued convincingly that work on middle-class political radicalism[48] has shown that political convictions tend to influence occupational choice and not the other way around. It is therefore perhaps not surprising that we find more on the left in some professions than in others.[49] The same argument can convincingly, I would suggest, be applied to where people decide to live particularly amongst a class who, almost by definition, are socially mobile – having left home to go to university where for the most part they cannot stay, they have to seek employment in professional and managerial posts elsewhere. As Savage and Fielding have shown, the south east generally is an 'escalator region' which acts as a 'honeypot' for young service class graduates.[50] For many the attraction is the high tech R&D centres on the M4 or around Cambridge which have been studied by Savage *et al*[51] and Massey *et al*[52]; for others it is likely to be the various service industries in the public or private sector, including the media and the professions which are located in central London. For those with non-scientific or technical qualifications, and particularly for women, these occupations are likely to be particularly attractive for the reasons suggested earlier by Warde.[53] My argument is that such people are likely to seek out people like themselves in order to reinforce the cultural and political values they have acquired during their formative years in higher education. Hackney has become an area where 'people like us' tend to live and can find reaffirmation of these beliefs which have been an important element in their/our lives. In other words, what is being suggested is that political orientation is in fact a causal factor for both occupational and locational decision-making and not the other way around as sociologists and others have tended to assume.[54]

An extension of this argument is that we might expect to find different kinds of social groups living in different gentrified areas. This is an area which requires further comparative work, nevertheless I think that the gentrification of Docklands has attracted a very different 'type' to that described above.[55]

The second question arising out of this research concerns how permanent this phenomenon is likely to be. Those of us who were radicalised through the politics of the late 1960s and the 1970s grew used to being told that we would grow out of it. Nobody would deny the importance of both career and material possessions to the Hackney respondents, but my impression is that those living in Hackney had not prioritised material gains as much as they might have done during the boom years of the 1980s. They were mostly well established in careers and had nice homes, but maximising their position on either the housing or labour markets did not for them seem an end in itself. Viewed from the mid-1990s, this restraint would appear to have protected them from the worst of the recessions in the London labour and housing markets. Nevertheless, for the middle class – especially those with children – living in Hackney is not easy, particularly for those who have a commitment to radical, or at least redistributionist, forms of social justice. This becomes acute when faced with choices about secondary education. One option, widely adopted by respondents in De Beauvoir Town is private provision. Almost nobody that I interviewed sent their child to the local primary school, either schools in Islington or private schools were the preferred options. This was less common in Stoke Newington for several reasons: they had less disposable income, there were greater ideological objections, particularly by those working in state welfare services, and there were 'better' primary schools which the middle class had 'adopted'. In both areas, many respondents had considered moving out to the suburbs (particularly to Hertfordshire because of its good reputation for schooling). But the disadvantages when both partners worked seemed to be overwhelming. An increasing trend though appeared to be to move further out, to Haringey, for example, which seemed to have a more congenial educational system and yet be close enough to central London for both work and entertainment whilst still counting as 'London'. They would not be seen as having sold out to the suburbs! In fact most people seemed to talk either of making the move to Muswell Hill or to far out of London and a total change in lifestyle. It would therefore seem that the early years of family building do not inhibit continuing to live in Hackney but, as the children begin to move through the school system, many of these gentrifiers do consider moving on. In this sense, the gentrification of Hackney has been both a cohort and lifecycle phenomenon: young couples with families have begun to be replaced by others as their families have reached school age. On the other hand, there are plenty of others, with and without children, who have stayed – either opting out of the state school system or, more commonly, doing what the middle class have always done which is to use their social and 'political' skills both to improve provision and to ensure that their children get the best of what is available. This process is not just confined to education but to other areas of public provision:

> My husband has worked quite a lot to ensure that the Square is reasonably well looked after, when he has heard of cuts in the Parks Department, for example, he's always acted very strenuously to ensure that we don't lose our park-keeper who is a permanent park-keeper which is quite unusual for a little area like this; we are lucky to have a park and a permanent park-keeper but that doesn't stop him from doing all he can to keep it and so far he has been successful.

Generally speaking the middle class have taken on the council both from within and without and are less inhibited in dealing with bureaucrats than other local residents (having access to a daytime phone helps!).

It can, of course, be argued that this is very much a double-edged sword, and that middle-class assertiveness, far from increasing the resources and quality of life for the whole area merely appropriates scarce resources for the relatively advantaged. Another respondent summed up rather neatly the importance of local resources, in the following terms:

> *TB: Is the local infrastructure then of no importance to you?*
> It depends on what you mean by the local infrastructure, the restaurants are quite important! ... We use the library, the Mildmay Library (in Islington) and in fact we use the sports centre down at the Britannia, we use the swimming pool, but that's about it really, we use the leisure facilities.

She is typical of many in De Beauvoir Town, she has removed her children from the local school, she has a nanny and the family have private health insurance and a company car through her husband's job; both partners are devoted to the Labour Party at a national level. On the other hand, others either do not have these resources or are not prepared to deploy them in this way and for them the choice appears to be either to stay and put time into improving the facilities or leaving the area. There is evidence of both strategies particularly in Stoke Newington.

The third issue that I posed concerned relevance of the gentrification of Hackney to the wider regeneration of East London. In many ways the outlook is not a hopeful one. The research that I carried out showed that people liked living in Hackney, there was a sense of wanting to live on the 'frontier' but within limits and one of these was the Kingsland Road (see Figure 3). On the whole people tended to shop in Islington and the Holloway Road and not in the ethnic markets such as Dalston's Ridley Road. Local colour is all right but within strictly controlled boundaries.The inter-relationship between gentrification and ethnicity is complex. To some extent, gentrification has gone along with working-class white flight; the gentrified parts of Hackney are amongst those with the highest ethnic populations which provides the incoming middle classes, who have too much work in an area suffering from too little work,[56] with a source of domestic labour for childcare and cleaning. It is quite likely that, although the middle class may have made the local council more responsive, at least to persistent middle-class campaigners and complainers, this may have had the effect of merely diverting resources from more deprived areas. In Tower Hamlets there appears to be little interaction between the newcomers who spend little time or money in the area and the displaced working-class residents. Michael Rustin has suggested in his introductory chapter that the election of a fascist local councillor might be seen as an indication of this failure to achieve any form of social integration.[57] If suburbanisation led to the social and spatial separation of the classes, then in gentrified areas there is little evidence that spatial togetherness leads to any lessening of social distance. Indeed this social separation is increasingly acquiring an ethnic dimension.

The nature of the housing stock in East London as one moves eastward from Hackney and parts of Tower Hamlets (David Owen's Limehouse, for example) becomes less attractive to the kind of people living in Hackney and areas to the west. As the distance from the cultural and business centres increases, it seems that much of East London has many of the disadvantages of urban living (propinquity to deprivation and perceived danger) and none of the advantages (greater accessibility to work and entertainment). It is hard to see how gentrification will 'jump' the swathes of council estates in East Hackney to Newham, Waltham Forest and areas to the east.

It is difficult to draw any firm conclusions from this study of Hackney for other areas except to point out that what has emerged is that gentrification points to diversity amongst middle-class groups as opposed to the uniformity that was suburbia. It would therefore be a mistake to expect the pattern of development in East London to follow a pre-determined outcome and I regard this as basically optimistic for the development of East London as a multiclass and multiethnic area.

Notes

[1] Ruth Glass, *Introduction to London: Aspects of Change*, Centre for Urban Studies, London 1963, pviii.
[2] Sharon Zukin, 'Gentrification: culture and capital in the urban core', *Annual Review of Sociology* 13, 1987, pp129–147.
[3] See the following for an overview of this debate: Chris Hamnett, 'Gentrification and residential location theory: a review and assessment', in D. Herbert and R. Johnston (eds), *Geography and the Urban Environment: Progress in Research and Applications*, Volume VI, Wiley, London 1984, pp283–319; Chris Hamnett, 'The blind men and the elephant: the explanation of gentrification', *Transactions of the Institute of British Geographers*, NS 16, 1993, pp173–189.
[4] Indeed most 'gentrifiers' would probably not wish to use the term about themselves; the London Docklands Development Corporation (LDDC) appears to actively discourage the use of the term in its literature.
[5] Neil Smith, B. Duncan and L. Reid, 'Disinvestment, reinvestment and the economic frontier line in gentrifying neighbourhoods', Paper presented to the Housing Policy and Innovation Conference, Amsterdam, June 1988.
[6] Neil Smith, 'Towards a theory of gentrification: a back to the city movement

by capital not people', *American Planning Association Journal* 45, pp538–548.
[7] This approach is best exemplified in the work of David Ley, e.g. David Ley, 'Gentrification and the politics of the new class', *Environment and Planning D: Society and Space* 12, pp53–74.
[8] See Hamnett 1991, *op.cit.*, for a review of this debate.
[9] See Alan Warde, 'Gentrification as consumption: issues of class and gender', *Environment and Planning D: Society and Space* 9, 1991, pp223–232; Liz Bondi, 'Gender divisions and gentrification: a critique', *Transactions of the Institute of British Geographers*, NS 16, 1991, pp190–198. For a critique of this approach see Tim Butler and Chris Hamnett, 'Gentrification, class and gender: some comments on Warde's "gentrification of consumption" ', *Environment and Planning D: Society and Space* 12, 1994, pp477–493.
[10] Warde 1991, *op.cit.*, p228.
[11] Peter Williams, 'The role of institutions in the inner London housing market: the case of Islington', *Transactions of the Institute of British Geographers*, NS 1, 1976, pp72–82.
[12] For a case study see: Ian Munt, 'Economic restructuring, culture and gentrification: a case study of Battersea', *Environment and Planning A* 19, 1987, pp1175–1197.
[13] Smith *et al* 1988, *op.cit.*
[14] Damaris Rose, 'Rethinking gentrification: beyond the uneven development of Marxist urban theory', *Environment and Planning D: Society and Space* 2, 1984, pp47–74.
[15] A full account of this research and the findings is given in Tim Butler, *People Like Us: Gentrification and the Service Class in Hackney in the 1980s*, unpublished PhD Thesis, 1992. The Open University, Milton Keynes 1992.
[16] In fact, as I will show later the vast majority of this group are professionals with relatively few managers and even fewer employers!
[17] A new standard occupational classification was produced during the 1980s replacing the OPCS 1980 Classification of Occupations which was used in the 1981 Census. Therefore the occupations within the respective SEGs have changed which should be taken into account when making comparisons between the two years. It should not, however, affect the general trends shown in the table.
[18] See Chris Hamnett, 'London's turning', *Marxism Today*, July 1990, pp26–31; and Chris Hamnett, 'Social polarisation in global cities: theory and evidence', *Urban Studies* 31, 1994, pp401–424.
[19] See Butler 1992, *op.cit.* This work using the Longitudinal Study of the Census which 'tracks' a 1 per cent sample of the census population between census points, shows that there is a clear trend for men who leave Hackney to be upwardly mobile in occupational terms whilst for women the trend appeared to be to move out of the labour market. At the same time there was a clear trend towards owner occupation.
[20] OO = owner occupation; CR = council rented; RU = private rented (unfurnished); RF = private rented (furnished).
[21] The 1991 Census imputed wholly absent households and residents for the first time. This accounts in part at least for the increase in the number of households from 1981.
[22] Butler 1992, *op.cit.*

[23] This compares with New York, for example, where gentrified areas have very clear boundaries, see Loretta Lees, 'Gentrification in London and New York: An Atlantic Gap?', *Housing Studies* 9, 1994, pp199–217.
[24] Smith *et al* 1988, *op.cit*.
[25] Estate agents, particularly in the early and mid-1980s, marketed Stoke Newington as 'East Islington'.
[26] The use of the word 'Town' is probably significant and indicative of how residents feel about the area; in somewhat similar ways residents in the Stoke Newington area acquiesced in the estate agents' designation of it a 'village'. These distinctions are explored in more detail in Butler 1992, *op.cit*.
[27] The Benyon Trust.
[28] I recall the general sense of excitement when Fox's Wine bar opened on Church Street in the late 1970s which was a sign that the area had arrived and as one of my respondents put it much later, that 'we had not bought a dud'.
[29] Another prized local resource was Abney Park Cemetery which has become a wildlife centre and which is discussed by Martin Hoyles (this volume).
[30] As *The Guardian* readership figures indicate there are consistent differences between De Beauvoir Town and Stoke Newington, nevertheless whilst these are significant they also indicate that the two areas share a common socio-economic and cultural profile when compared to the middle class nationally.
[31] Peter Williams, 'Class constitution through spatial reconstruction: a re-evaluation of gentrification in Australia, Britain and the United States', in Neil Smith and Peter Williams (eds), *Gentrification of the City*, Allen and Unwin, London 1986, pp56–77.
[32] Warde 1991, *op.cit*., p221.
[33] John Goldthorpe, 'On the service class, its formation and future', in Anthony Giddens and Gavin Mackenzie (eds), *Social Class and the Division of Labour: Essays in Honour of Ilya Neustadt*, Cambridge University Press, Cambridge 1982, p175.
[34] Alvin Gouldner, *The Future of Intellectuals and the Rise of the New Class: A Frame of Reference, Theses, Conjectures, Argumentation and an Historical Perspective*, Macmillan, London 1979, p27.
[35] Ley 1994, *op.cit*., p56.
[36] Erik Olin Wright, *Classes*, Verso, London 1985.
[37] Mike Savage, James Barlow, Peter Dickens, and Tony Fielding, *Property, Bureaucracy and Culture: Middle Class Formation in Contemporary Britain*, Routledge, London 1992.
[38] Savage *et al* (*ibid*.) use the term 'cultural capital' in this context. This they derive from Pierre Bourdieu, *Distinction: a social critique of judgement*, Routledge, London 1984. In effect, they equate cultural capital in their work with the accumulation of higher educational qualifications.
[39] Mike Savage, Peter Dickens and Tony Fielding, 'Some social and political implications of the contemporary fragmentation of the "service class" in Britain', *International Journal of Urban and Regional Research*, 12, 1988, pp455–476.
[40] Central Statistical Office, *Social Trends*, Volume 19, HMSO, London 1989.
[41] Respondents were asked 'If there were to be a general election tomorrow, which party would you vote for?'

[42] Gordon Marshall, Howard Newby, David Rose and Carolyn Vogler, *Social Class in Modern Britain*, Hutchinson, London 1988.
[43] Ivor Crewe, 'A new class of politics', *The Guardian*, 15 June 1987.
[44] Crewe 1987, *ibid.*
[45] The response rate was low at around 35 per cent and the overall numbers were small at 245.
[46] See Savage *et al* 1992, *op.cit.*
[47] Paul Bagguley, 'Middle-class radicalism' in Tim Butler and Mike Savage (eds), *Social Change and the Middle-Classes*, UCL Press, London forthcoming.
[48] The main example is Frank Parkin, *Middle-Class Radicalism*, 1968.
[49] See Anthony Heath and Mike Savage, in Butler and Savage (eds), *op.cit.*, for a study of the relationship between occupation and party identification.
[50] Mike Savage and Tony Fielding, 'Class formation and regional development: the "service class" in south-east England', *Geoforum*, 20, 1989, pp203–218.
[51] Savage *et al*, 1988, *op.cit.*
[52] D. Massey, P. Quintas, D. Wield, 'Hightec Fantasies: Science parks in Society', *Sciences and Space*, Routledge, London 1992.
[53] Alan Warde *op.cit.*
[54] This approach is supported by the research being undertaken in Germany on 'social milieux' which suggests that lifestyles and patterns of association have a far greater independence of occupation than previously assumed.
[55] Darryl Crilley *et al*'s work would suggest a rather different profile for Dockland's 'gentrifiers': see D. Crilley, C. Bryce, R. Hall and P. Ogden, *New Migrants in London's Docklands*, Queen Mary College, London 1900.
[56] Nicky Gregson and Michelle Lowe, *Servicing the Middle Classes: class, gender and waged domestic labour in contemporary Britain*, Routledge, London 1994.
[57] See also Phil Cohen's chapter in this volume.

The Political Modernism of East London

John Marriott[1]

The political landscape of East London is perplexing, fraught with an unevenness likely to trap the unwary. While seeming to share a certain common history of industrialisation and immigration, its constituencies have inhabited political experiences traversing the entire spectrum of parliamentary and extra-parliamentary activity. Solid support for the Labour Party in local and parliamentary elections has existed alongside a tradition of Conservatism, and on the Tower Hamlets council in recent years, Liberalism. Even at borough level there are striking contrasts. West Ham, for example, which has been dominated by the Labour Party since 1919, has in the south experienced lately the threat of fascist activity from the British National Party.

To chart, let alone analyse, this shifting and uneasy landscape is a daunting task worthy of rather more attention than I can devote here. What I wish to attempt is little more than a provisional, speculative overview of certain themes that may help us to understand better something of the political trajectory of East London. More specifically, I explore the experience of West Ham[2] in contrast to that of the 'traditional' East End, arguing that distinct conditions prevailed to underpin the hegemony of the Labour Party. Not that the hegemony was complete. In spite of the unassailable authority of the party over the formal political terrain, its support was never popular. In West Ham, as in the East End as a whole, the urban poor remained politically volatile, arguably because they retained premodern cultures resistant to modern political discourses.

Labourism in West Ham

On 4 July 1992 a group of politicians, academics and local dignitaries assembled at Stratford Town Hall to commemorate a particular moment. From that site precisely one hundred years previously historic election results had been announced for the southern constituency of the borough of West Ham. They declared the return of James Keir Hardie, an Independent Labour candidate, for West Ham South.

His election may have owed much to historical contingency but it did signal a decisive new phase in the history of working-class politics. For the first time a working-class candidate without the patronage of the Liberal Party had been returned to Parliament with a mandate to represent working-class interests and hence herald parliamentary labourism, the most influential form of political involvement in the twentieth century.

And yet this centenary took place in the aftermath of a devastating Conservative victory in the April 1992 General Election. So damaging was it that not for the first time, but now with a quite new sense of urgency, prophets spoke of the demise of the Labour Party.[3] Should it be so, future historians would no doubt contemplate a rather tidy periodisation; the tradition of labourism existed for almost exactly one hundred years.

Rumours of the death of the Labour Party, however, have been greatly exaggerated. Parliamentary labourism has proved to be surprisingly adaptable not least because of a pragmatism built into its very foundations. And we need look no further than West Ham and Newham for evidence of this. West Ham returned not only the first Independent Labour MP some eight years before the foundation of the Labour Representation Committee, but also the first labour council in British electoral history in 1898. The council was short-lived; fatally weakened by the fragility of the alliance that constituted the labour group, and challenged by an increasingly vituperative and effective anti-socialist marriage of convenience between local Tories and Liberals, it was defeated in 1900. For a time power changed hands with a predictable regularity, until 1919 when a Labour council was elected together with two Labour MPs. In the course of the next decade the Labour Party was able to establish an almost complete hegemony on the formal political terrain – a hegemony that to the present has never been seriously challenged.[4]

The experience of West Ham stands in some contrast to that of other East London boroughs.[5] On the eve of the First World War the Labour Party had been quite unable to establish even a foothold in Bethnal Green, Stepney and Hackney. Only in Poplar was there evidence of significant support for the party on a scale comparable to

West Ham, but at the time the local Labour Party had been disaffiliated by the national party, the charismatic George Lansbury temporarily carrying the electorate with him into the political wilderness. After the war Labour advanced in all these boroughs, capturing control of Bethnal Green, Stepney and Poplar. Unlike West Ham, however, success here was relatively short-lived; by the mid-1930s Labour was once again a minority voice.

Overall, labourism in West Ham demonstrated a degree of continuity and resilience not witnessed in other areas of East London. What was true of the period leading up to the Second World War is true of the postwar period. Constituencies which displayed a political volatility have continued to do so.

This demands explanation. It is tempting to turn with a degree of inevitability to the touchstone of social composition. Perhaps detailed exploration of the industrial and social development of East London will reveal significant differences that can account for variations in political traditions. There is something in this. We cannot view East London as an entity with a common historical experience. That of West Ham was certainly distinct and separate. It emerged or rather thrust its way into industrial modernity in the last third of the nineteenth century with a staggering increase in population. Mid-century West Ham was essentially agricultural; by the turn of the century it was the industrial heartland of the south east. During this process the population has risen from 20,000 to over a quarter of a million.

Equally significantly, this expansion coincided with the onset of a protracted decline in the industrial structure of the older East End. Staple industries around shipbuilding, silk weaving and the docks collapsed or displayed telling signs of terminal illness, to be replaced by smaller-scale production of clothing and furniture, the so-called sweated trades. Toward the end of the century there was a net loss of population, much of it migrating over the River Lea in the hope of finding work in neighbouring West Ham.

The remarkable development of West Ham does explain in part its unique position in British political history. Its relatively stable industrial base and the trade union tradition to which it gave rise did, it has been argued, provide propitious conditions for a mature class consciousness lacking in other areas of East London.[6] Similarly, the growth in strength and stature of the trade unions during the First World War promoted the subsequent success of the Labour Party. But such explanations are partial, and tend to beg rather more questions than they answer. Social conditions do not automatically generate particular forms of political consciousness; we need to have a rather more refined sense of how these conditions were perceived by those who inhabited them, what grievances were defined and how they were defined, and what solutions were sought. And for this we have to look at their construction through language, more specifically the political rhetoric of the protagonists.

We have also to guard against the tendency to overemphasise difference. Contrasts in industrial development and composition there were, but certain features were common to the whole of East London. Most notably, the wretched system of casual labour pervaded, transcending industrial and administrative boundaries. A massive reservoir of labour existed. It existed because no industry was immune to seasonality of production and demand, and employers found the reservoir a most convenient means of varying at will the size of their workforce. This population became a vital element in the political equation.

Early Fortunes of the Labour Party

In the period leading up to the First World War the Tory and Liberal Parties had measures of success, and it is impossible to account for the fortunes of the nascent Labour Party without due reference to this complex political landscape. What is evident is that the Labour Party cannot be understood as the natural and inevitable voice of the East London electorate. The picture is further complicated by the uncertainty of Labour's identity. Before the formation of the London Labour Party and later a central organisation provided the semblance of a framework for campaigns and strategies in local politics, constituency parties possessed autonomy. They could decide on programmes and tactics, and produce their own propaganda without reference to a higher authority. The result was Labour Parties of considerable diversity.

The advance of Labour in East London was hampered by the older rival parties which were capable of promoting and sustaining radical programmes.[7] Liberals in particular, drawing on a radical metropolitan heritage, pursued policies of municipal intervention and social reform that continued to attract significant support from a deprived working-class electorate, and made it difficult for Labour to forge a recognisably distinct presence. Tories, whilst more cautious in municipal intervention, exploited racial tensions, promoted a strong sense of Englishness and adopted a less proselytising attitude to working-class culture.

Labour owed its relatively successful development in West Ham to a number of factors. Structural conditions imparted certain advantages. The industrial base gave rise to a powerful tradition of trade unionism. Three unions in particular came to dominate, namely, the railway workers based around the locomotive centre at Stratford, the dockers at the Royal Docks south of the borough, and the gasworkers at the Beckton Gasworks. Not that there was an easy equation between trade union strength and Labour Party success. Unions branches were not entirely convinced of the merits of political representation, seeking to redress grievances through industrial struggle. When this faltered, members turned with renewed vigour to struggle through political representation. The consequence was that unions were not always prepared to support Labour either financially or in terms of active electoral work.

But these unions had a local membership which in composition and ideology was removed from the traditional craft élite and its Liberal sympathies. Almost without exception the key figures in the early moves to Independent Labour representation came from their ranks. Will Thorne, Jack Jones, Arthur Devanay, Joe Terret and Richard White dominated the unions and came to exercise a powerful hold over the formal political terrain, never relinquishing it to those middle-class radicals who were attracted to the cause. The appeal of Labour to a working-class electorate was immediate and direct. The response may have been based on an untheorised, unreflective sense of us and them, but it did serve the interests of the Labour Party.

Elements of the political culture that gave birth to and sustained these unions also promoted the dramatic growth of the Co-operative Movement. Originally founded by railway workers in 1860, the Stratford Co-operative Society expanded through amalgamation with smaller local societies. By 1903 it had a membership of nearly 13,000 and was, with the society at the Royal Arsenal in Woolwich, the only one in the south able to challenge the co-operative might of the north. From the outset and as the movement expanded its ideals attracted members from across the political spectrum. Under such circumstances any form of involvement in politics, particularly political representation, threatened disruption. Alliance with the liberal cause, for example, would have engendered disaffection among the movement's conservative membership. But with the ascent of labour representation such involvement was forced onto the agenda by trade union co-operators and others who saw parliamentary struggle as a vital weapon in the co-operative armoury.

Nowhere was this more apparent than in the Women's Co-operative Guild. From its inception in 1883 the Guild had remained self-governing and self-financing. This meant that although it continued to operate within the co-operative movement, it was able to pursue strategies unhampered by the conservatism of the parent body. In the 1890s, for example, it worked assiduously to promote closer relationships with the trade unions, and embarked on an effective campaign to increase female representation on public bodies. In the period leading up to 1918 it focused its energies on maternity benefits, divorce reform and child and maternity care. Guild members may not have had the municipal or parliamentary franchise, but the ground was being laid for a female Labour vote when it was eventually won.

The existence of powerful currents of trade unionism and co-operation, a discredited Liberal Party and an absence of middle-class involvement in the local Labour parties provided the foundation for the subsequent triumph of Labour in impoverished West Ham. In no other East London borough did these conditions prevail.

The First World War and its Aftermath

There is little consensus on the nature of the impact of the First World War on the fortunes of the Labour Party. McKibbin's stress on the ante-bellum character of the Labour Party and the strong continuities into the interwar years, and Nairn's thesis that war *made* the Party through promotion of Labour's role in government and a sense amongst the working-class electorate of a profound need for change have been replaced by a more considered appreciation of the complex and uneven development of the party over this period.[8] The conditions of war effected structural changes that were propitious neither to a class consciousness which Labour could exploit nor to a strengthening of Labour's position in the state apparatus.

War did provide opportunities for Labour in localities where it could harness patriotic sentiment and resist Liberal charges of collectivism and extravagance. It emerged strongest in areas where it had been able to establish a social and economic base before 1914.[9] In no area was this more apparent than in East London where in the elections of 1919 every borough passed into the control of Labour.

Labour's advance in East London during the immediate postwar period has been recognised for some time. Thompson[10] saw it as the result of the party's new found ability to build upon a new class consciousness engendered by the displacement of small-scale production, and a heightened sense of the importance of effective electioneering pioneered by Herbert Morrison's London Labour Party (LLP). More recently Bush has argued that socialist activity and an increasingly solid trade union movement enabled the LLP to establish an electoral base which it mobilised effectively when the war ceased.[11]

Gillespie confronts what he sees as the implicit teleology of these arguments.[12] The growth of the party in East London was not based on a putative class unity forged at the workplace but on the opportunities that opened up for intervention in the local state. Trade unionism had remained weak in the old East End throughout the war, and if it was to become more firmly established in the interwar period this was due not to structural change in the local economies but to political intervention, particularly in issues related to employment and relief. Thus while decasualisation of dock labour was attempted by both the Ministry of Labour and the Transport and General Workers Union with little success, Labour councils were able to encourage decasualisation by intervening in employment policies to set wage rates and conditions of service which often exceeded those demanded by the unions.

But it was the question of unemployment that came to dominate the political agenda:

> The success of local Labour parties in the East End in the early 1920s was a function of their ability to bridge the gap between different categories of the unemployed and those potential supporters still in the workforce. The unemployed became a significant component of Labour's organisational base throughout East London. However, where the party appeared to subsume its interests with those of the organised unemployed, this provided a recipe for disaster.[13]

Poplar and Bethnal Green provide test cases for this thesis. Poplar had a powerful Labour council, leaders of which went to prison for refusing its precepts from the London County Council (LCC) in defence of adequate scales of relief for the unemployed. But they demanded the burden of relief to be carried at a national or metropolitan level with an attendant equalisation of rates; in this they had the support of both Liberal and Conservative councillors. In Bethnal Green, on the other hand, Labour identified much more closely with the unemployed themselves; as a result it had relatively little success in Board of Guardians elections, and lost control of the council in 1928. Overall, the more Labour allied itself to the unemployed the worse it fared.

Toward the close of the 1920s the locus of political power, particularly around unemployment, shifted to the national level. In 1926 the state superseded the West Ham Board of Guardians in an unprecedented attack on local representational democracy. Wholesale cuts in relief ensued as East London guardians were forced to retreat. Three years later the administration of relief was taken over by new LCC Public Assistance Committees, severing the link between relief and local politics, and undermining Labour's base by destroying the alliance between the unemployed, skilled workers and casual labour. Labour abandoned the political agenda that had underpinned its advance and moved onto a terrain inhabited by its opponents. By 1930 it had lost control of the East London boroughs.

This experience stood in some contrast to that of West Ham. Labour emerged from the war with renewed strength and vigour. Bitter rivalries between pacifist and patriotic elements had threatened a split. For a brief moment in the period leading up to the 1918 General Election, an alliance of Independent Labour Party and British Socialist Party succeeded in having their members selected as parliamentary candidates. In itself this may not have been unexpected, but what was surprising was the defeat inflicted on Will Thorne by these more radical elements in the party. Thorne was the single most influential figure in local politics. A founder member of the Gasworkers Union, MP for West Ham South since 1906 and a leading councillor, he had during the war demonstrated a rabid jingoism which attracted tacit support of the other union leaders and substantial sections of their membership, but which antagonised pacifists. Thomas Kirk, union secretary and councillor complained of the

> perpetual insults that every decent labour man has endured through standing up for his country in the hour of her crisis from men who have foisted themselves on the Labour movement by wirepulling tactics. These men have no industrial history and owe their presence there to men like Will Thorne, Jack Jones, etc, who in the past gave labour the footing that it has attained ... To be associated with them you must be either a square-headed German or a bearded Bolshevik. I have resigned membership of the West Ham Town Council Labour Group and in future will answer to the West Ham Branch of the National Union of Railwaymen.[14]

Pressure from the unions forced ILP candidates to withdraw leaving Thorne as the Labour candidate. He, together with Jones, was returned with a huge majority in the election. There followed a period of reconciliation in the interests of unity for the forthcoming municipal election, and Labour embarked on its seemingly inexorable ascent to power.

It was the populist discourse expressed by Kirk that was to prove decisive in moulding the political agenda. Aggressively asserting a (male) working-class identity built on industrial power in opposition to middle-class involvement, it strengthened links with influential sections of the local electorate and the unions in a way that other parties could not.

At the end of the First World War local trade unions were powerful bodies. West Ham's industrial base had continued to expand in the course of the war as a result of which membership in local branches of the NUR stood at 6280 and the National Union of Gasworkers was 6,013 in 1918, and that of the Transport and General Workers Union in 1922 was 7,378 – more than enough to dominate completely the arena of electoral politics through use of delegate power. Union membership, however, never translated itself automatically into electoral support for Labour. Unions had quite different perspectives on the need for parliamentary representation. The NUR looked most favourably on it, forging close ties with party leaders and backing the party financially. The NUGW, on the other hand, remained suspicious of the middle-class, nonconformist, pacifist elements among the party leadership, and the TGWU continued to trust in industrial rather than political struggle as a means of furthering the interests of their members.

Locally, branches provided the ballast behind the party leadership which emerged, not in financial terms, but by endowing them with credibility and legitimacy. At times of difficulty councillors could always appeal to their union branches for support which then exerted pressure through the influential West Ham Trades Council.

Potentially of greater importance to Labour was the co-operative movement. Largely as a result of grievances provoked by discrimination of the Food Controller against the movement during the war, the 1917 Congress voted overwhelmingly for the principle of political representation as a means of furthering their interests and to that end formed the Co-operative Party. The Stratford Society, whose membership now stood at over 44,000, lost no time in implementing the decision. The jealously guarded independence from the Labour

Party was preserved, but the programme of social and political reform adopted was so close to Labour's that both entered future elections with strategies that were mutually beneficial.

This alliance was vital to Labour's ascent; in no area was this more evident than in its ability to secure the newly enfranchised female electorate.[15] By the end of the war the Women's Co-operative Guild was a national body with a considerable presence. Under Margaret Llewellyn Davies its membership had risen sharply from 1800 in 1889 to over 51,000 in 1921. Campaigns during the war, particularly around child and maternity welfare, touched the lives of working-class women in a direct way and led to a massive expansion. Financial resources in an impoverished area like West Ham were meagre, but guild members had an influence disproportionate to their numbers. Not only did they determine the agenda of public health committees, but provided fertile ground for Labour to exploit. Thus election propaganda promised that the Party would attend to the interests of women and children by pursuing with vigour the powers made available under the new Maternity and Child Welfare Acts.

Labour in West Ham in the immediate postwar period was able to consolidate power around a populist programme of social reform. A commonsensical assertion of working-class identity, supported – albeit in complex and indirect ways – by powerful trade union and co-operative movements, secured hegemonic control over the formal political terrain not evident in other East London boroughs. This hegemony, however, was exercised by a relatively small elite of skilled and semi-skilled workers. In spite of Labour's success it failed to engage with different constituencies of the working class; the overwhelming mood of the electorate, not only in West Ham but East London as a whole, was one of profound apathy.

Casualisation and the Modern

Two constituencies in particular lay outside Labour's domain, namely, the unemployed and the casual poor. There was a large measure of overlap in that the casual poor contributed massively to the ranks of the unemployed, but the unemployed comprised also skilled and semiskilled workers who conferred a political dimension on unemployment with far reaching consequences.

West Ham was disastrously affected by the economic downturn in the immediate postwar years. Levels of unemployment throughout the interwar period were consistently higher than those of London, although they did not quite match those experienced by the devastated coal communities of the north-east and Wales. As levels increased, sections of the unemployed, largely inspired by the National Unemployed Workers Movement (NUWM) and the example of Poplar, began to mobilise against the West Ham Board of Guardians. The unemployed organised meetings, took to the streets and beseiged meetings of the guardians. Leadership of the local Labour Party, favouring constitutional action, invited scorn and ridicule from the militant unemployed.

Demands of the unemployed challenged directly discourses around relief that had been installed by the 1834 Poor Law Act. In response the guardians granted scales of relief that flouted government guidelines. The Ministry of Health reluctantly agreed to lend the necessary funds to finance relief until the Government, confident after the failure of the general strike, rushed an act through Parliament empowering it to supersede errant boards of guardians. In July 1926 administration of relief was taken over by three Government-appointed commissioners.

Widespread cuts in relief followed, and yet resistance from the unemployed evaporated with a rapidity which many who recalled their previous militancy found surprising. But it was evident that the large body of the unemployed had fought alone. Most skilled workers received benefits from labour exchanges during periods of unemployment and so had no real stake in the struggle. The rank and file of the labour movement tended to be indifferent to the plight of the unemployed; unions at best provided benefits for their members, while the Labour Party refused to take any responsibility.

For a while this intransigence attracted the vehemence of communist members in the NUWM, but the party was secure. As in Poplar it lost no ground on the political terrain of unemployment. Indirectly it gained, for in the period leading to supersession, Conservative opposition on the council in the form of the Municipal Alliance had argued for cuts in relief and lost considerable electoral support.

The politics of unemployment suggests that the constituency of casual labour was remote from labourist discourse. This applies also to the formal political terrain. There was an inverse relationship between turnout at elections and the extent of casualism; crudely speaking, the poorer the area the lower the turnout. If we need to understand the nature of electoral apathy in this period, then, it is to the political culture of casual labour that we have to direct attention.

I would wish to argue that casual labour lay outside the experience of modernity. However we might think of modernity, be it economic, social or political, casual labour was able to resist its inexorable logic and retain premodern forms well into the interwar period.[16] Much of this resistance derived from its relationship to the market. Casualism as a distinctly urban phenomenon was created by the forces of modernisation, but then occupied an ambivalent position in the labour market. Since by definition casual labourers had only intermittent work they were never subject wholly to its discipline; the temporal and spatial re-ordering promoted by new forms of work rarely impinged on the lives of casual labourers. They took responsibility for where and when they worked; for many, and in spite of attendant want, this provided a degree of independence that was consciously retained over time.

But it was within the political that the separation was most evident. All of the forces that contributed to the ascent of Labour were modern. The Labour Party itself would have been inconceivable without recognition of the need within a capitalist state to establish forms of democracy, citizenship, rights and welfare that were recognisably modern.

These arguments apply also to trade unionism and co-operation. Trade unions for much of the nineteenth century were dominated by and acted in the interests of a craft élite enshrined within a respectable Liberal creed, but as the structure of the labour force changed so attention was devoted to the establishment of so-called new unions. These encompassed a much wider membership of semiskilled and occasionally unskilled workers, and were largely committed to the ideal of labour representation.

The co-operative movement was initially founded on the principles of a radical Owenism, but in the course of the century became increasingly occupied with the modern ideal of consumer power. Capitalism, the argument went, was to be challenged not at the point of production but at the point of consumption. Through co-operative endeavour the whole structure of retail distribution would be gradually annexed and eventually organised to promote political redistribution. It was within the Women's Co-operative Guild that this modern impulse was most strongly evident. 'Basket power' remained at the centre of its work but this was seen increasingly in terms of the necessity to promote female suffrage and welfare.

Casual labour was effectively (self)-excluded from these modernist tendencies. It inhabited a premodernism at the heart of which lay the carnivalesque. The medieval carnival was the greatest popular festival.

Characterised by excessive consumption of alcohol, meat and sex, and the transgression of hierarchical social and political structures, it celebrated a collective folk identity against political and moral restraint. Subjected to assaults from church and state from the time of the Reformation, the carnival was displaced from the public domain, but survived in rearticulated, less visible and more privatised forms.

We can detect the carnival in many instances of collective action right up to the twentieth century. It was evident, for example, in struggles of the Waltham Blacks against enclosure and the redefinition of property rights, in bread and unemployed riots, and early forms of new unionism. The dock strike of 1889 owed rather more to the carnival than to modern forms of industrial struggle. At a local level collective social norms were asserted through carnivalesque rituals such as rough music.[17] And carnival is abundantly evident in Mayhew's account of the cultures of costermongers and other sections on the fringes of the metropolitan labour market. Indeed, on the entire subcultural landscape – in sport, language, 'crime', theatre, street entertainment, humour – elements of the carnivalesque survived among the urban poor.

This culture was never engaged by the modernism of the Labour Party, co-operation or trade unionism. Labour meetings and demonstrations in West Ham may have attracted the support of sections of casual labour, but this derived from a sense of public spectacle and celebration rather than from a mature political consciousness. In spite of the Labour Party's success individual membership was minute and turnout at elections remained exceptionally low, particularly in wards south of the borough where the docks and industry were concentrated; the party remained one of a skilled and semiskilled working class.

Likewise co-operation. The co-operative movement could not appeal on the basis of consumer power to a constituency which had so little. The poor could not even afford to buy goods at local co-ops, relying instead on corner shops which were prepared to sell small, non-standard quantities and offer limited credit. The guild's efforts to establish a 'people's store' selling food at cheap prices and in small quantities failed. Campaigns to improve child and maternity welfare had greater success but resources were totally inadequate to the task and the poor were forced to rely on the older traditions of mutual support.

There was no trade union for the casual labourer. Structural constraints were prohibitive – financial stability depended on regular subscriptions from members in relatively secure employment. But more importantly unions demanded discipline and promoted political representation that could have no appeal. Union leaders expressed despair at their inability to organise casual labour for anything more than the short term. They did have some success during the 1889 dock strike, but once it was over membership of the dockers' union plummeted.

Any allegiance to the Labour Party amongst the constituency of the casual poor was fragile, passive, instinctive and untheorised. Based on little more than a sense that Labour stood for us against them, the allegiance was volatile and at particular moments could be articulated readily to other political discourses around nation and Englishness.

In recent years the East End has suffered protracted economic decline and experienced massive demographic change resulting in large-scale settlement of a highly mixed ethnic population. And yet the area has inherited something of an older political legacy. Labour has continued to dominate Newham at municipal and parliamentary levels. Tower Hamlets, on the other hand, has had a rather more complex political trajectory, with a much stronger Conservative and Liberal presence. The menace of neo-fascism has resurfaced since the 1960s.

Casualism and unemployment once again haunt the East End. There is talk of a new, modernising Labour Party. In the meantime, electoral apathy prevails, and local councils tend to be dominated by entrenched, insulated and select groups of party activists with little popular support. It all looks strangely familiar.

Notes

[1] I would like to dedicate this chapter to the memory of Martin Lewis, 1967–1995.

[2] West Ham was amalgamated with East Ham in 1964 to form the London Borough of Newham. It was not a felicitous process since the two older boroughs were quite different in social and political composition, producing tensions that are still apparent. Whether they can be considered as part of the East End is an open question.

[3] See, for example, Gregory Elliot, *Labourism and the English Genius: The Strange Death of Labour England*, Verso, London 1993; A. Heath, R. Jowell and J. Curtice (eds), *Labour's Last Chance? The 1992 Election and Beyond*, Dartmouth, Aldershot 1994; Willie Thompson, *The Long Death of British Labourism: Interpreting a political culture*, Pluto, London 1993.

[4] For details of West Ham's rather particular political development see my *London Over the Border: A Study of West Ham During Rapid Growth, 1840–1910*, unpublished PhD thesis, University of Cambridge, 1984; *The*

Culture of Labourism: The East End Between the Wars, Edinburgh University Press, Edinburgh 1991.

[5] For accounts of East London politics in the metropolitan context see Jim Gillespie, 'Poplarism and Proletarianism: Unemployment and Labour Politics in London, 1918–34', in David Feldman and Gareth Stedman Jones (eds), *Metropolis: London, Histories and Representations Since 1800*, Routledge, London 1989; Duncan Tanner, *Political Change and the Labour Party, 1900–1918*, Cambridge University Press, Cambridge 1990; Paul Thompson, *Socialists, Liberals and Labour: The Struggle for London, 1887–1914*, Routledge, London 1967.

[6] Gareth Stedman Jones, *Outcast London*, Clarendon Press, Oxford, 1972; Thompson, *op.cit.*

[7] Tanner, *op.cit.*, Chapter 6.

[8] Ross McKibbin, *The Evolution of the Labour Party, 1910–24*, Oxford University Press, Oxford 1974; Tom Nairn, 'The nature of the Labour Party', in New Left Review (ed), *Toward Socialism*, Fontana, London 1965.

[9] Tanner, *op.cit.*, p382.

[10] Thompson, *op.cit.*

[11] Julia Bush, *Behind the Lines*, Merlin Press, London 1984.

[12] Gillespie, *op.cit.*

[13] *Ibid.*, pp178–9.

[14] *Stratford Express*, 19 January 1918, cited in Marriott, *The Culture of Labourism*, pp31–2.

[15] Pamela Graves, *Labour Women: Women in British Working-Class Politics, 1919–1939*, Cambridge University Press, Cambridge 1994.

[16] This is explored in rather more detail in my 'Sensation of the Abyss: The Urban Poor and Modernity', in Mica Nava and Alan O'Shea (eds), *Modern Times: The British Experience of Modernity*, Routledge, London 1996.

[17] E.P. Thompson, 'Rough music' in *Customs in Common*, Merlin Press, London 1991.

The New Ethnic Diversity

The Unsecular City: The Revival of Religion in East London

Greg Smith

Introduction

Studies of religion in the East End of London usually begin with the familiar hypothesis that urban people are less religious, that city life brings only church decline, and indeed that the city itself is a dark and evil place. Urbanisation has been equated with secularisation and many devout people have a wistful nostalgia for a mythical age of rural innocence in which (allegedly) 'the chapels were full and the prisons were empty' and everyone lived in close harmony with creation and its Creator. Of course this simplistic and nostalgic view can be challenged on the evidence of history.[1] This chapter, however, uses contemporary evidence from local research to question such received wisdom, and concludes that East London, far from being a secular city, is an increasingly religious community.

In addition there is now a respectable alternative hypothesis to the 'urban equals secular' assumption in the sociology of religion literature. This suggests on the basis of data from the USA that religious attendance increases in a plural market situation.[2] In this view, competition between religious groups leads to greater efforts and efficiency to recruit members, and niche marketing in a fragmented society makes membership of particular religious groups attractive to a varied range of individuals drawn from the general population. Easy travel and geographically dispersed personal networks in larger urban areas allow this diversity to flourish. If neighbourhood and kinship loyalties are diminishing, the basic sense of belonging can be found for many people in religious or ethnic communities. Therefore, cities can be strongly religious places. There has been relatively little research or comment on these issues in Britain but evidence from Newham would seem to support Finke and Stark's view that competition is beneficial to the church.[3]

Christendom in Decline

In the nineteenth century the urbanisation which accompanied the industrial revolution sent waves of panic through the religious establishment (especially as they looked across the Channel and saw the results of Enlightenment philosophy in the secular revolution of 1789). Despite the successful evangelism of the Methodists among some sections of the working classes, the 1851 religious census showed how unchurched the urban masses remained.[4] The second half of the century saw ambitious programmes of church-building and urban mission.[5] *The Daily News* census of 1903 showed the same picture.[6] Inner urban areas of London (especially the East End) still reported much lower church attendance than the emerging suburbs or the West End. As the twentieth century proceeded churches saw numerical decline both nationally and locally. From 1945 churches were closed and demolished at an ever increasing rate. When I came to live in East London in 1975 and began employment as a community worker with a Christian organisation, I was told that if current trends continued and Christians continued to migrate towards the coast (like lemmings!) there would be no churches left in Newham by the year 2000.[7] As late as 1985 the *Faith in the City* report was bemoaning the continuing decline of urban congregations; in urban priority areas Anglican attendance averaged 0.85 per cent or half the national average.[8]

In none of these statistics was there any attempt to control for population decline, the age profile of urban areas, or to analyse in any depth the effect of social class or ethnic composition of communities and congregations. It was taken as gospel that 'urban' was bad news for the church, and when Colin Marchant and I began to suggest that a new wave of urban church-planting was beginning to transform the Christian scene in Newham, and other parts of London, our observations were hard for many people to accept.[9] Evidence in our favour is now building up as this paper will attempt to show.

A Re-emergence of Religion?

The borough of Newham according to the 1991 Census is the second most ethnically diverse in the whole of Britain, with only 58 per cent of its people describing themselves as white.[10] Religious pluralism is unparalleled and recognised by the local authority in the provision of school holidays at festivals such as Eid-ul-Fitr (Islam), Diwali (Hindu), Guru Nanak's Birthday (Sikh), as well as the traditional Christian ones of Christmas and Easter. Local politics increasingly reflects religious interests; recent arguments in Newham Council and Labour Party have focused on the following issues:

- the sale of land to provide car parking for a mosque as opposed to a building site for housing;
- the inappropriateness of scheduling a race equality sub-committee on the eve of Eid;
- whether Muslim representation on the Standing Advisory Committee for Religious Education should be increased;
- selection contests in the Labour Party for council candidates involving Muslim, Hindu and Sikh candidates, sometimes with accusations of dubious membership recruitment practices within religious communities;
- the nomination of two Christian Independent candidates for the May 1994 Council elections;
- conflicts over the funding of community centres; the Council substantially funds what in practice is a Hindu centre, but is uneasy about the prospect of backing a Muslim women's centre (rather than an Asian women's centre), while at least one Christian centre has ceased to be funded by the Council following a debate over religious/moral values around equal opportunities for gay and lesbian people and equal access to Muslim groups;[11]
- churches taking a lead in campaigns against the neo-Nazi BNP in Docklands, and in support of asylum seekers and refugees fighting deportation, to the extent of offering sanctuary in their buildings.

Numbers of Religious Groups

The history of religious institutions in the borough of Newham is a rapidly changing one and is well documented, especially in the writing of Colin Marchant[12] and in historical studies such as the volume edited by F. Sainsbury.[13] Before 1850 there were the three ancient parish churches of Little Ilford, West Ham and East Ham, a congregational chapel and not much else. The second half of the nineteenth century saw the establishment of over forty Church of England parishes, five large Roman Catholic parishes, and a very strong Free church presence with ninety-seven Methodist, Baptist and Independent churches ... as well as numerous settlements and mission halls. There was also a significant Jewish presence with several synagogues and cemeteries. The post-1945 exodus and decline in local population on top of a general decline in church-going habits, and the loss of a number of church buildings in the blitz, led to rationalisation and closures on the part of the denominations, the Church of England merging parishes and the Free Churches selling off buildings. There were by the mid-1970s only eighteen Anglican buildings and twenty Free Churches. However, by the mid-1980s Colin Marchant, a local Baptist minister whose doctoral research produced the groundbreaking study of the religious history of Newham, was becoming less pessimistic as he had noticed a wave of church-planting.[14] David Driscoll (a local Anglican vicar) and I, in a report submitted to the Archbishop's Commission on UPAs, documented some of the new church-planting and the renewal of congregational life in some parts of the mainline churches.[15]

Several factors have contributed to the stemming of the tide of secularisation in Newham. The first of the 'black Pentecostal' churches were founded in the area before 1970 by immigrants from the Caribbean. By about 1975 a new awareness of East London as a mission field was emerging in the mainline churches spurred on by David Sheppard's book *Built as a City*[16] and the creation of groups such as the Newham Community Renewal Programme and In Contact. A wave of educated Christian incomers (including the present author) moved into the area, full of zeal to do evangelism and/or community work, and many of them have now stayed nearly 20 years. They have been joined more recently by several groups of 'religious' from the Roman Catholic orders. From 1975 to the present several new independent congregations have emerged in the 'white led' evangelical charismatic sector of the church. Many mainline denominational churches which were on the verge of closure in the mid-1970s have found new congregational life. These include both charismatic/evangelical congregations and (more recently) broad and Anglo-Catholic congregations. Caribbean-led majority black Pentecostal churches continue to be formed, although there is some evidence that their growth had peaked by the mid-1980s. In the last ten years the most significant growth point has been among African Christians.[17] Many mainline denominational churches have doubled in numbers because of the involvement of African Anglicans, Methodists, Baptists and Pentecostals, while a thriving independent African-led sector has mushroomed. These newer churches are mainly from Pentecostal/Holiness or the Aladura/African indigenous traditions and serve Ghanaians, Nigerians, Ugandans, Zaireans and Zimbabweans usually in their national or ethnic grouping.[18]

Alongside this Christian growth has been the development of Hindu, Sikh, Muslim and other faith communities. There are now more than a dozen mosques, at least three Sikh and four Hindu temples in Newham. There are also two Buddhist centres and Bahai, Pagan, Rastafarian and other groups. In the white community there is a traditional Spiritualist presence, which is arguably a product of Cockney folk religion with its excessive reverence for departed relatives.[19] Similar informal, folk or implicit religions are to be found in the various ethnic minority communities, although there is little research in this hidden and sensitive area. There are, in addition, some proponents of New Age spirituality, although because of its privatised and consumerist nature and local focus in more 'trendy' places such as Glastonbury and Brighton, little organised activity is to be observed in Newham.

The Newham Directory of Religious Groups (Second Edition) published in 1994 lists 275 groups. Statistics for all faith communities (based on a survey with a response rate of 78 per cent of all congregations, and 96.5 per cent for the mainline Christian churches) show that in Newham in 1994 there were:

- 198 'congregations', 117 of whom owned their own meeting places;
- 163 of these congregations were in the broadest sense of the term 'Christian';
- 77 religious organisations, centres, agencies, orders, networks etc.

A breakdown by denomination shows that Pentecostal congregations are by far the most numerous category, followed by Anglicans (Church of England), independent evangelicals and Muslims. But when it comes to owning their own buildings the Anglicans are in a league of their own, although almost all Muslim, Baptist, Methodist, Salvation Army and United Reform Church (URC) groups do own

Table 1 Denominations within Christian Tradition

	Congregations	Organizations	Congregations owning building	Estimated Attendance
African	7	0	4	882
Baptist	12	1	12	972
C of E	28	10	27	2,072
Ecumenical	2	17	2	100
Independent Evangelical	17	5	8	1,268
Methodist	6	2	6	372
Moravian	1	0	0	40
Orthodox	2	0	1	300
Pentecostal	56	4	7	3,416
Quaker	0	1	0	0
Roman Catholic	12	15	8	7,812
Salvation Army	3	0	3	51
Seventh Day Adventists	3	1	2	480
United Reformed	4	2	4	164
Total				17,929
Non Trinitarian	11	0	8	
None	0	5	0	
Other Faith Communities				
Bahai	1	0	0	
Buddhist	2	0	1	
Hindu	8	4	5	
Ravidassi	1	0	1	
Universal	2	0	0	
Jewish	1	0	1	
Inter Faith	0	4	0	
Muslim	14	5	13	
Pagan	1	0	0	
Sikh	5	0	4	
Total	198	77	117	

Note: Estimates for attendance are based on the replies of church leaders to the question 'How many people usually attend the largest meeting/service you regularly hold, (e.g. for Christians this would be the main Sunday Service, for Muslims Friday prayers).' The 'high' estimate is given here which assumes non-responding churches to have the mean attendance for their denomination.
Source: Newham Directory of Religious Groups.

their buildings. Many of the newer Pentecostals and Independent Evangelicals and some of the Roman Catholic groups meet in rented church halls and community centres. There are also a handful of examples where two or more congregations of different denominations have a formal agreement to share a church building such as the ecumenical St Mark's Centre in Beckton.

Table 1 above illustrates the proportion of Christian congregations in each denomination including information about building ownership and attendance estimates.

Church Attendance Statistics

Church attendance figures are one of the most frequently used measures of trends in secularisation, perhaps because the measurement is relatively easy to put into operation (usually by counting all attenders on a given Sunday) and is therefore thought to be reliable and replicable at different times. The only national religious census for England in 1851 showed that in West Ham, there was a 40 per cent church attendance rate (65 per cent of it Anglican). Since urbanisation had hardly begun in the area in 1851 this can hardly be used as a baseline for later comparisons.

In London in 1903 *The Daily News* survey of religious life indicated that the attendance rates in inner, and especially East, London were low.[20] In West Ham church attendance was put at 20 per cent (55,649 people in 137 churches and chapels). Nonconformists accounted for 65 per cent of the church-goers, 32 per cent were Church of England and the Roman Catholic congregation had grown to 12 per cent. There was also one synagogue with 68 worshippers. The church authorities were most concerned over even lower attendances in the southern working-class neighbourhoods of the borough. Marchant's doctoral work suggested the pattern continued in the 1970s and he summarised the historical situation by saying that in East London the decline in national church attendance was reflected locally, but rates were consistently half to a third of the national average.[21] Yet by 1988 my own research was suggesting that in Forest Gate church attendance rates were not far behind the national average, and really quite high in a community where around half the population was from Muslim, Hindu and Sikh communities.[22] My estimates of numbers for the mid-1980s, based on extensive visiting and participant observation, were that about 2 per cent of the predominantly white working-class population of Plaistow and Canning Town might be regular attenders at Christian churches, while at least 7 per cent of the multiracial, more socially mixed population of Forest Gate might attend.

The most recent church censuses with any claim to comprehensive national coverage were those of 1985 and 1989 conducted by MARC Europe based on a head count on a specified Sunday in each year.[23] They showed a 10 per cent increase over four years in adult attenders in Newham from 6800 to 7500 and a growth in membership of 16 per cent from 13,300 to 15,400. But this attendance level still only represented some 5 per cent of the adult population. There are many problems about the reliability and coverage of this data, but it does not seem implausible to those with local knowledge of the churches, and it is matched by similar trends in other parts of inner London especially the inner south-east and inner north-east sectors.[24] The 1989 MARC census put church attendance rates for England as a whole at 9 per cent and follow up work suggests they are still declining.[25]

Table 2 Estimates of Church Attendance. Newham 1994

	High Estimate†	Low Estimate†
Total estimated church attendance	17,929	15,388
As % of Newham's population	8.26	7.09
As % of non-Asian population	10.99	9.44

† Estimates are based on the following assumptions in order to allow for the cases where the information had not been received.

The high estimate assumes that churches with missing information have numbers equivalent to the mean average of the churches in their denomination for which we have figures.

The low estimate allows for the possibility that smaller less established congregations are over-represented among the missing data and also incorporates some 'local knowledge' about the likely size of particular congregations.

The 1994 *Newham Directory of Religious Groups* gives estimates of attenders at congregations in the Christian tradition which are at least one and a half times as high as the 1989 Census figures. Between 15,000 and 18,000 people are likely to attend services in the borough. This is around 8 per cent of the whole population and 10 per cent of the non-Asian population (See Table 2 above).

It is important to ask why even our lower estimate for church attendance in Newham is so much higher than the MARC Europe 1989 figures. The research discovered many churches which were not included in the MARC census and elicited a much higher response rate. MARC researchers worked from a list of only 65 churches and achieved only a 65 per cent response rate. The directory's key question invited church leaders to estimate the number who usually attended the largest worship event regularly held, rather than insisting on an actual count on a given Sunday. The temptation to round up numbers and to count every person who might attend would have been irresistible for many. Despite this caveat it is impossible to discount the possibility that there has been a substantial growth in religious observance among Christian groups in Newham in recent years.

The major growth area has been among Pentecostal and African Independent congregations. Almost all of these churches are black-led, and have predominantly black congregations. In the last decade the African element has predominated, and in addition many mainline white-led congregations have benefited from an influx of African Christians, and the lively faith and style of worship they bring with them.

But even the predominantly white communities of Docklands are affected. A recent local study by Oliver[26] has looked at adult Christian learning and church attendance in Canning Town and Custom House, an area of council estates, which is well researched and documented in earlier urban mission literature.[27] Oliver estimated 2.86 per cent of the local population were church-goers (230 of them attending 7 local churches). Nearly three quarters of them were female and just under a quarter were black. Oliver characterises church-going as 'deviant' behaviour in the local (white) working-class Cockney culture, especially for men. Yet significantly he reports growth in attendance; a doubling of estimated numbers from 150 (in 8 buildings) in the early 1980s to 300 (in 7 buildings) in 1991/2. Only a small part of the growth can be put down to active Christian incomers including black people. There has been some significant 'conversion' growth, of which Oliver documents a number of individual cases.[28]

Non-Christian Faiths

The following estimates for the main religious communities are based on the author's reworking of ethnicity and birth place data in the 1991 Census.

- Muslims: between 25,000 and 30,000 people.
- Hindus: approx 20,700
- Sikhs: approx 4,150

Attendance Patterns

The data collected for the directory does not allow us to measure attendance rates at non-Christian worship. Indeed cultural differences around the patterns and meaning of attendance at worship in the various faith communities make it hard to use as a comparable measure of belonging. However, a survey by the Newham Association of Faiths did produce some relevant results.[29]

Of 75 adult Muslims questioned 33 (41 per cent) said they attended their mosque at least weekly of whom 16 (21 per cent) said they went daily. But 23 (31 per cent) never attended. However, among the 37 men over 75 per cent attended at least weekly and only one man never went, while among women less than 10 per cent were weekly or daily attenders and 58 per cent never went.

Of 47 Hindus 20 (42 per cent) attended worship at least weekly and 7 (15 per cent) never. Slightly more men (47 per cent) than women (40 per cent) were weekly or daily attenders. Of 27 Sikhs 10 (37 per cent) attended worship at least weekly but 6 (22 per cent) never attended. Attenders included 50 per cent of the men and 22 per cent of the women. Clearly this gender difference, which is most marked among Muslims and Sikhs, indicates a cultural pattern rather than a lower level of faith among Asian women.

Religious Attitudes and Practice

While attendance at worship may be the most appropriate measure of belonging to a religious community, measures of believing (to use Davie's terms) are more commonly based on repsonses to attitudinal questions in survey research.[30] As a baseline for local comparisons the British Social Attitudes Survey discovered that 69 per cent of the population believed in God, 27 per cent claimed to pray at least weekly and 16 per cent to attend a service at least two or three times a month.[31]

West Ham Parish Survey

Between August 1992 and January 1993 185 residents of the inner city parish of All Saints, West Ham were interviewed in households selected by a two-stage stratified and geographically clustered sampling process. Low contact and response rates compelled the interviewers to use substitution at neighbouring addresses in order to complete many interviews. Nonetheless it can be shown that the resulting set of respondents match very closely the social profile of the parish population as indicated by the 1991 Census. And while it is necessary to concede that the topic of the survey and the fact that the volunteer interviewers introduced themselves as coming from the church may have biased the replies to a degree in favour of over-reporting of religious practice and belief, the findings presented in Table 3 (below) show that religion is an important part of the lives of a substantial minority of the population and that self-reported religious practice is higher than would have been expected on the hypothesis that inner city areas are 'unchurched'. Moreover local levels of belief and practice may well be higher than the national average.

It is no surprise that in a neighbourhood with very few Asian residents 73 per cent called themselves 'Christian', or in view of national findings that 73 per cent 'definitely' believed in God. It is, however, remarkable that 30 per cent claimed to go to church or other religious centres, and that 18 per cent said they had attended within the last week. This compares with figures from the same survey of 28 per cent visiting pubs, 39 per cent entertainment venues such as theatres/cinema/concerts, 32 per cent car boot sales, 81 per cent going to shopping centres or markets, 19 per cent to sporting events, 23 per cent taking part in sport and 11 per cent going to adult education classes. Private religious practice defined as prayers, scripture reading, worship at home etc. produced a considerably higher figure of 43 per cent participation in the previous week.

Breaking the findings down by denominational affiliation and race gives some interesting insights. Nominality, which is defined here as no public practice in the last year, is widespread. It reached about 60 per cent among respondents who identified themselves as 'Church of England' and 42 per cent among Roman Catholics. However, while 18 per cent of whites claimed to have been to public worship in the previous month the figure among black respondents rose to nearly half. Yet even among whites in West Ham there is no evidence here to suggest that religious activism is below the national rates.

Table 3 Religious Practice by Denomination

(ALL includes those claiming no religious affiliation and Non Christian Faiths)

	COFE	%	RC	%	FREE	%	ALL	%
Going to Church								
Already	18	24	12	48	13	59	56	30
Interested	4	5	3	12	6	27	22	12
Not Interested	53	71	10	40	3	14	107	58
Total	75	100	25	100	22	100	185	100
Public Practice								
Last Week	8	10	8	31	9	36	32	18
Last Month	9	11	3	12	1	4	19	11
Last Year	15	19	4	15	4	16	28	16
Over a Year Ago	41	51	11	42	11	44	75	43
Never	8	10	0	0	0	0	22	13
Total	81	100	26	100	25	100	176	100
Private Practice								
Last Week	31	39	10	42	16	76	72	43
Last Month	7	9	3	13	2	10	15	9
Last Year	6	8	1	4	0	0	9	5
Over a Year Ago	9	11	6	25	2	10	21	13
Never	26	33	4	17	1	5	50	30
Total	79	100	24	100	21	100	167	100
Believe in God								
Definitely	56	69	22	85	22	88	130	73
Some Sort Of	11	14	2	8	2	8	19	11
Not Sure	6	7	2	8	1	4	15	8
Definitely Not	8	10	0	0	0	0	14	8
Total	81	100	26	100	25	100	178	100
Consider Spiritual things								
Very Important	20	25	11	41	16	64	64	36
Important	37	46	13	48	6	24	69	39
Not Important	23	29	3	11	3	12	45	25
Total	80	100	27	100	25	100	178	100

Source: West Ham Parish Survey.

In order to verify these findings and to control for the possible influence of other demographic variables, multivariate statistical techniques were used. First an index of religious practice was created, on the basis of a factor analysis of most of the items in the questionnaire, which showed the replies to the individual questions listed in Tables 3 and 4 to be highly correlated. A multiple regression analysis on this index suggested that over 40 per cent of the variance could be accounted for by three independent factors.[32] Firstly, white respondents were far less likely than others to be religiously active. Secondly, older respondents were more likely to be religiously active than younger ones. Finally, women who were mothers of small children were more likely than other people to be religiously active; a variable specified in this way appeared to have more explanatory power than a simple male/female dichotomy. Variables based on denominational and faith affiliation, social class or its proxies (such as housing tenure and education) or length of residence or residence close to the church were found to play no significant part in explaining rates of religious activism when the three main factors were held constant.

Analysis of variance methods produced broadly similar findings with the following exceptions. Denominational or faith affiliation appeared also to be a significant factor with the groups ranked from 'no religious affiliation' (lowest) through 'Church of England', 'Roman Catholic', 'non-Christian Faiths' to 'other Christian' (i.e. Free Church and Pentecostal etc) as most religious. Clearly the high correlations between faith/denomination group and ethnicity have meant that the effect of faith/denomination group is overwhelmed statistically by the effect of ethnicity. A three-way analysis of variance using the factors gender, white/non-white and four age groups showed that the gender difference (women are more religious) is confined to the white group. It also revealed that among men the least religious activism is among the 26–40 year olds, while among women this childrearing age group is the most religious of all. It is interesting to speculate as to why young mothers are more likely to attend church. Is it that anyone who has been involved in childbearing and childcare is inevitably more 'spiritual'? Or are they more concerned to ensure that their children are given some early exposure to the Church and its values, and therefore bring them to Sunday school? Perhaps they have a more practical motivation, that of seeking support networks and direct social help from the parish and its organisations, including quite significantly in this parish, the church primary school.

Table 4 Religious Practice by Ethnicity

	White	*%*	*Black*	*%*	*Asian*	*Other*
Going To Church						
Already	21	19	20	47	4	11
Interested	8	7	11	26	1	2
Not Interested	80	73	12	28	2	2
Total	109	100	43	100	7	15
Public Practice						
Last Week	9	8	14	34	3	6
Last Month	12	10	6	15	1	0
Last Year	20	17	5	12	2	1
Over a Year Ago	59	50	13	32	1	2
Never	17	15	3	7	0	2
Total	117	100	41	100	7	11
Private Practice						
Last Week	34	30	27	69	5	6
Last Month	12	11	3	8	0	0
Last Year	7	6	2	5	0	0
Over a Year Ago	16	14	4	10	0	1
Never	43	38	3	8	1	3
Total	112	100	39	100	6	10
Believe in God						
Definitely	76	64	37	88	6	11
Some Sort Of	15	13	4	10	0	0
Not Sure	14	12	1	2	0	0
Definitely Not	14	12	0	0	0	0
Total	119	100	42	100	6	11
Consider Spiritual Things						
Very Important	24	21	27	63	6	7
Important	52	45	12	28	1	4
Not Important	40	34	4	9	0	1
Total	116	100	43	100	7	12

Source: West Ham Parish Survey 1992.

Newham Association of Faiths Survey

The findings of the West Ham parish survey were confirmed by another local survey of 513 Newham residents, which was carried out by the Newham Association of Faiths in 1993. In this research 32 per cent of the respondents claimed that they usually attended a public gathering for worship/prayer etc. at least weekly, and 54 per cent claimed to belong to a local religious body (a church, mosque, temple or other group). The ethnic patterns were replicated, and it was possible to see more clearly the pattern in the Asian communities, as Table 5 makes clear.

Table 5 Attendance at Religious Groups by Ethnicity

Ethnic Group	N	% attending or belonging	% attending at least weekly
White (UK)	190	35	19
Irish	23	65	52
African	35	75	54
Caribbean	44	52	21
Indian	108	72	46
Pakistani	40	80	35
Bangladeshi	10	40	40
Other	35	66	49
Overall	511	54	32

Source: Newham Association of Faiths 1993

Multivariate analysis on a slightly different index of religious activism, which included a question as to whether the respondent held any office in a religious group, showed once again that both gender and ethnic group produced highly significant variations in the index scores, but also an interaction between the two. Broadly speaking the Asian, African and Irish groups were more religiously active than the White and Caribbean groups in the sample. In this sample and with this index, however, it was the men who were more active than women in religion. But this gender difference was concentrated in the South Asian and African groups, while among Whites there was no observable difference and among Caribbean respondents women were slightly (but not significantly) more active. A multiple regression model using four independent variables accounts for 29 per cent of the variance of this index. It suggests that the least religiously active people are likely to be those claiming no religion (trivial!), UK whites, and women (for cultural reasons about public participation rather than religious views). A social class dimension was also identified, with those in professional occupations (across all religious and ethnic groups) more likely to be activists or leaders than non-professional people.

Summary

The findings of the two surveys can be summarised as follows:

1. White UK respondents are more likely to have no religion or be nominal Christians than are other ethnic groups and therefore to have lower scores on a religious activism index (RCs, Free Church and Pentecostal adherents being more active than people who call themselves 'C of E'). Among them the younger age groups, and younger men in particular are likely to be additionally less religious.
2. People from a Caribbean background will be somewhat more religiously active than whites (mostly within the Christian tradition) and older people and women are likely to be more active.
3. Among Africans there is a high likelihood of being Christian (probably Free Church or Pentecostal) and very active religiously. Men are likely to be more active than women.
4. Among South Asians there is a high likelihood of being very religiously active, with Pakistanis and Bangladeshis being predominantly Muslim, Indians being Hindu, Sikh, or in a minority of cases, Muslim, Christian or Buddhist. Activism is especially high among males, with Muslims being slightly more active than Hindus or Sikhs. Mosque attendance is particularly high among Muslim men regardless of age, but is not a good measure of religiosity for women.
5. In the Christian community women with young children, be they black or white are more likely than other people to be religiously active.
6. In all groups professionals are more likely to be religiously active than other classes.

Reflections

What then can we say about religion in Newham, and more widely about religion in the inner city?

In the first place, whatever Newham is in the 1990s it is not a godless or unchurched community. Although religion is by no means a majority interest and attendance at worship is far below Irish or American levels, faith persists and if anything is growing in numbers, influence and significance. New churches, mosques, temples and organisations are being formed to cater for unmet religious and community need. Some important questions are raised which I will address in the remainder of this section:

Is the revival of religion purely a result of ethnic diversity? This is a compelling suggestion in as far as the tendency for religious organisations to be ethnically homogeneous. Indeed there is a case that in many plural urban settings around the world the prime focus for belonging, identity, community, *gemeinschaft* is located in some notion of ethno-religious-linguistic identity. However, there may be some counterevidence especially if the growth of churches, mosques and other religious communities which cut across some of the ethnic, national and tribal identities can be sustained. Yet even in Christian congregations which have attracted roughly equal numbers of black and white worshippers, there are often observable social divides, cliques with ethnic boundaries, and an imbalance in patterns of participation and power that can be seen as racist exclusion. The same may be true in some of the other faith communities that cross ethnic lines.

The answer to the ethnic question and the future of Christianity in Newham will depend on whether a long term measurable revival in religious activity among the deprived white communities in Newham can be sustained. At this moment there are only hopes and hints to counter long established trends. Will church attendance, or 'getting religion', continue to be deviant behaviour in the Cockney culture? Will young white people start to attend church, or will older congregations simply die out? If numerical growth is established among both white and black communities, and the church can overcome its own racism, then religious community identity might become a significant factor in its own right. Specifically it could emerge as the polar opposition to the sense of Islamic identity found among some young local Muslims. For Christians at least the dream of evangelical unity which rests on the vision of 'people of every language tribe and nation worshipping before the throne of the Lamb' (Revelation 7) could just be realised in Newham as it is in heaven.

More generally will religion diminish in significance as immigrant communities mature and become established in Britain? There are inevitably many pressures towards secularisation including economic forces, the professed value neutrality of the state and its education system (which is now being questioned), the mass media and the McDonaldisation of global culture. But all of these forces encounter some resistance at the level of human communities, and a feature of postmodern culture is that there is some recognition and space in which subcultural forms can flourish. In North America it is significant that ethnicity has undergone a strong revival in recent decades, and that for many ethnic groups it is their churches which maintain ancestral traditions, values, cultural forms and 'roots' long after other markers of ethnic community identity have gone. The same forces could be at work in Britain. In addition, there is the dimension of racism. As minority groups, most of them 'Black' in the political sense of the word, continue to meet hostility, discrimination and social exclusion, their religious identities and organisations will prove to be a powerful resource in their struggles. Already we are seeing a mobilisation of Islamic (rather than Asian or Pakistani) identity around such issues as the publication of *The Satanic Verses*, and the Muslim Parliament. In this setting it is hard to believe that an irresistible force of secularisation will sweep away the religious aspects of minority cultures.

The ethnic dimensions of religion clearly portray faith as a social phenomenon, involving belonging as much as believing. An alternative approach to religion, quite widely held in mainstream white British culture in the twentieth century is that faith is a purely personal matter between the individual and God. In this view, derived in large part from the Protestant view of individual conscience, the role of the church is merely to be available as a solace in time of need. One can certainly be a good Christian without attending church, and the congregation as community, or the church as a political force is not on the agenda. Undoubtedly there are many people in Newham, particularly among older white nominal Christians who subscribe to this view of believing in an ordinary God, as opposed to a supernatural interventionist one, without belonging to any church. However, most churches in Newham, of all denominations, are increasingly operating on the model of the congregation as the gathered community of God's people, distinct from the non-Christian world, but committed to being involved in that wider world according to the Biblical metaphors of salt and light, in service and evangelism. This trend has theological roots, but also resonates with an important social need. As neighbourhood community and kinship networks have fragmented, perhaps more rapidly in East London than elsewhere, many people recognise a deep personal need for belonging, for solidarity, for social support, for communion. At the local level it is churches and other religious groups that are best placed to meet such needs.

In a deprived urban area such as Newham a crucial question must be the relationship of poverty and religion. Religion was criticised by Marx as 'the opium of the people' and with some justification as an ideological tool of the ruling classes. But in the light of collapse of Soviet-style communism and the resurgence of religion in Eastern Europe and in the Islamic world it is time to re-evaluate. There is a long Christian tradition of concern for and involvement alongside the poor, of voluntary poverty for the sake of the Gospel, and of struggling to see the Kingdom of God established as social and economic reality on earth. That tradition continues in Newham as church and other groups play a major, and growing role in community development work, anti-poverty programmes and the provision of social services. It would appear that such social involvement is widely spread across the denominations in Newham. Pentecostals, Adventists, Catholics, Methodists and Anglicans all play a part. The media stereotypes of a church divided between the evangelical fundamentalists who reject social involvement and the liberals who have lost all confidence in God and the Gospel do not in my experience seem to fit. There are differences in emphasis, more among clergy than lay people, and some Christians see their social mission as little more than 'bait' with which to entice converts. For them church growth and numerical success is a priority. On the other hand, there are those who put political action as a high priority and who are very cautious about evangelism, especially in its American mass meeting form, or when it targets people from other faith communities. Such Christians stress faithfulness to the Gospel and quality of discipleship over numerical growth. But there are many individuals and congregations that seek to bridge these divides and there are a range of projects, organisations and networks that enable Christians of diverse viewpoints to co-exist and even collaborate.

It would appear that the social context in which the church operates is having an increasingly strong influence on its theology. Internationally there is a vigorous theological debate both in Catholic and evangelical circles about social justice and the Gospel, in which Christians in the 'Two Thirds World' and in British inner cities often make common cause on 'the option for the poor' and the need to root the gospel in local realities. Some Muslims too are exploring their traditions in the light of longings for equality and liberation. As the social and economic statistics about Newham show that it is consistently the African, Pakistani and Bangladeshi groups that are bottom of all the deprivation leagues, and it is these very groups that are most religiously active, then we can expect struggles for racial and social justice to take on a religious form. There may still be some vestiges of the 'pie in the sky when you die' syndrome, a reluctance among heavenly-minded people to engage with the everyday world, and a global culture which seeks to privatise spirituality, but it seems to me unlikely that this will be the dominant feature of religion in East London in years to come.

A final question is whether religious and ethnic divisions will sharpen and lead to conflict, segregation, and the brutality of competing fundamentalisms. In short will Newham become like Belfast or Beirut? Clearly there are such dangers, especially if the discourse of nationalism, racism and tribal loyalties are superimposed on deeply held religious, social and 'moral' values in a context of conflict over diminishing economic and social resources. At the time of writing, a recent murder in Newham has been reported as having some such dimensions of religious conflict. However, such fragmentation might be mitigated by the inability to avoid contact with a common mass culture, the complexity of ethnic interaction in Newham (compared with say the bipolar conflict in Belfast) and by deliberate policies in education, housing and community relations work.

Will the majority of Muslims in Newham follow a line that can be described as 'fundamentalist'? Will Hindus and Sikhs develop radical versions of their own religions? Will Christians be pushed towards a fundamentalism of their own, or will the liberal tolerance of broad church Anglicanism and the Free Churches survive and grow? Interestingly enough the material from the Newham Association of Faiths survey does not suggest that the majority of people are willing to go to war over religion, but rather see religion potentially as a force for harmony. Although 75 per cent of respondents agreed that 'there are always going to be conflicts between religions' only 10 per cent agreed with the statement 'I think of other faiths as the enemy of my own'. By contrast 69 per cent agreed that 'all religions have a lot in common' and an overwhelming majority of 92 per cent agreed that 'different religions should work together to help people in need'. There is in these findings a potentially more hopeful scenario in which religion, in all its diversity, becomes the building blocks out of which a new wider sense of community can be constructed.

Conclusion

The evidence presented in this paper has shown that there is a persistence, and in all probability a growth in religious activity in at least one inner city London borough. This adds substantially if not conclusively to the case that religious pluralism, perhaps through the operation of market forces and competition, is helpful to the survival and growth of religious organisations. Religion in Newham has arguably reached the level of 'critical mass' beyond which it can only continue to flourish. Furthermore postmodern urban pluralism is a relatively tolerant milieu in which 'deviant' behaviours such as religious practice are likely to be acceptable, as long as they do not challenge the 'rights' of others to choose their own lifestyle. Clearly this runs counter to any simple version of the secularisation thesis, and especially to versions which link urbanisation with inevitable secularisation.

However, the case against secularisation in the realm of ideas and values remains unproven for it is possible to argue that the persistence of traditional outward forms and discourses masks fundamental changes of function and belief. It is logically possible, as the long history of religious hypocrisy shows, to belong to a faith community without believing. And in an age where modern science, and economic rationality remain important, belief in traditional dogmas about the supernatural is for many people not as easy as joining a church. But this approach is to reduce secularisation from a testable hypothesis to no more than a problematic to be explored and repeatedly recast.

However, even modern (and especially postmodern) human beings find it almost impossible to live in a world without enchantment. There are conflicting and irrational mixtures of the traditional and modern in many current forms of religious practice; for example in Christian churches that use management and advertising techniques in planning prayer and evangelism, or in the pick and mix theology of the New Age, where computer programmes making astrological predictions are devised and marketed. In a world where virtual reality is a common experience and consumer choice is infinite, the market is likely to produce experiential religions individually tailored to suit every possible taste.

Pluralism, individualism and privatisation in a postmodern urban world makes it harder to live as though there were any religious (or indeed any other) certainties. Many people would give up the search for a public basis of truth, or shared meaning and values for society as a whole. Indeed this is a logical step, unless perhaps, as both committed Christians and Muslims might argue, one of the religious products on offer in the market place has been fundamentally right all along, and actually is the ultimate truth as revealed by the creator of the Universe. East London could well be at the leading edge in dealing with such basic religious questions in the coming century.

Notes

[1] D. Martain, *A General Theory of Secularization*, Basil Blackwell, Oxford 1978; D. Lyon, *The Steeple's Shadow*, Third Way/SPCK Books, London 1985.
[2] R. Finke and R. Stark, 'Religious Economies and Sacred Canopies: Religious Mobilisation in American Cities 1906' in *American Sociological Review*, Volume 53, 1988. K.D. Breault, 'New Evidence on Religious Pluralism, Urbanism and Religious Participation' in *American Sociological Review*, Volume 54, 1989. R. Finke and R. Stark, 'Re-evaluating the Evidence' comment on Breault's article in *American Sociological Review*, Volume 54, 1989.
[3] M.R.D. Johnson, 'Religious Observance in the West Midlands' in *Ethnic and Racial Studies*, Volume 8, Number 3, July 1985.
[4] R. Currie, A. Gilbert and L. Horsley, *Churches and Church-goers: Patterns of Church Growth in the British Isles Since 1700*, Clarendon Press, Oxford 1977; E. Wickham, *Church and People in an Industrial City*, Lutterworth 1957.
[5] H. McCleod, *Class and Religion in the Late Victorian City*, Croom Helm, London 1974. H. Walker, *East London: Sketches of Christian Work and Workers*, (1896) republished in 1987 by Peter Marcan Books, High Wycombe.
[6] J. Hart, *The Religious Life of London 1903*, EUTP, PO Box 83, Liverpool L69 8AN; C. Marchant 'Religion' in *A Marsh and a Gas Works: One Hundred Years of Life in West Ham*, W.E.A./Newham Parents Centre Publications, 745 Barking Road London E13 9ER, 1986.
[7] C. Hill, *Renewal in the Inner City*, Methodist Home Mission Dept., London 1976.
[8] ACUPA – Archbishop's Commission on Urban Priority Areas, *Faith in the city*, Church Information Office, London 1988.
[9] Marchant *op.cit.*, G. Smith, *God's in E7*, Evangelical Coalition for Urban Mission/British Growth Association, London 1986. G. Smith, *Inner City Christianity: Some Sociological Issues*, MARC monograph series, Number 17, London 1988.
[10] G. Smith, '(Almost) All You Could Ever Want To Know: Newham in the 1991 Census, Implications for Community Work' in *Newham Needs and*

Responses; CIU Annual for 1994, Aston Community Involvement Unit, London 1994.
[11] P. Watherston, *A Different Kind of Church: the Mayflower Family Centre Story*, Marshall Pickering, London 1994.
[12] Marchant 1986, *op.cit.*, C. Marchant, *The Inter-relationship of Church and Society in a London Borough*, unpublished Ph.D. Thesis, London School of Economics, 1974.
[13] F. Sainsbury (ed), *West Ham 1886–1986*, London Borough of Newham, 1986.
[14] Marchant 1986, *op.cit.*
[15] G. Smith, and D. Driscoll, *West Ham Christians: 1984*, Evangelical Coalition for Urban Mission, London 1985.
[16] David Sheppard, *Built as a City* (2nd edition), Hodder, London 1975.
[17] J. Ashdown, *Guide to Ethnic Christianity in London*, Zebra Project, London 1993.
[18] Booth (1985), *We True Christians*, unpublished Ph.D. thesis, Birmingham University.
[19] G. Ahern, 'Cockneys and Clergy Speak', in G. Ahern and G. Davie, *Inner City God*, Hodder & Stoughton, London 1987.
[20] Marchant (1986), *op.cit.*
[21] Marchant (1974), *op.cit.*
[22] Greg Smith, *Inner City Christianity: Some Sociological Issues*, MARC monograph series Number 17, London 1988.
[23] P. Brierley, *Prospects for the Nineties: Trends and Tables from 1989 Census of Churches in England*, (especially Volume on Greater London, including commentary by G. Smith, MARC Europe, London 1991. P. Brierly (personal communication) Data for LB Newham in 1989 Churches Census.
[24] Brierley (1991), *op.cit.*
[25] P. Brierley, V. Hiscock, *UK Christian Handbook*, 1994/95 edition, Christian Research Association/Evangelical Alliance, London 1993.
[26] J.K. Oliver, *Christian Lay Learning in an East London Community*, Unpublished MA dissertation, Youth and Community Work, Faculty of Education & Design, Brunel University, 1992.
[27] Marchant (1970), *op.cit.*; Sheppard (1975), *op.cit.*; Smith and Driscoll (1984), *op.cit.*
[28] There is a (spurious?) correlation between the take-off of this growth and the fact that the present author ceased to be a pastor in the area in 1984!
[29] Newham Association of Faiths, *Inter-Faith Relationships: What Do Newham People Think?*, NAF, Froud Centre, 1 Toronto Avenue, London E12 9JF, 1994.
[30] G. Davie, *Religion in Britain Since 1945: Believing Without Belonging*, Blackwell, Oxford 1994.
[31] A. Greely, 'Religion in Britain, Ireland and the USA' in R. Jowell, *et al. British Social Attitudes: The 9th Report*, SCPR, London 1992.
[32] Adjusted R2 = .41 n valid cases 146, Significant factors white/non-white Beta = -.64, age Beta = .45, young mothers Beta = .175.

Refugees in Newham

Alice Bloch

Introduction

The East End of London has, for many centuries, been an area of migration: the Huguenots in the seventeenth century, the Irish in the eighteenth and nineteenth centuries and Russian and Polish Jews at the turn of the century.[1] Due to the presence of the docks, there are also long-standing Chinese and African communities resident in the East End. Since the 1950s there has been mass migration of people from West Indies, the Indian Sub-continent and East African Asians.[2] In addition to the long-standing migrants, there are recent migrants from all over the world who have arrived in the area as asylum seekers and refugees.

This chapter is concerned primarily with the experience of refugees in Newham. However, it is also important to recognise the diversity of background and experience of Newham's resident minority ethnic communities in order to ensure that social policy reflects the heterogeneous needs of the different communities. In order to place refugees in a wider context of migration, this chapter will summarise the demographic and geographic profile of Newham's minority ethnic groups. I shall also examine the role of the voluntary and statutory sectors in providing information and advice to people from refugee communities. Finally I shall consider some of the difficulties that refugees in Newham may experience in gaining access to services and suggest ways in which services could be improved.

The situation of refugees will be my focal point because there are many factors which affect the ease with which refugees are able to gain access to services. Some of these factors are a result of national legislation while others are due to local policy decisions. On a national level, government legislation can leave refugees isolated and marginalised from the rest of the society. For example, the system of reception and resettlement tends to be *ad hoc* which much of the responsibility falling on community groups who work both nationally and locally with refugees and asylum seekers.[3] The Government tends to grant asylum seekers exceptional leave to remain on humanitarian grounds rather than giving them full refugee status. In this situation the applicant is granted leave to stay for one year subject to renewal after that time and again after three years.[4] Figure 1 shows Home Office decisions on asylum applications for 1992.

Figure 1: 1992 Home Office Decisions on Asylum Applications

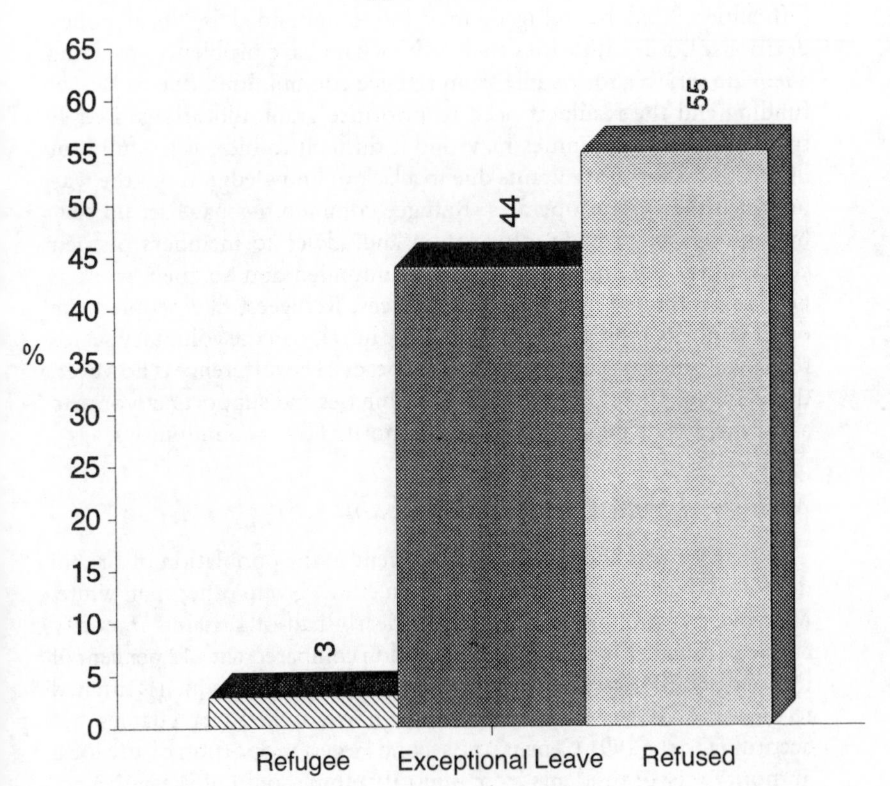

The proportion of applicants granted refugee status has dropped dramatically in recent years. In 1980 nearly two-thirds of applicants were granted refugee status, in 1990 23 per cent were accepted as refugees and, as Figure 1 shows, in 1992 the proportion had dropped to as few as 3 per cent.[5]

There are many problems associated with being granted exceptional leave to remain rather than full refugee status. These include: no family reunification rights, no security of settlement as the Home Office can refuse to renew leave to remain, only a proportion of social security benefits and no rights to student grants until three years of residency has been completed. In effect, the propensity to grant exceptional leave to remain means that refugees do not have full citizenship rights. The consequences of less than full citizenship are far reaching, resulting in social exclusion which has been linked to poverty.[6]

In addition to the problems caused by national policies, the difficulties faced by refugees may be compounded by local policy decisions. Local authorities such as Newham have problems providing adequate services for people from refugee communities, due to lack of funding and the resultant need to prioritise grant allocations. People from refugee communities may find it difficult to bid successfully for limited local authority grants due to a lack of knowledge about the way in which the system operates. Refugee communities have set up self-help groups to provide information and advice to members of their community, but these often remain unfunded and so their work is necessarily limited by a lack of resources. Refugees, like people from other minority ethnic communities, rely heavily on the voluntary sector to provide information, advice and advocacy. The difference is however, that refugees do not have the same kinship ties and support networks to assist them as do people from other minority ethnic communities.[7]

Minority Ethnic Groups in Newham

The 1991 Census showed that 5.5 per cent of the population of Britain described themselves as belonging to an ethnic group other than white. Moreover, at the time of the Census nearly half of Britain's minority ethnic population lived in Greater London compared with 12 per cent of the total population. The London Borough of Newham, which is situated to the east of Tower Hamlets and to the north of the River Thames, has according to the 1991 Census, the second largest proportion of any local authority area of residents from minority ethnic communities; 42.3 per cent in total.[8] In fact, Table 1 shows that three out of the four local authority districts in Britain with the highest proportion of residents from minority ethnic groups are situated in the London's East End.[9]

Comparisons with the national figures show that Newham has much higher than average proportions of people from all minority ethnic communities living in the borough. Table 2 compares the national results of the 1991 Census ethnic group question with the responses for Newham.[10]

Table 1 1991 Census: Local Authority Districts with the Highest Proportions of People from Minority Ethnic Communities

All minority ethnic groups	%
District	
Brent	44.8
Newham	42.3
Tower Hamlets	35.6
Hackney	33.6
Ealing	32.3
Lambeth	30.3
Haringey	29.0
Leicester	28.5
Slough	27.7
Harrow	26.2

Table 2 1991 Census: Resident Population by Ethnic Group – Great Britain and Newham

	% of total population of Great Britain	% of Newham's population
Ethnic Group		
White	94.5	57.7
Black – Caribbean	0.9	7.2
Black – African	0.4	5.6
Black – Other	0.3	1.2
Indian	1.5	13.0
Pakistan	0.9	5.9
Bangladesh	0.3	3.8
Chinese	0.3	0.8
Other Groups – Asian	0.4	3.0
Other	0.5	1.4
Total (number)	54,889,000	212,171

Within Newham itself, the ethnic composition of the wards differs substantially, showing the spatial polarisation within the borough. Spatial polarisation of minority ethnic communities is not restricted to Newham, it is evident nationally and varies by ethnic group.[11]

Examination of the census data shows that wards in the south of Newham have much higher than average white populations than the borough as a whole (see map p.169). Indeed, in the wards of Beckton, Canning Town, Customhouse and Silvertown, Greatfield, Hudsons, Ordnance and South at least three-quarters of the population described themselves as white. By contrast, the wards to the north-east of the borough have the highest proportions of residents from minority ethnic groups. In the wards of Kensington, Monega, St. Stephens and Upton more than two-thirds of the population described themselves as coming from a minority ethnic group.

The highest proportion of people who described themselves as Black Caribbean live in the wards of Forest Gate, West Ham, New Town and Park; over 10 per cent of the population from these wards described themselves as belonging to this ethnic group.

People reporting their ethnic group as Black African are more likely to be living in the wards of New Town, Park, Ordnance and Stratford than elsewhere. In these wards around 7 per cent or more of the population described their ethnic group as Black African.

Among people of South Asian origin over 30 per cent of people who live in the wards of Kensington, St. Stephens, Monega and Upton described their ethnic group as Indian. Eleven per cent or more of the population of Central, Kensington, St. Stephens, Monega and Upton described themselves as Pakistani and there are higher proportions of Bangladeshis living in Manor Park, Monega, Upton and Little Ilford than elsewhere in the borough. In these wards 8 per cent or more of the population described their ethnic group as Bangladeshi.

The Chinese community is more dispersed throughout the borough than are people from other minority ethnic groups although they tend to be slightly more concentrated in the wards of South, Stratford, West Ham and Canning Town. The wide distribution of the Chinese community is something that is evident nationally as well as locally with '... a more spatially even distribution and a lesser tendency to form local concentrations in urban areas'.[12]

The 1991 Census also asked people their country of birth which allows information to be obtained about migration and provides more detail about the ethnic composition of each area. For instance, while the ethnic group question breaks South Asian into Indian, Pakistani

Table 3 Country of Birth in Newham: 1981 and 1991

Country of Birth	% of 1981 population	% of 1991 population
United Kingdom	79.5	72.3
Irish Republic	1.7	1.7
Old Commonwealth	0.2	0.2
New Commonwealth:		
East Africa	2.8	2.6
Africa (remainder)	1.0	2.2
Caribbean	3.9	3.4
India	5.6	5.8
Bangladesh	0.2	2.5
Pakistan	2.1	2.9
Far East (Hong Kong, Malaysia, Singapore)	0.7	0.8
Mediterranean (Cyprus, Gibraltar, Malta, Gozo)	0.5	0.4
Remainder New Commonwealth	0.2	1.1
Other Europe	0.7	1.0
Rest of the World (Non-Commonwealth Africa, Asia and Turkey, USSR and America	0.8	3.1
Total residents (number)	209,128	212,170

and Bangladeshi, the country of birth question also provides information about people born in Sri Lanka, most of whom are refugees. Among the South Asian groups, Bangladeshis were less likely to have been born in the United Kingdom than were people who described their ethnic group as Indian or Pakistani. Thirty six per cent of those who described their ethnic group as Bangladeshi were born in the UK compared with 41 per cent of those of Indian origin and half of those of Pakistani origin. This reflects migration patterns as people from Bangladesh are among the most recently arrived migrants in Britain with immigration increasing after 1980.[13]

African Carribbeans are the longest established minority ethnic group in Britain with mass migration from West Indies to Britain taking place in the 1950s.[14] As a result, the highest proportion of people from this minority ethnic group were born in the UK (55 per cent). In fact, African Caribbean children aged under 16 are almost as likely to have been born in the United Kingdom as are white children.[15] In contrast, only 32 per cent of people who described their ethnic group as Black African were born in the UK, reflecting the increased migration from Africa in the 1980s due to civil unrest in some African countries.

Comparison of the country of birth question from the 1981 and 1991 Censuses (Table 3) shows that there has been an increase in the proportion of Newham residents who were born in Bangladesh. There is also an increase in the numbers who fall in the 'Rest of the World' category. This would include refugees from non-Commonwealth countries such as Somalia and Zaire, as well as Kurdish refugees from Iraq and Turkey.

Refugees in Newham

Migration to avoid persecution is an age old phenomenon which has become politicised and internationalised in the twentieth century.[16] Refugees have been coming to the East End for many centuries but the first acknowledgement of an international responsibility towards refugees did not come until 1921 with the appointment of Fridtjof Nansen as the first United Nations High Commissioner for Refugees.[17] World War II resulted in millions of displaced persons although the first international legislation which concerned refugees and asylum seekers was not until the 1951 Geneva Convention.[18] The Convention defined refugees as, 'persons who are outside their country because of a well-founded fear of persecution for reasons of race, religion, nationality, membership of a particular social group or political opinion'.

The Bellagio Protocol (1967), which was signed by nearly one hundred countries, removed the geographical and temporal limitations of the Geneva Convention in order to extend its applicability to refugees from all over the world. This change reflected the fact that the refugees were generated all over the world, not just in Europe.

The 1970s and 1980s saw an increase in refugees from crisis areas in Africa, Asia and the Middle East. The reason for this increase was due, in part, to the attainment of independence from European control which resulted in territorial conflicts as colonisers created boundaries that did not necessarily reflect the cultural composition of an area.[19] According to the Independent Commission on International and Humanitarian Issues (ICIHI), ' … the arrival of many refugees from geographically and culturally distant areas constituted an unprecedented challenge to the legal machinery and conscience of the receiving countries'.[20]

The new refugees were culturally and ethnically different from the host society and they lacked kinship ties and support groups in their country of settlement.[21] Moreover, the new refugees often arrived in their new country under traumatic circumstances which affected their ability to adapt to the host society. This has resulted in a series of measures to restrict entry to Britain. Measures have included the imposition of visas on Sri Lankan and Turkish nationals after an increase in the number of Tamils from Sri Lanka and Kurds from Turkey applying for asylum.[22]

In reality, only a tiny proportion of Britain's population are refugees but the Government's fear of bogus applications resulted in the Asylum and Immigration Appeals Act 1993. Table 4 shows that there was a large decrease in the number of asylum applications even before the Asylum and Immigration Appeals Act 1993 came into force. The decrease in numbers is partly due to the reduction in applicants from Zaire and Angola.[23]

Table 4: Asylum Applications, Excluding Dependants, by Area and Main Nationality

	1991 Number	%	1992 Number	%
Sri Lanka	3,754	8.4	2,085	8.5
Pakistan	3,245	7.2	1,700	6.9
India	2,075	4.6	1,450	5.9
Turkey	2,110	4.7	1,865	7.6
Zaire	7,010	15.6	880	3.6
Angola	5,780	12.9	245	1.0
Ghana	2,405	5.4	1,600	6.5
Somalia	1,995	4.4	1,575	6.4
Uganda	1,450	3.2	295	1.2
Ethiopia	1,685	3.8	680	2.8
Other Africa	7,177	16.0	2,355	9.6
Former Yugoslavia	320	0.7	5,635	22.9
Rest of world	5,834	13.0	4,241	17.2
Total	44,840	99.9*	24,606	100.1*

* Percentages have been rounded up so the totals do not add up to 100.

Home office statistics show that asylum applicants tend to be male and younger than the population as a whole. In 1992 around 70 per cent of applicants were male while Figure 2 shows that in 1992, 83 per cent of applicants were under 40 years of age.[24]

Figure 2: Applications for Asylum in the United Kingdom, by age, 1992

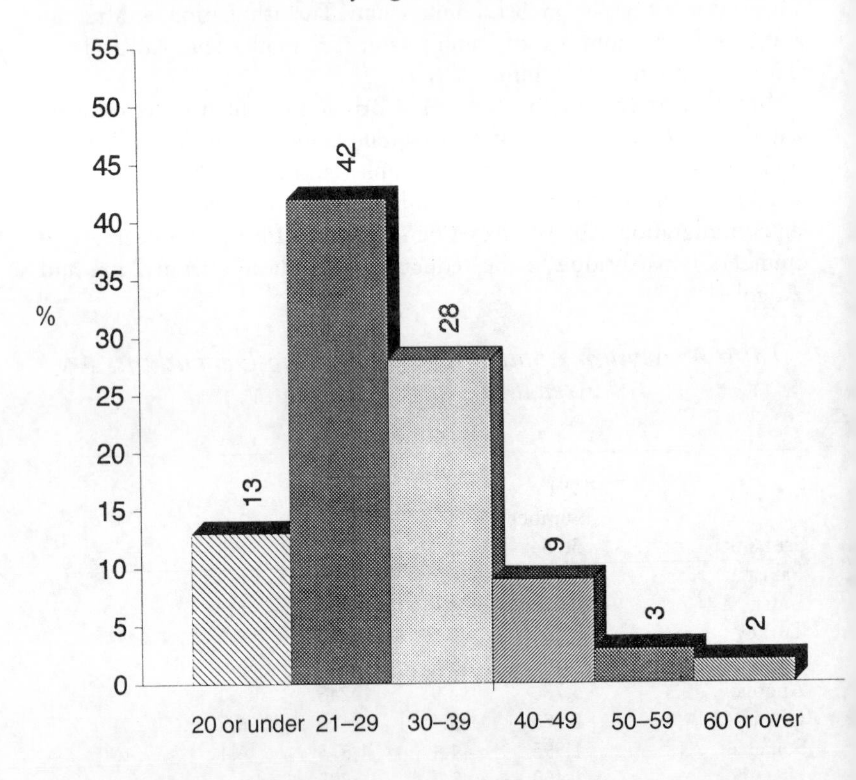

One of the major problems faced by policy-makers in relation to refugees is that of obtaining accurate information about the numbers and ethnic origin of refugees in any given locality. The problems in gaining accurate information are fivefold. First, Home Office statistics are not available by local authority area. Secondly, it can be difficult to distinguish between migrants and refugees. For instance, Somalis have been resident in the East End of London, and other shipping areas in Britain, for over a hundred years but when they applied for citizenship, they were included in the asylum statistics. Thirdly, refugees are an extremely mobile group and there is much secondary migration in Britain. This has been particularly apparent among Vietnamese refugees who were initially dispersed around the country but have since regrouped in a few large centres.[25] Fourthly, the Census information does not allow refugees to be distinguished from other minority ethnic groups. Finally, information provided by community groups are merely estimates and the data are subject to problems of validity. As a result, a combination of different sources which included interviews with representatives from voluntary and statutory agencies, secondary analysis of the Census and documentary sources were used in order to provide the best estimate about the number and ethnic composition of refugees in Newham.[26]

It is estimated, based on figures provided by the Benefits Agency and a formula devised by Griffiths, that the number of refugees in Newham is over 9,000.[27] This is similar to the 9,000 refugees estimated after research was carried out by the Health and Ethnicity programme of the North West and North East Thames Regional Health Authority.[28] Table 5 shows the distribution of refugees in the North East Thames Regional Health Authority area.[29]

Table 5: Estimated Figures for Refugees in the North East Thames Region of Health Authority Area

District	Number
Islington and Bloomsbury	20,000
City and Hackney	15,000
Haringey	15,000
Tower Hamlets	12,000
Newham	9,000
Enfield	3,000
Waltham Forest	3,000
Hampstead	2,000
Total	79,000

The two largest refugee groups in Newham are Somalis and Tamils.

Somalis form the largest group and estimates about the number of Somalis resident in the borough vary from 6,000 (representative from the Somali Welfare Association) to 8,000.[30] The size of the Somali community in Newham has increased since 1965 for two reasons. First, between 1965 and 1977 many Somali seafarers brought their families over to Britain and secondly, since the late 1980s civil unrest in Somalia has forced people to seek asylum in other African countries and in the West. People from Somalia are most likely to live in the wards of Forest Gate, Stratford, Manor Park and Plaistow.

Tamils from Sri Lanka form the second largest refugee group in Newham. Tamils began to arrive in Britain in the mid 1980s and in larger numbers since 1987 when the Indian army sent troops to Sri Lanka to end the conflict between the Tamils and the Government. Estimates about the number of Tamils in the borough vary quite substantially, ranging from between 10,000 (representative of the Tamil Welfare Association) to 1,835 which is the number of people resident in Newham who were born in Sri Lanka at the time of the 1991 Census. People from Sri Lanka are dispersed throughout Newham although the highest proportion, over a quarter, live in Wall End.

The Census also provides information about the number of people born in Uganda (2,029). The number of people of Ugandan origin would be greater if the number of children born in Britain of Ugandan parents were taken into account. A small proportion of those born in Uganda will be of Asian origin and a few may be of English origin. Given that the Refugee Council estimates the total number of Ugandan refugees in the United Kingdom to be around 10,000 and Bell estimates the number to be 8090, it is apparent that over a fifth of all Ugandan refugees in the United Kingdom live in Newham.[31] People born in Uganda and living in Newham are dispersed around the borough, although slightly higher proportions live in Upton (12 per cent) and Manor Park (9 per cent) than elsewhere.

Other African refugee communities resident in Newham are from Zaire, Ethiopia, Eritrea, Angola, Liberia, Gambia and Sierra Leone. According to the Census, 213 people resident in Newham were born in Sierra Leone and 54 people were born in Gambia. Numbers remain unknown for the other African refugee groups although a survey of languages spoken at secondary schools, which was carried out by Newham Education Department in 1993, provides an estimate of the relative size of each group. The survey found that 33 children in secondary schools spoke Lingala, a language spoken in Zaire. Portuguese was spoken by 31 children; the majority of whom are refugees from Angola and Mozambique. Kurdish and Turkish is spoken by 116 children, 35 children speak Vietnamese while Serbo-Croat is spoken by four secondary school children.

It is thought that there are around 300 families of Kurdish origin living in Newham while the Census shows that there are 402 people living in Newham who were born in Turkey. Kurds have been arriving in Britain since 1988 having fled oppression in Kurdistan. The Census also shows that there were 247 people living in Newham who were born in Vietnam, 183 from Iran, 37 from the former Yugoslavia, 83 from Romania, 247 from Poland 28 from Hungary and 27 from Czechoslovakia.

Clearly the refugee population in Newham is very diverse. Refugees are also spread around the borough in all areas except for the south. This has implications for service providers who need to try and meet the needs of all residents in the borough.

The Changing Role of the Voluntary Sector

There are a number of national and locally based organisations that assist refugees on arrival in Britain. Nationally, there is the Refugee Arrivals Project at Heathrow Airport and the Refugee Council who not only provide practical support, but also participate in policy and campaigning work. On a local level in Newham, there are a number of specialist refugee groups who assist people from particular communities such as the Newham Somali Association and the Uganda Asylum Seekers Association. There is much networking and communication between the national and the local groups with the latter assisting in finding housing and providing interpretation services for new arrivals.

Although there are a large number of voluntary agencies providing a service to refugees, at a local level advice services have developed in response to local need rather than in line with a national strategy. The development of local services has tended to rely on the willingness of the local authority to fund services.[32] This can be problematic for small voluntary sector organisations working with refugees for two reasons. First, because resources are necessarily limited and because the groups they are working with tend to be small, some refugee organisations depend on volunteers working from home rather than paid staff in rented offices. Secondly, in order to gain access to funds, small voluntary sector organisations need knowledge of the workings of the local authority and of the resources that they can bid for.[33] It follows that refugee organisations will be at a disadvantage as they would be less likely to have the knowledge and understanding of a system in which they have only recently become involved. Lack of knowledge is an issue that the Wolfenden Committee alluded to in the late 1970s when it stated that:

> We have obtained a picture of the difficulties experienced by voluntary organisations in their relationships with local authorities. The difficulties related mainly to finance and duration of grants but we also had the impression that many organisations, especially the smaller ones at a local level, find it hard to obtain the information they need about the statutory side and its workings in general, as well as the particular details about the criteria to be met in order to qualify for grant aiding.[34]

In Britain the voluntary sector has a number of roles: the voluntary sector can speak for the consumer, act as a watchdog, act as a catalyst for change and cater for the diversity of need in the community (which includes the interests of minority ethnic communities). Moreover, community and user organisations have sprung up in order to fill the gaps they see in mainstream provision. This is particularly apparent with voluntary organisations who work with people from refugee communities as their needs and experiences can be unique and are often not catered for by the statutory sector. This includes the provision of interpretation services, the recognition of cultural differences, an understanding of health needs and experience prior to migration.

Services for Refugees and Problems Gaining Access to Services

There are many agencies, both statutory and voluntary, that provide information and advice services for refugees in Newham. However, research in Newham, along with other research, shows that refugees rely heavily on community groups and other contacts they might have in an area where they settle.[35] This section will review some of the services available to refugee communities in Newham and will demonstrate the ways in which refugees may be disadvantaged when it comes to obtaining basic services.

There is a wide range of voluntary sector organisations in Newham; some of the organisations are funded either wholly or in part by the local authority while others receive no funding at all. Most of the enquiries received by the voluntary groups concern basic social welfare advice about social security benefits, housing, education and immigration. A minority of the community groups also organise English language classes and interpretation services but these services are not extensive enough to meet the needs of the communities who require them.

In addition to the community groups working with refugees in Newham there are also three umbrella refugee organisations: the Refugee Union, Refugee Consortium and the Refugee Forum. Although the role of these umbrella groups varies they all serve one very important role; they help to ensure that information is properly disseminated among the different communities.

The statutory sector organisations also provide a service to refugees and fund services which work within the statutory sector. The most recent development is a new Refugee Centre in Manor Park, which is funded by Newham. The Centre is in its developmental stage but it is anticipated that it will house at least 17 refugee groups and provide a range of other services including a resource centre, an immigration legal adviser and a counselling service. The Centre has set up a number of working groups focusing on key issues that affect refugees. They are planning to carry out research to inform service provision and service delivery for refugees.

The Social Services Department has, since the end of 1993, employed a refugee worker whose role is to identify the needs of refugees in the borough and suggest ways of improving services to refugees. The Social Services Department has also started an Initial Contact Service which acts as an information and referral service. The ultimate aim is to make it into a 'one stop shop' for all Newham residents.

The Family Health Service Authority of the East London and the City Health Authority operate a health advocacy service around linguistic groups which include some languages which are spoken by refugee communities. Languages include: Hindi, Punjabi, Bengali, Urdu, Gujerati, Turkish, Arabic, French, Vietnamese and Chinese. The health advocates bridge the gap between non-English speakers and English health professionals and primary health providers. They also give information and advice and refer clients to other services.

Access to services

Refugees may be disadvantaged when it comes to obtaining basic services such as housing, education, health and social security. This section will examine some of the national and local factors which affect refugees' access to services.

Housing: Gaining access to suitable housing is a difficulty faced by many refugees.[36] With the exception of programme refugees, such as the Vietnamese in the late 1970s and early 1980s, most refugees on arrival in Britain are dependent on voluntary sector organisations assisting them in their effort to find accommodation. Moreover, the Asylum and Immigration Appeals Act 1993 withdrew asylum seekers' rights to housing as local authorities said that they could not fulfil their statutory obligations.[37] This will put even more pressure on voluntary sector organisations.

Many refugees come to Newham because of cheap housing in the private rented sector and refugees who have been placed in other boroughs by the Refugee Arrivals Project migrate to Newham as housing is cheaper. In Newham, the Tamil Welfare Association has links with a local letting agency and assists with deposits where necessary so that refugees can be housed on arrival. There are housing associations in Newham that provide housing to refugees, such as ARHAG Housing Association but their provision can only go some of the way towards meeting the housing needs of refugees.

As a result of insufficient social housing and the inability of refugees to gain council housing due to the length of residence rule in local housing departments, the housing tenure pattern of refugees differs from the population as a whole. According to the 1991 Census, in Newham around half the population in the borough were owner occupiers while 31 per cent were council tenants. A survey carried out by Gammel and her colleagues found that housing tenure among refugees differed from the population at large. Only 6 per cent of refugees were owner occupiers, 55 per cent were living in housing which was privately rented but paid for by the council, 21 per cent were in council housing, 7 per cent in bed and breakfast and 24 per cent lived in hostel accommodation. Moreover, the survey found that 68 per cent of refugees were probably living in housing that was deemed to be overcrowded.[38]

The Refugee Council has identified homelessness as a crisis among refugees. Of the 22,000 refugees who approached the Refugee Council for help in 1991, 60 per cent needed urgent help with housing.[39] In 1991/92 it was estimated that there were 47 homeless refugee families in Newham.[40]

Education: It can be very difficult, as we have seen, for refugees to gain access to higher education because of the restrictions surrounding funding. Only those with full refugee status are entitled to mandatory educational grants for higher education while those with exceptional leave to remain have to wait three years before they are entitled to a grant and asylum seekers are not entitled to a grant at all. This means that it is difficult for refugees to be educated as they are required to pay prohibitive overseas fees. Most refugees are under forty years old (83 per cent) and therefore the delay in their education can be very destructive. This is shown by a study carried out in Lambeth which found that a lack of education was seen as the main barrier preventing employment among refugees.[41]

Many refugees are already highly qualified and skilled before arrival in Britain but have difficulties gaining employment for two reasons. First, their qualifications are not recognised in Britain and secondly, most employers require references from a previous employer which can be almost impossible to produce. Indeed, in 1992 the Refugee Council reported that 70 per cent of refugees in London were unemployed.[42] The link between education and employment is vital and this is demonstrated by a case reported by Gambell:

> Asylum seeker: qualified dentist from University of Baghdad. She has been told by the British Dental Council that she must requalify or complete a dental course in order to practice in United Kingdom. She has been considered for a university place but as an asylum seeker she would have to pay overseas student fees, and does not qualify for a grant.[43]

The Education Department in Newham has put in place a number of initiatives to assist refugee children in schools. First, newly qualified teachers and managers are trained in refugee issues and awareness in an attempt to help them better understand the emotional and psychological needs of refugee children. Secondly, they provide English language classes for refugee children. Thirdly, they try to meet training and employment needs by working closely with local colleges and businesses and by arranging training for 16 to 19 year olds.

Health: Gaining access to appropriate health care can be difficult and this is borne out by research which shows a low take-up of health services among members of minority ethnic communities for a number of reasons including: lack of knowledge about services,[44] lack of understanding about the system and ways of obtaining services,[45] difficulties communicating with health professionals[46] and the inappropriateness of some services due to religious and cultural beliefs.[47]

In the case of refugees, the physical and mental health needs can be greater than those of people from other minority ethnic communities due to their experiences before arrival and on arrival in the United Kingdom. Gammel *et al* in their survey of refugees found that only 6 per cent of refugees who said they were depressed had taken up counselling services, while nearly three-quarters said they would like to talk to a professional counsellor in their own language.[48] One of the problems already mentioned was lack of knowledge about health services and of how to gain access to them. Gammel and her colleagues found that only 7 per cent of refugees had been given information about how to register with a General Practitioner while 3 per cent had been given information about how to use hospital services.[49]

The Patient's Charter published by the Department of Health[50] recognised the need to make sure that all users were informed about services so that they are able to make an informed choice about the treatment and care they receive. What is clear is that refugees are not well informed about service provision or about access to services. This needs to be addressed if the Department of Health is to fulfil its charter. The Health Advocacy service goes some way towards meeting the needs of different communities but is necessarily limited. For instance, there are two health advocates who work with Turkish speakers in the City and East London Health Authority. It is estimated that there are around 300 Kurdish families in the area who are Turkish speakers, with five or six family members in each family, so it is impossible for them to provide the level of service that is needed for people from this community, as their role ranges from providing information to attending doctor's appointments with clients in the role of translator.

Social security: Most refugees arrive in Britain with little or no money and so they are immediately dependent on social security as they are unable to study or work. As new arrivals are classified as 'persons from abroad', they only receive a reduced level of Income Support (90 per cent). Some refugees will be put off claiming benefits because personal documents can be requested by the Benefits Agency as a way of checking eligibility. Research on access to benefits for minority ethnic groups found that over a third of claimants had been asked to produce their passport in support of their claim, while over one-fifth had to produce their birth certificate and one-fifth had to show their marriage certificate as part of the claiming process.[51] It can be very difficult for refugees to produce official documentation and when they are able to produce official documentation it is usually in a language other than English.

Some refugees are asked to produce a Standard Acknowledgement Letter (SAL) from the Home Office as evidence of status and identity before benefits will be paid. The process of issuing SALs can be a lengthy one involving many interviews and this affects the claiming process. Gambell gives examples of cases where payment of social security has been delayed due to problems obtaining documentation. 'Asylum seeker who arrived in the United Kingdom in July 1992. Income Support was claimed in August but not awarded until Home Office papers were issued in November.'[52]

Research also showed that some refugees were put off claiming benefits because of fears that the Benefits Agency would want information about immigration status and rights of abode. According to one Kurdish refugee, 'There is stigma attached to being a refugee, and people often act indifferently towards you. That is one of the reasons why my husband did not claim benefits when we were together'.[53]

The claiming process can be extremely difficult for refugees, especially those without English language skills. The Benefits Agency in Newham has installed Language Line in the reception areas of their local offices in Stratford, Plaistow and Canning Town and have noticed an increase in the number of requests for Serbo-Croat, Turkish and Polish interpreters. Staff from the Benefits Agency also work closely with voluntary organisations and carry out outreach sessions in community centres around the borough. It is known that this approach is successful as it enables people to claim in an environment that they feel comfortable in rather than going to offices of the Benefits Agency.[54] In Newham however, staff at the Benefits Agency cannot cover the range of refugee languages that are spoken in the borough and so this service is not widely available to members of refugee groups.

Policy Implications

There were a number of recommendations for policy initiatives that emerged from interviews with representatives from both statutory and voluntary sector organisations. The initiatives included the provision of interpreters, more culturally sensitive services which recognise the heterogeneity of different groups, employment of refugees in statutory agencies, more training for voluntary sector workers and more outreach work.

Interpreters: People who do not speak English or do not feel confident speaking English face more difficulties and often depend on interpreters to assist them through the process. In fact a survey carried out in Islington found that nearly two-thirds of refugees would approach family, friends and community advisers for help.[55] This may be problematic for two reasons. First, for an interpretation service to be successful then it needs to be professional and therefore the interpreters need to be trained.[56] This is not the case with the informal arrangements that are the norm. Secondly, reliance on family members, particularly children, can put a great deal of strain on family relationships. Children find themselves privy to information that they would not normally have access to and it is difficult for the parents as it changes the normal dynamic of familial relations. This is especially true in dealings with social workers, health professionals and the Benefits Agency.

Recognition of the diversity of need: At present, service providers tend to adopt blanket service delivery strategies rather than recognising that each group has different needs. For instance, the Benefits Agency found that their Ethnic Freeline Service, a free telephone advice service, was thought useful among some groups while others preferred face to face information and advice.[57] The Punjabi and Urdu lines were valued because people who spoke these languages said they preferred telephone advice to visiting the office. In addition, people who spoke these languages liked the feeling that the advice providers were from the same minority ethnic community as themselves and could therefore relate better to the enquiry. By contrast, the Freeline Service was not an effective way to reach the Chinese community who expressed preference for face-to-face meetings.

Another example of the blanket approach to service delivery is the tendency to translate leaflets and information packs into a range of different languages without properly assessing language and literacy in the different languages. Translated materials may be appropriate for some groups and sub-groups but not for others.

Services need to be more culturally sensitive if they are to meet the needs of different groups. In dealings with the DSS one Kurdish refugee stated that, 'Although I come from Turkey I am Kurdish. We have a slightly different culture to Turkish people. We should not be grouped together as one community, we have our own identity'.[58]

Staff who work at the statutory agencies need to be better informed about different cultures and experiences as a means of combating racism. The problems of prejudice were expressed by one Kurdish refugee when he stated that, 'When most Kurdish people inform the DSS of their difficulties and tell workers they are political refugees, they are faced with hostility. A lot of my family and friends have had to put up with DSS workers' prejudice regarding our status'.[59]

There is also a need for more cultural sensitivity in the provision of health services. For example, Sadler documents a case where an Asian woman was fitted with a contraceptive coil by a male practitioner in front of a group of medical students. She was unaware of her right to ask for a female practitioner and more privacy. In her culture the experience was a violation of her personal dignity.[60]

Employment of refugees in statutory agencies: A favoured initiative was more staff employed in statutory organisations from the different refugee communities. The value of this would be three-fold. First, it would create more employment for refugees, a group with high levels of unemployment. Secondly, it would mean that refugees would know that there was someone working at the agency with whom they could communicate in their first language. Thirdly, it would mean that the experience of going to the agency would not be so alienating as there would be someone there who would understand the refugee's particular culture and experience.

Training of voluntary sector workers: It was suggested that an increase in the provision of training for voluntary sector workers would be a very valuable policy initiative as some are without basic welfare rights training. The implication of the lack of training is that clients may receive inaccurate advice. Moreover, many voluntary sector workers operate on their own in an organisation and in some cases this means that they do not have the time to keep up-to-date with the leglislation as they are seeing clients all the time.

Outreach work: There is a need for more basic advice provision so that refugees can receive information and advice in an environment in which they feel comfortable. It was argued by voluntary sector workers that it was not sufficient to have different language speakers in what are thought of as predominantly white agencies because refugees do not feel comfortable in that environment. One of the ways around the problem is to increase the amount of outreach work carried out by the statutory agencies. Outreach work carried out by the statutory agencies like the Benefits Agency and the health authority are held in high regard, but as we have seen, do not go all the way to meet the needs of refugee communities due to resource constraints. Ideally, outreach work should take place regularly at a number of locations around the borough and it would help to make up for the limited number of funded community groups providing a service to refugees in Newham.

Summary

Most refugees are not programme refugees and so they have not had the benefit of a formal reception and resettlement operation. Instead, they rely heavily on community groups and family members and friends to inform them about service entitlements and to assist them through the process of gaining access to services. If services are to be improved for refugees then national and local policy initiatives need to be put into place.

Nationally, a more organised approach to the reception and resettlement of refugees would assist refugees in learning about the system and finding out about their rights to services. Moreover, much of the restrictive legislation on rights to employment and educational grants should be reconsidered as these force refugees to put their lives on hold at the start of their settlement in the United Kingdom. It would also be useful if the Home Office released facts about numbers and location of refugees on a locality basis so that service providers could better plan for the communities they serve.

On a local level, in Newham, there were a number of service delivery initiatives identified by representatives of community groups and statutory organisations that would assist refugees on settlement in the United Kingdom. Some initiatives require a financial input while others require a reshaping of current policies to help to ensure that refugees have equal access to services.

Notes

[1] W. Fishman, *The Streets of East London*, Duckworth, London 1979.
[2] C. Holmes, *John Bull's Island – Immigration and British Society 1871–1971*, Macmillan, Basingstoke 1988.
[3] T. Renton, 'Refugees: the Responsibilities of the UK Government', Chapter 3 in V. Robinson (ed), *The International Refugee Crisis: British and Canadian Responses*, Macmillan, Basingstoke 1993.
[4] Due to the difficulties in differentiating people with refugee status, those who are seeking asylum and those with exceptional leave to remain, the term

'refugee' is used as a generic one to encompass people in all three categories.

[5] HMSO, 'Asylum Statistics United Kingdom 1992', *Home Office Statistical Bulletin*, HMSO, London 1993, p7.

[6] P. Close, *Citizenship, Europe and Change*, Macmillan, Basingstoke 1995.

[7] A. Bloch, *Access to Benefits: the Information Needs of Minority Ethnic Groups*, Policy Studies Institute, London 1993.

[8] A. Teague, 'Ethnic group: first results from the 1991 Census', *Population Trends*, Summer 72, HMSO, London 1993.

[9] *Ibid.*, p14.

[10] A. Bloch, *Refugees and Migrants in Newham: Access to Services*, London Borough of Newham, London 1994a, p15.

[11] M. Cross, 'Race and ethnicity', Chapter 8 in A. Thornley (ed), *The Crisis of London*, Routledge, London 1992.

[12] D. Owen, 'Spatial Variations in Ethnic Minority Group Populations in Great Britain', *Population Trends*, Number 78, Winter 1994, HMSO, London 1994.

[13] T. Jones, *Britain's Ethnic Minorities*, Policy Studies Institute, London 1993.

[14] Holmes, *op.cit.*

[15] Jones, *op.cit.*

[16] D. Joly and R. Cohen (eds), *Reluctant Hosts: Europe and its Refugees*, Avebury 1989.

[17] G. Loescher, *Beyond Charity: International Co-operation and the Global Refugee Crisis*, Oxford University Press, Oxford 1993.

[18] D. Joly, C. Nettleton and H. Poulton, *Refugees: Asylum in Europe*, Minority Rights Publications, London 1992.

[19] J.Hein, *States and International Migration: The Incorporation of Indochinese Refugees in the United States and France*, Westview Press, Boulder, Colorado 1993.

[20] ICIHI, *Refugees: Dynamics of Displacement*, Zed Books, London 1986, p33.

[21]B.N. Stein (1981), 'The refugee experience: defining the parameters of a field of study', *International Migration Review*, Volume 15, Number 1, pp320–30.

[22] D. Joly *et al*, (1992), *op.cit.*

[23] HMSO, *op.cit.*, Table 2.2.

[24] *Ibid.*, p11.

[25]J. Bell and L. Clinton, *The Unheard Community: A Look at Housing Conditions and Needs of Refugees from Vietnam Living in London*, Refugee Action, Derby 1993: Joly *et al* (1992), *op.cit.*

[26] A. Bloch (1994a), *op.cit.*

[27] S. Griffiths, *Poverty on Your Doorstep: London Borough of Newham Poverty Profile*, London Borough of Newham, London 1994.

[28] G. Karmi (ed), *Refugees and the National Health Service*, The Health and Ethnicity Programme, North West and North East Thames Regional Health Authority, London 1992.

[29] *Ibid.*, p21.

[30] Race Equality Section, *Refugee Families*, Social Services, London Borough of Newham, London 1993.

31 J. Bell, *Ugandan Refugees: A Study of Housing Conditions and the Circumstances of Children*, Community Development Foundation, London 1993.

[32] Policy Studies Institute, *Review of Advice Services in Leicester*, Leicester City Council, Leicester 1993.
[33] D. Deacon and P. Golding, *The Information Needs of Voluntary and Community Groups*, University of Leicester, Centre for Mass Communication research, Leicester 1988.
[34] Wolfenden, *The Future of Voluntary Organisations*, Croom Helm, 1978, p91.
[35] S. Balloch, *Refugees in the Inner City: A study of Refugees and Service Provision in the London Borough of Lewisham*, Centre for Inner City Studies, Goldsmiths College, University of London, London 1993.
[36]J. Gambell, *Welcome to the UK*, NACAB, London 1993.
[37] R. Cohen, *Frontiers of Identity*, Longman, New York 1994.
[38] H. Gammel, A. Ndahiro, N. Nicholas and J. Windsor, *Refugees (Political Asylum Seekers): Service Provision and Access to the NHS*, College of Health, London 1993.
[39] Refugee Council, 'Sanctuary on the streets', *Exile*, September 1992.
[40] London Research Centre, *London Housing Statistics*, LRC 1992.
[41] H. Rolfe, *Careers Guidance and the Employment, Training or Educational Needs of Young Unemployed People in Lambeth*, Policy Studies Institute, London, 1993.
[42] Refugee Council 'Careers Guidance – When and Where it is Needed', *Exile*, November 1992.
[43] Gambell, *op.cit.*, p34.
[44] A. Atkin, E. Cameron, F. Badger and H. Evers, H., 'Asian Elders' Knowledge and Future Use of Community Social and Health Services' *New Community*, April 1989, pp439–45.
[45] C. Sadler, 'Women's Voices', *Nursing Times*, July 15 1992.
[46] Adult Literacy and Basic Skills Unit, *A Nation's Neglect: Research into the Needs of English Among Speakers of Other Languages*, London 1989.
[47] C. Pharoah and E. Redmond, 'Care for Ethnic Elders' *The Health Service Journal*, 16 May 1992, pp52–64; E. McFarland, M. Dalton and D. Walsh, 'Ethnic Minority Needs and Service Delivery: the Barriers to Access in a Glasgow Inner City Area', *New Community*, April 1989, pp405–15.
[48] Gamell, *op.cit.*
[49] *Ibid.*
[50] Department of Health, *The Patient's Charter*, HMSO, London 1991.
[51] Bloch (1993), *op.cit.*
[52] Gambell, *op.cit.*, p9.
[53] Bloch (1993), *op.cit.*, p32.
[54] *Ibid.*
[55] Islington Refugee Working Party, *Refugee Questionnaire Survey*, London 1992.
[56] Saddler, *op.cit.*; Bloch (1994), *op.cit.*
[57] A. Bloch, 'Improving Access to Benefits for Minority Ethnic Groups', *Benefits*, Issue 9, January 1994.
[58] Bloch (1993) *op.cit.*, p42.
[59] *Ibid.*, p44.
[60] Sadler, *op.cit.*

Appendix: Newham Ward Boundaries 1991

All White on the Night? Narratives of nativism on the Isle of Dogs

Phil Cohen
with the assistance of Tarek Qureshi and Ian Toon

Starting points

> People do not live not in places
> but in the description of places
> Wallace Stevens

Today every estate agent subscribes to Wallace Stevens's adage, and practises a corrupted poetics of place. As a result, the reputation of an area, whether it is seen as desirable or undesirable, has a direct material impact on the lives of its inhabitants. This not only affects the value of their properties, the cost of their insurance premiums, or their ability to get hire purchase, but the quality of schooling which is available to their children and the pattern of their everyday lives.

This 'urban imagineering' is not just a matter of private enterprise. Local authorities frequently spend as much money on promoting positive images of particular cities, regions or even neighbourhoods, in order to attract tourism or investment, as they do on improving amenities for those who live there. And it is not just a question of images, but of narratives. For we are concerned here with local gossip and rumour as well as media news stories and public mythology, all of which weave a tangled web of anecdote through which a certain social fiction about habits, habitats and inhabitants is maintained.

What then happens to those whose faces do not feature or fit within these official spaces of representation? In the narrative cartographies which link modernity, progress and urban regeneration, the poor, the unemployed, and other large minorities find their inconvenient existence all too easily and often glossed over or written out of the picture. How then do those who have been made invisible put themselves back on the map? How do those who are silenced by the script make themselves heard, if only between the official lines?

It was with these questions in mind that we started the investigation which is reported, in part, in this chapter. The project arose out of work which the New Ethnicities Unit at UEL undertook on the Isle of Dogs in 1992, with students and staff at George Green School, to develop a new approach to multicultural art education.[1] It became clear from analysing students' material that the identity work in which both white and black or Asian adolescents were engaged had a lot to do with local antagonisms within and between their respective communities. We decided to follow up the educational work with a more concerted piece of research. This took the form of a series of lengthy interviews with a small but representative sample of local Bangladeshi and white working-class residents, carried out over the summer and early autumn of 1993.[2] The interviews focused on the sense of home and belonging, and on what or who was felt to threaten it. We were interested in where and how that sense of home was located, its relation to particular kinds of gender, class and ethnic identity, and how this in turn interacted with community relations on the Island. As we were completing the analysis of this material, racial violence in the area intensified, and the BNP began to gain the electoral ground which culminated in its temporary success in the Millwall by-election of 1994. More than is usually the case therefore, this research is shaped by political events which were not its primary focus of attention, but which constitute, nevertheless, the ultimate object of explanation.

It should also be stressed that this was a pilot study designed to evaluate a particular methodology which we subsequently hoped to employ in a larger and more comparative study into models of community safety and racial danger.[3] For this purpose we took a leaf out of Wallace Stevens's book, and set out to explore possible ways of mapping a popular poetics of place. Through the stories that are told about places, and the people in them, some of the most far-reaching and far-fetched ideas about the structure of social relationships are given a local habitation and a name. Our task then was to serve as earwitnesses to the stories which were being told amongst different groups on the island about each other, about the places where they met, and the places they did not. Our premise was that whether in the form of private or public anecdote, these narratives mapped out a symbolic landscape of shared and contested territories, places of safety and danger, in a way which governed actual patterns of social encounter. It is through this grid of symbolic representation that struggles over access and entitlement to public amenity and resources – housing, education, jobs, leisure facilities, transport – are largely articulated and racialised.

The fact that we were on the right track was borne in on us at the very outset when we were looking for the more literal kind of premises from which to conduct the field work. We were put in touch with a number of organisations which might provide us with some temporary house-room. It quickly became clear that where we located ourselves would send specific messages to different interest groups on the Island about where the project was coming from. If we had been based at Jack Dash House, then we would have been placed as belonging in the camp of municipal anti-racism and as such subject to distrust from sections of both communities; if we had managed to get a room in a multi-ethnic community centre used by Vietnamese/Chinese and Bangladeshi families amongst others, then we would have been identified by white islanders as siding with 'the ethnics'. If we set up shop in the Docklands settlement, then we would be seen as siding with the white cause. There was, it seemed, no neutral ground.

How much this positioning has to do with the actual policies and practices of these different organisations is an interesting question in its own right, but one which we do not tackle here. Our primary concern was to find out how these agencies were located in a symbolic landscape of race, place and identity. It was clear there was little room for manoeuvre here. Our address was made to tell its own story about where we stood on the issues dividing the communities, irrespective of what we might actually want to say.

Partly as a result of this experience, and partly as a result of the events that began to unfold on the Island, we became increasingly aware of the link between what were being told to us as 'inside stories' circulating within and between the different Island communities, and the grand narratives of race, nation, and the body politic, which were being elaborated by 'outsiders'. These included political parties, the mass media, anti-racist organisations, and academic researchers, all of whom converged on the area in search of the 'inside story' and in the process created, if not a great debate, then at least a grand soap opera about East Enders.

As the research progressed we became concerned with the impact of these 'outside-in' accounts on individuals and groups living on the Isle of Dogs. How far did the locals ignore, internalise, rework or exploit these more or less officially authorised stories as part of a strategy which variously aimed to defend or deny the area's public reputation, or put it and themselves back on the political map?

The more we pondered this question, the more evident it became that we were not simply dealing with an immediate issue of media saturation and moral panic, but with a much wider and longer running issue concerning the East End and the politics of its representation within dominant discourses of class, nation and white ethnicity. And it is to this we must now turn.

Myths of Explanation

For almost two centuries conditions in the East End have been an obsessive concern of outside commentators: social reformers, missionaries, philanthropists, novelists, journalists and social scientists of every kind. No area in Britain has been more written about, more exploited as a source and site for the projection of public anxieties about proletarian combination or sexual promiscuity, the state of the nation or the degeneration of the race.

In many cases the pictures of disease, depravity and disorder which were drawn with such lurid detail were the preamble and rationale for local schemes of moral education and social reform based upon no less imaginary communities of civic well-being, national health, or racial integrity. Whether it took the form of designing model dwellings, providing rational recreation, reforming the sweating system, or relieving poverty, the project of improving conditions of life and labour in the East End was intimately tied to the regulation of local family and community relations. Moral panics focusing on the spectacle of gangs of unemployed youths terrorising the neighbourhood, girls selling themselves on street corners, men brutalising or abandoning their wives and children through gambling or drink, ensured that whatever actual relief of distress was achieved by these means, remained secondary to the reduction of alarm amongst the middle classes.

Although similar images were applied to other working-class areas, and other parts of the country, they were articulated with particular vehemence in the East End of London. For here, in the heart of the metropolis, within a stone's throw of the City, and within walking distance of Parliament and the West End, was a dense concentration of dangerous difference, where poverty wore a foreign face, and where people from far flung corners of the empire might strike back.

In the last ten years these discourses and the interventions inspired by them, have been the object of an increasingly sophisticated re-reading, inspired by Marxist, post-structuralist and feminist critiques.[4] The slum novel, urban ethnography, and the popular press have all been grist to the mill of these various 'deconstructions'; these texts have provided rich pickings for inquirers into the 'other scenes' of knowledge and power which traverse representations of class, gender and race in the Victorian city.

In some recent accounts there has been a tendency to regard these outsider stories as pure hallucinations. The 'east end' of Besant and Gissing, Jack London and W.T. Snead, not to mention De Quincey and Oscar Wilde, is understood as a pure figment of the bourgeois imagination, a product of bad faith; even the investigations of Mayhew and Booth, it is argued, remain captive to the spell of ideological constructs which have no real bearing and little real impact on the actual inhabitants who live there.

Allon White and Peter Stallybrass, for example, in their book *The Politics and Poetics of Transgression* argue that when the top people in late Victorian society sought to get to the bottom of East End lives they discovered their own anal erotic phantasies which were unconsciously repressed as a condition for assuming a superior civilised posture. Hence the voyeuristic obsession with insanitary conditions, and the imagery of sewers, pollution, germs and dirt which were used to characterise the moral status of these 'lower orders' and to condemn their habitats as the breeding grounds of vice.

Certainly De Quincey's descriptions of East End street markets transform them into oriental bazaars where he sees the 'swarming masses of Asia' in the 'myriad of faces in the urban crowd.' They seem to owe more to opium-induced paranoia whipping up aristocratic terror of the working class than to actual observation.[5] But I think that to read the later Victorian literature in this way is to be carried away by its own, rather calculating, rhetoric. It would perhaps be more precise to say that the urban explorers were horrified to discover the open drains and middens, the slum tenements with no water, heating or light, the physical evidence of lives so different from their own, and the very evident signs of distress which accompanied these conditions. But this phenomenology of poverty also excited their sociological imagination about its causes and consequences in a way which provided, in some cases, a space of representation for more florid phantasies about the state of the body politic.

The hallucination model has the unacknowledged pay-off that it leaves the lives of real East Enders intact, if invisible. East End cultures remain unpolluted by the perverse imaginations of the civilising missionaries, as resistant to the oppressive disciplines of capital as they are to the corrupting delights of cosmopolitan modernity. The 'inside story' continues to rule OK as an index of a purely proletarian authenticity.

It follows that if there are 'impurities' (if, for example, there is a pronounced local history of racism), then they have to be explained by factors which are purely intrinsic to the East End itself; we must be dealing with a natural home-grown peculiarity of this particular section of the English working class.

This is the view advanced by Charles Husbands in his seminal study of East End racism.[6] His work takes in a broad sweep of local racisms: from the popular antisemitism which helped pioneer the Aliens Act of 1905 (Britain's first official immigration controls), through the Mosleyite agitations of the interwar years, to the dockers' support for Powell's 'Rivers of Blood' speech in 1968, and the mounting harassment of the Bangladeshi community during the 1980s. Husbands argues that underlying and linking all these instances is a common, and generationally transmitted culture of racism, which stems from the persistence of an ethnically homogeneous and inbred working-class community, centred originally in Hoxton and Bethnal Green and subsequently diffused to other areas through white flight. He describes this community as exhibiting:

> A profoundly materialistic culture, which implies a very limited and confused perception of social structure, and a corresponding readiness to apportion blame in inappropriate directions. Its political sophistication has been similarly limited; it was long resistant to sustained mobilisation by the left, and even in its more recent voting has had a narrowly pragmatic and poorly articulated ideological basis. A continual readiness to engage in rightwing racial exclusionism suggests the persistence of a 'rootless volatility' which was also a feature of working-class politics in the nineteenth century.

This characterisation seems to amalgamate Mayhew's model of 'wandering tribes' with a quasi-Marxist view of the 'lumpenproletariat' and its false consciousness. East End racism is put down to the persistence of an archaic, premodern and irrational streak in its inhabitants, consequent upon their 'inbreeding'.

There is, however, an alternative reading which completely reverses the terms of Husbands's argument. Far from failing, it is suggested that the civilising mission was all too successful. From the 1880s onwards the mass of East Enders were transformed, slowly and unevenly, from dangerous revolutionaries or denizens of the underworld, into cheerful patriotic Cockneys. This was achieved through the combined and cumulative influence of the labour movement, the church, state education, better housing and sanitation, and strategies of self-improvement provided by settlements, clubs and missions. Even the music hall played its part. The emergence of a conservative, inward looking, but above all respectable culture of labourism in the East End is held to epitomise a wider process in the remaking of the English working class in and through the late Victorian culture of imperialism.[7]

Race is again a key motif in this story, but now it is seen as something injected into the proletarian body politic from outside, as part of its transition to modernity. The emergence of local support for Little Englander nationalism, or white supremacism, in the post-1945 period is put down to the fact that East Enders have internalised the aspirations and values prescribed by the civilising missionaries, whilst being systematically deprived of the means to achieve them. According to this line of argument, these once-upon-a-time immigrants have learnt only too well how to defend themselves against the discrepancy between the official success story, and the actual outcome of their lives, by drawing a line under their own feet and constructing a racialised ethnicity which both excludes Asians and blacks and blames them for a general failure of white working-class expectations.

Simplified versions of both the intrinsic and extrinsic explanations of East End racism were much in evidence in press coverage of the events leading up to the election of Derek Beackon in Millwall. One storyline adopted by the *Sun*, the *Daily Mirror* and *The Guardian*, if for rather different reasons, pursued the theme of a decent and law abiding community driven into the arms of the BNP out of desperation caused by high unemployment consequent on the closure of the docks, and the failure of the LDDC, the local council or the Tory government to fulfil their promises to regenerate the local economy. The subtext in much of this concerned the political betrayal of an otherwise loyalist working class, a betrayal which had turned it from being the backbone of the nation into a dangerous underclass or race apart.

This theme was taken up from the opposite direction in intrinsic explanations offered by the *Independent*, the *Daily Telegraph*, and the rest of the Tory press. These stressed the peculiar nature of the area, its physical and social isolation from the rest of the East End and, by extension, from the rest of 'mainland' Britain. Local support for the BNP, and racial attacks on Bangladeshis were then conveniently just one more symptom of this exceptionalism. The *Telegraph* asked, 'What is it that makes this area so distinctive, so potent in the imagination, and to outsiders so frightening?' And answered that it was the fact that it had developed a ingrown culture cut off from the modern world. In other words the inhabitants of the Isle of Dogs, whatever their ethnic origins, were always and already a race apart.

It is interesting that a paper known for its anti-European stance, and the Little Englander chauvinism of its readers, should in this instance emphasise the pathological nature of insularity. Even without this ideological baggage, the *Independent* took a similar line, characterising the area as:

> subdued and mistrustful, simmering with hostility, its resentments easily exploited by the far right. Says Andrew Davies, who conducts walks round the East End, 'The Isle of Dogs is different, more introspective and empty. There is much less street life than anywhere else in the East End, and Canary Wharf has cut it off more than ever'.

This image of the East End as a drab, soulless, monoculture has a long historical provenance; perhaps its most famous exponent was Jack London who wrote in *People of the Abyss*:

> No more dreary spectacle can be found on this earth than the whole of the 'awful east' with its Whitechapel, Hoxton, Spitalfields, Bethnal Green and Wapping to the East India Docks. The colour of life is grey and drab. Everything is helpless, hopeless, unrelieved and dirty. Here lives a population as dull and unimaginative as its long grey miles of dingy brick.

In contemporary reporting by the liberal press this imagery was drawn upon to contrast the Isle of Dogs invidiously with Whitechapel, now portrayed as an ideal multicultural society; as in this account from the *Independent*:

> Brick Lane perhaps offers one model of what the East End might become. One of the all-night bagel shops has a poster for a Gujerati dance company; the other has a poster asking for information about Quaddus Ali's stabbing. Through these shops move Bengali artists (the East End, and this part in particular, is home to the largest group of artists outside New York), whites, blacks, City executives and tourists, mingling happily over their smoked salmon and cream cheese rolls. But Brick Lane is different from the rest of the East End, and fashionable in its exoticism.

This trendy hybridity – the postmodern equivalent of the bohemian cosmopolitanism of the cultural avant-garde – is thus set up as constituting an essentially anti-racist environment. *The Guardian* extolled its virtues in the following terms:

> Today Brick Lane exudes the confidence of a community that no longer cowers in the face of hostility. Its marriage of Asian and English customs is unabashed and potent. Smells of coriander, cardamom and incense merge with that of Beackon's steak and chips. On one corner stands a Fried Chicken Store marked Al-Halal. Brick Lane is as much of an oasis as the Isle of Dogs, with its own mores and loyalties. Yet, unlike the island, its doors are not closed to outsiders. It has become a popular residence for successful artists like Gilbert and George, whose presence in Fournier Street, an adjoining terrace of ramshackle Georgian properties, has earned it the title of London's new Millionaires' Row. The tranquillity is punctured normally only by BNP supporters who sell white supremacist literature on Brick Lane every weekend.

Racism is identified entirely with the activities of the BNP, and thus can be seen as an alien outside force rather than as part of the local landscape, which would endanger the myth of multiculturalism. This manoeuvre involves normalising the presence of the BNP itself, in a way which would not be much appreciated by the local Bangladeshi youth who are the 'normal' objects of their attacks.

Mimicry and Masquerade

It may be the case that given the massive burden of representation which the East End, and by proxy East Enders, have had to carry, it is not possible for young people especially to ignore or turn their backs on it anymore. These images and narratives have to be taken up in various ways, manipulated and invested with other meanings, exploited so that political or cultural capital can be made out of them.

East End youth cultures have been particularly good at this game.[8] From the masher and swell of the 1890s to the mod and crombie of the 1960s, impersonations of upper or middle-class styles of dress and deportment, have been a strong card to play. Unlike the ritual transvestism of the early urban explorers, who dressed up in carefully disinfected second-hand clothes bought from the street market in order to pass as one of the labouring poor, these youth styles contained elements of irony and parody aimed at the very cultures they sought to emulate. The masher's scarf was part of coster rig, not the rich young man about town. The cut of the crombie coat, combined with jeans, caricatured the well-dressed city gent. Such features signal the presence of mimicry and disturb the social simulation game, even as they convey the message, 'this is play'.

There are other strategies for turning the official story inside out; the very features which are picked on by outside middle-class observers as characterising the essential Cockney or authentic East End can be exaggerated in ways which simultaneously make nonsense of the stereotype and confirm it. The original boot boys were Victorian shoeshine boys, orphans and destitutes picked off the street by child rescue missions such as Dr Barnardo's in Stepney and organised into brigades to go out and mend or polish the boots of the bourgeoisie in Regent Street or Pall Mall. There was no more effective image of child rescue for fundraising purposes than the spectacle of the erstwhile waif and stray transformed into honest service, and happy with his lot.

We may suspect that even the original bootboys had a somewhat different inside story of their lives as they spat on these well-to-do shoes and rubbed them up to a shine, a story perhaps closer to what is in the back of the minds of latter-day bootboys and skinheads who wear their Doc Martens as a symbol of physical hardness historically associated with costers and dockers. For this now almost defunct culture of manual labour and its increasingly dysfunctional version of masculinity is precisely what has so fascinated generations of middle-class observers of the East End, a male physicality at once envied, feared and despised, especially by those who secretly or openly wished to participate in a bit of male bonding with the rough trade as part of their moral reclamation of the working class.

Another model of narrative transformation is to be found in certain postwar romanticisations of the old East End in various films and TV series, and in the autobiographies of professional East Enders like Dan Farson, Ralf Finn, Dolly Scannell and a host of others. The picture of the slums as redeemed by warm, close-knit family and neighbourhood life; the cosy Cockney village, with its friendly pubs and markets spiced with a bit of safe ethnicity, and naughty but nice sex; communities united against adversity, but not usually against class adversaries; the heroic stories of self-help, self-sacrifice and self-improvement, all this seems not only to have touched a chord of nostalgia amongst the yuppies, but amongst working-class people as well. The defence of traditional East End values of solidarity and tolerance is as common a refrain in left wing propaganda, as is mourning for their passing in the life stories of the older generation who grew up in the area between the wars.

It is difficult to know whether we are dealing here with simply invented traditions; sentimental idealisations which owe their origin and power to the workings of political rhetoric and collective false memory. Or whether this sense of imagined community draws on real historical material, structures of life and labour which have been dismantled by the malign confluence of post-Fordism and Thatcherism, but which are being remembered selectively to dramatise feelings of loss.

Even if we shelve the issue of whether these accounts of a 'world we have lost' do correspond in some way to 'the way it really was,' we are still left with the question of their symbolic function in the present. Do these stories offer the new generation of East Enders a more engaging image of the area than the narratives of drabness and dereliction, exotic multiculturalism, or gothic horror which are otherwise on offer? Or is the evocation of a lost community spirit really a coded statement for a racism which refuses to recognise the black and Asian presence as an integral part of it, and blames this presence for its demise? In the most general terms does the attempt to construct a 'real' East End from below, through some kind of 'authentic' inside story, really break with the dominant representations? Or does it rather function as a manic defence against the anxiety of outside influence, and necessarily produce a racially exclusive definition of who belongs, in a way which mimics the larger narratives of nation in which the East End story has traditionally been told?

Localising Identity

In order to begin to address some of these questions empirically, we asked our sample of informants to talk to us about their sense of 'where they were coming from' in their dealings with everyday life on the Isle of Dogs. We were interested in the relationship between their real face-to-face community, the people and places they visited or avoided, and the stories they told, listened to or read and through which they imagined their social participation and entitlement in terms of locality, ethnicity, nationality and various kinds of transnational identity.

Quite early on in the interview we asked them whether they identified with being an East Ender, or an Islander, or some other descriptor, and what they associated with these terms. The sample were virtually unanimous in associating the term Islander exclusively with white people living on the Isle of Dogs. The older generation of whites were proud to call themselves Islanders; they associated it with long-term residence in the area and keeping up traditional values. They also thought that Islanders were the true East Enders, a term which for most of them was also synonymous with Cockney. This was an equation which the under 25s tended to reject, though most of them still strongly identified with being Islanders. In the white sample as a whole there was considerable agreement across the generations that East Ender was a much less easily definable term and that it had mixed connotations; it transpired that in many cases this was because people thought the East End had been taken over by newer, non-white immigrants, and had therefore become a mixed race or hybrid category. In some cases this caused the respondent to reject the term altogether, or to prefer Islander as a metonym which carried the same meaning.

Not surprisingly none of the Bangladeshis interviewed identified with being Islanders; for most it held negative connotations, of being not only white, but racist. Length of residence in the area was not seen by them as an enabling criterion. Some of the younger Bengalis felt more positive about 'East Ender' which for them was a wider, more racially inclusive, term. Two were quite insistent that they were Cockneys – a term which they associated with being smart and streetwise. For young Bangladeshis who claimed these terms (and there were still a significant number who did not), East Ender and Cockney were quite compatible with being black, Asian, Bengali, Muslim, British, Sylheti, or any combination of these terms. There was considerable variation in which of these descriptions were felt to be most self-defining. There were some quite marked generational differences, with the under twenty-fives, who had been born and/or grown up in the area, being more likely to twin a local (i.e. East Ender) identity with a global one (i.e. Muslim), whereas their parents were less likely to use local descriptors and to prefer British and Asian as general terms of self-reference. Black was not a popular category amongst the Bengali sample of any age, nor was it used by the whites to refer to them.

The type and extent of informants' actual social networks and their patterns of geographical mobility were not strongly correlated with these identifications. For example, those who preferred islander to East Ender were not noticeably more tied to the immediate area; they travelled to other parts of the East End and further abroad just as much or as little as those of the same age, gender and status who saw themselves firstly as East Enders. It was a question of cultural geography, not physical, imagined, not real community.

This point is underlined by a major difference in the way the white sample talked about the Isle of Dogs. There were those who were primarily concerned to construct what they saw as an insider's account of what had happened to the area, and for whom Islander or East Ender meant not just a social description of a certain kind of people or place, but a deeply felt source of autobiographical anchorage and personal identity. As might be expected this orientation was most frequently found amongst the older, grandparent and parent generation, who had grown up in the area or lived most of their lives there. There were, however, a significant number of young people and newcomers who adopted a similar stance. They were often defensive about the area's public reputation, but dismissed such reports, especially those emanating from the national press or TV as being ill-informed and prejudiced.

The second orientation was much more concerned with how outsiders saw the area, and the kinds of stories generated by outside sources which might give a wrong or bad impression to people who did not know it. From this perspective East Ender or Islander were positional rather than personal terms of identification – they placed people in a wider social structure, and ascribed certain moral characteristics to them. For most of this group the terms also projected a largely negative image to the outside world, for example as being a yuppie area, or a hotbed of racial violence, or being full of yobs. A few dissociated themselves from the Islander/East Ender labels altogether for that reason. Others still held to these localisations, but dealt with possible cognitive dissonance by adopting a strategy of narrative impression management – telling stories to us which would show up the area in a true/good light and hence convince us as outsiders that most of the media reports were exaggerated and untrue. For example, they would tell us anecdotes designed to reassure us that there was little or no racist feeling amongst whites, citing examples of their own good neighbourliness, whilst at the same time portraying the Bangladeshis as ungrateful or unresponsive to these overtures, keeping themselves to themselves, and gaining unfair advantage in housing.

On the whole, young people (under twenty-five) were more highly sensitised to the area's public image and reputation than their elders. They were correspondingly more likely to take these 'outside-in' stories directly into account in constructing their own versions. But there was one significant exception. Those with the most pronounced and unambiguous racist views were invariably committed to the insider view and dismissed media, and indeed all other accounts as examples of wilful prejudice on the part of ignorant outsiders.

The Bangladeshi sample had a quite different set of orientations. Their accounts varied chiefly in the extent to which they explained the racism they or their children suffered in terms of the peculiarities of the Isle of Dogs or the East End, or whether they saw it as a local instance of a wider phenomenon affecting the whole of British society. On the whole the older generation took a more particularistic view, and felt that in other areas of London, or the country as a whole, things were not nearly so bad for Asian people. Their children tended to see racism as something more structural or inherent, although many also thought there were important exceptions to this permeation rule.

The most obvious case where the particularisms of place took on a wider media-generated resonance, in a way which was hard for 'locals' to ignore is, of course, TV's *East Enders*. Here is the ultimate outside-in story whose authenticity relies on its claim to portray vernacular cultures which in all their diversity remain 'home grown'. A large number (60per cent) of the older Bangladeshis watched the programme on a regular basis, a much higher percentage than the whites. One interesting reason for this which was put to us by one of our informants was that it showed that East End people could get along together, and that they weren't all racists or hooligans. If only the real East End were as good as it was shown on TV! In other words, it was the perceived utopianism of its multiracial *mise-en-scène* which appealed.

Their children took the opposite view. They were much more critical of what they saw as its patronising, tokenistic or stereotypical portrayal of ethnic minorities. They also thought that the programme ignored or downplayed the extent of racial tension, and unlike their parents were critical of its lack of realism on this score. Their white counterparts also criticised the programme, but on grounds of class stereotyping rather than race. 'It shows us all up as being thick, spending all our time in the pub, having rows, and working in street markets' was the gist of one frequent complaint.

In characterising these various strategies of narrativisation, we found it useful to draw on the distinction made by the American sociologist David Riesman, in the 1960s, between inner and other directed judgements.[9] In the first case, value judgements are asserted on the basis of a strong sense of personal morality validated by custom and community; in the second case, expressions of attitude and opinion are manipulated to create a desirable impression in the eyes of significant others. In the jargon of the era, Riesman was talking about a shift in 'general value orientations' from inner to other directed 'personality types' and seems to have had in mind the decline of rugged individualism as an American cultural ideal, exemplified by John Wayne, and its replacement by the opportunistic narcissism of Andy Warhol. But for our purposes, the distinction has less to do with normative values than with different strategies of authorisation at work in constructing narrative identity. In particular the concepts helped us make a distinction between two articulations of racist discourse. The first (inner-directed) is based on asserting a privileged moral entitlement to represent custom and community 'from the inside'; all other statements on race are automatically invalidated as those of 'outsiders', and ethnic minorities who try to become 'insiders' are marked down for 'special treatment'. The second (other-directed) approach is organised around denying attributions of racism made by influential 'outsiders' through various kinds of narrative impression management whilst at the same time constructing accounts which portray ethnic minorities as failing or refusing to conform to 'insider' norms.

The discourses of aversive and assimilative racism thus have distinctive storylines and styles or strategies of authorisation. The distinction is, of course, an ideal typical one. In the actual repertoire of stories which people told or cited, it was a question of relative emphasis not total 'value orientation'. But it helped us to recognise certain patterns of negotiated meaning around local identity which were useful when we came to probe our informants' sense of home in greater depth.

Island Racism and Fictive Kinship

We decided, in a second phase of the research, to look at how narratives were organised in the case of one particular group. We interviewed a small sample of white residents who supported a local campaign to promote the rights of the indigenous Islander over and against the claims of the Bangladeshi community. This campaign was entirely composed and led by self-identified Islanders. It initially rejected overtures from the BNP, and was never affiliated to any political party, though it did for a time have the tacit support of a local Liberal Democrat councillor. In what follows we have concentrated on the views of the older, parent and grandparent generations, rather than the voice of youth.

A refrain running through all these accounts is the decline in traditional or 'old' East End values which are associated with certain moral qualities of community. This old East End was always contrasted favourably with the new. Here is one very typical comment:

> It used to be a nice place. I mean it wasn't very well known, but it was a warm and friendly place, where people looked out for each other and stuck together through thick and thin. If you said you came from the Isle of Dogs they wanted to know where it was. Other people thought it was a terrible, rough sort of place, but now it's regarded as one of the best places, everyone knows about it because of Canary Wharf, and you get all these notices – 'Welcome to the Isle of Dogs!' But I don't like it. We've had enough. Our houses have all been made dirty with the lorries coming by and all the building work. And people have kind of shrunk into their shells.

The comment is interesting in the way in combines inner- and other-directed narrative. Public ignorance or bad impressions of the area, containing perhaps an echo of the 'drab wasteland' theme, is contrasted with its rich inner life available only to those who live there. There is a double inversion at work here – a working-class area which used to be regarded as rubbish by outsiders, but which was prized by those who lived there, is now seen to have been transformed into a 'high class' area for yuppies, but ruined for 'the real insider'.

In the process, the more negative aspects of the 'old East End' are glossed over as in this comment, which contrasts the 'good old days' of the Krays, with the present state of local crime:

> We've always had villains on the island, but the attitude was, 'don't shit on your own doorstep.' So it was safe to leave your door open or the window open. But as the years have gone by the old Island people have moved off and it's got worse and they've put in the new housing, especially where the yuppies are. People think if you live on the Island you must be well off and have something to take. So you don't feel safe going out as you used to. In the old days down our way if you saw someone who wasn't supposed to be there you'd ask them what they was doing. But now there's so many strangers in the area, people coming from outside, you don't know who they are.

So even the villains observed local protocols of public propriety, and indeed policed them. The general point being argued here is the Durkheimian one, that internal moral regulation exercised informally through social networks has given way to a state of anomie caused by rapid social change.[10] The idea that what planners see as urban regeneration has in fact resulted in moral degeneration is a common refrain in many of the Islanders' interviews.

The old East End is invested with an exclusive aura of cultural authenticity which by definition newer habitats – and newer inhabitants – cannot possess. To some the very notion of 'Docklands' was a newfangled and suspect bit of urban imagineering. As an Islander community leader put it:

> Docklands is an industrial term, and increasingly it's an advertising term, used as a marketing device by the LDDC. There is no such place as Docklands. I mean people identify Docklands as being where they are. Beckton is not Docklands you know, 'cos Beckton is a very different sort of place from the island. The term just doesn't recognise that Wapping, the Isle of Dogs, Surrey Docks, Shadwell, these are all distinct areas with their own histories and identities.

Docklands as a generic signifier of the new East End is seen as erasing the older, territorial and matrilocal cultures, and their prides of place. These accounts continually evoked the power of collective memory to landscape the area with personal meanings. It was this sense of immanent belonging which allowed these storytellers to symbolically own the island and construct it as the locus of a fixed, almost biological sense of identity:

> I'm an Islander and proud of it. It's in your blood. We were born here, we've grown up together, we all help each other, and we stick together. I mean you go to some places and no one wants to talk to you, but if you're an Islander you know you're an Islander.

In this example the sense of historical generation, rooted in local custom and circumstance becomes like a blood tie and furnishes what might be called a genealogy of place – the sense that one's social destiny is almost congenitally linked to one's place of birth and early life. This sense of identity could be extended to the East End as a whole:

> I think that Islanders have a sense of identity, a bit like being working-class – you identify with a particular group and a particular place – it's seen as a negative term by other people, but not by us. And

> with East Ender again there is a certain affinity, I can't quite define it but it's there. It has something to do with the shared experience of being brought up during the Blitz and living through all the changes in the East End.

In many cases this kind of genealogy supported a nostalgic myth of origin to the effect that once upon a time, in some golden age, Islanders and/or East Enders were one big family, where everyone was on good terms with their neighbours and lived happily ever afterwards. But this myth is only mobilised in order to be counterposed with another in which this cockney village idyll is shattered by the invasion of the Others who are variously referred to as 'the immigrants', 'the ethnics', or 'the coloureds'. Here is a typical statement in this genre:

> Our street is very friendly, and they're good neighbours, and they'll always help you out, but a lot of the atmosphere has gone, a lot of it is dog eat dog which doesn't make for friendly relationships. They're moving a lot of immigrants into the island, which, though I've got nothing against them, they're moving so many it's causing problems.

In these and many similar accounts, we are presented with an image of an 'island paradise', a state of perfect self-contained social harmony which has been suddenly, almost overnight, invaded and destroyed by aliens. This island exists in people's minds as occupying a homogeneous time and space: it is a place where the population is supposed to have reproduced itself identically from generation to generation, through a process of local endogamy, and where its cultures of kinship and community have somehow survived despite the closure of the docks, and remained immune, or at least highly resistant, to wider changes in society.

> Our family have been living around here since well before the war. We've seen a lot of changes, not all of them for the better, but we survived them. We've had our ups and downs like any family ... the docks going but we've pulled through. What has always kept us going is the desire to get the best for our kids, and to make sure as far as we can that this is a good area for them to grow up in.

The family is central to this version of local history and geography – it binds the transmission of values and the patrimonies of place into a fixed sense of home. An ex-docker remembers:

> Those members of my family who have moved away, still come back as often as they can to re-establish their roots. Home is where the heart is and my heart is here on the island. If I could imagine myself at home

> anywhere, I'd be sitting in an easy chair, writing or reading, doing some paperwork and I'd be gazing out over the river. I wouldn't live anywhere else, I'm happy here. This is where my home is. This is where all my activities are and I'll fight my corner here.

Insofar as family provided a model and a metaphor for all other kinds of social relationships, it could be deployed to naturalise practices of exclusion which might otherwise look like all-too-familiar examples of racial discrimination:

> Every family has its black sheep, the odd ones out, who don't really belong; you don't get on with them so well, so you try to avoid them, or keep them at arm's length. Well it's like that with some of the ethnics – we don't tend to mix with them.

This notion of kinship, and of everyone sticking up for their own kind allowed Islanders both to celebrate their own insularities and ignore their effect in freezing out 'the ethnics'. How is this for a version of the open society:

> In the old days before the ethnics came this used to be a really friendly place. People used to leave their doors open, anyone was welcome to drop in for a cup of tea and a chat, you wouldn't think twice about it. But since they came, with all the problems of vandalism, mugging, and all that they brought, people are afraid to go out and you certainly wouldn't leave your door open nowadays. It's a great shame.

This 'open doors' policy only applied to those who were regarded as indigenous, not to 'immigrants'. 'Open doors' in this context is always a misnomer since it is based on a strategy of social closure within restricted networks of family and friends. In its racialised form, as here, it becomes a device for blaming the 'ethnics' for the very exclusions which they suffer. More than that, they are accused of turning the Islanders' 'natural open mindedness' into fearful prejudice.

All White on the Night

The fact that the island was invented as a haven of 'old East End values' meant that any local change was seen as a sudden and catastrophic advent of the new:

> What really saddens me is the breakdown in warmth, in the old social structure. The slums have gone and good riddance to them, but so has the positive sense of solidarity. In its place you've got racism. I don't go to Bow very much now, because the area is so changed. I'm a stranger in my own land in that sense.

The idea that 'immigrants' are making the 'indigenous' strangers or second-class citizens in their own land was another common refrain. At the same time, there is a continual search for some little bit of the Island which has somehow remained pure and uncontaminated by the undesirable changes associated with the Bangladeshi presence. Mostly this phantasy is centred on Cubitt Town:

> I know the area and I've always lived round here. I used to know everybody on the island when I was on a milk round during the war, but it's altered tremendously. This part of the island around Cubitt Town is the only part that's not really altered.

Historically, Cubitt Town was where the stevedores, the higher paid skilled dockworkers and their families lived, most of them Irish Catholics. Millwall, by contrast, was more industrialised, more 'Protestant' and regarded as an altogether rougher area.[11]

> The two sides of the island were quite different and where anyone talked about Cubitt Town to people living in Millwall, it was as remote as talking about people who lived in Hackney. The Cubitt Town people looked upon the people of Millwall as belonging to another world.

That distinction has been carried over and reworked so that Cubitt Town is now regarded as the core of the Islanders' community. The distinction, however, is no longer one of religion or relative socio-economic status but of race. Cubitt Town is seen as a white area – an area which is safe for whites.

We asked our informants to mark the areas which they felt were safe or dangerous and to explain why. Cubitt Town was invariably marked safe by this group:

> It's safe because you've got the police station nearby, the Docklands Settlement which is always open, you've got George Green school which has always got a caretaker that you can get to if you're in trouble – they'll always let you pop in and use the loo or whatever. It's a very well-lit area, you've got the takeaway shops which are always open. The area is used mainly by whites and yuppies. My aunt lives there too.

On many of the personal maps drawn by the sample, the association between space and race is very close. In one interview, one of our informants let this slip; when she was asked about how she felt about her immediate neighbourhood she replied, 'it's all white, I mean, its all right down our way'.

But why is the safety of Cubbitt Town described in terms of a series of bolt holes? It seems that even 'down our way' has its hidden dangers because this 'white space' is invariably seen as being increasingly threatened internally by invasion from the 'ethnics':

> I always used to feel safe round here [Cubitt Town] but not any longer. There's a lot of racial nastiness about. I don't feel easy with my children walking down the street. Last year my youngest daughter [seventeen] was walking down the street by George Green and a lot of Asians spat at her. I mean luckily one of the boys in the group, she had this Asian boyfriend for a time, he was there so she was safe. But it does make you wonder.

It did not apparently make her wonder that maybe her daughter walking down the street with an Asian boy might be seen as a threat or a challenge to the authority of the Asian elders. But the narrative does allow her to portray her family as being entirely free of racism, whilst all the prejudice is on the side of the Asians.

The sense of creeping invasion is present is most of the accounts:

> For as long as I can remember there have been certain places on the island where the Bangladeshis predominate. As I've got older the amount of them seems to have grown. Perhaps it's just that I've become more aware of it. I mean when I went to Cubitt Town School, there was just a couple of Asian people and black people, but now when I walk down there, there's big clusters of Asians.

The construction of Cubitt Town as the core of the Isle of Dogs which is itself imagined to contain the essence of the old East End, has become central to the racialisation of space in this area. This was not just about the demarcation of territory; it served to articulate a particular autobiographical claim on the part of these self-styled Islanders to represent an authentically indigenous population. What distinguished this group from other residents, both white and Asian, was the sense that 'being born and bred' on the Island gave them special rights and privileges in relation to education, housing, and local amenities, which others groups did not have:

> There's a saying first come first served, and when it comes to housing, jobs, schools its only fair that people who have been here a long time, sometimes for generations, should have their fair share of things, especially so that their sons and daughters can go on living in the area.

Here the role of the family, and in particular the principle of matrilocal residence, is yoked to a myth of indigenous origins in order to naturalise a racist 'rights for whites' position. The Council's own 'sons and daughters' housing policy was often taken by islanders as vindicating their claims.[12]

Reasons to Be Racist

Almost all the Islanders rejected the suggestion that their feelings of antagonism towards the Bangladeshi community were racially motivated, or that they held racist beliefs. Their rationalisations took a number of different forms. The first was the classical ploy of dissociating oneself from any personal implication in these views by attributing them to others, and then providing a justification as to why other people might feel or think like that:

> It's understandable, people see the Bangladeshis coming in and getting all the housing, you've got to expect some people who've been living here all their lives and have got a son or daughter on the housing list to feel a bit narked. It doesn't make for friendly relations.

Then there was the equivalence argument, applied here to suggest that racism is normative, and the result of peer pressure:

> If you're white you seem to have to hate Asian people and blacks, and if you're Asian, black or Chinese you seem to have to dislike white people. The pre-eminent white feeling is that the Asians get the best everything – housing, grants, clubs, and the ethnics no doubt feel the same way about us.

Sometimes the media are blamed for stirring up racial hatred:

> To be fair I don't visit many parts of the island. I go by what people tell me. You pick up the local papers and it's the Asians getting this, that, and the other. We see pictures of George Green and it's 'spot the white face' and it gets a lot of the older people annoyed. I mean they're living on the breadline with their pension and they see the council giving all this money to Bangladeshi clubs and outings and housing.

In many cases people cited stories about things that had supposedly happened to friends, or neighbours, as a justification for their own attitudes or perceptions. The role of rumour and gossip in constructing racist mythologies was sometimes recognised:

> People nowadays are frightened of being frightened – they scare themselves with all these rumours and stories about what goes on in this place or that place. It's almost a self-fulfilling prophecy.

The amplifying power of rumour lent credence to a general sense of being overwhelmed by events beyond their control:

> You hear stories about people being mugged, about gangs coming down from Brick Lane, and nobody seems to care or do anything to stop it. Nobody tells us what's going on, and even the police don't seem that bothered.

One of the most common lines conveys the sense of a community whose initial tolerance gave way to prejudice under the pressure of numbers:

> We had quite a few Asians in our flats and they mixed in well with the white kids, brown kids, black kids and yellow kids. But in the last few years since they've moved in more it's got worse, since you've got a big mass of them.

The shift from assimilation to aversion (i.e. between two modes of racism) is thus indexed to the numbers game, and to the white rights refrain of 'enough is enough'.

An alternative explanation was sometimes based on the intrinsic and inner-directed model stressing the peculiar history and material circumstances of the East End. A local community activist argued:

> There is a strong prevailing racist element. There has always been a basic underlying racism in the East End. The Irish went through it, and the Jews went through it, and now the Bangladeshis, it's everyone in their turn. It's because the East End was treated as the arsehole of Europe, and then it was treated as the arsehole of London. When you get that kind of situation people struggle to get out, to climb over each other's backs and some people get trodden on.

In this account, racism in the East End is always the same old story, as homogeneous in its way as the community itself is imagined to be. The dumping ground thesis is used to provide a rationale for this tradition.

At the same time the experience of racial harassment and discrimination is made almost a rite of passage into full membership of the community.

However, some of the Islanders made it very clear where the line was being drawn under their own feet:

> Everyone here is an immigrant, there are no true-blooded Englishmen, there were Huguenots, Irish, Jews. But they became English first. But the Bangladeshis don't try and fit in. They put Bangladeshi not English down as their nationality. Now they are in the West, they should try and behave like westerners, not easterners. But the trouble is their culture is so different, its just not European.

The Culture of Complaint

As we've seen, the Islanders' sense of imagined community included a view of themselves as constituting an autonomous self-regulating civil society, defining and defending its own territory, and policing its own protocols of public propriety. This went hand in glove with a conspiracy theory of the role of the local state as interfering busybodies, especially in the sphere of local 'race relations':

> The social services and the local council and the school have got to be seen to be doing the right things and all the do-gooders say that if you're coloured you can't do a thing wrong. They're trying to close down a lot of the old places, the places we used to go, and giving the money to Bangladeshis for clubs and that which is just for them.

Many islanders felt betrayed by the local Labour Party, which they thought had also been taken over by middle-class do-gooders, who treated them like pariahs:

> They just look down at you as if you don't know anything, even though you lived in the area all your life. And they treat you like dirt, as if you've got some kind of disease they might catch. What do they know about it? They just read a load of books about racism, working-class this, working-class that. But they don't have to live with them. When they knock off work they go off to their nice little flats in Hampstead.

The sense that many Islanders had of being the backbone of the nation (as well as of the East End) but of being treated as a race apart by the powers that be, comes across strongly in this statement:

> The people here, they've been through the lot. They're honest, they're hard working, they're the salt of the earth. They've struggled, and what have they got to show for it? Nothing. They're treated by the LDDC and the council like they were scum. As if they were just an unsightly nuisance, which should be swept away so the yuppies don't have to see how the other half live.

Here we can see how an inner-directed narrative connects up with the 'liberal' media interpretation of events. In both cases a picture is drawn of a beleaguered community betrayed by the authorities. The way in which the themes of besiegement and betrayal could be articulated into a version of Custer's (or Cockney's) last stand against the Indians (or Bangladeshis) illustrated in the following:

> It's gone too far. Enough is enough. There is no more room for them. We are being driven under. We are becoming extinct. At this rate we'll all end up on Canvey Island. Our hands are tied. We want the rights of the locals put first. But they ignore us. They call us racists when we protest about being discriminated against. But us Cockneys have become an ethnic minority in our own country…

This ethno-demographic inversion is central to 'white rights' rhetoric, and was often linked to imagery of an island race being overwhelmed by a tidal wave of immigration. Given its ideological provenance this imagery makes the connection between the local and the global space of population flows all too easily: 'It's a flood, and if it's a flood there is only one way to stop it and that's to turn off the main.'[13] The homely image of do-it-yourself plumbing is a characteristic device of popular racism: it shows us that what may begin at people's front doors, or backyards, does not necessarily end there.

What emerged in the Isle of Dogs was a culture of complaint articulated by a racialised vision of the area's special history and geography. The prevailing sense of impotence and isolation was easily connected to the experience which this group had of being excluded from due political processes, and being subjected to forms of prejudice and discrimination:

> We're not getting anywhere in the Island, we're knocking our heads against a brick wall. They just shut us out. It's like we're lepers when all we're trying to do is stand up for our rights. So we got to do something to get central government and the mass media to sit up and take notice. We've got to put the Island back on the map.

This claim to indigenous entitlement pulled easily on a language of popular patriotism historically associated with the birthright of the 'freeborn Englishmen', a language which belongs to a rather larger island story.[14]

In fact, this connection had already been made implicitly in the campaign which the islanders had organised against the LDDC plans for Canary Wharf. For all its socialist inspiration, the campaign increasingly fell back in desperation on a populist rhetoric which relied subliminally on the 'Falkland factor'; the image struck was of an long-established, indigenous population of British stock being brutally attacked and driven from their own land by the dictatorship of foreign capital and requiring all patriotic freeborn Englishmen and women to come to its rescue in the hour of need.[15]

In a sense the campaign and its rhetoric provided the essential missing link between the grand narratives of race and nation relayed in media coverage, and a myth of local origins and entitlement which drew on an oppositional discourse of popular rights and sovereignties. It was this fatal connection which facilitated the growth of white working-class nativism on the Isle of Dogs. This dual process of racialisation inevitably gave a new lease of life to the self-image of Islanders as belonging to a tight-knit, homogeneous, and long-established community which had been deserted or betrayed by its traditional friends and besieged by alien forces of change.

Instead of explaining this outcome as the simple triggering of an immanent local peculiarity by a conjuncture of disadvantage or as the expression of a generalised false consciousness within a historically declining manual working-class culture, our analysis focuses on a specific, racialised, articulation of the East End. But by the same token, there is nothing inevitable or permanent about this way of thinking, or its local hegemony. It is made up of different elements whose internal tensions can be exploited and ultimately unravelled. Its rationale can be challenged. There are alternative versions of the East End and even the Cockney which point the search for a viable white working-class identity in another less racialised direction. But that, as they say, is another story.[16]

Notes

1 See 'Tricks of the Trade', a video and sampler curriculum available from the New Ethnicities Unit at UEL. This project is discussed in P. Cohen, 'Teaching Art in and Against Multiculturalism' in D. Buckingham (1996).

2 This research project was funded through a PCFC grant made by the Faculty

of Social Science at UEL, and we would like to thank Michael Rustin for his support. The field work was carried out by Ian Toon and Tarek Qureshi, and the data analysis by Phil Cohen. We would like to thank the many organisations and individuals on the Isle of Dogs who made it possible for this work to be carried out.

[3] 'Finding the Way Home' is an ESRC funded project which is currently being carried out jointly with the Centre for Urban and Community Studies at Goldsmith's College and the Institute for Migration and Racism Research in Hamburg.

[4] See, for example, Stedman Jones (1983), Epstein (1985), Humphries (1989). For a more recent feminist and post-structuralist perspective see Walkovitz (1992), Wilson (1991). See also the studies in Feldman and Stedman Jones (1991).

[5] On the excremental vision and its links to urban imagery see Bataille (1989). On De Quincey and the barbaresque, see the study, by Barrell (1991).

[6] See Husbands (1982).

[7] This is the argument advanced by Stedman Jones (1989). For an alternative reading of the conjuncture which stresses the continuities rather than the breaks with the mid-Victorian period see Marriott (1995) and Bourke (1994).

[8] See the discussion in Walkovitz, *op.cit.*

[9] The history of these youth cultures has yet to be written but there are some suggestive elements in Hobbs (1989) and Samuel (1981).

[10] For a discussion of the role of retrospective community as an invented class tradition, see Bourke (*op.cit.*) and Bauman (1991). On the relationship between symbolic loss and real deprivation, see Bloch (1988). On the general role of memory in the construction of 'imagined community', see Anderson (1983).

[11] See Riesman, (1974). A somewhat similar distinction between different narrative orientations has been made by Young (1992). See also Shotter and Geiger (1989).

[12] See Foster (1992) and Cohen (1996).

[13] On internal divisions on the Isle of Dogs see Cole (1987) and Morgan (1993).

[14] On the racialisation of housing see Smith (1989) and Docklands Forum (1993).

[15] On the local/global and its relation to cultural and community politics see Appadurai (1987), Castells (1989) Hall (1991) and Eade (1994).

[16] For a general discussion of the connection between micro and macro narratives of home in popular racism and nationalism see Cohen (1994); on the gendered dimension see Massey (1994).

[17] On Thatcherism see the contributions to Hall and Jacques (1991).

[18] On the role which the Bangladeshi community are playing in reconstructing East End cultures and politics see Neveu (1991) and Eade (1989). For the view of youth see A. Lam (1995). For a general discussion of this point see Cohen *et al*, (1996).

The Echoing Corridor: Music in the Postmodern East End

Andrew Blake

One of London's many contemporary troubles is a crisis of spatial/geographical identity. The shambolic, relatively unplanned development of the metropolis has often caused problems (for example, of access) for people living to the east of the City; to the aggregate shambles of the centuries has been added the twentieth century gifts of the bomb and the overflow town, to produce an 'East London' whose boundaries are limited neither by the conventional postcodes nor by the more recent physical limit of the M25 motorway. Parts of Essex are, no doubt, rural, agricultural, and as 'traditional' as any country farmed by the descendants of recent Scottish immigrants may be. Many urban areas in this county, on the other hand, are parts of London – and this does not just apply to places which are contiguous with or part of London boroughs such as Barking and Dagenham, Havering, and Redbridge. Basildon, Southend and so on are not only parts of the East Thames Corridor; they are parts of London.

For all its insights, the recent work on the city in postmodernity has not paid much attention to this phenomenon of displaced urbanity, of commuter-distance areas which are themselves parts of the urbs, rather than the suburbs, of the city. Whatever their differences, common constructions of the postmodern city (the work of *inter alia* Harvey and Jameson on the spatialisation of postmodernity, and Soja and Davis more specifically on the most thoroughly imagined postmodern city, Los Angeles[1]), including the debates covered in the first chapter of this book, substantiate the fluidity of the city; its continuing developmental crisis. Work specifically on London has noted the consistent underdevelopment of the east, its comparative lack of infrastructure and the comparative isolation, therefore, of many of its communities.[2] This chapter will by contrast examine ways in which, through the technologies of postmodernity, cultures may be drawn together, held together, created and recreated through music.

In his recent text *Dangerous Crossroads: Popular Music, Postmodernism and the Poetics of Place*, George Lipsitz has argued that 'while the nation state recedes as a source of identity and identification, popular culture becomes an ever more important public sphere'.[3] Drawing on the work of Arjun Appadurai, Lipsitz claims that transnational capital has worked both with and against patterns of migration; thanks to the development and use of new technologies of communication, and the creation of new multilingual spaces and continuities, not only the nation state but also the 'country' may be an obsolete formant of identity. Instead of conceptualising countries, Lipsitz remarks, we should think about 'ethnoscapes, mediascapes, technoscapes, finanscapes, ideoscapes: through which we can all inhabit many different "places" at once'.[4] Music is a constantly present aspect of this multiscape. This is, in other words, one way of seeing through the vexed question of the global and the local, of seeing them simultaneously: the global availability of musics such as rai and reggae have meant not the presence of a series of universal signs or the creation of universal cultures, but their incorporation into syncretised local cultures.

This has been the case in East London, which has been spatially extended beyond geographical continuity, but which is continually recreated through music. The growth of holiday resorts in the late nineteenth century, ribbon-development expansion until the 1930s, the development of the new towns from the 1950s, the continuing suburbanisation of most of Essex, and the developing commuter culture of the M25 hinterland, have all impacted on the idea of East London and the affiliations and identities of people who live outside the greater London postal area. London as an idea, an imagined space, and a source of identity, has grown and continues to grow. Musicians originating in various parts of Essex such as Southend and Canvey Island (e.g. pub rockers Dr Feelgood), Chelmsford (witty songsmiths Blur), as well as areas nearer Greater London such as Grays (jazz-influenced classical composer Mark-Anthony Turnage), Romford (live-techno band Underworld) and Dagenham (the amateur tradition as represented by the Dagenham Girl Pipers), use the relatively undifferentiated mode of pronunciation known as Estuarial English, and claim or have claimed London as their focus of identity (e.g. Turnage is an Arsenal supporter). 'East London', therefore, should be read as an urban/suburban entity which, through cultural, transport and communication links, certainly extends east as far as Southend.

This should not be taken to indicate the imposition of a grid of cultural coherence, or even of the easy alignment of age, gender, ethnicity and cultural allegiance. A paradox typical of postmodern cultural politics may serve to underline the point. As the above identification of the extended East End indicates, 'Essex Man', *homo Basildonensis*, and 'Essex Girl', the female equivalent (both of whom were the butt of much terrified, reactionary humour in the late 1980s), are a particular form of East London identity. Which is not to say that such an identity is or could be simple or uniform. This overwhelmingly white grouping is in part responsible for the introduction of a great deal of black-influenced dance music to the ears of the nation. At the high moment of late 1980s 'enterprise culture', under the (very brief) apparent hegemony of Thatcherism, the sound systems of Ford XR3Is being driven around Essex London were annoying older residents with the soul/dance music mix which was then provided by pirate radio stations, but not by the official national broadcasting networks of BBC radio. As the Government began to offer new licenses for local and national radio services, one station seeking legitimacy, the former London pirate Kiss FM, actually boasted that it would have access principally to the young C2s of the area. Kiss FM's PR exercise argued to potential advertisers that this group, usually mortgage-free before mid-20s marriage, had as much disposable income as people higher up the social-scale alphabet, and a greater willingness to spend it. Advertisers were impressed, Kiss FM was duly licensed, and the pattern of officially sanctioned broadcast music changed, with the mainstream BBC Radio 1 reacting to the presence of Kiss by increasing its output of dance and black-influenced music (as it has continued to do: in January 1995, for example, Radio 1 appointed black MTV VJ Lisa l'Anson to a daytime slot aimed at precisely the young, fun-seeking C2 Kiss audience).[5]

The general point is that musics of this wide area, what might be called the greater East Thames corridor, must be interrogated both as evidence of East London's cultural diversity – of the affinity of certain musics with certain specific ethnic groups and cultures – and, equally, of the ways in which barriers cannot hold, and musics have impacts and influences well beyond their points of origin. Looking at the influences of American, Caribbean and Asian music, and at the traces of English musical history (e.g. music hall) present in late twentieth century music made in East London and its extended 'suburbs', the chapter will comment in particular on the location and development of musical forms; and on the nature and extent of music provision by the music business, by educational institutions and by local government.

The Location and Development of Musical Forms

Any survey, however brief, must start with music hall.[6] There are specific continuities and developments in staged variety entertainment by and for East Londoners, from the beginnings in the 1840s, through the mid-twentieth century heyday of Flanagan and Allen, to the 291 Club, an all-black variety show which was held at the Hackney Empire (and televised therefrom) in 1991. This theatre was built specifically for music hall in 1901, and still hosts regular Old Time Music Hall shows aimed at older residents.[7] Music hall also remains in a more portable form. The borough of Redbridge and the London Boroughs Grants Committee support the work of Gilt and Gaslight, a small company which provides music hall-style entertainment for people in residential and day centres and which works all over East London.[8]

Music hall began in pubs; the connection between the alcohol business and leisure in the East End was continued in the development of Southend as a bank holiday resort for the East London working class. It was these seaside resorts which, as White and Stallybrass claimed in *The Politics and Poetics of Transgression*, their rather naive celebration of the uninhibited, saw the last vestiges of the early modern reversal of social order, the Carnival.[9] Here in the early 1960s mods were threatened by rockers, to the prurient delight of the national press. And here, a decade later, the most important of the proto-punk pub bands, Dr Feelgood and Eddie and the Hot Rods, thrashed around in an ostentatiously semi-pro answer to pomp rock's concert-hall respectability (including that of Southend's very own progressive rock band, Procul Harum, whose greatest success, the single 'Whiter Shade of Pale', had brought Bach to the Top Ten in 1968). The pub bands' national success was based on their working a circuit of Essex and London pubs; the Dr Feelgood album *Stupidity* headed the charts in 1976, heralding the breakthrough of the punk ideology of DIY, high energy, and lack of respect for major-label rock. This moment underlined again the importance of Southend and Canvey Island as centres of carnival, of the reversal of order, of East London on Holiday, and of the crucial connection between the public house and other aspects of popular culture.

There are times when popular culture's oppositional tendency is more openly political than carnivalesque celebration. In a similar musical configuration to the R'n'B-based success of the Feelgood-type pub bands, the charismatic Ian Dury began to explore his Upminster inheritance, working with pub bands like Kilburn and the High Roads and (with Chaz Jankel) the Blockheads. Dury's staples have always included songs of East London life, such as 'Billericay Dickie', 'Plaistow Patricia' and 'Upminster Kid'. Dury's 1981 album *Lord Upminster* was made with Jankel, again, but also the innovative backing of Sly and Robbie, a West Indian rhythm section much in demand in the early years of Thatcherism as attempts were made to counterpose, and sometimes to combine or fuse, the musics of the oppressed – punk and reggae – in the interests of left politics. Dury's political astuteness has remained part of his appeal. Rock Against Racism, and its politicised detritus (notably Red Wedge's attempt to market the Labour Party to young people through music) also helped to throw up the rather more aggressive singer-songwriter Billy Bragg, a denizen of Barking and reliable supporter of left causes.

Yet in the end the carnival inheritance may serve as a more important sign of the refusal of established values than the 1980s attempts to dragoon music into line with political causes. There is more to the music of East London than politics considered in this narrow sense of party or union-based activity – indeed, if Lipsitz is to be believed, 'the political' as a sphere even of potential democratic action has been replaced by 'the cultural'.[10] To explore this point in a more general sense, I shall form a history of post-war popular music from the contributions of East London and its environs, and then interrogate that story.

In the late 1950s Joe Brown attempted both to use rock'n'roll, and to find a slot in the fading light music/music hall scene which was more recently reoccupied by heritage culture cockneys Chas'n'Dave. At the same time trumpeter Kenny Ball (born in Ilford) helped launch the trad jazz revival in pre-Beatles Britain, while straight outta nearby Romford Graham Bond was one of the leaders of the more arcane practices of the British blues scene which eventually, through the Yardbirds and then Cream, saw the beginnings of British rock. While during the mid-1960s Chris Farlowe effectively aped black American soul singers, another Romforder, Chris Andrews, wrote equally effective bubblegum pop for Sandie Shaw; a couple of years later Procul Harum's pomp rock was paralleled by the noisier offerings of

Uriah Heep, one of the very few successful heavy rock acts from London and its environs. When all this became too much, the pub bands anticipated punk, and Billy Bragg kept its aggression going into the 1980s.

In the meantime pop had made a comeback. The gloomily robotic, underproduced synthesiser sound of early 1980s, Basildon-based band Depeche Mode demonstrated the physical alienation of Basildon Man. The gradual disappearance of the drummer and then other live performers (replaced firstly by drum machines and synthesisers, then tapes, then samplers and sequencers), is an interesting analogue (!) of the replacement of skilled East End labour such as typesetting; of the concomitant breaking of the unions which had dominated Fleet Street; and of the Essex turn to consumerism, self-employment and individual ownership. There was nothing very dominating about synth pop, though when Depeche Mode's founder, Vince Clarke, got bored with the band and went back to Basildon to search for something different, he found the imposing musical and physical presence of Alison Moyet, whose wonderful voice illuminated Clarke's electronic doodlings in the bizarre, but successful, Yazoo. (Moyet's career quietened after two goodish solo albums, though the appearance of a 1995 *Greatest Hits* album with three new tracks is a hopeful sign; Clarke's later outlet, the splendidly camp Erasure, features a vocalist, Andy Bell, whose talents match Clarke's more aptly.)

To interpret. What we have here in microcosm, from the late 1950s on, is an important aural history of British post-coloniality in two directions. Throughout the post-war period there has been increasing cultural interaction with the USA; especially with American music. American products have inspired British popular culture, to the resentment and hostility of many on the left who, for all the xenophobia of a reaction such as Richard Hoggart's diatribe *The Uses of Literacy*,[11] could at least see that this was a power relationship. Elsewhere American music was welcomed and used; Brown, Ball and Bond each worked with a different aspect of American jazz and popular music. But it is not a simple story of everyday cultural imperialism globalising away and destroying indigenous cultures. The Andrews/Sandie Shaw material was less reliant on American models (and had at least something to do with local popular musics from a music hall/light entertainment tradition), while Procul Harum were at first part of progressive rock's turn away from R'n'B and engagement with European classical and folk musics – though in later incarnations their sound became more Americanised. The pub bands, for all Dury's local humour, were musically back in the territory of R'n'B and American rock; synth bands such as Depeche Mode qualified the Americanism once again.

British musical culture has been formed in part through this narrative of engagement, rejection, and incorporation of American musics. But this is not the only story of British music, which has also been formed through a parallel relation with the former colonies, their people and their musics. The arrival in Britain since 1945 of many musicians and musics from the former colonial and imperial territories, including West Indies, India and South Africa, has meant moments of cultural miscegenation which have been massively productive for the development of British music. (Partly because of this it was to London that the American Jimi Hendrix came in 1966, to forge a new expressive language of guitar playing within a song-writing context which did not rely merely on blues harmonies or the controlled rhythmic repetition of R'n'B or soul, but also paid respect to white popular musics.[12]) The saxophonist Joe Harriott was one of the first wave of Caribbean immigrants to Britain. As well as playing in the accepted styles of the late 1950s and after, Harriott attempted in the mid-1960s to create a specifically post-colonial music using Indian musicians and instruments as well as Caribbean and white musicians and styles: the result he called Indo-Jazz Fusions – releasing an album by that title at the same time as the exposure given to the sounds of sitar and tabla on 1967 albums by the Beatles, *Sergeant Pepper*, and batter drums and bamboo flutes on the Rolling Stones's *Their Satanic Majesties Request*.[13] Again, it was through London that this postcolonial interaction took place, as it was from London that white Jamaican entrepreneur Chris Blackwell's Island label launched reggae as a worldwide musical form, principally through the elevation of Bob Marley to 'rock' superstar.[14]

The examples of Joe Harriott and Bob Marley point to the reason for the importance of Britain as site for the transformation of popular musics: the nature and extent of post-war, post-colonial immigration. Since 1945, millions of people from the Caribbean, from India, Pakistan and Africa, have settled permanently in London and other big cities. While there has been a black presence in Britain since at least the sixteenth century, and while there have *always* been musical cultures associated with black people in Britain,[15] the concentration of peoples in the last fifty years has created new markets for musical forms developed by and for specific ethnic groups, and provided the site for the interaction of these with existing forms and the consequent re-production of musics. Reggae, for example, was re-created in Britain partly because there were substantial numbers of British people of West Indian origin prepared to buy the resulting concert tickets and albums. But reggae did not remain a specifically West Indian form. It was used in other music: important points of crossover include the moment of punk in 1976, and the subsequent infusion of reggae in the Rock Against Racism movement of the late 1970s; the continuing importance of dance music of all kinds to the pop charts; in particular, the astonishing success in Britain of House-derived musics since 1988 is due partly to the presence of a reggae aesthetic making bass and drums the most important part of the mix. The typical House band name Bomb the Bass, and typical acid-house track title 'Bass: how low can you go?' emphasise this, while the revival of dub reggae in 1993 was often led by white DJs fascinated by the possibilities of detuned bass guitars, rather than young blacks who dismissed it as 'parents's music'.[16] The summer of 1994 saw the commercial popularity of Jungle, a hybrid reggae/ragga/rave music, in which techno drum patterns, dub and techno bass lines, and soul samples interact in a music claimed by its innovators to be specifically a London product; several emphasise the impossibility of such open black/white cultural interaction in New York, for example.[17]

This perception by practitioners suggests a qualification to the arguments put forward in Paul Gilroy's recent book *The Black Atlantic*.[18] Gilroy claims that music has a particular importance to African-American and Caribbean people because of its power to go beyond the verbal and express the black experience of modernity in ways unavailable to language. Gilroy's argument is signalled by his subtitle, 'modernity and double consciousness'. The legacy of slavery, and the continuing pervasiveness of racism, means that feelings of placed identity are both local and African, mediated by the Atlantic as both the historic site of the middle passage and the current site of cultural interchange between the Americas, the Caribbean and Europe. Music is one of the crucial registers of this double consciousness.[19]

I want to make two points in relation to this very important argument. One, African-American music has a commanding place in British popular culture; it is continuously available as a marker of the black presence, whatever the relative absence of black faces from mainstream visual culture in film and television. This relative absence from visual representation, together with the expressive power of the music, underlines the alternative, even the subversive status of black cultures in such a way as to attract many white people who wish to reject the dominant values of their societies, whether young white Americans who buy rap records or the young white Britons who were claimed by Dick Hebdige to have engaged in a 'phantom dialogue' with black American and Caribbean cultures.[20] The ethnographic work of Simon Jones on young whites who identify themselves as culturally black, the spiralling multiculturalism of jungle and its derivatives, perhaps most notably the chart success of cultural hybrids, for example, Apache Indian's Handsworth-originated dancehall/ragga-with-Indian-percussion, have indicated the availability of a performed black identity to young British whites and Asians, in the inner cities at least.[21] This could also be theorised as a form of double consciousness.

Secondly, there is more to American culture than music. Hebdige's classic work on subcultures has been followed by *Hiding in the Light*, in which a broader view is taken of the Anglo-American relationship.[22] Cars and other products, films and film stars, the whole panoply of American culture is present in this latter text – not just African-American culture. And so is their impact on Britain and British culture, in a positive assessment of the cultural pollution which was the object of hostility in that influential early cultural studies text, *The Uses of Literacy*. British culture is deeply imbricated with American products and values. There is a White Atlantic, through which the present and future are visualised, and heard, in Americanised terms. The Kiss FM C2s with their house-derived dance music, and the pub rockers of the Dr Feelgood era, are part of this continuing 'phantom dialogue' – though it should be recognised that in the case of dance music, there is also a phantom dialogue with Europe and an envisioned European future.[23]

We should, then, go beyond the Atlantic in assessing the sense(s) of place available in the postmodern East End. Musical fusions made in Britain have involved many different cultural interactions. New Asian musics have been created, in relation to African-American, Afro-Caribbean and Anglo-American forms among others. The politicised and ethnicised indie of Cornershop, the junglish ragga of the (East London based) Asian Dub Foundation, and the post-punk rock of Echobelly, indicate the range of musics currently being reworked through British Asian participation. At the time of writing there is much talk of the 'rebirth of Asian cool', musically underwritten by new jazz fusions.[24] One of the most commercially successful of these hybrids is bhangra, a development of a Punjabi folk idiom which has kept its drums, it basic rhythms, and the language and intonation of Punjabi in its songs, while also incorporating western pop, African-American and African-Caribbean harmonies and instruments. Bhangra is a nodal point in a large bilingual (occasionally non-English speaking) Asian commercial culture, in which flourishing record labels and all-day parties rival the sales of English-monolingual urban culture. While bhangra may be said to be principally a north and west London development, it is popular in the Asian communities of East London.[25] But it is not the only syncretic Asian pop performed here. Members of the Bangladeshi community in Tower Hamlets have produced 'Joi-Bangla', a music which, like bhangra, blends traditional instruments and performing styles (played mainly by older people) with high technology instruments played by youngsters.[26] In this case, unlike in bhangra, there is also an obvious inflection by rock music, the Anglo-American form which as the success of the pub bands and Uriah Heep may indicate, is arguably more important in the east than elsewhere in London. The location for this music remains a point of concern, especially since the takeover of the Tenor Clef, a small venue in Hoxton which had provided a regular public outlet for this music, by the proprietors of the Acid Jazz label (which was set up in Hackney). Newham local authority's widening of their provision for music education, which will for the first time in 1995 include funding for community-based ethnic musics, may begin to make good this deficiency.[27]

The Greater East End has also played a part in the continuing transformations of the British music scene. One important tendency should be noted. Proclamations of the death of rock'n'roll have often based their verdicts on the impact of new technology. The 1980s hegemony of first the drum machine and synthesiser, then the sampler and computer sequencer, have apparently made live-performance popular music as we knew and put up with it a thing of the past, or will do so imminently.[28] Not so; from the land of the pub bands has come music which uses new technologies to transform and extend the possibilities of live performance, not to replace it. Disco Inferno, for example (a trio from Essex, currently based in West Ham, whose voices betray the usual estuarial characteristics), use samplers not to provide endless drum loops but new banks of sounds which can be triggered from the fretboards of their guitars or the skins of their drums. The result can confuse the onlooker, since the common expectation is that bass guitars will produce bass guitar sounds and not those of the bass drum, the horn section, well known television tunes, or the building site. Their music often, however, reverts to its roots: a version of the jangly-guitar 'indie' music beloved by the students of the late 1980s, the journalists who wrote for the inkies, and hardly anyone else, but which might claim spiritual kinship with (even at a stretch, parenthood of) the Seattle grunge sound and its derivatives.

A more routine use of new technologies is in the broad post-House genre which can loosely be called Dance Music. This too can involve the use of live instruments in recording and even, occasionally, in performance, though it is basically a music of the sequencer and sampler, the shortlife white label mix and the club – and therefore a music which, like pub rock, tends to subvert the conventional, deeply overcapitalised, political economy of the music business. At the time of writing one of the most successful of these new-tech outfits is the Essex-based band The Prodigy – indeed their success has crossed into mainstream sales. A more typical, low-budget, East London example is Medium High, a partnership between Georgina Dark and Kristian Rutter, whose work is typically programmed at home, recorded and mixed in professional studios, and then transferred to white label 12″ vinyl discs for use in clubs.

I shall end this section with the story of Underworld, a band based in Romford whose musical and extra-musical activities embody the present and predict the future rather more than the Heritage Pop, pseudo-cockney impishness of those lovable creatures of Colchester art college, Blur. Like Disco Inferno, Underworld incorporate live instrumental performance with the manipulation of high technology samples and sequences. Starting in the late 1980s as a funk/blues/rock outfit, the band have been joined by a DJ, and are associated with video and multimedia production facilities (which have produced television advertisements for Nike among other things). Like Disco Inferno, and a few other acts like Bark Psychosis and Ultramarine, Underworld have combined mixed and layered samples with live instrumental performance, thus again keeping touch with the audience interaction and unpredictability which have always informed popular entertainment. Underworld's highly acclaimed 1994 album, *Dubnobasswithmyheadman*, reflects this interest in all the parameters of performance and composition.[29]

The Nature and Extent of Music Provision

Interactions with America and the former colonies have produced changes at every level of British musical life. The continuing presence of pop music, and the music of the Asian and Caribbean communities, on radio and in record stores, and the presence of the children of the Commonwealth immigrants in the schools of British urban centres, have led gradually to the reformation of senior school music teaching away from music appreciation and classical composition and instrumental technique, and towards the technologies and practices of popular music. The GCSE syllabuses introduced in 1985 stressed the learning of compositional and performance skills, including the use of synthesisers, samplers and recording equipment.[30] More recently the Interim Report of the Working Group on the place of music in the national education curriculum was published in March 1991.[31] Enthusing in its multicultural brief, the committee's report assumed the equal value in education of musics as different as reggae and ragas, sambas and serialism. The skills of performance and composition were stressed rather more than the critical appreciation of the work of previous generations. Again, the use of synthesisers, computer-based composition packages and multi-track tape recorders, African drumming techniques, and jazz improvisation were placed alongside baroque counterpoint and sonata form. The only composer from the European tradition mentioned by name was Mozart. There followed a furore in the pages of the broadsheet newspapers. The Working Group was arraigned for betrayal of the classical music tradition, and a series of letters and articles rallied the intellectuals of both old and new right in defence of 'traditional' musical education, i.e. the appreciation of the techniques and achievements of previous generations of male Europeans.[32]

Too late, thankfully. In most East London schools, this battle had already been decided in the interests of multiculturalism. In Tower Hamlets (and from September 1995 in Newham) music teaching is provided on the basis of 'relevance' and interest.[33] Peripatetic instrumental tuition is available in western, African and Asian musics. In Tower Hamlets, schools with a majority Bengali population will usually provide lessons in tabla, tanpura, harmonium and other South Asian instruments; all children are taught to sing the work of Rabindranath Tagore, the Nobel Prize winning writer, Indian nationalist and composer of the Indian national anthem, in a popular Bengali style known as 'Rabindrasangheet'. Most of the children who take to these musics, however, have ambitions beyond the classical or folk styles they are taught – they want to play bhangra, and/or Hindi film music, when they grow up.[34] Throughout East London, the pattern repeats itself: the musics studied by the majority of the pupils at primary or GCSE level are popular and/or ethnic-classical, rather than the carefully preserved western classical canon.

It is particularly unfortunate, then, that music education in these skills at higher levels is unavailable locally. Some colleges provide basic introductory courses in rock music, and/or in soul, reggae, and the new computer-based technologies. There has been for many years liaison between local government and independent recording studios, and though the budgets for these activities are never less than tight, such investments have continued. The Tower Hamlets Youth Music Workshop, for example, was launched in 1982 as a council-supported educational charity. It employed an administrator and, on a part-time basis, teaching staff who were themselves active in music recording and performance. A small 16-track recording studio was built in a disused public swimming bath. The facilities, and the expertise of the staff, were made available at very low cost to target groups such as the unemployed; women taking access courses in music and music production; adults in further education; and local arts and community organisations. The studio was also available for hire at full professional rates for the making of commercial recordings. The charity has continued to operate, and has sought European funding for its redevelopment.[35] A decade later, Tower Hamlets supported the setting up of ATUM, another training project based around recording studio skills. By this time there was no question of council funding for startup costs, though from the start it was clear European Social Fund moneys would be available for staffing costs. In order to claim these it was necessary to be specific about the types of training offered and the eventual vocational destination of trainees. Liaison with the BBC, and with local further and higher education institutions such as Guildhall University, produced a range of specifically tailored pre-vocational courses and access to higher education courses, in music production and music/video production.[36]

What is not currently provided in the East London area itself is degree-level work which provides theoretical study as well as practical hands-on experience. Such courses are provided in many parts of London (the nearest to East London being at City University in Clerkenwell, and the Guildhall School of Music and Drama, at the Barbican). African-American and African-Caribbean forms and their local derivatives are comparatively well provided for in these courses – the Guildhall School's big band was one of the sources for the successful professional big band of the mid-1980s, Loose Tubes. However, Asian musics are not available in the same ways. Provision is sorely needed which will build on the primary education in South Asian music, and provide insight into the interactions between these forms of basic training, and the popular musics which so many of the schoolchildren who take them up wish to perform. The University of East London has a particular opportunity to develop work in this field – and, in pursuit of its claimed mission, to become thereby truly a centre for the creation and maintenance of local musical excellence.

The changing nature of local government arts provision, under increasing central budget-limiting control, underlines the importance of the expansion of musical provision by the new educational corporations. Local government has for long played a pro-active role in local musical cultures: including *inter alia* support for festivals and other subsidised concerts; adult education in musical appreciation and performance; the provision of training opportunities for local people in recording studios, as discussed above; and the provision of facilities for rehearsal and performance.

Predictably, Thatcherism impacted at the local level on the conceptualisation of cultural policy. Recently, Arts policy has been seen as an arm of general economic policy: the arts, in other words, are seen as an industry, employing people and attracting both local and sometimes national tourists, and local or global inward investors seeking 'lifestyle' for their employees. They have become, therefore, an adjunct of the commercial lives of areas and communities. These issues have been raised recently in East London. The borough of Havering, concerned at the economic impact of the loss of consumers to the Lakeside shopping complex, has invested in brighter shopping facilities, and at the end of 1994 was considering regular outdoor musical events in its town centres, in an attempt to win back the shoppers who had been seduced by the motorway leisure city.[37] But central government has constantly attacked the possibilities even of such commerce-related provision indirectly, through stringent budgetary control.

To take the borough of Havering as an example. Havering regularly supports concert series in libraries and parks, including a showcase for local popular music bands on National Music Day. The borough subsidises a range of professional and semi-professional musical events in the Queens' Theatre. There is an annual free orchestral concert (sponsored in full by accountants Kingston Smith) in the grounds of The Langtons, what was once a country house in Hornchurch. Regular cheap coach parties attend shows in central London. The borough's arts officer liaises with amateur and semi-professional performers – there are twelve choirs, ten troops of majorettes, and seven marching bands, for example – publicising gigs, and arranging rehearsals and making personal contacts when possible. All this is done on a shoestring – the 1993-4 annual budget was £250,000 for all the arts (inner London boroughs such as Tower Hamlets are currently funded more generously). But much more could be done even within this budget if the borough had a suitable venue for concert music. At present it does not; there is nothing suitable for large orchestras, nothing for the better-known rock performers (there are of course plenty of pubs, but few enough offer gigs). All over East London, in fact, arts officers told me that there was a need for regular performance venues, and for large venues in particular. A site is needed somewhere in outer East London to match the excellent facilities of the Fairfield Halls in Croydon. Havering may be able to develop the empty site of the former Romford Brewery in Hornchurch; the funds necessary could come from the National Lottery's capital spending for the arts.[38] The University of East London should also be cognizant of the need for suitable performing spaces, as well as for rehearsal space and teaching/production facilities. Any development of the proposed Docklands site, for instance, must include a fully equipped medium-sized concert hall and general performance space.

One useful source in addressing this problem of provision is John Street's article 'Local Differences? Popular Music and the Local State', which discusses the planning, conversion, and the first few years' running of a new medium-sized rock venue in Norwich. 'In Britain, much of the public provision of culture falls to elected local authorities.'[39] Yet whereas this obligation has usually been taken to include musical entertainments such as brass bands in parks on Sunday afternoons, and orchestral concerts in town halls, it has seldom extended to pop. Local subsidy of pop and its derivatives has been provided only through the students' unions of the universities and colleges: as a leisure function of further and higher education, with all the implicit elitism of this distinction.[40]

The Norwich Venue Campaign started in 1985. Local musicians and fans claimed that the only local popular music venue of any size, the University of East Anglia (UEA), was too far from the city (three miles!), and the local arts centre too small (a maximum capacity of 300). With the endorsement of local resident John Peel, but the opposition of many other local residents, basic plans to convert an abandoned warehouse got nowhere before the intervention of UEA itself, which wished to relocate its own drama centre. So with university and council co-funding the project, a 700-person rock venue was set up. Prices were low, and booking policy tended to the indie sector; some local performers were given support, but overall the local consumption of a national and transnational culture was fed through the choice of live performers. It was not a great financial success, went into receivership, and eventually the University took over its management completely. The venue is now both an urban students' union and an important space for local and student music and drama. This, too, is a model which should be considered by those planning future developments by East London educational institutions.

The East Thames corridor will, no doubt, continue to echo with new sounds even if the public and corporate provision for the making of music remains at its present low level. Pop, rock, reggae, rave, jungle and whatever is next can and will be made in garages and bedrooms, in pubs and schoolrooms. But more could and should be done, especially for those South Asian musics currently underprivileged within the hierarchy of educational and broadcasting values, and which lack the Atlantic connections which have proved so fruitful for Anglo-American music-making in all its twentieth century forms.[41]

Notes

1 D. Harvey, *The Condition of Postmodernity*, Basil Blackwell, Oxford 1989; F. Jameson, *Postmodernism or The Cultural Logic of Late Capitalism*, Verso, London 1991; E. Soja, *Postmodern Geographies*, Verso, London 1987; M. Davis, *City of Quartz*, Verso, London 1990.

2 See e.g. A. Thornley (ed), *The Crisis of London*, Routledge, London 1992; B. Schwarz, 'Where Horses Shit a Hundred Sparrows Feed: Docklands and East London during the Thatcher Years', in J. Harvey and S. Corner (eds), *Enterprise and Heritage*, Routledge, London 1991, pp76–92.

3 G. Lipsitz, *Dangerous Crossroads: Popular Music, Postmodernism and the Poetics of Place*, Verso, London 1994, p5.

4 *ibid.*, p5.

5 A move discussed wittily by Emma Forrest in the *Independent*, 5 January 1995.

6 For general studies of music hall see P. Bailey (ed), *Music Hall: the Business of Pleasure*, Open University Press, Buckingham 1989 and J.S. Bratton (ed), *Music Hall: Performance and Style*, Open University Press, Buckingham 1990.

7 I am grateful to University of East London Cultural Studies graduate Helen Noake for permission to use material from her 1991 dissertation on local music hall. See also Fiona Beckett, 'Opportunity Knocks for the Young, Gifted and Black', the *Independent*, 6 December 1990.

8 My thanks to Havering Arts Officer Chris Cole for this information. Tower Hamlets also supports music hall for the elderly: see *Tower Hamlets Arts Strategy*, a council paper originated by B. Oakaby, 14 February 1995.

9 P. Stallybrass and A. White, *The Politics and Poetics of Transgression*, Methuen, London 1987.

[10] Lipsitz, *op.cit.*, pp12–13.
[11] R. Hoggart, *The Uses of Literacy*, Penguin, Harmondsworth 1957.
[12] See A. Blake, 'Re-Placing British Music', in M. Nava and A. O'Shea, (eds), *Modern Times: Reflections on the Experience of Modernity in Britain*, Routledge, London 1995. The least worst book on Hendrix is C.S. Murray, *Crosstown Traffic: Jimi Hendrix and Post-War Pop*, Faber, London 1989.
[13] It is worth mentioning one current London-based attempt to cross these boundaries from the rather different direction of the European classical tradition, Pritti Paintal's ensemble Shiva Nova.
[14] S. Clarke, *Jah Music*, Heinemann, London 1980; D. Hebdige, *Cut'n'Mix: Culture, Identity and Caribbean Music*, Methuen, London 1987.
[15] P. Fryer, *Staying Power*, Pluto, London 1984; P. Gilroy, *There Ain't no Black in the Union Jack*, Hutchinson, London 1989; P. Oliver, (ed), *Black Music in Britain*, Open University Press, Buckingham 1990.
[16] On black musics and cultural hybridity, see G. Stephens, 'Interracial Dialogue in Rap Music', *New Formations*, Spring 1992, pp62–79.
[17] See Tony Marcus interviewing Rebel MC, General Levy, DJ Ron and Jumpin' Jack Frost, all exponents of jungle, in *Mixmag*, July 1994, pp32-36; the phenomenon is discussed briefly in A. Blake, 'Village Green, Urban Jungle', *New Statesman and Society*, 12 August 1994, p32.
[18] P. Gilroy, *The Black Atlantic*, Verso, London 1993. For a broader version of my argument about modernity and consciousness see A. Blake, 'Listening to Britain', paper given at the conference 'Advertising and Consumption since the 1950s', held at the University of East London, 8 September 1994, to be published in a book of this conference's proceedings edited by Blake, M.Nava, B. Richards and I. McRury.
[19] Gilroy, *Black Atlantic*, p74.
[20] The classic text here is of course D. Hebdige, *Subculture: the Meaning of Style*, Methuen, London 1979.
[21] S.Jones, *Black Culture, White Youth*, Macmillan, London 1989.
[22] D. Hebdige, *Hiding in the Light*, Comedia, London 1988.
[23] Much dance music is European (German, Belgian and Italian especially) in origin; the use of gregorian chant in the very successful first *Enigma* album (*MCMXC* a.D, Virgin CD 262 029, 1991), and the quite casual comparison made between the work of ambient techno wizard The Aphex Twin and the German avant-garde composer Karlheinz Stockhausen signal, I suspect, an attempt to distance this music from its American heritage.
[24] A brief treatment of Asians in 'rock' is R. Huq, 'Rock of Asia', *Red Pepper*, October 1994, p40.
[25] There is very little academic work on bhangra. See S. Banerji and G. Baumann, 'Bhangra 1984-8', in Oliver (ed), *op.cit.*, 137-152; S. and A. Sharma (eds), *New Asian Dance Music*, Zed, London 1996.
[26] Joi is discussed briefly by Lipsitz, *op.cit.*, p119.
[27] My thanks to Bill Romford, director of the Newham Music Trust, for this information.
[28] See A. Goodwin, 'Sample and Hold: Pop Music in the Age of Digital Reproduction', in S. Frith and A. Goodwin (eds), *On Record*, Routledge, London 1990, pp258–274.
[29] I am indebted to Underworld's publicity agent, Robin Turner, and to

Sophie Zante, a University of East London Cultural Studies graduate who interviewed Underworld for her final year dissertation in 1994. See also C. Larkin (ed), *The Guinness Who's Who of Rap, Dance and Techno*, Guinness Publishing, London 1994, pp336–7; S. Masters, 'Underworld' *The Lizard*, Summer 1995 pp30–33.

[30] For the prehistory of this moment, see G. Vulliamy and E. Lee (eds), *Pop, Rock and Ethnic Music in Schools*, Cambridge University Press, Cambridge 1982. A fuller discussion of these issues is in A. Blake, *The Music Business*, Batsford, London 1992.

[31] The National Curriculum Music Working Group produced its final report in October 1991.

[32] See the *Independent*, 18 January 1992; 23 January 1992; 28 January 1992; 29 January 1992; 24 February 1992.

[33] See Vulliamy and Lee, *Pop, Rock and Ethnic Music in Schools*, and in general on the question of music education L. Green, *Music on Deaf Ears*, Manchester University Press, Manchester 1988. A particular example of best practice in this field is the teaching of African-derived musics at the Leo Mason School, Birmingham. See Val Wilmer, 'On the School Trip', the *Independent*, 27 June 1990.

[34] Gerry Farrell, 'South Asian Music Teaching in Change', unpublished paper given at the conference *Music, Performance and Identity*, held under the auspices of the International Council for Traditional Music at King's College, Cambridge, 7 December 1994.

[35] Boyden Smith Arts Media Leisure consultants, 'Tower Hamlets Music Charity Business Plan 1991-4' available from Boyden Smith, 11-15 Betterton Street, London WC2H 9BP. My thanks to Jon Wilkinson for this paper and a discussion of the charity's work.

[36] Personal communication from David Richardson at Tower Hamlets – my thanks.

[37] My thanks again to Chris Cole, Borough of Havering Arts officer, for a useful discussion.

[38] I am grateful once again to Chris Cole.

[39] J. Street, 'Local Differences? Popular Music and the Local State', *Popular Music* Vol.12 No.1, 1993, p43.

[40] The county of Essex, for instance, remains wedded to the hierarchy of performing arts, organising an impressive list of classical concerts and festivals, and an increasing range of jazz activities. It does not subsidise rock or other popular musics, arguing that they are 'commercial'. (I should perhaps make it clear that I am not arguing *against* classical or jazz provision, but *in favour* of the setting up and maintenance of venues for popular musics.) My thanks to David Dougan, Arts Officer for Essex.

[41] For a broader discussion of the issues raised in this paper see A. Blake, 'Re-Placing British Music', *op.cit.*; and A. Blake, *The Land Without Music*, Manchester University Press, Manchester 1996.

Culture and Space

Architecture in East London

Bill Risebero

Limehouse, in East London, is an old working-class town centre. Against a background of post-war council housing, local shops huddle along the edge of Commercial Road, Hawksmoor's imposing but dilapidated church of St Anne offers shelter to the destitute, and the staff of the Gill Street health centre struggle with the chronic illnesses of the East End.

If you walk south-east from Limehouse, you soon move from one world to another. First you have to cross a traffic intersection, whose huge geometry cracks the old town centre apart, with acres of left-over spaces. The reason for the junction soon becomes clear; Commercial Road now delivers traffic from the City of London onto the newly-built Limehouse Link, and thence to the office city of Canary Wharf, which you can see in front of you.

It is not a route for pedestrians, for whom it is tortuous and dangerous, but arrival at Canary Wharf offers its own kind of rewards. New trees, well-kept lawns, wide views of the river, and a fountained plaza lead on to a conference hall, a shopping mall full of designer clothes and leather luggage, and to the shining towers themselves, the first phase of an intended 12 million square feet of office floorspace.

Canary Wharf is relentlessly commercial, offering much to its entrepreneurs but nothing, either economically or socially, to the people of Limehouse. And not only is it alien to East London – it also looks it. Its style is seductively, but in the geographical context meaninglessly, American – the style of Battery Park City or Bunker Hill. Among the many questions it raises is an architectural one: what connections are there between the economic forces which create such massive physical changes in places like East London, and the architectural style in which these changes are clothed?

We might begin to answer this by noting the dual nature of the building process. Buildings, in Marx's terms, are use-values, providing shelter and other human needs. But they also operate as exchange-values – commodities produced for profit – a function which, under capitalism, will always predominate. The building process will be aimed mainly at maximising surplus-value for entrepreneurs; labour will be exploited; users will be alienated from the production process; human need will be subordinated to profit.

This was the system which, at least from the sixteenth century, produced the East End of London. Its people were exploited economically, and their physical environment was a reflection of this exploitation. Even steps taken to improve the living conditions of the working class – the charity housing of the nineteenth century, the council estates of the post-war years – took place within the capitalist mode of production; the meeting of local need was often compromised by the demand for profit.

The choice of architectural style plays a part in this process. To begin to see how this is so, let us distinguish between 'buildings' and 'architecture'. Pevsner's famous aphorism was

> A bicycle shed is a building; Lincoln Cathedral is a piece of architecture. Nearly everything that encloses space on a scale sufficient for a human being to move in, is a building; the term architecture applies only to buildings designed with a view to aesthetic appeal.[1]

Whatever the limitations of this definition, it does emphasise that architecture belongs not only to the material world of production, but also to the world of ideas. Marx recognises this. For him, the connection between ideas and actions – theory and practice – is fundamental to human development, and he uses architecture as a metaphor for this process.

> The architect will construct in his imagination that which he will ultimately erect in reality. At the end of every labour process we get that which existed in the consciousness of the labourer at its commencement.[2]

If theory and practice are closely allied in this way, then human beings have the potential to take control of their circumstances – to shape their environment for the better and, in the process, to develop themselves.

In a class society, however, both theory and practice become appropriated. Under capitalism, practice is controlled by capital, while theory is dominated by ruling-class ideology. Theory and practice are still linked, it is true, but in a way that is not conducive to equality or to social progress. The production process exploits, while the ideological superstructure supports and, when necessary, 'mystifies' that process.

Out of this, the built environment emerges. Building is a matter of production. Through it, the quantitative issues are addressed: what should be built, how much of it and at what cost. The practicality of the building process gives a fairly clear picture of, for example, a society's technological capability, or its ability to organise itself.

Architectural theory and design, on the other hand, address the qualitative issues; architecture is a language, which can and does transmit ideological messages. Architecture uses form to express ideas – true or false – about a society, its class structure and its political priorities. And the most dominant of these ideas, the 'ruling ideas' of any given period of history, have always been 'the ideas of the ruling class'.[3]

The relationship between production on the one hand and the ruling ideology on the other can clearly be seen in many famous buildings. Take Chartres, one of Europe's most celebrated medieval cathedrals. The practicalities of its construction – the great size, the materials used, the structural system – tell us much about the abilities of the builders of the Middle Ages and the feats of organisation of which they were capable. The architecture of the building – its form, designed for very specific liturgical functions, and its persistent use of religious symbolism and iconography – seem to tell us that it was built by a uniquely religious society. This is ideology. The architecture speaks of the enduring power of the Church and of feudalism but belies certain realities of the building's production: that it was paid for by bourgeois merchants and designed by specialist master-masons whose lives and careers now lay outside the enclosed world of the Church, and even of Christianity itself. In short, it was the product of a rapidly secularising, increasingly capitalist society.

The use of ideology as a mask for economic realities can be seen in almost all architecture. You see it, for example, in the huge changes, both economic and physical, which East London has undergone since the Second World War. The fate of the Docks, of course, has been central to the economic changes. The Docks had provided the East End's main economic purpose and had been the centre of its social life. As the target for enemy bombers they had also been the main reason for its wartime destruction. During the general post-war revival, they were in a state of gradual and debilitating decline. Following the economic crisis of the 1970s, their eventual closure provided both the excuse and the opportunity for uninhibited commercial exploitation. And along with these major economic changes went successive phases of physical change, in which architectural form was used to express the 'prevailing' ideas.

Immediately after the war, three main tasks were apparent. One, self-evidently, was that of physical reconstruction following the bombing. Another was the task of social reconstruction, along the lines of the Beveridge proposals, to banish for ever, it was hoped, the inequalities of the 1930s. And most fundamental of all was the task of developing a system of economic management, to deal with the recurrent crises of over-production, which had so bedevilled the inter-war period and were widely seen as capitalism's last remaining basic defect. The adoption of Keynesianism as a means of managing the economy would involve the creation of a huge public sector. This in turn would help in the tasks of physical and social reconstruction. But the first priority was to save capitalism; the creation of the Welfare State was desirable of course, but to be tolerated only if it did not compromise capital accumulation and profitability.

During the war there had been much debate about the new egalitarian society that would be created. After the war, however, the framework for the new society fell far short of the aims. Property relations went unchallenged: inheritance persisted, land and the building industry went un-nationalised. Private schools and private medicine remained. The new planning system did introduce a tax on property speculators but this was soon repealed.

Based on the new technologies developed during the war – electronics, nuclear fission, aerospace and the automobile – the western economies quickly grew. In Britain, growth was uneven. Finance capital prospered, but it invested in industry only when short-term profits were to be made. Sunrise industries on greenfield sites were able to benefit, both from investment and from encouragement by decentralist planning policies, but the traditional heavy industries continued their gradual long-term decline.

Whether or not the decline of London's Docks was recognised, nothing effective was done about it. In the 1950s, the County of London Plan predicted a gradual expansion of the Docks. In the early 1960s the South-East Study said the Port of London would maintain its dominant position. Contemporary planning debate was almost all about dealing with the challenge of growth rather than the problems of decline.[4] Yet meanwhile the Docks were losing trade: to Tilbury, to the airlines, to other docks in Europe. During the 1960s they began to close.

As a whole, though, the British economy was buoyant, and the Welfare State was able to benefit from the proceeds. In the 1950s, a huge national building programme began: New Towns, city centre redevelopments, hospitals, schools, universities, roads and, above all, a housing programme which aimed at, and frequently achieved, an annual output of 300,000 dwellings.

The East End of London was physically reconstructed. Two square miles of the badly bombed Poplar area became the largest Comprehensive Development Area in Britain, housing a population larger than that of many a New Town. Chrisp Street Market, the Lansbury estate, the Balfron Tower, the Robin Hood Gardens estate, presented

> a totally new world, dominated by the tall blocks of flats and by the lower terraces of three- and four-storey maisonettes, standing in spacious gardens and landscaped squares.[5]

The mood, as can be seen, was intensely hopeful. The architectural style was modern, derived from the heroic theorists of the 1920s and 30s – the Russian Constructivists, Le Corbusier, Walter Gropius and the Bauhaus school – for whom modern architecture was synonymous with social progress. During the 1930s, these ideas had not been put into practice on any large scale; the 1950s seemed to offer the opportunity of doing so.

High-rise flats would free up ground space for public gardens and walks. Industrialised building techniques would increase both housing output and housing quality. Nationally-agreed standards would improve housing design. The principle of comprehensive development would improve living conditions, providing the opportunity to segregate housing from industry and to reduce residential densities. Community facilities would be built to match the needs of the residential population. Public ownership would ensure a coherent housing policy, and the subsidisation of both building costs and rents

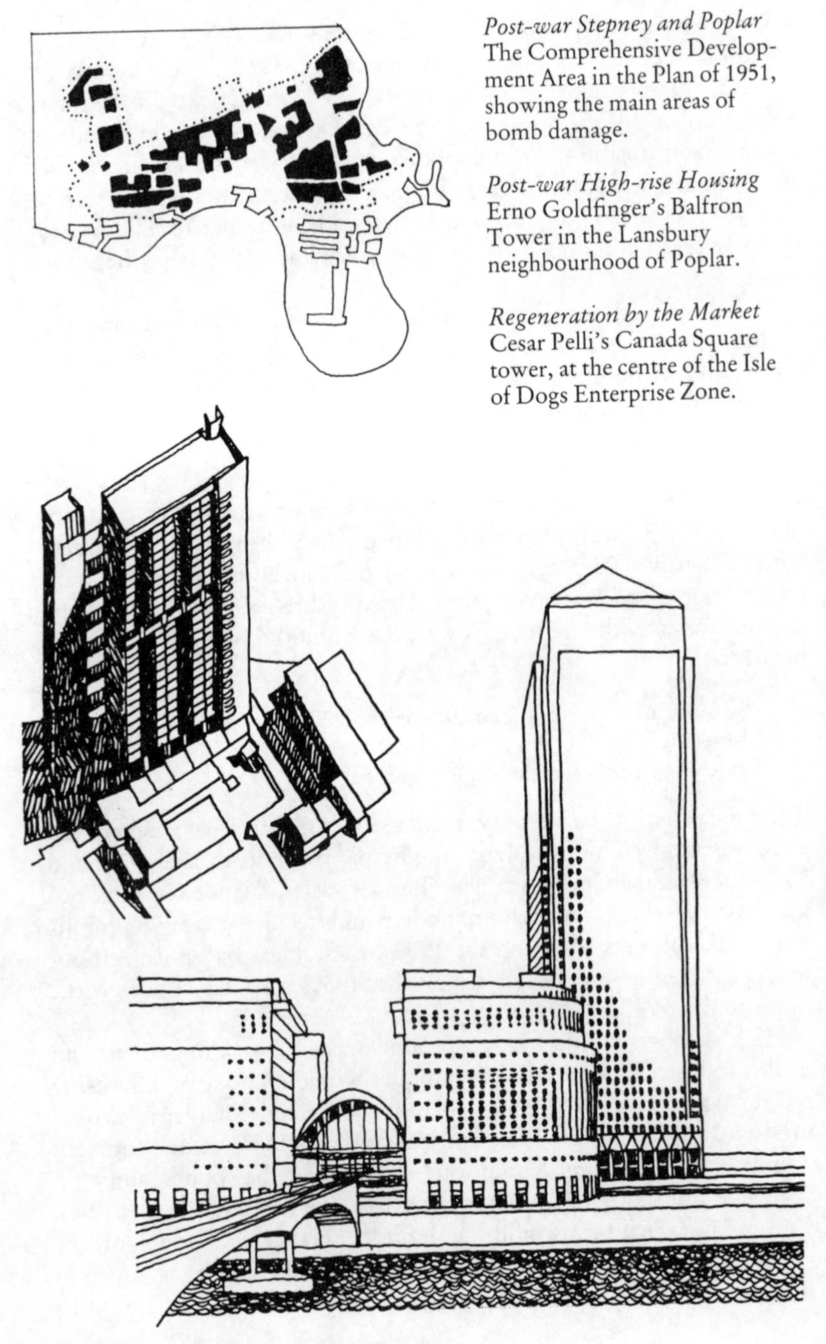

Post-war Stepney and Poplar
The Comprehensive Development Area in the Plan of 1951, showing the main areas of bomb damage.

Post-war High-rise Housing
Erno Goldfinger's Balfron Tower in the Lansbury neighbourhood of Poplar.

Regeneration by the Market
Cesar Pelli's Canada Square tower, at the centre of the Isle of Dogs Enterprise Zone.

Community Care
A window detail from the Matrix Co-operative's Jagonari Centre in Whitechapel Road.

Community Theatre
Florian Beigel's design for the Half Moon Theatre in Mile End Road; the main theatre is on the left, a smaller childrens' theatre on the right.

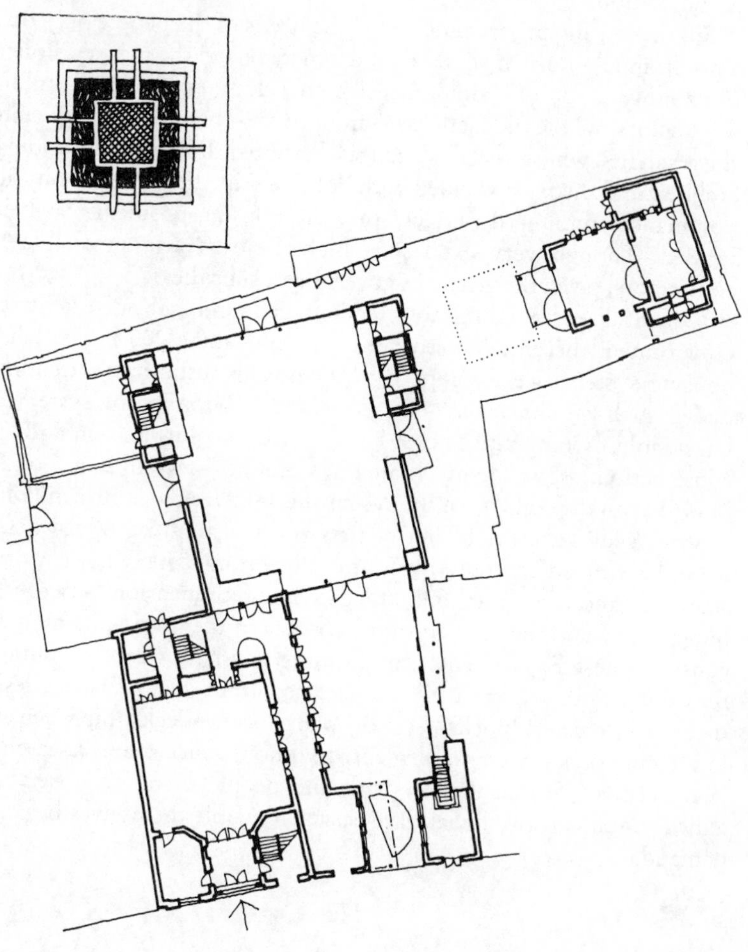

would ensure that housing was available to those who needed it. In the event, the gains were very real; the great housing estates were often an undoubted improvement on pre-war living conditions. And ideologically they were a conspicuous architectural statement that a new world was being born. Behind the physical change lay the implication that a social and economic change was also taking place. There was a strong conviction that physical reconstruction was in itself a means of achieving social reconstruction. 'Architecture or Revolution', Le Corbusier had said. 'Revolution can be avoided.'[6]

This was far from true. A new physical environment was no substitute for social revolution. The economic system, the class structure, the state and its ideological machinery remained much as before, operating as always according to the imperatives of capital accumulation.

So the housing programme suited the needs of the people only up to a point; much more, it suited the bureaucracy and the market. Policies of zoning and of comprehensive development suited building contractors' wholesale methods – and profits – better than they suited the residents, whose social fabric was disrupted. In high-rise buildings, architectural theory coincided with political expediency; their physical dominance announced publicly that the housing problem was being tackled. Though very expensive, high-rise was also profitable for contractors, given the generous government subsidies.

Industrialised building too, encouraged and subsidised by the Government, became lucrative. At one time some 200 industrialised housing systems were competing for housing authorities' attentions; under such circumstances efficiency and economies of scale were impossible. Competitive cost-cutting led to lower standards of construction, as was demonstrated in Canning Town in East London in 1968 with the collapse of the system-built tower block Ronan Point.

Space standards, the layout of flats and the minutiae of flat design were determined centrally by Whitehall, through the 'Parker Morris' standards and other methods; the gap in comprehension between the bureaucracy and the needs of those for whom they were planning was considerable. Experiments in housing design were encouraged regardless. Such was the drive to increase output, many suspect design theories – 'cluster' blocks, 'scissor' plans, access decks, high-density-low-rise estates – were implemented without much prior research or later feedback. Consultation with the people being rehoused was almost unknown till the late 1960s, when people themselves began to demand it.

In East London, one of the biggest ironies was that while the living environment was being reshaped, its architectural forms trumpeting the arrival of Utopia, the economic environment was being allowed to collapse. Over a twenty-year period, some 20,000 jobs were lost from the Docks themselves, together with many more in associated industries like ship repair, road haulage and manufacturing. Today unemployment among men of working age is around 9.7 per cent for England and Wales, and 12.0 per cent for Greater London. The corresponding figure for the East London borough of Tower Hamlets is 21.8 per cent.

A number of factors have contributed to this: the national long-term decline of traditional industries; the economic crisis of the 1970s, which hit all industry hard; the planning policies of successive governments since the war which have contributed to the relative decline of the Docks and failed to provide any alternative. By the time the Greater London Council made a belated attempt in the 1970s to prepare a co-ordinated plan for the Docklands area, it was too late. In 1979, the Thatcher government began to establish a completely different set of priorities for British industry in general and for East London in particular.

The only response capitalism has to a major crisis is to allow some capital to be destroyed. Thatcherite policy was to protect finance capital – specifically the City of London – at the expense of all other sectors, including industry, for which monetarism became a major burden. This, together with the erosion of the Welfare State, the abolition of the GLC along with its strategic planning role and its re-distributive policies, the virtual termination of the housing programme, and a spate of anti-working class legislation, has been to the great disadvantage of the East End of London.

It has also led to the second major physical change in the area since the War. In 1980 the London Docklands Development Corporation was set up to control the old Port of London Authority areas of Tower Hamlets, Newham and Southwark. Like the New Town corporations, the LDDC was able to override the local authorities. It was given sweeping powers to raise money, acquire sites, build infrastructure, take planning decisions and carry out development. Its task was simply 'the regeneration of the area'.

Given this wide brief and the LDDC's powers, to say nothing of huge amounts of public subsidy, it was one of the scandals of post-war planning that almost nothing was done to improve the employment situation for local people, or to confront local problems of housing need and social deprivation. Instead, an 'enterprise culture' was created in which commercial development, restricted as little as possible by planning controls, was encouraged. At the centre of the Isle of Dogs lies an Enterprise Zone, where the least control and the greatest inducements were exercised. Within this area, the construction of Canary Wharf came to symbolise the very essence of Thatcherite urban policy.

Canary Wharf looks like a small city centre, and indeed it lies at the centre of three existing working-class communities – the Isle of Dogs to the south and Limehouse and Poplar to the north. To them, given different circumstances, it could have brought appropriate employment, low-cost housing, community facilities, schools, improved health care and many other benefits. However, Canary Wharf is not a city centre, but an agglomeration of office blocks, and consequently has little relevance to local people's needs.

The Canada Square tower is a landmark all over London. It is a conspicuous statement that something significant has happened in East London, that 'regeneration' has occurred. Once again, the appearance belies the reality. Canary Wharf is merely a continuation of a long and discredited post-war trend, that of office speculation for profit. Socially, it changes nothing, regenerates nothing.

Architecturally, Canary Wharf is eclectic. Different blocks of offices have been designed by a variety of hands in a variety of styles, most of them consciously historicist. The styles are as 'traditional' as those of the post-war housing estates were assertively modern. Here again it seems that a point is being made. If modernism is equated, however debatably, with social progress, historicism expresses 'traditional values'.

Claiming 'traditional values' is a common tactic among the adventitious, and their architects have always been ready to respond. In the early nineteenth century gentlemen's clubs in Pall Mall were designed like Italian Renaissance palaces, implying that their upstart, bourgeois clients, elbowing their way into positions of power, were inheritors of a long historical tradition. Traditional-looking buildings – and by implication, what goes on in them – are easier for us all to accept, because they look as if they have been there a long time. Colonial architects have always used traditional forms to dignify the colonial process. There is a sense in which the implanted Canary Wharf is colonial.

In long-established towns, a wide variety of buildings reflects a wide variety of uses. The architectural style of Canary Wharf also changes from building to building, disguising the fact that behind the different façades lies a huge, monolithic office city. This kind of reticence is not confined to architecture. LDDC's recently published planning studies of the Isle of Dogs, Limehouse and Leamouth, contain almost no hint that millions of square feet of new office floorspace lie in the midst of the area.[7]

Clearly it was important to the developers to create commercial confidence in Canary Wharf. Monolithic land-uses and traditional design appeal to financial institutions, as ways of minimising investment risk. One of the design paradoxes, of course, is that the traditional-looking outer skins conceal very up-to-date buildings. The steel-framed construction, erected by 'fast-track' building methods, designed or supervised by American architects and contract managers, connotes speed and efficiency, and makes its own kind of appeal to investors.

The physical dominance of Canary Wharf is clearly intentional. The whole Docklands development was intended to be conspicuous, a demonstration that inner city regeneration could be achieved by the private sector. Having informed LDDC's thinking throughout the 1980s, this ideology became a general government policy in 1988 with the publication of 'Action for Cities'. The inner cities, it was stated, should be

> [P]laces where businessmen want to invest. They also want to be able to get on with their business; to press ahead with sensible development without unnecessary red tape; to keep their costs as low as possible, and not to be punished by excessive rate demands; to be made welcome. For this to happen, the inner cities need to rediscover the sense of civic pride which once united residents and business.[8]

The regenerative effect of private investment has not been proved by Canary Wharf. It has needed large amounts of direct and indirect public subsidy yet, even commercially, it has been less than successful, with large amounts of floorspace remaining unlet. Socially, it has been a failure, not only locally, but also for the wider community.

Since the war, both welfare capitalism and enterprise capitalism, in their different ways, have failed to measure up to the scale of East London's environmental problems.

The reasons for this are largely economic: East London's recent abrupt economic decline is one aspect of this; another is the gradual decline of Britain's traditional industries throughout this century; both are matters which capitalism has been unable to remedy. The economic regeneration of East London is a huge task, bound up as it is with the future of London as a whole and of all so-called 'post-industrial' cities, and is dependent ultimately on the creation of a productive, crisis-free economic system.

There are also political reasons for the failures. Even when the Docks were thriving, social inequalities marked out the East End as a deprived area. The inability of successive governments to respond adequately to the East End's environmental problems at any time in its history – during times of prosperity, times of decline and times of depression – merely emphasises how far apart the interests of capital and labour lie, and how powerful is the hegemony of the ruling class.

What prospects are there for a better urban environment in East London? The two successive waves of post-war urban intervention, first under welfare capitalism and then under Thatcherism, have raised as many problems as they have solved. They have had their own kind of achievements, but have destroyed much in the process.

East London has been left a wasteland, not only environmentally but economically and socially too; traditional methods of attempting positive urban change have been dismantled without being replaced. London now has no effective strategic planning authority, no public housing programme, no co-ordination of its transport systems, no programme of environmental improvement, no clear economic direction. Problematic as it is, this vacuum also provides an opportunity; so many wilfully destroyed institutions need to be replaced that they can now be reconstructed anew, to meet present and future rather than past needs. In inverse proportion to the official inaction, there is increasing unofficial debate about the future of London.

This debate is diverse. It encompasses long-standing pressure groups like Shelter, the Campaign for the Homeless in Central London, and Transport 2000, but also involves new campaigns around specific issues, such as the defence of Oxleas Wood or the building of the M11 link or ethnicity and housing in the Isle of Dogs. Books, magazines and newspapers, after a period of indifference, are now starting to address the issues with greater urgency.[9]

Some of these contributions are, perhaps inevitably, self-serving, but others raise important general issues and are beginning to allow an alternative picture of London's future to emerge, which lies neither with welfare capitalism nor with the enterprise culture, but is economically more pluralistic, and politically more democratic and participatory, than either of them.

Central to such a future would be a restructured economy, in which finance capital was not allowed to carry all before it, and industrial capital played a much bigger part. Industry would not be monolithic, but based on co-operation, devolved power, local organisation and control: instead of large blocks of capital, there would be multifarious small ones. Central too, would be the overhaul of property relations – especially in the property market and the building industry – aimed at breaking down the commodity fetishism which at present compromises all attempts to build for social need.

A new housing programme would be needed. There is a huge backlog of unimproved dwellings, a major residual problem of energy-inefficiency in the existing building stock, and an urgent need to expand the stock of low-cost rented accommodation on a scale unprecedented since the 1960s. The huge, co-ordinated programme needed to confront such problems would at the same time need to allow real democratic control of housing at local level, making much greater use of co-operative and communal solutions.

And it is essential to create a new planning system for London, in which effective action at strategic level does not preclude the devolution of real power to the local communities of which London is composed. A co-ordinated transport system, in which the overwhelming emphasis would be on public transport, energy conservation and environmental protection, would be high on the list of planning priorities. So would be the creation of a well-resourced and democratic system for the provision of community facilities, hospitals and schools.

If such changes were to take place within society as a whole, architecture would be dramatically affected. The profession, with its top-heavy, elitist structures, would be challenged. Architects would begin to surrender control of architecture to those who use it. Architecture would become less of a vehicle for bourgeois ideology. Buildings would begin to lose their role as exchange-values and their use-value would be strengthened.

Their appearance would change. The anti-social aspects of high-tech, commercially-conceived buildings – their expensive materials replete with embodied, non-renewable energy, their heavily-serviced environments creating a constant energy demand – would be recognised as anachronistic. In their place, sustainable buildings, using appropriate materials and renewable energy sources, would alter the appearance of London, and the quality of its everyday environment, very much for the better.

Here and there in East London, one can get glimpses of this other world, including hints of what its architecture might be like. As yet, produced within the confines of capitalism, and all the worse for it, they are only hints, but there are enough examples of humane, alternative architecture to demonstrate some of the key issues.

Spitalfields Health Centre in Brick Lane was designed by Avanti Architects as long ago as 1975. It incorporates a number of GPs and a dental practice, serving a population of 16,000. Built on a tight urban site in the middle of the 'old' East End, it is intended to act as a 'social condenser', that is, a focus for and stimulus to community activity. Its architectural form reflects this. It is a functional building whose purpose-designed forms are different from anything in the locality, and make it a recognisable local landmark; and at the same time it is respectful of the local context. The steep slopes of its cluster of roofs match the heights of the surrounding buildings: high on the Brick Lane frontage and against the now empty industrial building to the south; low towards the Asian restaurant on the north side and the housing at the rear.

Just round the corner, the Whitechapel Art Gallery in Whitechapel High Street is one of the East End's most distinguished buildings. Designed by Charles Harrison Townsend in 1901, it was a part, along with all those other settlements and institutes, of the cultural network devised by Victorian philanthropists for East London. Recently, in response to present-day cultural needs, its role was reappraised. A sensitive conversion of the building by Colquohoun and Miller was opened in 1985. The fine Art Nouveau façade remains, but the galleries behind have been substantially remodelled, to make greater use of natural lighting. The staircase has been moved, to improve circulation through the galleries. A lecture theatre, classroom, audio-visual facilities, a meeting room and a cafe have been provided in a discreet, and humanely designed extension at the rear. The changes have made the building much more accessible, in every sense, to the local community, and reflect the gallery's wide-ranging exhibition policy, to include among others the work of working-class, ethnic minority and Third World artists.

Also in 1985, not far away in Mile End Road, the Half-Moon Theatre was built. Funded by the GLC, ILEA, the Arts Council and other organisations, the Half-Moon represented a new direction in community theatre to which the architect, Florian Beigel, responded with an innovative design incorporating both a theatre and a young people's theatre on either side of a public courtyard. Accessibility was again the key; the free-flowing space, from street, to courtyard, to entrance, to auditorium, to acting area, was intended to present as few barriers as possible to the public. The close link between actors and audience was a consciously Brechtian conception, whereby the onlooker was to be confronted with the material realities of life. The auditorium is near the main road, but its high-tech walls, incorporating specially-developed glass panels, let in the light while reducing both traffic noise and heat-loss to an extraordinary degree.

It is typical of the fate of public sector community building under Thatcherism that the Half-Moon was never fully completed, had to be sold and has now changed its use. Another imaginative building by the same architect was never even started. This was a mini-Town Hall in Marsh Wall in the Isle of Dogs, designed by Beigel and by Nasser Golzari of Tower Hamlets Department of Architecture to house the Council's Isle of Dogs neighbourhood services. The architects took this community brief as far as possible. In consultation with the local residents, they designed a building to provide a series of public spaces, including a covered 'town square', an accessible council chamber and a multi-purpose hall suitable for anything from prayer meetings to physiotherapy. For festivals the building would be opened up to a larger public space outside. A pedestrian route would run through the site, a public garden was planned next to the existing houses in nearby Glen Terrace, and even the council offices in the building were designed to be converted to housing at a later date, if circumstances changed. For political reasons, however, this interesting scheme was replaced by a much more commercial office block designed by an outside architect, which the council eventually took over and named Jack Dash House.

All these examples consciously use the architectural language of Modernism, not only because it is functional but also for the ideological associations it has with social progress. There is another local building, however, which though just as progressive in concept, has an architecture much more difficult to categorise. This is the Jagonari Centre in Whitechapel Road, a community centre for Asian women in the Spitalfields area. On the main road is a high, gabled façade of sand-coloured brick, punctured only by a decorative doorway and some high-level windows protected with iron grilles. The appearance is slightly Islamic, but the building also fits well into the Victorian street scene of Whitechapel Road. Behind the façade, a complex of rooms of different sizes and types leads through to a garden at the rear. The firm of architects responsible for the building is described as having

> [I]dentified among its women clients an interest in connecting spaces and activities in buildings and in connecting the people who use the building. Thus ... large windows in an interior wall allow people to see activities inside a work shop.[10]

The building is the work of Matrix, the feminist architectural co-op well-known for the close working relationship it develops with the clients and users of its buildings. The Matrix architects

> [D]raw upon their own experience and that of their clients so that daily experiences rather than abstract concepts become the source material for design.[11]

The eclectic, almost historicist, architectural style of the Jagonari Centre has been criticised by some modernist architects who would otherwise share many of Matrix's progressive political views. This, however, is to miss the point. If architects are prepared to discover and respect the wishes of building-users to the extent that Matrix are, prescriptive or purist design decisions – of the kind often associated with Modernism – are inappropriate.

Genuine community architecture is about the empowerment of ordinary people to take control of their own environment. Matrix takes this task seriously, and does its best to break down the conventions of the bourgeois architectural process. The same applies to the architects involved in the growing self-build movement, whereby groups of people form into co-operatives physically to build their own houses or community centres, saving on labour costs and gaining a considerable sense of achievement. The architect most associated with this movement was the late Walter Segal who developed a timber-frame self-build system, flexible enough to provide for all kinds of space needs, and simple enough to be erected by unskilled labour. Several self-build projects have been carried out in East London, including the Isle of Dogs. Here they have enabled people to emerge from otherwise difficult housing conditions and stand as a permanent reminder of the alternatives that exist to the grossness of the area's commercial developments.

Notes

1 Nikolaus Pevsner, *An Outline of European Architecture*, Penguin, Harmondsworth 1943.
2 Karl Marx, *Capital*, Vol.1, Lawrence & Wishart, London 1977.

[3] Karl Marx and Friedrich Engels, *The German Ideology*, C.J. Arthur (ed), Lawrence & Wishart, London 1970.
[4] See, for example, Peter Hall, *The World Cities*, Weidenfeld & Nicolson, London 1966.
[5] *Ibid*.
[6] Le Corbusier, trans. Frederick Etchells, *Towards a New Architecture*, Architectural Press, London 1946.
[7] London Docklands Development Corporation, *Development Framework for the Isle of Dogs, Limehouse and Leamouth*, LDDC, London 1994.
[8] 'Action for Cities' (White Paper), HMSO, London 1988.
[9] See, for example, Andy Thornley (ed), *The Crisis of London*, Routledge, London 1992.
[10] Karen A. Frank, 'A Feminist Approach to Architecture', in Ellen Perry Berkeley (ed), *Architecture: A Place for Women*, Smithsonian Institute, Washington 1989.
[11] *Ibid*.

Hints of Open Country

Martin Hoyles

> Who, that has reason, and his smell,
> Would not 'mong roses and jasmin dwell,
> Rather than all his spirits choke,
> With exhalations of dirt and smoke
> And all th' uncleanness which does drown
> In pestilential clouds a pop'lous town?
> **Abraham Cowley** (1618–67) *The Garden*

Many public parks in the East End of London are under threat. The maintenance of all urban greenspace in Britain has been estimated to cost almost a billion pounds a year but local authorities have no statutory duty to provide parks. Compulsory competitive tendering and contracting out have led to less local authority involvement and these amenities are often the first to be cut when financial savings are to be made. Flower-beds are particularly vulnerable as they are labour intensive. Victoria Park in Hackney, for example, had a high reputation for its bedding displays but these have now been replaced by roses and other perennial flowering shrubs. One of Barking Park's main bedding areas is now largely grass, with a few beds of snapdragons. In Philips Park, Manchester, the beds have all been grassed over.

People have more access to the countryside, take holidays abroad and engage in other leisure pursuits. The Conservatives' emphasis on the private sphere has often led to an open ethos of selfishness and a frequent abandonment of public space. There is a crisis of confidence as to what public parks and open spaces are for. Often they are places of fear, where violence, theft and rape take place. There are particular threats to women, children and ethnic minorities. The decrease in park wardens, poor lighting and vandalism have contributed to a spiral of neglect and less regular use.

Do people no longer want or need the parks, or can they be renewed and reinvigorated?

Historical Background

Between the middle of the eighteenth and the middle of the nineteenth centuries, seven million acres of common land, the equivalent of ten English counties, was enclosed or privatised. This period corresponded with the industrial revolution and the massive growth of the population of towns (Manchester from 17,000 in 1760 to 400,000 in 1844; London from 750,000 in 1760 to 5 million in 1881).

The lack of contact with nature and the countryside was keenly felt but the initial impetus for creating green space was more drastic. There was nowhere to bury the dead. The graveyards and church crypts were full to bursting and many corpses were dug up before they had rotted. This led to the movement to build cemeteries, which preceded the first public parks. In 1830, the General Cemetery Company was established in London and the next year it purchased 54 acres at Kensal Green. The cemetery which was built there shows the influence of the eighteenth century landscape garden but a key incentive was profit. By 1839 the original shares had doubled in value.

Pleasure Gardens

There had been pleasure gardens in the eighteenth century which were open to the public but they were privately owned and usually charged for admission. Ranelagh Gardens in Chelsea, for example, charged one shilling for most of the eighteenth century, rising to two shillings in 1792. A protest against charging took place at the opening of the 1764 season at Vauxhall Gardens when a group of 50 young men tore up the railings in order to lay the walks open.

Many were built around wells, for instance Islington Spa, where there were mineral springs and people went to drink the water or meet in the tea gardens. There were often places to play games like bowls, skittles, archery or cricket, and also various performances such as fire-eating, juggling, tight-rope walking or acrobatics. Concerts and firework displays took place while people could also eat, drink and dance. The fact that many of these activities took place in the evening is revealing, as most of our modern public parks close at nightfall.

The gardens consisted of shaded walks and arbours, shrubs and fruit trees. At Sadler's Wells there were poplars and willows and sloping banks of flowers. Bagnigge Wells had formal walks with hedges of box and holly, a flower garden, elder bushes and other shrubs, and also gooseberry and currant bushes. Ranelagh Gardens, one of the most fashionable resorts, had gravel walks shaded by elms and yews and a flower garden. It was here, on 29 June 1764, that the eight-year-old Mozart played several of his own compositions on the harpsichord and organ.

Most of these pleasure gardens had ceased to exist by the end of the eighteenth century as the industrial revolution began to get under way. Land was needed to house the increasing population, to build roads and railways and also to bury the dead. The Spa Fields Pantheon, for example, was turned into a Church of England chapel in 1777 and the gardens converted into a burial ground. Cuper's Gardens were destroyed in order to build Waterloo Road, the southern approach to Waterloo Bridge, and Pancras Wells were taken over by the Midland Railway to build St Pancras Station.

Public Parks

The increasing population of the cities in the nineteenth century led to more enclosure of land to build houses. The danger of losing touch with the country was clearly seen by Engels:

> A town, such as London, where a man may wander for hours together without reaching the beginning of the end, without meeting the slightest hint which could lead to the inference that there is open country within reach, is a strange thing.

Agitation over the Reform Bill eventually led to the Municipal Reform Act of 1835 which created locally elected town councils, though with a very limited franchise. The 1848 Public Health Act eventually empowered councils to establish public walks and open spaces, a 'means of exercise for the middle and humbler classes', though it was not until 1860 that local authorities were allowed to levy rates to maintain such spaces.

The movement for public parks in the nineteenth century had many motives. In Edinburgh recreation in a park was thought to cure drunkenness; in Macclesfield, they considered that it led to a decrease in crime and a fall in the death rate; and after Leeds Botanical Gardens had been opened to the public on Sundays, drunkenness was said to have decreased and manners improved. The object of the Derby Arboretum, designed by John Loudon, was 'to give the people of Derby an opportunity to learn botany, to enjoy the pure air of the park as an alternative to the debasing pursuits and brutalising pleasure of drinking and cockfighting'.

There was also a shrewd economic motive for building parks,

connected with land speculation and development. Nash's improvement scheme for the West End of London, which included Regent's Park and St James's Park, had three aims, in this order: 'to assure the greatest possible revenue to the crown, secondly to add to the beauty of the metropolis and thirdly to study the health and convenience of the public'. The villas built next to Regent's Park gave the inhabitants the illusion of living in country houses and their values, in property terms, were correspondingly enhanced.

Victoria Park

Victoria Park, in the East End of London, originated from working-class pressure. In 1838, an organisation called the London Democratic Association was formed with a radical programme of reform. It found support amongst some of the poorest-paid workers in the East End; weavers, dockers and labourers. The society campaigned for a public park and recreation area. Land was eventually acquired in Hackney, called at first Tower Hamlets Park, later to become Victoria Park.

The East End of London, at this time, had the same population as the whole of Manchester, about 400,000. Industry and the new railways had brought smoke and pollution. Overcrowding, unemployment and poverty led to insanitary conditions, death and disease. In 1839, the newly-appointed Registrar-General of Births, Deaths and Marriages made his first report. It shows that the mortality rate in East London far exceeded that of the rest of the city. The appendix of the report contains recommendations from William Farr, a well known reformer and authority on public health:

> A park in the East End of London would probably diminish the annual deaths by several thousands and add several years to the lives of the entire population. The poorer classes would be benefited by these measures and the poor taxes reduced. But all classes of the community are directly interested, for the epidemics which arise in the east end of the town do not stay there, they travel to the west end and prove fatal in wide streets and squares: the registers show this.

Although the Municipal Reform Act was passed in 1835, it did not apply to London. There was no overall London local authority. The only authority to appeal to was Parliament or the Queen. In 1840, a local MP, George Frederick Young, got involved in the campaign. After a public meeting 'to advocate the formation of an East London

Park', he was given the task of drawing up a petition to Queen Victoria, who was then 21 years old and in the third year of her reign.

The petition refers to the 'Poor People, closely crowded in confined districts', who 'have no open spaces in the vicinity of their humble dwellings for air, exercise or healthful recreation; circumstances which produce the most painful effects on their physical and moral condition.' It continues: 'From official documents it appears that the mortality in towns, in general, from epidemic diseases, is double that of agricultural districts. But, in the neighbourhood for which we implore your majesty's gracious interposition, the mortality is more than double that of those parts of the Metropolis which are more effectually ventilated. Fever is constantly prevailing in these places, which are indeed declared on competent authority to be "the main sources and seats of the Fevers of the Metropolis".' After the petition was circulated throughout Tower Hamlets for a few weeks it collected more than 30,000 signatures.

Other reasons for creating a park were put forward. It would reduce drinking and gambling and it would raise land values and rents. The tone of the East End would be raised by attracting middle-class people to live in the area, as a local magistrate, George Offer, explained:

> To land and house owners in this Eastern district it is of the greatest importance that emigration to the west should be checked by providing a rational and wholesome place of recreation similar to those enjoyed by the Northern and Western districts. A Public Park, surrounded by good houses, would attract wealthier residents, improving the tone and behaviour of the area.

Construction of the Park

By 1841, the decision to build the park had been taken by the government and it was decided to sell some Crown property to raise the money to finance it. It was initially a royal park, though in 1887 it lost its royal title and was financed from the rates. The workers who built it were paid 3s 3d a day if they were unskilled labourers and 5s 5d if skilled workers, such as bricklayers, carpenters and painters.

The park was designed by James Pennethorne, who had worked with Nash on Regent's Park and the post of chief horticulturist was given to Samuel Curtiss, on the recommendation of William Hooker. Pennethorne envisaged the park in two distinct halves, divided by class. One half would contain lawns and flower-beds, winding paths and clumps of trees, with its western side surrounded by large middle-class houses whose ground rents would help finance the park.

The sites for these villas were advertised for sale but not one was actually sold. The wealthy were not convinced of the desirability of living in the East End, even with a park next door! The other half of the park, to the east, would be mostly open grass for working-class games and recreation.

Nothing much was done till 1845 when the park fences were erected and Curtiss started his planting. He had to cover 16 acres with tree-clumps, at about 2,000 trees to the acre. The 32,000 trees cost £640 and he also bought 400 larger trees, 'for dotting about the park', at a cost of one shilling each. He needed 240 elms and 120 limes for the drives and 550 hornbeams to screen the canal. As the *Illustrated London News* of 3 January 1846 recorded: '70-80 men are employed daily, over 10,000 trees and shrubs are planted, the avenues lined with elms and hornbeams, intermixed with laurels, chestnuts and the true cockspur thorn.'

The park never had an official opening. Local people just took it over in 1845 while it was being built. As Nathan Cole later wrote: 'They look on the park as their own property.'

Sport and Horticulture

The park was certainly popular and surprise was expressed in the *Illustrated London News* of 2 May 1846, at the small amount of damage done by its working-class visitors:

> We are happy to find that this newly-formed 'Public Walk' is progressing well, so as already to afford the Eastern inhabitants of the Metropolis an amusement to which they have, till lately, been strangers ... We may state that on Good Friday, the new park was visited by 25,000 persons, and by a considerably greater number on Easter Monday. Excellent order was kept and very trifling injury or damage was done.

The Rev. Suter of All Saints, Bethnal Green, thought that use of the park prevented suicide and praised it in glowing terms: 'It is our sanatorium for invalids, the gymnasium for our young men, the playground for our children, and the only place where our unemployed can go, walk and sit and enjoy God's fresh air without paying for it, and thus be saved, in many cases, from the despair that leads to suicide.'

People also came in their carriages from the West End to visit the park. In 1851, music was allowed in the park as a result of a petition drawn up by 'the inhabitants of Hackney, Old Ford and Bethnal

Green', and in 1865 a permanent bandstand was erected. When the band played, crowds of 100,000 might be present in the park. On Whit Monday 1892 the number of recorded visitors reached a total of 303,516.

The park was used for sports and recreation, such as cricket, rounders, archery and boating. Football was not allowed until 1888. A gymnasium was built and, when the lake was constructed, swimming became very popular. It was allowed between 4.00 am and 8.00 am in the summer, though only for men and boys. As many as 25,000 went swimming on a single day. The swimming was in the nude, swimming costumes not yet having been invented. A request by a group of women for a tennis court was turned down.

The flower-beds were also very popular and Victoria Park became famous for its bedding-out schemes which were displayed without railings, unlike in Hyde Park where they were kept behind bars. Carpet-gardening became fashionable, using plants such as coleus and various cacti to form a continuous pattern like a carpet. By the end of the century, 200,000 plants were being bedded out annually.

There was a friendly rivalry between the professional gardeners of the park and the local amateurs, as J.J. Sexby records: 'At Victoria Park the hard-working artisan is a bit of a horticultural critic in his way. Somehow, in the small back gardens and crowded yards he manages to rear many a choice specimen, so that the flowers in the adjoining park have to be kept up to the mark.' Every spring, after the young plants had been bedded out, the remainder were given away free to anyone who asked for them.

Political Demonstrations

The other main use of the park, besides sport and horticulture, was for politics. In 1848, Victoria Park witnessed the final great Chartist demonstration in support of the third presentation of the Charter which contained two million signatures. On Whit Monday a demonstration was called to take place in the park, to be followed by a march through London linking up with other contingents of Chartists. The Government took it very seriously, reacting with organised force and turning Victoria Park into an armed camp. Some 1,600 foot police were stationed in the park, 500 of them armed with cutlasses, 100 mounted police and 500 recalled police pensioners. A large detachment of cavalry also stood by. Even the park-keepers were sworn in as special police and issued with cutlasses. Facing this threat of violence, the organisers tried to cancel the demonstration but people had already begun to assemble and speeches had started. The demonstrators were charged by the mounted police and this, along with torrential rain, eventually dispersed the crowd.

A part of the park called the Forum was traditionally used for open-air public meetings, whether religious or political. Famous socialists, such as Henry Hyndman, Bernard Shaw, William Morris, John Burns, Tom Mann and Ben Tillett, were frequent speakers. William Morris wrote to his daughter Jenny in 1886: 'Eastward Ho to Victoria Park. It is rather a pretty place with water (though dirty) and lots of trees. Had a good meeting, spoke for an hour in a place made noisy by other meetings near, also a brass band not far off.' South of the Forum was a large assembly place used for mass meetings of dockers and other industrial workers. Suffragettes also demonstrated here. It was to this spot too that Oswald Mosley was leading his fascists in 1936 when they were stopped in Whitechapel by a counter-demonstration.

Contemporary Use

One of the key controversies today is about how to structure the public park for contemporary use. There is clearly no single solution but it would seem desirable for each local authority to have a variety of provision. Vast expanses of grass, as in Barking's Mayesbrook Park, for example, are clearly cheap to maintain but they do not encourage different activities.

There is also the issue of proximity to open space. Some parts of the East End are distinctly lacking in green areas and there is a pressing need to create new parks. In *Nature Areas for City People* (1990) Jacklyn Johnston writes: 'The exact distance from a nature area that researchers have found to be significant varies but what is clear is that people need contact with wildlife on an everyday basis and on a scale which fits in with their everyday living pattern: most people need a nature area within a five or ten minute walk of home.' In her handbook, produced by the London Ecology Unit, which should be required reading for every local councillor, the author goes on to deal with how to establish, manage and protect nature areas, also discussing their educational and recreational use.

Environmental Gardens

A growing interest in nature conservancy and ecology has led to the idea of the natural park, like that in Camley Street, behind King's Cross station which is internationally renowned, visited by 10,000 pupils a year and for the time being saved from demolition by developers. With the nearby canal, it is a haven for wildlife and plants, and its existence encourages an interest in natural history amongst those who visit.

In Newham's newest parks there are 'natural' areas with trees and plants which give food and shelter to encourage birds, insects and other wildlife. The 118 acre Beckton District Park, for example, funded by the London Dockland Development Corporation and opened in 1981, has extensive natural shrub areas, a woodland walk and a large artificial lake. Barking Park has a similar area with its boating lake. Likewise, the new Forest Lane Park in Forest Gate is being developed as a centre for environmental education for children.

This kind of development could be introduced into other parks. Some already have such areas, wild gardens which stimulate the growth of a variety of more unusual plants. It is not necessarily the case, however, that such a project is labour-saving, as it has to be carefully managed, not just allowed to run wild.

City Farms

A similar attempt to bring the countryside into the town is represented by city farms. They began in 1972 with the opening of Kentish Town City Farm, which is financed by Camden Council. There are now about 20 such farms in London.

Newham City Farm in Custom House was founded in the late 1970s and in the 1980s received capital funding from the LDDC. Now it is financed by Newham Council and run by the Play Section of the Leisure Services Department. It is visited by around 50,000 people every year. The manager of the farm maintains that local community involvement helps to minimise vandalism but there is still a warning which advertises the use of anti-vandal paint. On the other hand, Plashet Park Zoo, in the north of the borough, is regularly vandalised, with animals stolen and even killed. It has a derelict appearance and it is difficult to locate the entrance to the Butterfly House. A park-keeper told me that this park has the worst reputation in the borough. There are no informational leaflets available and the cafe buildings in the middle of the park are boarded up and covered in graffiti.

City farms not only introduce town people to farm animals and activities such as horse-riding and milking, but also to their interaction with vegetation, types of food, etc. They are very popular with children and well used by schools. A section of a large park could be converted to this type of use.

Top: Security measure at Newham City Farm, Custom House
Below: Local Community involvement helps to minimise vandalism at Newham City Farm

Allotments

There are usually long waiting lists for local authority allotments, for instance, two years in Stepney. A recent television programme about this area showed how various women used the allotments for growing flowers and vegetables and also for creating a wild garden. Gardening was often a family activity and illustrated the multicultural make-up of the area.

During the two world wars, allotments became essential to the war effort. In the First World War their number rose from about half a million in 1913 to one and a half million by the end of the war. In the Second World War numbers nearly doubled from about 815,000 in England and Wales in 1939 to about 1,500,000 in 1945 when 4,000 local societies were affiliated to the National Society of Allotment and Leisure Gardeners.

Today the number of affiliations is only about a third of that figure, with just over 100,000 members, though in 1988 the allotment movement began to grow for the first time since the Second World War. In that year there were about half a million allotment holders. They have to be ever vigilant, however, for even on statutory, protected sites allotments are continually under threat. In 1987 the National Society was approached by over 60 local societies objecting to proposed changes of land use which threatened their allotments.

If there is a shortage of allotments, why not create more in a local park? It would certainly be one way of saving money on maintenance and would even provide a small income. It could be organised on a co-operative basis by a kind of garden club, producing different styles of garden, like the Culpeper Garden in Islington. This kind of activity might be very popular for those with no garden or those who have just acquired one.

The Culpeper Community Garden is situated in the heart of London, near Chapel Market (1 Cloudesley Road, N1 0EJ). It was designed from a triangle of derelict ground in 1982 and there are now 46 plots, most held by individuals or families who have no garden. Two schools and a playgroup also feature among its organic gardeners and three plots are reserved for the disabled. In addition to the plots, there is a pond with a cascade, a small lawn, some formal planting and a nature area. The garden provides the opportunity for relaxation of an informal kind: for some it is a regular lunching place, for others a sunbasking spot. There are also barbecues and parties for senior citizens, children and local residents. The Culpeper Community Garden Association is a registered charity, run by a committee of eleven members elected annually. The site is owned by Islington Council who, along with the Cripplegate Foundation, fund a gardener. She works three days a week. There are problems with vandalism and theft but when I visited it in May 1994, it looked in very good shape.

Education

One of the difficulties schools face is the lack of space and what exists is under threat. The National Playing Fields Association estimates that as many as 300 school playing fields are currently under threat. Many schools have no green areas. According to the Government's own figures, 15 per cent of primary schools have grounds which are almost entirely hard-surfaced. Its own bulletin 'The Outdoor Classroom' (1990) suggests many uses for school grounds, including vegetable plots, herb gardens, wild flower meadows, ponds, butterfly gardens, flower-beds, orchards and copses. But with the school population set to increase by over a million in the next fifteen years, there is likely to be less room for such developments, not more.

Learning Through Landscape is an organisation that partners the World Wildlife Fund and in their recent report, 'Special Places, Special People', the author, Wendy Titman, researched 12 primary schools and 216 pupils. The children found tarmac and concrete boring and what they wanted were trees, grass and chances to develop imaginative play. She quotes the evidence of environmental psychologists that landscaped and well-managed grounds produce healthier and more caring individuals.

Several schools in Newham have nature areas, including Dersingham infants and St Bonaventure's secondary school, and many more visit East Ham Nature Reserve for their environmental work. As it is always fully booked, however, there is, according to Archer and Yarham, 'an urgent need for another educational nature reserve in the borough'. Similarly, pupils from Barking and Dagenham schools regularly visit The Chase Nature Reserve and a number have their own nature areas such as Richard Alibon and Dorothy Barley junior schools. Grants for school nature areas are available from the Nature Conservancy Council for England (English Nature). Free advice on design and management is available from the London Ecology Unit.

Another key educational function of parks was envisaged by John Loudon. In 1811 he presented a scheme to the Linnean Society for a 'living museum', a garden of about 100 acres, containing every known species and variety of plant. The collection of plants would be arranged so as to appeal to the general public as well as the scientist. Nowadays, it is rare to find any plants with labels in public parks. On a recent visit to West Ham Park, run by the Corporation of London, I found only one, and that was because it was a tree that had been planted by the mayor!

Multicultural Gardens

'Every known species' is a tall order! But the Royal Botanic Garden in Edinburgh, for example, has the largest collection of Chinese plants outside China. What a local park could concentrate on might be the geographical origins of a selection of plants. There could be a display of plants from India, for example, as in the Asian Horticulture Centre in Derby, or from the West Indies, as in Burgess Park, Southwark. This could stimulate interest in the historical introduction of plants, colonialism and the plant-hunters, economic botany, aesthetic and utilitarian uses of plants, medicinal and culinary practices.

In 1984, the Newham Allotment and Wasteland Project planned to sow emmer, a bearded wheat grown by ancient Egyptians and neolithic peoples, on part of the wasteground between Sarah Bonnell's sports hall and the Civic Centre car park in Stratford. As Julian Agyeman writes:

> A 'cultural ecological garden' is a place where flowers, ferns, trees and vegetables representing pupils' countries of origin, can be grown. This provides a valuable ecological, cultural and educational resource for parents, pupils and the local community. Such plants as red hot pokers and stonecrops (Africa), passion flower and pampas grass (South America), jasmine and buddleia (China), mullein (Turkey) and a wide range of Mediterranean aromatics (rosemary, sage and lavender) are hardy in Britain and are readily obtainable through the Royal Horticultural Society and other outlets.

A list of plants which could be used to develop a cultural ecological garden can be obtained from the Black Environment Network, c/o National Council for Voluntary Organisations, 26 Bedford Square, London, WC1B 3HU.

There is also an opportunity to create gardens of different styles representing various national traditions. Obvious examples are a Japanese garden, Chinese (e.g. in Leicester), Italian and Swiss (e.g. in Bedfordshire). More revolutionary would be to construct an Arab, Aztec or American Indian garden. This would help us to see our gardening in cross-cultural perspective.

Garden History

Another educational function would be served by looking at our native gardening tradition. This is often represented as consisting mainly of the landscape garden. Clearly, this would be difficult to recreate! Anyway, there are plenty of existing examples for people to visit. But a Tudor knot garden would be relatively easy to reconstruct and it could be done in a small space, as in the churchyard of the Museum of Garden History in Lambeth Palace Road. Similarly, it would be possible to create a traditional English cottage garden, introducing the typical plants that it contained, or William Robinson's idea of the wild garden.

Victorian bedding-out is fairly familiar as it persists in many local authority parks and roundabouts. But more could be done to relate its introduction to the social conditions of the times – industrial and domestic pollution, the creation of new kinds of glass, colonialism and plant-hunting. This could be tied up with contemporary environmental issues such as lead poisoning and carbon monoxide pollution.

Cemeteries

Garden cemeteries are another historical resource related to public parks. These can serve not only as a place of recreation but also of education (e.g. famous people buried in them, architecture, Victorian way of death, plants, wildlife). Abney Park Cemetery in Stoke Newington was originally laid out as an arboretum in 1840, with each tree labelled for the 'edification of the working classes'. Overgrown and neglected for many years, it has recently been taken over by a Friends of Abney Park Cemetery Trust, under a management agreement with the local council, and is being developed as a wildlife site.

Similarly, people visit Highgate Cemetery to see the Victorian mausoleums, the trees and undergrowth, as well as Karl Marx's grave. Many old cemeteries now have organisations which help to maintain them, such as the Friends of Tower Hamlets Cemetery Park who manage the wooded 27 acre site for nature conservation, history and education. East Ham Nature Reserve organises activities in East London's largest churchyard. There is a fully accessible nature trail and visitor centre, wildlife display and handling table, specialist natural history advice and seasonal guided walks.

Gardens for the Disabled

One of the most successful modern developments has been the creation of gardens for the disabled though on a limited scale. At the beginning of the eighteenth century when Repton was disabled and confined to a wheelchair, he designed raised beds but it is only fairly recently that they have been introduced to public parks.

Other improvements involve making safer paths with tapping-rails, handrails and tactile junction indicators and providing braille labels, audio cassettes and embossed maps. There are two demonstration gardens in London for disabled people run by the Disabled Living Foundation (380/384 Harrow Road, London, W9 2HU), in Battersea Park and at Syon Park. Another, in Dulwich Park, was begun in 1986, planned and built by disabled people. There is also one at the Royal Horticultural Society's gardens at Wisley, near Woking in Surrey.

Audrey Upton and Peter Thoday of the Department of Horticulture at Bath University have produced *A Bibliography of Horticulture and Out-Door Amenities for the Handicapped and Disadvantaged*, referencing nearly 300 books and articles. There is also an illustrated book called *Landscape Design for Disabled People in Public Open Space* which deals with access, provision and design. The authors, Rowson and Thoday, argue against separate gardens for the disabled and for 'integrated landscape provision'.

An organisation called Horticultural Therapy (Goulds Ground, Vallis Way, Frome, Somerset, BA11 3DW) which was established in 1978, has a comprehensive collection of printed material on gardening for disabled people. They produce a quarterly magazine called *Growth Point* which includes articles on subjects such as planning a garden for children with special needs, how horticulture could be used by community-based services for people with mental health problems, and advice for those with special needs seeking a job in horticulture.

The Fieldfare Trust (67A The Wicker, Sheffield, S3 8HZ) gives advice on facilities for disabled people and more information can also be obtained from The Greater London Association for Disabled People (336 Brixton Road, London, SW9 7AA). The Advisory Committee for Blind Gardeners, working with the support of the South Regional Association for the Blind, has produced guidelines to be borne in mind when designing gardens. They make it clear that they do not support the idea of gardens exclusively for people with visual impairment but say that 'all gardens should be designed with the enjoyment of everyone alike in mind'. Attached to the guidelines is a list of fragrant plants recommended by the Royal Horticultural Society. There is a directory of scented gardens and gardens suitable for disabled people. This has been prepared for the Royal National Institute for the Blind and lists over one hundred parks and gardens throughout the country.

Top: Vandalism in Plashet Park, Newham
Below: Disabled people planting daffodil bulbs in Plashet Park, Newham

Sometimes these gardens appear to be tokenistic. Plashet Garden for the Blind, for example, which was opened in 1976, has some scented shrubs but no braille labels or any other aid for the blind. The irony of the visual notice at the entrance has been spotted, as the graffiti reads 'they won't be able to see this so it's here'! The garden was deserted when I visited it in the autumn of 1994 but in the south of the park I came across an animated band of disabled people from Greenhill Day Centre. They were gardening in a small triangle of lawn, digging holes and planting daffodil bulbs. The group planned to return in the spring.

Festivals

Concerts and festivals are still popular and could well be held more often in parks. Admittedly, there is the problem of the unpredictable weather but fairs still manage to draw large crowds. Local arts councils could be drawn in to organise music, dance and drama festivals. Medieval plays, after all, were performed in the open air on moveable stages and spectators would walk round from one stage to the next. Finsbury Park, in north London, does something similar with its annual summer concert providing four stages for music and comedy acts. Likewise, bandstands can still serve a variety of uses, not just for brass bands, as shown by the one on Parliament Hill. Nearby, the Kenwood open air concerts are a great success story.

Bonfires and fireworks are common on November 5th, for example on Primrose Hill, but could well take place on other occasions, accompanied by refreshments, stalls, clowns, acrobats, magicians, etc. The Greenwich Festival, for example, opens with a firework display. Fairs are still held during holiday periods on open spaces, such as Wanstead Flats and Barking Park.

On a more private level, gardens could be used for celebrations such as children's birthday parties, weddings and anniversaries. When I visited Birmingham Botanic Gardens, a wedding reception was taking place on the lawn below the conservatory.

Politics and Religion

The long tradition of political meetings and demonstrations held in parks could well be revived. The television dominates national elections but there is no reason why candidates standing for election should not hold open air meetings in parks. It would be even more worthwhile for local elections which are hardly covered at all by television. There could be hustings at which the local candidates would speak and answer questions, accompanied by stalls with political material and refreshments.

Similarly with religious meetings and festivals. Sunday schools used to congregate in local parks. On Whit Monday in Sheffield's Meersbrook Park, for example, long processions from all the chapels would wend their way along roads lined with large numbers of people and go into their own roped-out enclosures. Each Sunday School had it own banner and the afternoon was devoted to sports with each chapel having its own area for games and races. Today, various youth organisations sometimes use parks for similar events.

Sports

Sport is a major activity in public parks and open spaces. One of the problems, however, is that it is largely a male preserve. Women and girls often feel alienated. It is like the school playground where the whole of the middle part is normally taken up by boys playing football, with the girls congregating round the edges. There is a need to 'feminise' public space, making some of it safer and less aggressive. More facilities for 'female' sports are also required. Newham 'parks for sport' policy is trying to do something about this problem and residents are encouraged to get in touch with the sports development team: 'We work anywhere we can run a session. You only have to ask. Young or old, black or white, men or women, people with a disability, there is something for everyone – all year round.'

It may be necessary to create single sex areas. The free open air swimming pools made from natural ponds on Hampstead Heath, for example, are very popular. There is one solely for women, one for men and one that is mixed.

Play areas in parks have often changed, with the introduction of adventure playgrounds and safer surfaces. Lappset, from Kettering in Northamptonshire, provide a large range of play equipment suitable for children of all ages and physical abilities. They can create environments accessible to wheelchairs and pushchairs. Too often, however, play areas are found to be derelict, with missing swings and an air of desolation. It may be that the best design is one which can be changed fairly often, to fit in with crazes and fashions, such as skate-boarding, roller-skating, and so on.

Hooky and Nooky

A friend of mine told me how she used to play hooky from her school in Leeds and indulge in nooky in Roundhay Park. According to a report in *The Guardian* of 5 August 1994 'sex and drinking in a local park formed the main social activity of the 15 and 16-year olds' who were interviewed by Julia Hirst from Sheffield Hallam University. She comments that sex in the park tends to be nasty, brutish and short. One girl dreamed wistfully of being able to make love in a bed: 'I'd take all my clothes off and there'd be loads of time.'

Though not advocating truancy, it is probably preferable that children play hooky in parks than in shopping malls. It might be possible to set up projects in the park which would encourage truants to take part, rather like free schools. They could do certain school subjects such as sport, art, gardening, botany, history and geography in what they might think were more congenial surroundings than their school building.

Books, such as those produced by Southgate Publishers from Crediton in Devon, would be helpful in this context. As well as those subjects already mentioned, they have published environmental education books on maths, English, science and technology. Their series *In the School Grounds* shows the range of practical work possible in playgrounds, all related to the National Curriculum.

There should certainly be the opportunity for nooky. It is surely one of the main functions of parks to celebrate love. One of the few writers to recognise this is George Chadwick in *The Park and the Town* (1966) where he writes: 'The need for withdrawn places for seclusion and courtship is an essential which is totally ignored by the modern town in general and by the design of its public places in particular.'

Walking and Cycling

Perhaps the main use of public parks is always going to be simply walking. It is the exercise and relaxation many need after work or to escape from the house. One way to maximise use for this purpose is to make a walk through the park the normal way of getting from A to B. This may involve more entries and exits. Sponsored walks and runs could also be organised in parks. The fact that many people take dogs for walks in parks means that facilities have to be provided and fences erected to protect children's play areas.

There has been some progress recently in making cycle routes. It should be possible to make some of them continue through parks without inconveniencing pedestrians. It is perhaps a sign of the times that Cambridge's experiment of providing free green bicycles has just been abandoned. The original white bike scheme in Amsterdam in the 1960s, on the other hand, proved very successful.

Organisation and Control
When the working classes were admitted to parks in the nineteenth century, reporters continually sounded amazed that there was so little vandalism. In 1840, after the opening day of the Derby Arboretum for the working-class inhabitants, the local paper reported: 'Not a single tree or shrub has been destroyed.' The next day, after the children's celebration, they dispersed as 'orderly and quietly as if they were retiring from a place of worship'.

It would be naive, however, to think that vandalism is not a major problem today. The toilets in Plashet Park are threatened with closure because of vandalism and the wire fences round the tennis courts in Barking Park are continually being torn open to let people get in. Conway and Lambert (1993) trace the origins of this problem to the 'removal of many cast-iron railings and park gates during the Second World War. Without their gates and railings, parks could not be secured at night and this opened the way to a major shift in the way parks were treated.' Some way of breaking the vicious circle of neglect is required. The initial effort almost definitely needs resources, though these may be able to be mobilised on a community basis, firstly, to clean up derelict parks and secondly, to maintain and develop them. Thereafter, if people start coming back in numbers, part of the problem will be solved, for it is their desertion and abandonment that often leads to the destruction.

Numerous organisations exist in the East End to look after open spaces, plant trees, bulbs and wild flowers, and learn about the natural environment. Their activities are published regularly in 'Wildlife East' which contains an East London Directory of local environmental groups. It is produced by volunteers working with staff from The Environment Trust and London Wildlife Trust.

Research carried out by Suki Pryce in 1987 shows that some community groups manage the landscape to a much higher standard than that of most local authorities, that community-managed landscapes tend to be richer in horticultural interest, and 'in the case of community gardens, sites also tend to be much richer in features and styles, and to be more zany, "fun" and interesting in general'. She also found that communities who look after their own landscapes treat them 'much better than the "public" normally treats local authority open space'.

It is probable, however, that there also need to be personnel, women as well as men, actively engaged on a regular basis working in the parks. West Ham Park has one woman gardener but that is out of a complement of 15 staff, as the park is well funded by the Corporation of London. Horticultural skills as well as social and educational expertise is required from these workers. This is not to take away the responsibility of local people to help in creating a congenial atmosphere and deciding how the parks should be used. The more actively involved they are, the safer the parks will be. Those who run the parks should be held accountable in an accessible way.

The fact that there is so much interest in private gardening could surely be harnessed to more public, communal events and activities. Many new gardeners need help and advice as to which plants to grow and what seeds to sow. What they see in public parks could aid that process if there were labels, more information, advice centres, exchanges of plants and cuttings, garden waste recycling and flower shows. They could also have an input into which trees and shrubs are planted in the parks, how they are arranged, what gardening styles are preferred.

Clearly, there is a need for much greater interaction, not only between local people but also between the local council and the people, and within the council between different departments. If some of the projects I have mentioned are to take place, it will require the active co-operation of each borough's Parks' Department, Education, Social Services, Sports, Arts and Leisure Services.

Advance planning is essential. If the East Thames Corridor is to be regenerated, parks need to be integrated into any development plan. Philips Park in east Manchester, right next to an urban renewal area which was being developed for the Olympic bid, was virtually ignored in the plans, when it could have been a focal point for redevelopment. By contrast, in Barcelona, the parks and open spaces were seen as fundamental to the city's Olympic bid, with a ten-year regeneration programme as part of the preparations.

Traversing the Great Divide: The North London Line and East London

Bruce Jerram and Richard Wells

This chapter argues that the much-derided North London Line (NLL) could deliver significant economic and amenity benefits to areas of East London, by developing as a major tourist and leisure asset for London as a whole. The NLL runs from Richmond in the west of London to North Woolwich in the east, with an adjoining but separate spur of the line branching off from Gospel Oak eastwards to Barking. Beginning and ending beside the Thames, the line is unique both in providing an orbital rail route through outer London north of the river, and as an overground service that has retained a strongly localised character. Our stylised map (see p252) indicates the appeal of this circuit, which links the better-known visitor attractions of the west and north to localities in the east of comparable interest, both actual and potential. Such a representation of the line challenges the symbolic polarisation of London into a rich, desirable west and a poor, dull, possibly dangerous east: but these deep-seated perceptions are also a pre-emptive threat to the serious consideration of our proposals. For however vaguely defined, East London is almost invariably discussed *only* in terms of a depressed or deprived area, demanding external intervention in the form of massively expensive 'regeneration' and 'urban renewal' programmes. Relatively modest investment in existing assets is not considered when the area is seen as a problem, with nothing positive to offer. In our view, these perceived negativities, as well as reflecting some grim realities on the ground, are also an aspect of divisive social processes which serve to isolate the east of London socially, economically, and culturally from the west.[1] Similar dynamics are at work, masking special interests and

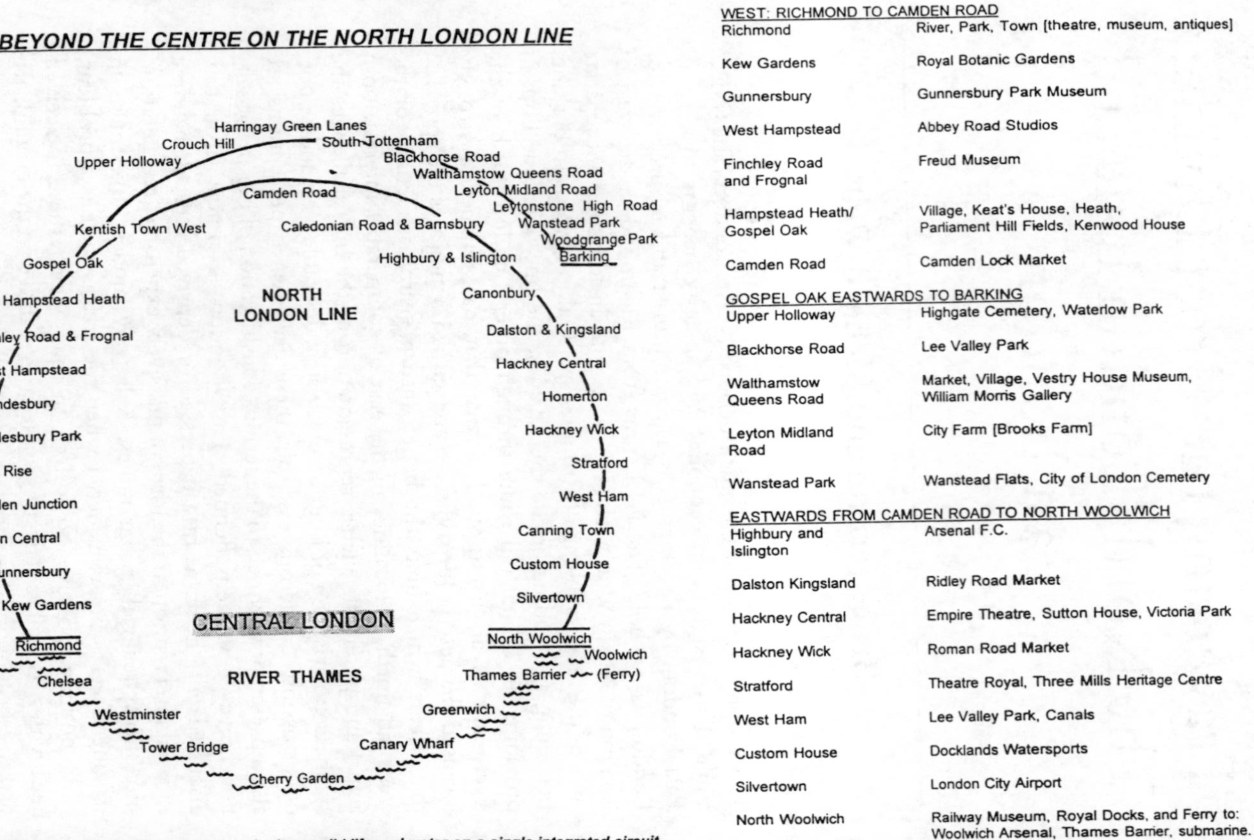

WEST: RICHMOND TO CAMDEN ROAD	
Richmond	River, Park, Town [theatre, museum, antiques]
Kew Gardens	Royal Botanic Gardens
Gunnersbury	Gunnersbury Park Museum
West Hampstead	Abbey Road Studios
Finchley Road and Frognal	Freud Museum
Hampstead Heath/ Gospel Oak	Village, Keat's House, Heath, Parliament Hill Fields, Kenwood House
Camden Road	Camden Lock Market
GOSPEL OAK EASTWARDS TO BARKING	
Upper Holloway	Highgate Cemetery, Waterlow Park
Blackhorse Road	Lee Valley Park
Walthamstow Queens Road	Market, Village, Vestry House Museum, William Morris Gallery
Leyton Midland Road	City Farm [Brooks Farm]
Wanstead Park	Wanstead Flats, City of London Cemetery
EASTWARDS FROM CAMDEN ROAD TO NORTH WOOLWICH	
Highbury and Islington	Arsenal F.C.
Dalston Kingsland	Ridley Road Market
Hackney Central	Empire Theatre, Sutton House, Victoria Park
Hackney Wick	Roman Road Market
Stratford	Theatre Royal, Three Mills Heritage Centre
West Ham	Lee Valley Park, Canals
Custom House	Docklands Watersports
Silvertown	London City Airport
North Woolwich	Railway Museum, Royal Docks, and Ferry to: Woolwich Arsenal, Thames Barrier, submarine.

Walks, sports, theatres, markets, museums, heritage, wild life and water on a single integrated circuit.

undermining public transport provision, when the NLL is referred to only in dismissive terms – as uneconomic, unreliable, threatened with closure. The insidious effects of these negative assumptions, as well as the real problems, need to be acknowledged before more positive arguments can plausibly be brought to bear.

Missing Links

'Italians don't grow up wanting to be engine drivers' proclaims the lettering on the hoarding near Barking station, beside a dramatic depiction of a yellow Fiat sportscar. The implications of the slogan may in reality be false or damaging, in relation to trains and cars, or Italians and the British, or growing up: but it exploits an unease that is genuine enough. In Britain today to propose the social, economic, and even imaginative potential of a 150 year-old overground railway line, whose low-capacity carriages clatter along a twenty-five mile loop through the outer suburbs of western, northern and eastern London without ever approaching the centre, stopping every few minutes at obscure and often dilapidated platforms, does at times feel a bit foolish; as if we were ... trainspotters, with ideas above our station. Add a perspective which links the prospects for this line with those of a notional entity as persistently disparaged as East London, and our project may indeed appear wistfully displaced, irreducibly marginal.

To make matters worse, the twentieth-century operation and the current state of the NLL make up a particularly sad case.[2] Linked to the great trading and commercial successes of the expanding imperial city, the line had become one of the successes of the nineteenth-century railway boom. Since the annual passenger numbers peaked at an extraordinary 46.3 million in 1896, they have fallen relentlessly, throughout various operational changes and reconfigurations. By 1930 the total was down to 12 million. In March 1963 the Beeching Report recommended the withdrawal of the only remaining service, between Richmond and Broad Street (in the City, adjacent to Liverpool Street). Protests organised at various localities along the line eventually prevailed, but had to be re-activated in the 1970s to counter British Rail's periodic closure threats. In the later 1970s the Greater London Council at last provided a strategic London-wide overview and reaffirmed the importance of orbital routes. The GLC itself provided a substantial investment in the eastern end of the line. In May 1985 a section from Dalston to North Woolwich, which had carried no passengers since war damage in 1943, was officially opened as newly-electrified track, and dubbed the North London Link, opening up a continuous service between Richmond and North Woolwich. However, this proved to be one of the GLC's last acts, before abolition by the Thatcher government. With no unifying metropolitan authority to 'think' the connection between east and west London, let alone promote the redistribution of the social wage through public transport policy, pan-London rail strategy lost impetus. The term Link is no longer used to designate the line.

Today, the NLL is a physically and administratively distinct service of North London Railways, which is a not-yet-privatised 'train operating unit of the British Railways Board'.[3] The timetable provides for a train every fifteen minutes between Richmond and North Woolwich, and every half-hour between Gospel Oak and Barking. But, notoriously, these trains do not run on time. They may not run at all, especially at weekends, because of engineering works. During the morning and afternoon rush-hours, the two or three-carriage trains only approach capacity over some sections of the line, with commuting schoolchildren, workers and students (the NLL serves both of the main University of East London campuses, at Barking and Stratford). At other times, especially on the Barking branch, there is a mere scattering of the typically low-income clientele who are dependent on public transport, as also to be found on any London bus: women with small children, older people, and members of ethnic minorities, making short journeys.[4] Freight business accounts for half of all traffic, but has attracted publicity for controversial cargoes of nuclear waste rather than for keeping lorry-loads off London roads. Some small stations which only serve the NLL, particularly in the leafier western suburbs, have a pleasantly rural character, but generally speaking there is dereliction, graffiti and vandalism enough to generate unease (e.g. at Woodgrange Park; Wanstead Park; Leyton Midland Road). That's if you can locate the line in the first place: station entrances are usually poorly marked and signposted (e.g. Walthamstow Queens Rd.; Upper Holloway). Even where there are station interchanges with British Rail or Underground lines, the NLL is often annexed to an off-site cutting via an obscure tunnel or footbridge, or a tiresome stretch of open road, thanks to the historic vicissitudes of track construction (e.g. Willesden Junction; West Hampstead; Stratford).

Such a catalogue of deficiences can all too easily be taken as an index of terminal decline. It seems so plausible to identify the viability of the line with the functions current during its period of spectacular growth and prosperity through the second half of the nineteenth century:

delivering goods to and from the busiest docks in the world, and then also transporting commuting workers to the City. With the docks finally abandoned twenty years ago, and the closure of the commuter connection to Broad Street in 1986, it may seem apparent that the line is now redundant – its fate assimilated to the rhetoric surrounding the collapse of maritime and associated industries in East London. But a little market history can be a dangerous thing. Transport infrastructure is not necessarily built to supply a pre-existing demand, and nor are the relative merits of public investment and private speculation as easy to disentangle as current government ideology would have us believe. Some of the historical particularities of the development of the NLL themselves demonstrate that these interrelationships – between supply and demand, between public and private provision – are more complicated, more symbiotic, and altogether less predictable than that.

An Infrastructure and its 'happy afterthoughts'

The current NLL route is but the latest consolidation of a service from among a maze of tracks which have varied historically in their precise configuration and extent, but which have remained identifiable as an orbital east/west route since the middle of the nineteenth century. We owe the origins of the unique orbital character of the line to the 1846 Royal Commission on railways in the London area, which successfully blocked yet another proposal for a competing radial route carving into central London from the north, and encouraged instead an orbital link across the existing arteries.[5] Like most early railways, the line was originally intended only for the transport of goods. It took legislation such as Gladstone's Railway Act of 1844, and the Cheap Trains Act of 1883, to impose mass passenger transport on reluctant rail companies.[6] In the event, the company directors of the NLL had riches thrust upon them by public policy, in the form of annual passenger figures approaching an astonishing fifty million at the turn of the century. In 1922 the chairman calculated that in the previous fifty years the line had carried thirty-three times the population of Great Britain.[7] Delighted directors apparently referred to their construction of Broad Street station in 1865, which provided the terminus for most of this traffic and became the third busiest in London, as 'the happy afterthought'.[8]

However, it would not be true to say that the speculator who created what is now the Stratford to North Woolwich section of the line prospered in the main by identifying an existing demand. Rather,

George Parker Bidder created that demand. When the line first snaked out across the empty marshland to the few poor houses and a tavern which comprised North Woolwich, a contemporary remarked on the eerie effect of the clanking of carriages across the desolate wastes where 'the heron, the bittern and the plover roamed in almost undisturbed solitude'.[9] Admittedly it is likely that the rail company involved with Bidder anticipated the potential for traffic across the river to the Royal Arsenal at Woolwich, using their own ferry service. This traffic soon declined, however, with the construction of rail links south of the river. The company responded by building the Royal Pavilion Gardens (now the Royal Victoria Gardens) at North Woolwich, to give passengers another reason to use the line.[10] But the truly momentous development involved Bidder's speculative plans to create a dock in the area. By 1855 the Royal Victoria Dock had been opened, followed in 1880 by the Royal Albert. With the establishment of the Port of London Authority in 1909 these unprecedentedly massive docks and their associated railway sidings became, in turn, a public asset. The final dock of the Royals complex, the George V, was built in 1921 as a public venture.

These railway and dock developments changed the character of social life and labour in East London.[11] Riverside crafts and traditional trades gave way to heavier industrial concerns. The more prosperous workers moved out to protect the whiteness of their collars from the soot and grime, confirming the character of the area as a transit camp for the casual labourer, and attracting incoming waves of immigrants and refugees. Not that the railways and docks always encouraged mobility. Railway cuttings and embankments, dock swing-bridges and warehouse walls also contributed to the formation of highly localised enclosed working communities which became a distinctive feature of the area.

More generally, the outer London suburbs through which the NLL now runs, and which it serves, were often themselves, at least to some extent, the creation of the railways, through the stimulation of speculative house-building.[12] Less happily, not all these new residents of outer London were the result of natural growth. It is estimated that between 1853 and 1885 at least 56,000 workers were evicted from within London by railway construction programmes, mostly from the city centre: often only to find themselves commuting back in to their workplaces, by rail.[13]

Global Prospects

The historical perspectives above indicate that there is nothing necessarily nostalgic or impractical about saying in 1995, here is a major item of railway infrastructure, with a particular location and characteristics, what significant social and economic developments can it promote in order to generate traffic for itself, given investment in both the development and the rail service? This always has been the question, irrespective of whether private profit or public benefit was the initial focus. At any given time answers have proved to be unexpected, or have had to be created, or have failed to materialise. But before elaborating where the most beneficial synergies might now be discovered, some wider contemporary factors, which are also very much in the line's favour, need to be noted.

The environmental and economic case for making the most of existing railways in London is by this point in the century surely overwhelming.[14] These factors alone should be enough to change for good the terms in which the NLL is considered: away from mere survival, as in recent decades, and towards maximising the potential of an undoubted asset. Whichever projections of overall passenger transport demand in London turn out to be accurate, they all presume an increase in demand over the next decade.

The NLL is extremely well placed to take advantage of major transport and development proposals in East London. The proposed Woolwich Tunnel rail scheme would link the NLL at Silvertown in the Royal Docks with the North Kent Line at Woolwich Arsenal, to make it possible to run new cross-river services linking East London and the Thames Gateway development areas.[15] Silvertown is also the nearest station to London City Airport, so the NLL would benefit from any increase in air traffic there. Development plans for the Royal Docks themselves include the Royals University College and Business Park, and the London International Exhibition Centre, as well as residential areas.[16] Most dramatically of all, if Stratford is chosen as an international rail passenger transport station for the Channel Tunnel link, the NLL would be connected to one of the busiest rail interchanges in Europe.

Although it is conceivable that some of these proposals will not materialise, the NLL infrastructure is already benefiting from major projects which are underway on other services. The East London end of the Jubilee Line Extension is being constructed on the old freight track alignment alongside the NLR tracks, and will result in new stations at Canning Town and West Ham, terminating at Stratford alongside the NLL platforms at a new western concourse. On the western section of the NLL, Eurostar are paying for the upgrading of the track between Acton and Camden Road, to provide a relief route for their northbound services from Waterloo. Closure of sections of the NLL in order to accommodate construction work for these other routes does, of course, further confirm the NLL's reputation for unreliability, but will bring benefits in the longer term. Apart from the opening of the Stratford to North Woolwich service already referred to, the last major overhaul of the line was in 1921, and it is this lack of investment which to some extent accounts for the line's physical and operational failings.

The importance of sections of NLL track to these current projects and development proposals, especially in eastern London, does confirm strikingly the distinctive contribution of the line to the wider network. It is the only east/west orbital route north of the underground Circle Line, providing links between overground and underground routes as they radiate from central London. Presumably in recognition of the importance of this function, the Richmond to Woolwich section (but not the Barking spur) has recently been incorporated within the famous London Transport Underground map. Enhanced integration of the NLL with the rest of the network is clearly one way forward, but even if its present operational and infrastructural limitations were substantially overcome, the NLL is inherently ill-suited to develop as an anonymous but fast mass passenger transit system – it is now an essentially localised service with frequent stops and a unique overground character. Nor is piecemeal upgrading of the line off the back of other services, as detailed in the paragraph above, any substitute for investment in the line as a whole with an overall strategy in view. Only a renewed vision for the line itself, which starts with its distinctive features, is likely to stimulate investment synergies comparable to those which characterised the building of industrial and commercial traffic in the last century. Ironically, it is precisely the de-industrialisation of the eastern end of the line which provides the opportunity for a fresh assessment of the line's potential. For one contemporary economic equivalent of the industrial and trading boom of the last century is undoubtedly the tourism and leisure industries of today, both in terms of volume and of growth.[17] To point this out has become something of a commonplace. The response is often less than enthusiastic, and sometimes hostile. Like regeneration, the term tourism can refer to a great variety of possible practices, not all of them welcome to everybody. We share this wariness, but suggest that promoting and investing in both the NLL and the attractions adjacent to it, as a co-ordinated strategy, is one practical way of ensuring that the improvement of local services, amenities and job opportunities is not neglected in the pursuit of income from visitors. That said, investment which encouraged regional and international visitors away from the 'overheated' traditional sites of central London is very much in line with recent thinking on tourism policy for the capital as a whole.[18]

Locomotion, Locality, Conviviality

Viewed in terms of visitor potential, the NLL can be seen as a semi-circular arc linking many of the most attractive, interesting and lively localities in the whole capital, and connecting directly to the River Thames at both ends (see Figure 1).

To the west and north, the stations at Richmond (for the River, Hill, Park, antiques and other retail outlets), at Kew Gardens (for the Royal Botanic Gardens, and river), at Hampstead Heath (also for Hampstead Village), and at Gospel Oak (also for Hampstead Heath, lido and adventure playground) are all resorts of long standing. Camden Lock market (accessible from Camden Road station) has also become a very major attraction over the last decade. Topographically, the value of river and canalside sites is very marked. Even Hampstead Heath, where the topographical value is most obviously that of high ground and fresh air, has significant lakes, ponds and bathing facilities, while Hampstead Village owed its original resort status to medicinal springs.

The eastern section of the line is, if anything, more richly endowed with waterside sites, and now that their dominance by industrial use has declined, they present actual or potential attractions which are quite as distinctive. However dubious the philosophy of urban regeneration for the inner docks in the form of office property speculation at Canary Wharf has proved, the spectacular nature of the buildings and the waterside site has generated a significant tourist interest: another 'happy afterthought' perhaps.[19] The maritime theme in East London is also clearly central to the two currently shortlisted London bids for the Millennium exhibition site, the Greenwich peninsula and the Stratford proposals (the latter based around the tidal Abbey Mills buildings on the nearby River Lea, part of the Lee Valley Park). In the event of either bid (or of a combination of both) succeeding, East London would become the focus for the national Millennium celebrations, with major, and we would hope sustainable, regenerative effects. Even if the bids fail, the NLL is well located to exploit the potential of the 10,000 acre Lea Valley Park, a river and canalside site which has been developed since 1967 for a wide range of sports and leisure activities and for nature conservation, and is ripe for promotion in its own right. The stations at West Ham and at Blackhorse Road give access to different areas of the park.

Staying with the waterside theme, the station at North Woolwich leads straight to the ferry across the river to the Woolwich Arsenal, where the Ministry of Defence are developing three museums in the magnificent complex of existing buildings due to open in 1997. A little further upstream is the visitor centre for the Thames Barrier, and the recent addition of the Russian submarine. At this point, the more traditional attractions of Greenwich are only a short bus ride away. Back on the North Woolwich side of the river is the museum of the Great Eastern Railway in the original station building, to add to the proposed developments for the Royal Docks mentioned above. Further into the hinterland of East London along the lines from Barking and from North Woolwich, both Walthamstow and Hackney have clusters of sites and of activity which could be developed into destinations of more than local interest. Walthamstow Queens Road is near to the longest street market in Europe, with the William Morris Gallery and an attractive village area including the Vestry House Museum beyond. Hackney Central station serves the Hackney Empire theatre, as well as the only National Trust property in East London, the sixteenth-century Sutton House, with the broad expanse and facilities of Victoria Park a short walk away.

There are some signs that the potential for developing visitor attractions in East London is beginning to be recognised, by the local authorities, by such consortia as TourEast, and by the NLL itself. There is a long way to go, however, in developing the level of design, signposting, maintenance, and promotion that has long characterised the London Underground service. The image of the line cannot be turned round without this. Resources will also have to be committed to specialising in niche marketing, thematisation, packaging and collaboration with the localities and sites themselves, which is required if the line is to realise its visitor potential to the full. Further work on the significance of the ethnic diversity and cultural life of the region is likely to discover markets and attractions that are as yet untapped. These may yet turn out to be more important than anything in confirming East London as an enjoyable place to live and work in, and to visit. In the meantime, it is perhaps the social and psychological barriers to imaginative investment rather than the physical ones that are most daunting. Both upstream and downstream from North Woolwich are developments which undermine the very idea of the riverside as a high-value environment: plans for up to nine rubbish incinerators (some already built) and the recently-built Belmarsh Prison, the only new prison for men to be built this century. These are too uncomfortably reminiscent of persistent Victorian associations of East London, not just with industrial grime and impoverishment, but also with crime and with rubbish. Defining East London as a location worth visiting is perhaps the most effective way of countering the continuation of such social splitting and mythologising, and of its genuinely damaging and degrading effects.

Notes

[1] One historical dimension of these divisions, which argues that London experienced 'a crisis of social and industrial development in the last quarter of the nineteenth century and that the central place in that crisis was occupied by the problem of casual labour' is given in Gareth Stedman Jones, *Outcast London*, Oxford University Press, Oxford 1971.

[2] For this history see M. Robbins, *The North London Railway*, The Oakwood Press, London 1953; Tim Sherwood, *The Railways of Richmond Upon Thames*, Forge Books, London 1991; *Return to North Woolwich*, compiled by the Great Eastern Railway Society, PEMT Enterprises, London 1987.

[3] We should like to thank Dennis Lovett, External Relations Manager of North London Railways, for his assistance.

[4] Current passenger figures are considered commercially sensitive in the run-up to privatisation, and are not available from North London Railways.

[5] M. Robbins, *op.cit.*, p1.

[6] David Norman Smith, *The Railway and its Passengers*, David and Charles, Devon 1988 pp32–37.

[7] M. Robbins, *op.cit.*, p28.

[8] Tim Sherwood, *op.cit.*, p57.

[9] W.T. Vincent, *The Records of Woolwich District*, Vol 2., J.S. Virtue and Co. Ltd., London 1890, p475.

[10] *Ibid.*, p479, 'the local authorities voluntarily surrendered the public footpath along the river bank in order that the pleasure-ground might have its esplanade.'

[11] Alan Palmer, *The East End*, John Murray Ltd, London 1989, pp48–50.

[12] David Norman Smith, *op.cit.*, p95.

[13] *Ibid.*, p36.

[14] See, *The Case for Reducing Traffic Levels in London*, compiled and published by ALARM, in association with Transport 2000, and *Action Programme for London Transport*, by London First, October 1995.

[15] *Woolwich Tunnel Rail Scheme*, leaflet by BR, LDDC, LT, Railtrack, July 1995.
[16] The University of East London is the lead institution for the Royals University College, which has now received government funding.
[17] See John Urry, *The Tourist Gaze*, Sage, London 1990.
[18] See London Tourist Board, *Tourist Strategy for London 1994–7*; CBI, *Succeeding Tomorrow*, London 1994.
[19] See *London Docklands Visitor Strategy*, LDDC, London 1995.

Prospects and Interventions

London East: Gateway to Regeneration

Anna Whyatt

The management of strategic economic development in London has been in constant change over the last fifteen years. It has ranged from attempts to prescribe for all eventualities to a push for the market to operate unimpeded by any kind of public policy and finally led to an uneasy truce between the two. This last has taken the form of an underlying belief that the market would resolve all issues, but with a necessary adoption of planning and land-site regimes which then led the development process, and without the economic or industrial context to make sense of what was being suggested. During this period, the London market moved into boom within finance and business services in the late 1980s, masking a number of difficulties in other major sectors and also concealing its own subsequent down-turn. The 1991 Census figures revealed the extent of the difficulty and the effect on the labour market in particular, namely the most rapid growth of unemployment anywhere in the UK.

The result of this was the recognition by both private and public sectors of the need for a system of economic monitoring and evaluation in London, along the lines of that which had been adopted by other cities in the UK and Europe for the last decade – a recognition which came about primarily through the demand from government for a medium-term strategy for London – the London Pride Prospectus. The concern of leading business in the capital that London needs to achieve world class competitiveness in order to retain its leading edge as one of the foremost cities in the world, matched by an equal concern from local communities regarding the growth of unemployment, has persisted beyond the London Pride exercise. Currently a number of partnership initiatives are in place to develop a strategic economic view either at the sub-regional level (the West London Alliance, the Central London, North London and Lea Valley Partnerships, the Thames Gateway Partnership) or at the pan-London level, the London Pride Partnership, London First. Whilst the sub-regional strategies are crucial, there is a general recognition that they need to be developed within a framework of the London-wide economy.

This chapter describes some of the issues which need to be confronted in looking at the Thames Gateway from an economic/industrial, as opposed to a land-site or labour market, perspective, set within the context of London-wide development. It forms part of an overview which is currently being constructed of the Thames Gateway economy. This in turn will inform new economic strategy which is being developed through a partnership of London East Training and Enterprise Council, the eleven local authorities who make up the Gateway group, the London Docklands Development Corporation and the University of East London. Two follow-on studies are also being taken forward; to look at the potential for tourism and associated industries in the area and to conduct an in-depth analysis and projection of future prospects in the manufacturing industry. All three pieces of work are action-research – designed to assist in constructing strategy for implementation through the programmes which each of the partners will be able to put into place in the medium to long term. The emphasis of the work is to try to provide an economic framework and way forward in tackling the problems, as opposed to simply rehearsing what the problems are.

The Profile of the Thames Gateway

The London East Gateway area, in large part the East End, but also stretching along the Thames from the City of London boundary to the M25, across the river to Greenwich and north to the borders with Hertfordshire and Essex, is no stranger to controversy. Since 1993 and the Government's announcement of its inclusion in the Thames Gateway designation, its profile has developed an increasingly schizophrenic character. It has been hailed as the geographic opportunity *par excellence* for London if not the South East. Yet part of the area is sufficiently deprived to meet European Union criteria ranking it alongside the poorest areas of western Europe. The truth is somewhere between the two. But the tension of the opposing profiles, particularly for those who work to develop and promote the area, encourages despair and frustration as they seek a meeting point between specious and grandiose aspiration on the one hand, and poverty and decline on the other.

The traditionally held opinion of East London and its prospects was, until relatively recently, one of deprivation and decline. To a large extent it is a view based primarily on the economic profile of residents and fails to separate out economic performance from labour market position. The situation of local residents is undoubtedly depressed and one which needs radical attention. Historically driven by its twin functions as a port and major industrial location, London East once accommodated a range of distribution and manufacturing activities. Both have left an indelible mark on the physical and economic structure of the area and most particularly in the way in which they shape the skills base and employment potential of its residents. It is also one of the poorest urban areas in the UK and Northern Europe. The 1991 DOE index of deprivation shows that most of the East London boroughs score high and that Newham ranks first in deprivation in the country. The region is also characterised by having a large and diverse ethnic minority population, amongst whom unemployment is disproportionately high. Newham and Tower Hamlets have the second (42 per cent) and third (36 per cent) highest population of ethnic minority residents in the UK. Newham also has the highest proportion of households with children under five years of age (18 per cent) in the UK. Tower Hamlets and Barking and Dagenham are both notably high in this regard. Unsurprisingly, most East London residents are heavily dependent upon public transport. The 1981 Census showed that most of the East Thames Corridor authorities exported the majority of their labour force to work outside their area. Only Barking and Dagenham and Tower Hamlets were net importers of labour.

Although over the year 1993–4, there was a steady decrease in total unemployment, down by 9.4 per cent, there are still high levels (13.8 per cent) of unemployment within the 1.2 million population. Unemployment is particularly high amongst men in the twenty-five to thirty-four age group, with low levels of attainment. The geographical distribution of unemployment shows highest levels in Newham and Tower Hamlets where the level of unemployment in some wards has reached 32 per cent. Unemployment has had a disproportionate effect on ethnic minority communities, as is the case in London overall. The most striking example of this is within the Somali community where unemployment stands at 84 per cent. An increasing proportion of the unemployed are long-term unemployed; 63 per cent in 1994, compared with 35 per cent in London overall. This has resulted in considerable skill mismatch, with local residents unable to access high skill and craft-related jobs in the areas of professional, managerial, personal and engineering services.

There is a specific focus to the overall problem in London East given that its occupational structure is not representative of London as a whole, especially in the areas of management and administration, professional and associate professional. The vast proportion of residents in the area, and a much higher percentage than that for London as a whole, are employed in lower grade skill areas. GCSE attainment in London East amongst 15 year olds is also lower compared with the national average. The main difficulty cited by employers in respect of hard to fill vacancies in London was shortage of applicants with the right qualifications. This means that a considerable programme of training for local people related to job opportunity for the future would need to be established before local people would be able to access jobs in the growth sectors in London East, a pattern which would also apply in London as a whole. There are specific challenges in relation to this in London East where there is expected to be a rise in the number of those in the over 35 age group. (See Vikki Rix's chapter on the detailed analysis of social change and polarity in East London.)

In 1993 the Government introduced into this one-dimensional picture, an exactly opposite vision of the then named East Thames Corridor. It was to become no less than the main driver for the future regeneration of London. Vast stretches of hitherto derelict land were going to become the key venues for industry, commerce and tourism for the twenty-first century. In essence this view was informed by the extremely large expanse of vacant land in the area and a totally laudable desire to change the prospects of the East London area as well as London itself. Without an economic dimension, however, a strategic vision which was land-site led combined with the severe labour market problems that face East London was almost inevitably going to lead to disappointment and depression. It was impossible that the notion of transformation could come from a situation in which there was little assessment of the economic prospects which were needed to underpin any change. Disappointment has been accompanied by an increasing polarity of view between those who believe that the human problems of the area are the dominant and driving pointer for the future and those who take the position that East London will become the London for the Millennium. It is a polarity which obscures in both cases an economic reality which is more encouraging than depressing, but one which needs to be built on for what it is and what it offers if the dreams of the last five years are to come anywhere near realisation.

The first necessity is to understand the relationship which the area holds within the context of London as a whole and for there to be a recognition that, far from leading in all regards, the East London area will in large part be revitalised by building on and exploiting the strengths that London already possesses. At the same time the challenges which need to be addressed if the specific problems which face particular areas in London are to be resolved are particularly severe and trenchant in East London. Their resolution must come through a London-wide recognition and ownership of them.

The London Context

All areas of London, both inner and outer, form part of the wider economy of London and the south-east, economically, the single most important region in the UK. But London operates at all times on a three-fold level: as a global city with pre-eminence in international transport, communication and financial networks; as a European, national and regional centre and, for those who live and work in it, as a local area. It is the premier site for historical and cultural heritage internationally and a key command and control centre for national and international government. Forty per cent of the top 100 headquarters in the UK are located in London. The net contribution of the capital to the UK economy has been set at £10.6 billion. Its contribution to GDP, 17.2 per cent of national GDP, 32 per cent as part of the region, is double that of Greece and Portugal and greater than that of Finland. Nearly three million jobs in the UK depend upon London as a market. London's net benefit to the UK economy is likely to be 22.3 per cent higher than similar investment elsewhere in the UK and government investment in London can yield benefit to the country as a whole. Economic activity in London produces on average a net social benefit of over 20 per cent more than that in the rest of the UK.

London is at the heart of business networks worldwide. It has been placed as top European business centre for three successive years. Its finance and business services industry holds premier international status, contributing substantively to its position as the ninth richest European region. Central London alone supports over a million jobs. It is the academic capital of Europe, with twelve universities and ten colleges of higher education. London is a key national and European centre for retail, leisure and artistic excellence. Tourism is a major industry in the UK, employing over 1.5 million people and representing nearly 5 per cent of GDP. In London it attracts of the order of 17 million visitors per year, generating income in the region of £5.7 billion, rendering it fourth amongst the top invisible export earners, and sixth in the world league for tourism receipts. Its potential for growth in the area of leisure and tourism is substantial. The total figure projected in tourism numbers for London by 2005 is 23 million, but given the passenger use forecasts and the international growth projections for the industry of 8.5 per cent per year this could be much higher. London is already a primary transport interchange, nationally and internationally, with Heathrow the busiest of the world's airports. New projections, however, for visitor flow into London show estimates of 112 million passengers for Heathrow/Gatwick and Stansted and 17.1 million for Waterloo Terminal via Eurostar. The total passenger market growth predicted (excluding traffic generated by the opening of the tunnel) is 145 million by 2013.

All of these strengths need to be seen in the context of the challenges which face London which are extensive. A forthcoming profile of the London economy carried out by South Bank University in conjunction with GHK Ltd, shows clearly that although any analysis of the capital's economic position must take into account all three of the levels at which it operates, by far the dominant factor is a deepening and increasing globalisation, accompanied by a technological revolution. These shifts will have enormous consequences for the UK as a whole. But London, by virtue of its global position within most industrial sectors, its location and role within the UK economy, is already feeling these effects more swiftly and more keenly than any other region.

At the international level, the prognosis is clear, whether looked at from future trend predictions in management, economics or training and education. By the year 2000, a billion people will have been added to the world population, the majority of the growth taking place in the developing world. Meeting the aspirations and material needs of that demographic pressure will be at the heart of international economics for the next twenty years as a powerful driver for change. Scenarios prepared by Shell UK Ltd for business in the community suggest there could be a four-fold increase in world GNP, mainly in newly industrialising countries. Global competition and changes in communications technologies will force companies to change methods of operation and with them international markets. Information/communications revolutions will mean that jobs could be anywhere. Future jobs will require higher skill levels, often at international levels of excellence in order to compete effectively. This factor alone is already shifting London's labour market which already extends to the home counties and the south-east, to become a European and international labour market. The region rather than the individual city will become the focus of economic activity for the future, generating further radical changes in the roles and performances of major cities in the next decade. The Organization for Economic Co-operation and Development (OECD) identified three major processes of structural change which would affect urban systems:

* Low-skilled assembly work being relocated to countries offering low labour costs
* the replacement in central business districts of office and leisure development for industrial and residential property
* growth of the service sector, with tourism as a major growth sector, and services which serve national and global rather than local demand
* fragmentation of the process of production in services as well as manufacturing via new communications technologies
* Concern from both business and residents about the quality of infrastructure and environment.

In order to manage these changes effectively for cities, there will need to be a positive commitment to partnership and strategic intervention, to the development of competitiveness in specific sectors and to comprehensive skilling and re-skilling. The implications of not following through these changes are trenchant and potentially traumatic. But the full implication of what they entail, in practice, has yet to be understood fully, particularly in the international context. Before London, for example, is able to judge whether its skilling and re-skilling is of sufficient standard, it needs to understand the key sectors for the future and their labour market requirements, and what level of provision it currently makes. At present it understands neither.

For the UK, the creation of the Single European Market and the opening of central and eastern European markets has also created major change in business prospects. According to the 1994 OECD economic survey of the UK its economy overall is holding up well with a rise in output, and a decline in underlying inflation. By spring of 1994, the UK had retained its 1990 peak level of output. Output growth in the range of 2.75 per cent to 3.25 per cent is predicted by the OECD for Britain as a whole and it remains the preferred location within the European Union for inward investment. During 1993/4, almost 97,000 jobs were created via investment from the US, Germany, Japan and France.

London, however, is expected to have to work harder than almost any other region in the UK if it is not to fall back even further from its present position. Although a slight growth is predicted in the economy overall, growth in London is expected to rise less than any other region in the UK, an average of 1.9 per cent, compared with that of 2.9 per cent in the region and overall 2 per cent lower than the UK average. Over the last decade its decline, extensively in the manufacturing sector, but in other sectors as well, has been rapid. It is also, increasingly a city dependant upon the service sector. Seventy-nine-and a half per cent of London's value-added takes place in the service sector, which together with distribution, accounts for 73.2 per cent of London's exports. Without attention the capital will lose the variegated and broad industrial base on which the survival of all cities depends (50 per cent of all London's employees now work in two sectors – finance and business services, and public/personal services). This needs to be taken particular account of, given that the manufacturing sector is likely to be one of the fastest growing sectors in the UK economy over this period. In services, previously seen as a future substitute for manufacturing loss, employment fell by 3 per cent between 1981 and 1993, whereas it rose nationally by 16 per cent.

Half a million of those who work in the capital commute in from outside, effectively exporting back some £10 billion of the capital's regeneration capacity into the south-east region, almost thirty times more than the current public regeneration investment. This has been a contributory factor in an accelerated rise in unemployment, the fastest in any UK region. London now faces the highest level of unemployment (11 per cent compared with 9.1 per cent for the region as a whole) of any similar city in Europe. Unemployment has concentrated consistently in core areas of the city, creating a central crescent of decline. In some inner area boroughs, over 20 per cent of the available workforce is out of work. It embraces, partly in consequence, enormous polarity of income, unemployment, with, overall, a worsening of income levels. There is widespread skill mismatch, an imbalance which is likely to grow whilst one in five Londoners and one in three sixteen year olds hold no qualifications, and inadequate training – the London region ranks lowest of British regions in training record. The advent of greater labour mobility throughout Europe at present poses a threat rather than an opportunity when 42 per cent of young people in the EU already speak fluent English. Transport inadequacy has led to loss of business growth. Commitment to a long-term investment programme to secure the world-class infrastructure which the capital needs is urgently required, to reduce car-usage and to gain major improvements in public transport.

The implications of these issues combined are severe for London if they are not addressed. However, because London is also the linchpin of the UK economy, its economic development has ramifications for the entire economy in a way that is much less true of other regions. Tourism, financial and business services and international transport are all examples of industries for which London's global reach ensures that activity comes to the UK rather than being gained by another country. Nurturing this catalytic role is, in its own right, a key development issue for the UK economy. A reappraisal of policy in the UK as well as London context is called for to sustain and consolidate London's leading position. This is not only a question of money. Although investment is a vital component of redressing decline in London's economy, of much greater importance is to reassess and decide upon those investments which will actually make the difference to London's economic future. As the Audit Commission commented in 1989, with regard to urban policy, 'it is hard to escape the conclusion that at the level of the individual city there can be programme overkill within a strategic vacuum.'

At the same time, in order to combat decline, London must ascertain and build on its strengths in every regard. The contribution of West London with a thriving industrial base in information technology and headquarters and that of central London as cultural, governmental and heritage location must be placed alongside the potential which exists in North and East London for the future development of industry and commerce – not to set one region against another but to combine the potential of all to support and develop London's economic future. The decline facing the capital is such that every available opportunity will need to be enacted to ensure that a positive future is delivered to London's communities. To do this there must be an evaluation of the strengths of the capital which avoids a division between any of the sub-regional areas within its ambit. There is no doubt that the strongest clustering of the industrial base at present lies within Central and West London. As a current asset base, it would be counter productive to seek a weakening of that position in any way. Indeed, in order to provide for London's future, including within that the future of the north and east side of London, there needs to be continuous strengthening of that asset base.

The Contribution of East London

The future of London as a pre-eminent world city will depend on commercial and industrial prominence coupled with connections with the rest of Europe and internationally. What London East can uniquely offer to London's economic future is the potential to provide the land-site capacity for large-scale facilities and innovative new national and international centres to contribute to the status of London as a World City. This potential has been underplayed in some key regards, whilst being unrealistically inflated in others. London East offers the opportunity for a second strategic gateway both south and north of the Thames to Europe and the Channel Tunnel. The Royal Docks, Greenwich Peninsula and Stratford offer the possibility of major new centres for development at the London end of the Thames Gateway, with strong and complementary potential to link into the City and West End.

The area also has industrial and business clusters on which new industrial activity could be built which would be important to London's future prospects. Cambridge Econometrics and the Kent County Council study of the Thames Gateway area both argue that job creation in the Gateway area as a whole is best achieved through a combination of expansion of existing industries with development of new ones. They also show that already in existence is a defined increase in construction, distribution, financial and business services, and government and other services. And whilst there has been a decrease overall in manufacturing, utilities and transport and communications, the presence of manufacturing in East London is still far more substantial than London as a whole (18 per cent as compared with 11 per cent for London), as is construction sector employment. Finally, it is an area which is one of the most culturally diverse in Europe with a distinctive history and heritage base. So far little has been made of any of these assets aside from the land base in developing a robust economic context for the area.

This is not to under-estimate the magnitude of the task. At present, the economic activity of the various institutions shows a pendulum swing between land-site/individual project initiation and a generalised desire to assist business growth with little rationale or connection between the two. They need to be much more closely woven together if an economic strategy is to be achieved which engenders increased business activity. At the same time, there needs to be a much greater sense of the priorities for sector development in the area if resources are to be properly deployed and flagship projects utilised to promote and enhance the opportunity for that business in the relevant areas.

Real Options for Growth

One of the effects of the schizophrenic profile carried by East London is that it masks on all sides the reality of what is being dealt with, and the tasks that need to be undertaken for the future will be ignored. The pattern of future growth proposed for the East Thames Corridor reflects that for London as a whole, a lower rate of 9.6 per cent by 2006 compared with 14.1 per cent for the south-east. This forecast combined with the widespread deprivation and unemployment in London East and the preponderance of declining industries, should, nevertheless, not detract from a realistic appraisal of the growth indicators. The very real problems of deprivation and distress need to be understood in the context of the prospects for growth so that the key issue of linking communities to jobs can be addressed.

Building on these positive trends to create development on the scale that is needed in London East will require care, dedication, realism and focus. It is clear from the experience of the past ten years that such development and investment may not necessarily deliver job growth on the scale required in London East. The 1991 Census mapping showed that, unsurprisingly, the most rapid spread of unemployment took place in the boroughs least able to generate development, primarily because they were also the areas of greatest industrial decline in terms of outmoded industrial activity. There is no question, therefore, that a more sophisticated labour market strategy needs to be devised, alongside an investment and job generation strategy.

Similarly, as long as energy is diverted into projects which have little chance of implementation, there is a major risk that other opportunities more grounded in real terms will be lost. What is required is a more grounded strategy backed through by coherent labour market programmes that will be able to access the jobs which are realised for local people, whilst at the same time enabling them to achieve mobility.

In the Thames Gateway as a whole the number of businesses grew by 52 per cent between 1980–92, compared with the regional average of 44 per cent. The performance of industry in London East is better in all sectors compared to London as a whole except for transport and retail. Eighty per cent of employment growth recently in the UK has come from small- to medium-sized businesses which make up the bulk of the sector in London East. Above average growth is shown in finance and related services, and in construction. The sectors within the London East economy which are expected to perform better for the future are in financial and business services, government and other services, construction and distribution. Those identified for growth London-wide are finance and business services; education and academic services, telecommunications, computing and electronics; distribution; medical services; tourism; media and entertainment. The congruence within the fields of business and financial services, between London and London East and to some extent also, government and other services must be a primary start to any economic strategy. In business and financial services, for example, the office market in Docklands is finally beginning to stabilise and all boroughs report a slight uplift in this industry. Cambridge Econometrics also predicts a net increase in distribution, hotel and associated employment. There is also evidence of some de-centralisation into Hackney and Tower Hamlets of the publishing, audio-visual and advertising industries.

The base employment forecast, however, essentially reflects past and present patterns of growth. Experience in other areas of the UK and in some parts of London has shown that there is no reason, through the use of careful selection and united strategy, that growth cannot be achieved in industrial sectors previously not well represented in an area. To obtain growth in key sectors not predominant at present in London East – tourism, education and academic services, medical services – the London East partnerships will need to devise particular and specific strategies, connecting into programmes for London as a whole in order to access the opportunities for growth offered Londonwide. This involves more than simply developing a high profile marketing campaign.

The prognosis for success if this approach is adopted looks strong in tourism and related industries and academic services. In tourism, London East already possesses a strong base with potential to develop in the related industries of catering, the hotel business, distribution and communications, utilising the pivotal location for access to major European markets. These are all projected growth sectors. It has plans for a number of tourist and heritage flagships which, if promoted and developed more coherently, in relation to London as a whole, could assist in extending the 'boundary of acceptability' from central London to develop the right kind of profile and image for London East. There would be a need too, to look southwards at the projected growth in Kent. In 1993, tourism generated £348 million in the south east region and supported 30,000 jobs. If the projected Millennium festival were to take place on the Greenwich peninsula then the potential uplift in tourism and the associated industries could be on an unprecedented scale. This would have to be set in the context of wider development if it were to have any more than a short-term peripheral effect.

In education and academic services, there is an improving education infrastructure, backed by growth in further and higher education institutions in the area, for example, at London and Greenwich universities and the University of East London. The area has ten further education colleges and four universities based within its boundary. The proposal by the Royal Docks University Consortium for a new university college incorporating a technology institute is providing a new focus for this sector. However, there is insufficient information even in relation to present capacity to give any specific sense of what growth might be achieved within the sector as a service industry.

The planned emphasis of the Royal Docks University Consortium on applied technology, echoed by that in the University of Greenwich on environmental technology, could contribute meaningfully to development of applied manufacturing industry, if it were really linked into leading edge companies in the sector. London East is currently an internationally recognised centre for research into manufacturing. Research and development and technology transfer work accounts for 13 per cent of total employment in the area compared with 10 per cent for London. Twelve per cent of manufacturing employment is in high technology industries. The development of a strong manufacturing base is key to the continuing future of London as a world city. Expansion is predicted in the manufacturing industry in the rest of the

UK, though not in London. A 1994 report from Chesterton Planning and Consulting with the Henley Centre for the south east region Training and Enterprise Councils predicts that high technology manufacturing and services will see stronger growth in the future. Kent TEC has targeted a 21 per cent level for manufacturing in that region. In these circumstances, there is scope for developing a stronger strategy for manufacturing development in London East, building on the strong core already there in engineering, and associated manufacturing.

It is difficult at this stage to show how London East might take advantage of the OECD predicted growth in health and medical services, as there appears to be insufficient information on this sector for the London East area. However, the fact that it appears to be a key sector for Tower Hamlets and that the European Medical Evaluation Agency is to be based at Canary Wharf would suggest that it would be worth some examination – if only to establish whether there is sufficient market opportunity for the area.

Achieving Change

The potential value of the London East area to London for the future is enormous. However, in order to realise that potential, a number of key catalysts for change need to be identified and actioned.

Overall, there is a need for a strongly focused strategy, supported by all partners. Duplication and fragmentation needs to be avoided. There needs to be strong sense of ownership deciding which industries to support across the whole of the LETEC area. Further alliances and partnerships are needed to support particular flagship projects within industries, even if they are not located in the home borough, on the basis that these will benefit the area as a whole and diffusion of effort is likely to result in opportunities lost to London East. These need to be accompanied by consensus as to the right role to be adopted by different agencies, understanding that it is not necessarily the case that any initiative is better than nothing. There is currently arguably an over-supply of programmes and initiatives by individual boroughs, specific schemes within all sectors and at a regional level. Although extremely worthy in their own right, many bear little relation to each other nor do they sit inside an overall coherent strategy for the sub-region. The sum of the parts does not appear to combine to effect a whole. They need to be re-examined and re-focused, specifically in the light of the development required in particular industries. Currently there is no coherent and integrated strategy for Business Service delivery in London East. Business Link especially will assist in this regard but the opportunity it offers for focus needs to be extended to other areas of business development and activity.

Growth in all sectors, but particularly in tourism and communications is extensively dependent on appropriate transport innovation, particularly in public transport and the building of linkages between rail/tube and air transport. The £4.5 billion of transport enhancements in hand via the Jubilee and East London Line proposals to link Docklands, Stratford and West Ham to central London; the opening up of underground access in the north and the Docklands Light Railway extension under the Thames to connect into Greenwich and the waterfront are crucial to make the connections between Central London/West End and the east side of the capital. They will undoubtedly generate investment interest and there are indications that this is already happening. Further work needs to be done to look at greatly enhanced use of the river for leisure, passenger use and freight – an issue which is as important for central London as it is for London East. There are also indications of an uplift in trade in the ports in the Thames Gateway, with a projected increase of 23 per cent by 2010 and this needs further examination. There is also a need to look at how rail public transport connections into Docklands and London East can be better promoted (alongside better promotion of the area generally) and made more attractive and familiar to those who use them.

The most potentially significant transport project for London East is the Channel Tunnel Rail Link. But given that inward investment increasingly focuses on establishing links with global corporate networks, access to a leading international airport has increasingly become a critical locational factor for such functions. The growing success of City Airport and easy access of the area to Stansted is already introducing a profile for the area as an international transport point, particularly for same-day return journeys. The introduction of an international rail passenger transport station at Stratford would undoubtedly offer major regenerative impact for the area. Given that the reversal of decline is a major issue for London and that the bulk of decline in London continues to appear in the east side of the city, there would appear to be strong arguments for a London investment in Stratford. But in order to reverse decline, there must be sound economic arguments which emphasise the importance of the role which an international transport station at Stratford could play for London as well as offering easier access to the Channel Tunnel for

Essex and East London. Stratford must be a primary destination in its own right as well.

The third key lever for change in the future is Europe itself. The proximity of London East to Europe both by sea and by rail must be exploited. More work is needed in concert with Kent County Council and the Kent districts to look at the real as opposed to imagined potential of the corridor in relation to the Trans Manche region. Far more information needs to be investigated as to the potential both for attracting inward investment from Europe and the potential for London East-based business to expand into European markets. Many London East businesses have trading and partnership agreements with other firms throughout Europe but no study of this activity has yet been produced.

Finally, there is a need to consolidate and maximise the collective potential of the heritage and tourism attractions in the area and their ability to attract established markets both back into central London and out to Essex and Kent. At present these are operated on a borough by borough basis and marketed individually, if at all. Combined with this is a need to refocus the links between these. Although this may seem a relatively simple proposal, it will be crucial to any change in profile for the area as well as stimulating growth in the industry. This is not an issue of design and image – both are of high quality – but of rendering key locations and tourism destinations as familiar in people's thinking as the major London attractions, moving away from the current amorphous and generalised perception of London East.

An Economic Future

To build the capital, a strong economic base needs to be backed by a high quality infrastructure and environment, designed to maximise business opportunity, with the active participation of those who live and work there. These three areas of activity are interdependent. They are in all cases as crucial to the future of London as a World City as they are for local communities and residents.

The current partnerships, whether at sub-regional level or for individual programmes and schemes, which are attempting to develop the economic future of London East face some of the most difficult prospects in the London area. The industrial base is in decline, or fragmenting, unemployment levels are high and the local economy cannot be sustained through the income input of residents alone. To safeguard the future of the capital as a whole, decline in East London must be arrested. However, more than that, the East London site opportunities, some of them in the most attractive and futuristic settings which London can offer, and the industrial potential of London East must be maximised to extend out from the relatively buoyant base of West and Central London. Once a strategy for London East has been fully developed along these lines and a full picture of its potential contribution to London established, then a strategy for promotion of the area and its potential in real terms can be devised for delivery at local, European and international level. However, this should only be attempted following a strategy which shows clearly how the land-site potential and transport communications for the area relate to its industrial and economic prospects. Growth of existing business will not be sufficient to ensure full employment for the local labour market, underlined by the fact that 91 per cent of establishments in London East report no current vacancies. A three-fold strategy needs to be adopted:

* To develop, sustain and grow existing business in key identified industries to build a dynamic and variegated economy via the sector boards as they are established by LETEC
* To develop into other growth areas not currently predominant in London East
* To devise a labour market strategy to access jobs for local communities both internally and externally to the area.

This will require a re-thinking and re-orienting of the labour market strategy and an overview of programmes currently in operation by whichever agency or partnership. At present, in common with many parts of London, there is insufficient connection between programmes and prospects for job access. The complexity of movement within the London labour market and the region means that a much more sophisticated, Londonwide strategy is required to ensure that job generation is accessed by those in need of jobs in indigenous communities.

The key potential growth sectors for London East and for London as a whole are, as I have discussed earlier, tourism and related industries, distribution, business and financial services, and academic services. Applied manufacturing linked to research and development in IT and related fields is not identified in pure terms as a growth area for

London East. However, given the importance of its stabilisation to London and the fact that growth is identified for the UK as a whole, it is well worth attention and development in London East, particularly since there is a skilled direct labour force. There will be some uplift in construction due to the housing proposals at Barking Reach, the urban village in the Royals and development at Havering.

To access these opportunities, there needs to be a more widespread acceptance than exists at present that the future of the sub-region will depend upon the success or otherwise of the nexus of industrial sectors which make up its whole within the Londonwide, international and national context within which they operate. There needs to be a far more coherent economic strategy for the area, between both public and private sector and at a cross-borough level. But this can only happen if it is underpinned by realistic and consistent understanding of market opportunity for these key sectors and the development of programmes which can maximise that opportunity to the benefit of those resident and working in the area. In this, the approach goes beyond a blind assumption that the market will resolve all economic problems within the sub-region, or indeed within London. It has not in the last six years and is even less likely to do so in the future. The experience of urban regeneration in the last ten years has enabled us to understand that partnership between all sectors is crucial for success in this field. Partnership alone, however, is not a panacea. It must coalesce around a strategy of intervention which is opportunistic and directional at one and the same time. This will entail a mixture of complementary private and public sector initiatives in which all parties are trying not to control, since control is impossible, but to develop industrial and economic activity and generate opportunity for the area in the process. In this sense, this is a new economics which embraces growth within a context of appropriate development for the sub-region for the future.

Business and financial services already occupy a linchpin role in the area and are a forecast growth sector both for London and London East, specifically in banking, finance, insurance and leasing. Together with distribution, hotels and catering, they make up 73 per cent of employment in London East – one in six jobs. There is additional evidence of renewed activity and confidence at key regeneration sites across London East. Eighty per cent, for example, of 4.5 million square feet within Canary Wharf Phase 1 is now occupied, with some major players as tenants. However, it is by no means certain that the spread out from the City will continue unabated. Work needs to be put in hand, if not already done, to examine the surveys and recommendations of the City Research Project on Financial Services and to begin to work with the industry to see how those recommendations might be applied in London East and what further initiatives need to be taken to bolster the sector.

Manufacturing growth in the area is feasible in a context where London East holds a base of 18.4 per cent activity in manufacturing compared with 11.1 per cent in London, accounting for almost one in five jobs compared with little over one in ten for London as a whole. The contribution of Ford to the Barking and Dagenham economy is in the region of £200 million. To do this there will need to be identification of UK growth areas and how they might be applied in London East, especially in the sub-sectors where the area is showing strength in motor vehicles and parts, paper and printing, metals, clothing, chemicals and food. The CBI has suggested that the success of manufacturing will hinge on the ability to exploit five key interrelated areas of technology: information and communications, aerospace technology, pharmaceuticals, materials technology and bio-technology. Other London studies indicate that the changing nature of the industry is leading to demand for more space-extensive industrial sites. East London has much to offer in this regard, as long as it promotes good quality industrial sites which can attract modern and high technology industries. *London World City* published by the London Planning Advisory Committee in 1991 identified the lack of integration between higher education and business and the potential for science and business parks. From the literature surveyed so far, however, this prospect seems not to have been developed.

Consideration should be given to expansion of already existing manufacturing clusters at Barking and Dagenham, Tower Hamlets and in high technology at Redbridge. There needs to be stimulation of stronger links between flagship employers and local and small to medium sized firms and closer links between business and London East's training and education infrastructure. As shown above it would also be worth considering whether there is a market opportunity for London East in medical and health care services by looking at the current infrastructure already established in the area against the prospects for growth already identified by London First Centre.

Tourism and heritage offer a major opportunity to London East. The international prospects for growth identified by the OECD are of 8.5 per cent per annum and this is the target proposed by the *London Pride Prospectus*. However, London has lost market share (down from fourth to sixth place in the world league. Since the industry is now London's second industry after finance and business services, it is clear that new strategies need to be developed to increase the potential benefit to London. Recent reassessment of the potential visitor numbers to London by the year 2005 shows that a much higher number of visitors than that currently projected might be foreseeable. This takes into account higher yearly increases from current levels, the numbers projected by other international venues as a result of Millennium activity and passenger transport use projections. There has been a tendency up to now to regard increases in visitor numbers with suspicion and to respond to the prospect by concern with regard to congestion and overheating in the central area. East London, however, with heritage assets of potentially international standard, close proximity to the central London area and good transport links could offer another major sub-regional dimension to the industry in London. In addition to its flagships (Greenwich/Spitalfields), it also has a potential supporting infrastructure of other unheralded attractions (East London contains more museums and galleries than any other sub-region in London) and a growing, although as yet unmapped, concentration of sub-sectors such as the music industry which could be re-profiled and developed to provide a solid mass of attractions within the area. East London is also a main focus for ethnic minority culture in London. The depth of the activities promoted by these communities are not really seen or appreciated in London as a whole. There is a major opportunity for development which could potentially assist job generation within a group where unemployment is disproportionately high.

Two projected flagships which could change totally the potential for East London in this regard and accelerate the development process to an unprecedented degree – for London as a whole as well as for the sub-region – are the prospect of the international passenger station at Stratford and the possible siting of the Millennium festival at Greenwich. In these scenarios, there would be the additional dimension of international traffic via St Pancras, Stratford and City Airport and a major change in the use of the river, with the proposed disembarkation at Deptford Creek, and connections cross-river from Tower Hamlets and Newham to Greenwich and Woolwich. Decisions on both will be known soon and will, without doubt, set the entire context for future development of the industry in the area, giving some credence to the aspiration, which is unreal at present, of London East as 'a gateway to London'. The only rationale for a gateway is if it is actually used as an entry point. It will be crucial, however, in the event of the international station or the festival not proceeding, that other strategies are developed for the industry and associated industries such as the arts to be a focus of activity for the future.

A thorough review is being undertaken by the University of East London in conjunction with London East Training and Education Council and the London Docklands Development Corporation of all heritage and tourism attractions in the area, including those in the Lea Valley, and at Barking Town Centre, Island Gardens, Petticoat Lane, LDDC and Canary Wharf Visitors Centres, Spitalfields, Epping Forest, the public parks, at Rainham and at Havering Riverside as well as those centres already in existence such as Whitechapel Art Gallery and those proposed in the Royals and the heritage museum at Barking. We are trying to develop linkages between them, both thematically and in terms of transport connection. There are already potentially strong asset projects in Docklands and the Docklands City Conference Centre which could provide a further magnet attraction. A rationale cannot be defined for the whole of the LETEC area. What is needed is a re-profiling and a generation of clusters of activity at a more sub-regional level. There needs to be a move away from the mixture which exists at present between generalised aspiration for the whole of the East London area, interposed with proposals for individual projects. The prospects for linkage back to major heritage and tourism activity in central London and the West End, down river to link with Greenwich and Woolwich and cross-river between Tower Hamlets and Greenwich, will be crucial.

Associated industrial activity – in hotel and catering, retail and distribution will be key to provide a support structure for the magnet attractions and to ensure that the right level of income generation accrues to the area. Distribution accounts for the highest number of jobs in the London East area, some 39,000 and the total sector accounts for 18.6 per cent of employment locally (19.8 per cent in London). Forecasts for these industries are very positive for the area. In the light also of potential developments for the Millennium as well as predicted growth in visitor numbers to London, there could well be an increase in demand for hotel space beyond the 19,000 new spaces already predicted by LPAC. There would appear to be great potential to link these areas of prospective growth to the promotion and development of the tourist flagships detailed above. However, a great deal more exploratory work needs to be undertaken in the individual sectors to identify precisely where the opportunities such as, strategic distribution, will occur.

The other area of connected potential to tourism is in transport and communications. Predictions in this sector range from projected growth to projected job loss. It would be important to establish exactly what trends are showing in the first instance and then to construct further projections from the scenarios outlined above.

Higher education is a major employer and a growing sector of employment for the UK. Academic services currently accounts for 33,000 jobs in London East. The focus proposed for the Royals University College should be built on and connected with proposals for expansion in technology transfer and manufacturing. However, it is almost certainly the case that there may be other areas of strength within further and higher education in the area which can be built on and foreign and home markets which could be accessed. All of these issues need considerable examination and study, again across the whole of the sector, not just centring on individual institutions and their prospects.

Underpinning the main focuses of the development of the economy in London East are some issues of process which are fundamental to its successful achievement:

* The Gateway Partnership needs to be on a level with the Investors in Kent grouping of the south-east region. There should be agreement on an economic strategy for the area which links into and is consistently related to the opportunities offered by the wider London economy and the region. This process has now been started and those discussions and the process of consultation to follow should result in a strong and unified agreement.
* This should provide agreement on the priorities for action in the area with a determination to cease fragmentation and support those projects which will deliver maximum benefit to the sub-region on an agreed basis.
* Development of a sector monitoring system which will enable increased integration of programmes and regular checks on the outcomes of strategies across the area is crucial.
* There needs to be a separation out of funding regimes and strategy. At present, understandably, there appears to be a desire to enter funding regimes in order to access financial resources, in the absence of an overall strategy which would then guide and shape funding opportunities.
* Re-focusing and targeting of existing programmes such as Business Link, or European programmes is required to strengthen the effort in individual sectors.

* In all the sectors outlined there should be investigation of the infrastructural levers (transport/land-site development) which will encourage business to grow and locate. This should be tailored to business need, rather than land-assembly without use in view, which does not have an economic rationale behind it.
* The lack of integration of East London's ethnic communities into the future economy is not only divisive in human terms – it means that there is a failure to capitalise on future markets in a variety of ways – particularly in the cultural field. This needs to be addressed.
* The fact that several leading regeneration agencies in the area will be wound up over the next two or three years emphasises that the need for a strategy for the future within the reality of what is possible is not a luxury but of urgent importance for London as well as for East London.

Manufacturing in East London

Gavin Poynter

Introduction

With some justification, a leaflet produced by West Ham Council in 1910 claimed that the borough was the 'factory centre of the South of England'.[1] Over 300 manufacturing firms were located in the area with the largest number concentrated in the chemicals, engineering, metalwork and food, drink and tobacco industries. Fifty years later, researchers at the Barking College of Technology[2] could report that East London and South East Essex contained a higher concentration of manufacturing industries than any other part of south-east England. By the mid-1990s, despite thirty years of rationalisation, manufacturing continued to play a more significant part in the local economy than it did in other parts of London.[3] Arguably, manufacturing has had a central role in the shaping and scarring of the social and economic fabric of East London. A brief glimpse into its history illustrates this point.

The development of manufacturing industries in East London broadly divided into two phases – the second half of the nineteenth century and the first fifty years of the twentieth. In the nineteenth century manufacturing was concentrated in the areas to the east of the City of London, the boroughs bordering the River Lea and Docklands. This location offered three main advantages to the Victorian entrepreneur. First, nineteenth-century legislation pushed the 'obnoxious industries'[4] from the City to the suburbs where the absence of local by-laws, or, in the late nineteenth century, their lax application, provided the opportunity to locate factories in areas where there was an abundance of unskilled labour. Second, cheap land was available in East London for industrial development and, finally, the area was well served by waterways and a railway network constructed in the 1830s and 1840s. Stratford became a rail centre during this period when the North Woolwich line was constructed in 1847 and the Eastern Counties Rail Company located its carriage works in the town, also in 1847. During this phase the area became a centre for the chemicals, engineering and metals, food, drink and tobacco, textiles, leather, clothing and construction materials industries. By the end of the nineteenth century industrial expansion in the boroughs bordering the City slowed down because of economic depression and, when an upturn occurred, there was relatively little space left for expansion.[5]

The second wave of manufacturing development took place mainly in the inter-war years of the twentieth century and was located in the previously agricultural and marshland areas of south-east Essex. Manufacturing expanded eastward to spawn new towns and industrial centres in Dagenham, Havering and Harold Hill. This period saw the emergence of the automobile industry around the Ford plant at Dagenham and the establishment of companies engaged in making new electrical and photographic products as well as the expansion of the more traditional cement, chemicals and printing industries.

The pattern of manufacturing in the post-1945 period was developed as a mix of the old nineteenth century industries and the new twentieth century ones, with the latter mainly located furthest to the east of the City of London. The last three decades have been dominated by the rationalisation and relative decline of both the old and the new though the process of rationalisation has been modified by a strand of resilience which has ensured that East London remains a centre of manufacturing industry in the south-east of England.

Despite this resilience, East London in the mid-1990s offers a relatively bleak picture of acres of industrial wasteland and empty, decaying factory buildings especially in areas like Canning Town, Stratford and the Lea Valley. Contemporary decline tends to obscure from view a past rich with illustrations of industrial innovation and social change. For example, industrial development in the mid-nineteenth century received a considerable boost from the supply of cheap coal through the wharves constructed at Bow Creek in the 1850s. The abundant supply of coal facilitated the location of the Gas Light and Coke Company at the nearby Galleons Reach in 1868. The company, responding to a significant increase in demand, constructed a large gas plant on the site which later became known as Beckton Gas Works. The works, on completion in 1870, was then the largest gas plant in the world. In 1889 it became the focus for the birth of 'new' unionism amongst unskilled labourers. The National Union of Gas Workers and General Labourers was formed in July 1889. Following a march from Barking to Canning Town, a successful campaign was launched to reduce the working day from twelve to eight hours at Beckton and other London gas works. A year earlier, in 1888, the first women workers union had been formed as a result of a strike in another large workplace near to Canning Town in East London. Bryant and May had its Fairfield works located in Bow and employed over 1000 mainly women workers producing a range of safety, strike-anywhere, wax-vesta and vesuvian matches. Working conditions were poor, management discipline was harsh and a punitive piece rate payment system was in operation. The strike started in July 1888 as a result of a walk-out by the women employees following the disciplining of two of their number. The strike lasted about two weeks and received widespread support and publicity. The matchgirls won significant improvements in pay and conditions and gained recognition for the first union of women workers, the Union of Women Matchmakers. The Bryant and May plant continued to produce matches at Fairfield until the 1960s. The factory, an imposing Victorian brick building, now located to the north of the Bow flyover, remained empty until 1980 when, as part of the gentrification of the area, it was converted into a complex of luxury apartments designed to serve the anticipated housing needs of those attracted to work in the regenerated Docklands area.

In addition to being a centre of the emergence of new unionism amongst unskilled workers in the late nineteenth century, East London also provided the location for several companies that became household names in the twentieth century. For example, sugar-refining has been an important industry in West Ham since the mid-nineteenth century. The company Henry Tate and Sons was established in Silvertown in 1887 and concentrated initially on the production of cubed sugar whilst Abram Lyle and Sons was established in 1881 and produced golden syrup at its Plaistow Wharf plant. The two firms amalgamated in 1921 to form Tate and Lyle Ltd, one of the world's largest sugar refiners. Extensive reorganisation of the two Silvertown plants, involving significant job losses, took place in the late 1960s. However, the plant has survived into the 1990s and continues to provide employment for over 1,000 workers.

Different areas of East London have associations with specific companies and industries. In the mid-nineteenth century S.W. Silver and Sons moved its waterproof clothing factory from Greenwich to the North Thames where, in subsequent decades, the company moved into the production of a wide range of waterproofing and insulating materials. A new public company was formed, the India Rubber, Gutta Percha and Telegraph Works Ltd and, by the early 1920s, was producing a range of electrical products. In 1923 the plant covered twenty three acres and employed over 4000 workers. The company dominated employment in the area which became known as Silvertown. In the late 1920s the company fell into financial difficulties and was taken over by the British Goodrich Rubber Co. In the 1930s the plant was reorganised on a smaller scale. It was heavily bombed during the Second World War but continued production into the 1960s when it was sold for redevelopment as the Thames Industrial Estate. In the twentieth century a similarly close association between an area and a large manufacturing plant was established in Dagenham when Ford set up its automobile assembly plant in the 1920s. The expansion of the new plant was associated with the construction, for the growing workforce, of new London County Council housing estates in the area and, at its peak, employment at the plant rose to around 30,000 in the 1960s.

Particular areas of East London have been closely associated with the rise and relative decline of specific manufacturing industries as well as individual companies and plants. The Lea Valley area, for example, established itself as a centre of the furniture industry in the inter-war years. Furniture-making was an important, traditional East End industry in the nineteenth century and was largely concentrated in small, cramped workshops in which a handful of craft workers were employed. The boom in house-building after World War One created a rising demand for furniture and facilitated the expansion of production and the introduction of new machinery and new production techniques. Few East End furniture-makers had the capital or premises available for expansion. Those that did, including Levus, Bluestone and Elvin moved into the Lea Valley area in the period 1928–35. These companies brought together all aspects of furniture-making under one factory roof and began to use new woodcutting machinery and new production techniques. Their domination of the cheaper end of the furniture market enabled them to survive the 1930s slump and continue production into the 1950s and 60s when the use of new cheap materials, like plywood and particle board, helped the Lea Valley companies to sustain their UK market share in high volume, low cost furniture production. The Lea Valley companies produced in a sector of the furniture market, however, that became increasingly competitive. The 1970s recession led to excess capacity and price wars in the domestic and European furniture markets and by the early 1980s the Lea Valley furniture industry was in terminal decline. Undercut by foreign imports the industry in the Lea Valley was decimated by the mid-1980s.

Paradoxically, the few furniture producers that remain in the East End are now largely concentrated in the old, small workshops making reproduction furniture for the antiques market whilst the Lea Valley, the area in which the expansion and development of the industry took place, is now an industrial wasteland.

The rise and decline of specific industries and plants provides the backcloth to the present industrial landscape of East London. The main focus of this chapter, however, is upon the shape and structure of the contemporary manufacturing sector in the period 1990–94. I shall begin with a short introduction to the East London area and provide a brief overview of developments in the labour market, comparing shifts in employment patterns in East London with the city as a whole. The analysis then moves to workplace level and, via the use of a workplace survey, illustrates the diversity of experience of a number of workplaces that have survived the recessions of the early 1980s and 1990s. The chapter concludes with a review of the prospects for manufacturing in the context of increasingly competitive domestic and global markets and recent attempts by policy makers and planners to encourage the regeneration of East London and the East Thames Corridor.

The East London Area

For the casual visitor to the area two short train journeys would provide contrasting insights into the contemporary industrial and social structures of the East London region. The first trip could be taken on the British Rail North London Line which runs through Islington and Hackney and crosses the River Lea before going south-east to North Woolwich. The branch line from Stratford to North Woolwich opened in 1847 and enabled large numbers of workers to cross the river to gain employment at Woolwich Arsenal or at various newly established chemicals, shipbuilding and engineering plants that opened on the north side of the river in the latter part of the nineteenth century. The train journey today reveals vast acres of derelict land where once factories and workshops stood. Just visible from the train is the now redeveloped Fairfield plant of Bryant and

May at Bow. The journey reveals a ghostly pattern of closed rail lines and cuttings that once threaded their way to the great London Docks and the line dissects successive generations of public and private estates constructed to house the local working-class population.

By contrast the second rail journey could be taken on the Docklands Light Railway from Bank or Tower Gateway, in the City of London, to Island Gardens, situated at the southern tip of the Isle of Dogs. This journey is on a driverless monorail and takes the passenger through such stations as Heron Quay and Canary Wharf located in the heart of the Isle of Dogs Enterprise Zone. The train passes by a series of glass-fronted, ultra-modern office blocks and piazzas. The Enterprise Zone was the main focus of the Docklands regeneration project that commenced under the guidance of the London Docklands Development Corporation (LDDC) in the 1980s. The LDDC was entrusted by the Conservative government with the responsibility for the regeneration of the derelict London Docks area. A combination of public and private funding was designed to create vast office and housing complexes which aimed at enticing the expanding services industries, particularly the financial services, into the area. The project has achieved modest results in terms of employment generation and its housing programme was primarily designed for the upper end of the housing market. These developments rest uneasily alongside the pockets of older housing estates that continue to serve the local community.

The two journeys offer unique insights into the past and possible future of East London industry and employment. The North London Line was built to transport mainly manual labour to the manufacturing industries that emerged along the North and South Thames in the mid- and late-nineteenth century whilst the Docklands Light Railway was constructed to transport white collar workers from central London and the City to the expanding services-based industries newly relocated to the Isle of Dogs at the end of the twentieth century. The two train journeys provide visual evidence of the changing patterns of employment and industrial structure in East London. These patterns may also be more precisely charted through a brief examination of recent employment data covering each of the boroughs that make up the East London area.

East London consists of six boroughs – Barking and Dagenham, Havering, Newham, Redbridge, Tower Hamlets and Waltham Forest. In 1994 the population stood at a little over 1.2 million. Tower Hamlets includes parts of Docklands and the Lea Valley, localities in which employment levels have declined in the traditional manufacturing and docks areas. The project to regenerate Docklands has had mixed fortunes, partly because of the relative failure to extend the activities of the City eastwards[6] though, in recent years, the large office development at Canary Wharf has secured a rising occupancy level through the relocation of companies like Texaco, Mirror Group and some financial institutions. These developments led to a modest overall rise of 1 per cent in employment between 1989–1993 with the growth concentrated in the service industries whilst manufacturing employment continued to decline. Newham, like Tower Hamlets, experienced employment decline in manufacturing industries whilst modest growth took place in transport, communications and financial services. Overall, however, between 1989–93 employment fell by 4 per cent. Waltham Forest includes within its boundaries parts of the Lea Valley where manufacturing employment suffered significant decline in the period 1989–93, as did employment in construction and other service industries. The early 1990s saw a 13 per cent fall in employment in the borough.

Moving eastwards to the boroughs of Barking and Dagenham, Redbridge and Havering similar patterns of employment decline have been recorded between 1989–93. In Barking and Dagenham job losses in metals/vehicle manufacturing mainly contributed to a 5 per cent reduction in employment levels and in Havering, primarily due to job losses in the financial services sector, employment also fell by 5 per cent. Redbridge, unlike the other five boroughs, is predominantly residential with little manufacturing industry. Here employment rose by 7 per cent between 1989–93 mainly because of growth in services industries. The pattern of employment decline in manufacturing industries for the six boroughs between 1991–93 is set down in Table 1.

The relatively sharp decline in employment in vehicle manufacturing, arising from job reductions primarily at Ford's Dagenham plant, had a significant impact upon the local labour market in the Barking and Dagenham area. This pattern of rationalisation and job loss within large manufacturing plants has had a particularly important effect upon the East London area over the past three decades. It has created local pockets of relative economic decline from which specific communities have not recovered. Such areas rest uneasily alongside districts in which regeneration projects have arisen. This is the case for example, in those communities bordering the Docklands area. Canning Town exemplifies this pattern.

Canning Town was a classic location for the manufacturing

Table 1: Employment Levels in Manufacturing Industries 1991–93 in the Six East London Boroughs

	1991	*1993*	*Estimated Change 1991–93*
All Manufacturing	70400	54000	–23%
Extraction of minerals, ores other than fuels, manufacture of metal products, chemicals	5700	5200	–8.8%
Metal goods, engineering, vehicles	30,000	17,710	–41%
Other manufacturing (food, drink, textiles, paper,printing etc)	34,700	31,100	–10.4%

Source: LETEC London East Labour Market Assessment 1993–94 (figures for 1993 are estimates)

industries established in the second half of the nineteenth century and during the inter-war years of the twentieth. The proximity of London Docks and the location of companies like Tate and Lyle, Unilever, Harland and Wolff and Standard Telephone and Cables (STC) provided an employment base in the 1950s and early 1960s which offered the area relative stability, if not prosperity. During the period 1965-75 the traditional manufacturing industries located in Newham and Tower Hamlets experienced 24,000 job losses. In 1966 over half the employed residents in Canning Town worked in local industries. When, during the same period, Tate and Lyle shed over 3000 jobs the local community was heavily affected. Of those made redundant 1,730 lived in Newham and nearly 550 lived in Canning Town. Put another way, of 7,000 Canning Town residents working in manufacturing, 16 per cent worked at Tate and Lyle, the majority of whom were manual, process workers. The job losses at Tate & Lyle and other manufacturing plants within the area caused half the working population of Canning Town to experience redundancy during the period 1965-75, an experience from which the area was unable to recover over the following two decades.[7]

This pattern of job loss in manufacturing industry over the last three decades has contributed to the creation of pockets of severe unemployment and deprivation existing alongside those localities which have benefited from the growth in services sector employment and the process of gentrification. These changes have created a fragmented social structure and increasingly differentiated local labour markets in which it is likely that demand for skilled and unskilled manual employment will continue to decline and employment in professional, technical and managerial occupations will continue to rise.[8]

East and West

The re-engineering that took place in mid-Victorian London, involving new office development, the demolition of working-class housing areas and the construction of new road and rail links, largely shaped the social structure of the capital for the whole of the twentieth century. It left the West End as the centre of affluence and the east as an important location for the housing of its workforce, often in overcrowded and poor conditions.[9] The West End and City became great centres of commerce and finance and the east the location of the docks and manufacturing industries.

In the post-1945 period the distinction between west and east sharpened. An area of economic growth and expansion was created to the west of London with the development of the Heathrow/Gatwick/Thames Valley triangle. The triangle provided the infrastructure for the development of what came to be known as the 'M4 corridor' along which new industries emerged[10] whilst the east remained a focus for more traditional manufacturing industries, many of which were in decline, particularly those located in areas closest to the City of London. The closure of the London Docks in the 1970s only served to reinforce the disparity in economic fortunes between east and west. This disparity is reflected in a broad comparison of contemporary industrial structures and employment patterns.

When comparing the industrial structure of East London with the rest of the capital in the 1990s, three contrasting features arise. First, whilst East London and the capital as a whole have experienced increases in employment in service industries, manufacturing retains a greater share of employment in the east. Second, when comparing the size range of companies, East London has a higher percentage employed in smaller companies and, thirdly, a lower proportion are employed in workplaces of over 100 workers.

Table 2: Size Range of Companies: London and East London Compared

	E. London Employment	Companies	London Employment	Companies
Company Size				
under 25	1,800(37%)	3,400(90%)	934,300(29%)	176,800(89%)
25–100	36,300(9%)	14,500(30%)	300(8%)	778,700(24%)
over 100	16,200(33%)	100(2%)	1,515,016(47%)	5,100(2%)
Total	48,700(100%)	3,800(100%)	3,228,000(100%)	199,100(100%)

Source: 1991 Census of Employment.

The pattern of full and part-time employment also reveals a variation between East London and the rest of the capital. The proportion of full-time employees in London as a whole in 1991 was 82 per cent compared with 77 per cent for East London and part-time employment accounted for 23 per cent of the workforce in the east and 18 per cent for the capital as a whole. In manufacturing industries part-time employment consisted of less than 5 per cent of employees in both East London and all London. Finally, in relation to the workforce composition by sex, East London has a smaller percentage of women workers as a proportion of the total labour force compared to the capital as a whole.

Table 3: Workforce Composition by Sex: East London Compared to Whole of London

	London	East London
Male	53%	59%
Female	47%	41%

Source: 1991 Census of Employment

The broad picture of employment trends and industrial structure in East London reveals a pattern of de-industrialisation or decline that has more in common with localities in the industrial Midlands and North of Britain than they do with the rest of the south-east of England. The manufacturing sector has, however, demonstrated some strengths in coming through the recessions of the early 1980s and 1990s and continues to provide an important employment base for the local workforce. The rest of this chapter shifts the focus of study to the plant or workplace level and analyses the results of a survey of manufacturing companies located in East London. The survey was designed to identify recent trends and developments in labour and product markets and company ownership and organisation as well as indicating how East London employers are developing strategies for meeting the increasingly competitive conditions prevailing in all manufacturing industries in the 1990s.

The Survey

Aims

There were five main objectives of the survey. First, much of the recent academic literature on local economies has focused on the decline of traditional manufacturing centres in the Midlands and North with relatively little attention being given to the specific experiences of manufacturing industries in London and the south-east. The survey makes a contribution to filling this gap. Second, the survey offered the opportunity to focus on events at plant level in East London, a task not undertaken since the pioneering studies of Woodward in the 1950s and 1960s. Third, the local economy of East London is located within a broader geographical area in which considerable change is taking place as a result of the regeneration of London Docklands and the development of new communications links with the European Single Market. The survey provided an opportunity to evaluate the impact of these changes on a sample of manufacturing companies. Fourth, an extensive literature has suggested that manufacturing enterprises in the advanced industrial nations are experiencing significant changes in production techniques, management organisation and working patterns.[11] To what extent were enterprises in East London experiencing this transformation in the early 1990s? Finally, the survey was designed to be the first stage in a longer term research programme focused on society and industry in East London. The second phase of the research will use the survey data to identify workplaces that provide the opportunity for more in-depth case study analysis at workplace level.

Survey Approach
The geographical definition of East London coincided with the six boroughs covered by the London East Training and Enterprise Council (LETEC) and, therefore, offered the possibility of using recently published data from that organisation as well as from other sources, including census reports, as a basis of comparison with the data generated by the survey. Identifying firms presented some difficulties since the majority of manufacturing companies were small businesses that were less likely to participate in the survey. In 1991 East London had approximately 3000 manufacturing companies, of which about 90 per cent were small firms employing less than twenty-five workers. In constructing the sample, it was considered more important to include a significant percentage of the workforce than it was to obtain the participation of a large number of companies. The survey focused, therefore, on obtaining participation from mainly medium and large-scale plants whose fortunes would have the most impact on the local economy. A list of 100 companies was eventually compiled and the survey distributed to each. Twenty-one companies provided in-depth responses upon which the survey analysis is based. The response rate indicates that it is not possible to claim that the survey sample is representative of a cross section of companies by size or sector. Nonetheless, the data received was detailed and comprehensive covering many aspects of workplace activities and the twenty one enterprises participating in the survey accounted for approximately 30 per cent of the total employed in manufacturing in the East London area in 1994.

The survey requested information on a comprehensive set of topics including type and age of business, ownership and location of plants, product range, markets, performance and turnover. The survey also asked for information on changes in employment and working patterns, management organisation, employee relations, production techniques and training programmes. Finally, employers were asked about their attitudes toward, and reasons for, their location in East London. Respondents were asked to indicate the patterns of change over the period 1990–94. Questionnaires were completed in spring 1995. The following analysis offers a thematic appraisal of the data provided. Respondents were mainly senior management staff with key responsibilities within their companies. Wherever possible, data provided was checked against published annual reports and accounts and other company publications.

The Sample

Of the twenty-one respondents, six were multinational enterprises (MNEs) with manufacturing plants located in other continents, twelve were UK companies operating from single plants located in East London and three were UK enterprises with other plants located elsewhere within the country. Of the six MNEs, four were UK subsidiaries of overseas companies. All six MNEs had sister plants in the USA and two had plants in at least four continents. The sample was, therefore, heavily geared toward the medium and larger scale workplaces that, as Table 4 indicates, were well established within the area. The vast majority of the sample had been established for at least twenty-five years and many for a lot longer. One medium-sized workplace had been set up in the 1820s to provide agricultural implements for the local area and had evolved into a company producing valves, motors and pumps for a range of engineering purposes. Other companies in the chemicals and printing industries

Table 4: Respondents by Type and Age of Business and Ownership

Type			
A.	Extraction of minerals and ores other than fuels, manufacture of metals, mineral products and chemicals		6
B.	Metal goods, engineering and vehicles		12
C.	Other manufacturing (eg print, footwear textiles, publishing etc)		3
Age of Business			
Less Than 10 Years			1
Between 10–25 years			1
Between 25–50 years			8
Over 50 years			11
Ownership			
UK		17	
of which owner managed			6
Overseas			4

had associations with the East London area that dated back to the mid-nineteenth century. Six companies had their origins in the nineteenth century, one was founded in 1902 and most of the remainder were established during the inter-war period or shortly after.

Products, Markets and Performance

The companies surveyed broadly divided between component suppliers and those who assembled or produced finished goods. Two-thirds of respondents fell into the former category, making a diverse range of components for customers in industries such as pharmaceuticals, chemicals, food processing and vehicle and machine manufacture. Those assembling or producing finished goods, the remaining third, were associated with industries such as construction, food, printing and automobiles. The majority of companies within both these categories anticipated important changes taking place in their product range and product markets in future years (Table 5). Of those currently experiencing change or anticipating change, four main reasons were given. First, and most importantly, companies anticipated an increase in competitive conditions within their sector as a result of developments within UK and European markets. Second, companies were experiencing increasing demands from their customers in relation to product specification, delivery and quality. Third, component suppliers were seeking to diversify their customer base in an attempt to overcome dependence upon a specific industrial sector and, finally, a smaller proportion of companies reported that product development and innovation was associated with taking advantage of perceived improvements in export opportunities.

Table 5: Changes in Product Range and Markets

Changes in product range and markets (1990–94)	9 (43%)
No change in product range and markets (1990–94)	10 (48%)
Future change anticipated in product range and markets	16 (76%)
No future change anticipated in product range and markets	5 (24%)

Respondents were asked to indicate the proportionate shares of their products sold in UK, European and other markets. Only one plant supplied a significant proportion of its products to other plants within the company. Amongst the remaining twenty plants, the UK market took the largest percentage share of output with the European market some distance behind (Table 6). As might be expected, the plants of MNEs tended to sell a higher proportion of their output to European and other (global) markets. There was, however, evidence of a significant minority of plants that sought to increase sales of their products within the European market.

Table 6: % Share of Products Sold in UK, European and Other Markets in 1994

Market	*% Share*
United Kingdom	76
Rest of EU	17
Other	7

Of those whose products were mainly sold in the UK market, one company relied entirely upon the local London area. For the majority the local London market share of UK product sales varied between 25-75 per cent. From the evidence provided by respondents three main conclusions could be drawn concerning product markets. First, companies demonstrated an awareness of the necessity to adapt and change product ranges in order to meet new customer needs. From the evidence of responses, the changes to product range were driven primarily by customer needs rather than by innovations in product or process technologies, suggesting that most of the plants within the survey operated in relatively mature and stable product markets. Several respondents reported improvements in their strategies for customising products to more precisely fit customer needs and a minority of the component manufacturers indicated that they had been required, in recent years, to hold a greater proportion of their products in stock since their customers had adopted just-in-time (JIT) approaches to component supply.[12] Second, the UK market continued to be the main outlet for most companies and, within the UK, the local London area received a significant proportion of market share. Finally, the local plants of multinational corporations were responsible for the highest percentage share of products sold outside the UK, particularly in other countries of the European Union.

Data supplied on profitability and investment indicated that respondents had experienced mixed fortunes during the period 1990–94. Half of the companies reported that they had maintained an investment programme during 1990–94, four of these had seen a continuous rise in investment over the period. The remainder had seen a fall in investment in 1991–92 followed by a modest recovery in the subsequent two years. There was a correlation between size of plant and investment programmes. The larger plants (over 100 employees) tended to maintain modest investment levels throughout the period whilst medium and smaller plants recorded a falling off in investment between 1991–93 and a small improvement in 1994. Data on profitability was supplied by half of the respondents. For the period 1990–94, profit levels of these companies tended to fall during 1991–92 and make a slight recovery in 1993–94. Finally, in relation to output levels for the period 1990–94, over half of the respondents reported some growth for the period as a whole, with stronger increases taking place in 1993 and 1994.

Employment Patterns

Debate about the changing nature of the UK labour market has tended to focus on three main themes – industrial structure, occupational change and shifts in employers' labour-use strategies.[13] An extensive literature has emerged over the last decade. Discussion of industrial structure has drawn attention to the underlying shift in employment away from manufacturing and toward public and private services industries. The 'restructuring' debate has largely focused upon the changing character of the economies of advanced industrial countries with some concluding that a new post-industrial society has emerged based largely around the successful diffusion of new information and communication technologies[14]. These authors emphasise the importance of the technical and organisation transformation of productive industries and the emergence of a new international division of labour based upon the spatial disaggregation of the production process.[15] The historical context of this transformation is often represented as a shift from one dominant production paradigm, mass production, to a more specialised and consumer-oriented form of flexible production.[16]

The discussion over the characteristics of change in industrial structure has been accompanied by a parallel debate on the nature and extent of change in occupational structure. Studies have shown how, within the UK, blue collar occupations have been in decline since the early 1970s whilst white collar work has increased. Manufacturing has been particularly affected by this trend with a significant fall in the numbers of craft and manual jobs. This trend has only been partly offset by growth in professional/technical and clerical occupations within the sector.[17] The third area of debate on the changing character of employment has focused upon employers' labour-use strategies. Here the discussion centred upon the extent to which employers have consciously adopted policies designed to distinguish between core employees, with permanent, usually full-time, positions and peripheral workers whose employment status is characterised by part-time, casual and temporary contracts. The core-periphery strategy emerged as the dominant discourse in management literature in the late 1980s. Government legislation, designed to create a more flexible labour market, appeared to provide the climate in which the model could be operationalised.[18] Recently published evidence from a number of academics, however, has created some scepticism over the extent to which the model has been applied in the UK. Sceptics have argued that the core-periphery strategy has been adopted in some private and public services industries but in the manufacturing sector in which it was considered most relevant, it has not been widely utilised[19].

A brief review of these debates in relation to recent developments in the East London labour market provides evidence of the area broadly conforming to the UK pattern of change in industrial and occupational structure. In terms of the restructuring debate, the area has experienced many of the features of de-industrialisation, though there has been relatively little evidence of the influx of 'high technology' industries often associated with the new panacea of the post-industrial society.

In terms of employers' labour-use strategies there is evidence, from aggregate employment data and the manufacturing employers survey, to support the sceptics' view that employers in the manufacturing sector have not adopted the core-periphery strategy. In East London employment in the public and private services industries in 1993 accounted for over 80 per cent of total employment. Between 1991–93 the only sectors recording growth in employment were Banking, Finance, Insurance and Business Services (6 per cent), Other Services (7 per cent) and Transport and Communications (3 per cent). All other sectors experienced reductions in employment with manufacturing suffering particularly badly with a decrease of approximately 23 per cent.[20] Occupational structures in East London also appear, according to a 1993 survey[21], to be following national trends with the major occupational groupings being clerical and secretarial, managers, administrators and professional staff. Though the rate of growth in service sector employment and white collar occupations has not been as rapid in East London as compared to the rest of London, the underlying trends are consistent with London as a whole and the broader UK picture.

The data on part-time employment in East London indicates that the area has a slightly higher percentage of part-time workers than the rest of London and that they are concentrated in financial services, hotels and catering and distribution industries. Manufacturing industries have well below 5 per cent of employees on part-time contracts. This aggregate data suggests that the core-periphery strategy (where part-time employment is regarded as characteristic of the presence of a peripheral workforce) has been largely confined to services industries in East London and has not been adopted by local manufacturing employers (Table 7). The results of the manufacturing employers' survey also supports this conclusion.

Table 7: Full and Part-Time Employment in Industrial Sectors

	% Full Time	% Part Time
Extraction/Manufacture of minerals and metals	2	–
Metal goods, Engineering and Vehicles	5	1
Other Manufacturing	11	3
Construction	6	1
Distribution, Hotels and Catering, Repairs	17	35
Transport and Communications	10	2
Business and financial Services	19	10
Other Services	31	48

Source: London East Employment and Training Survey, LETEC 1993

The survey sample covered approximately 30 per cent of the total workforce employed in manufacturing in the East London area in 1994 (Table 8). Respondents provided evidence of change in employment patterns over the period 1990–94. From that evidence several points emerged. First, those plants covered by the survey experienced job losses over the period 1990–94 that were consistent with those levels incurred by the East London manufacturing sector as a whole (–23 per cent in both cases). Second, the sector retained a predominantly male workforce and, third, the proportion of temporary and part-time workers was less than 1 per cent of the total workforce covered by the survey with little change occurring in these categories during the period 1990–94 (Tables 9 and 10). This suggests that a core/periphery employment strategy was not adopted by companies employing nearly one-third of the East London manufacturing workforce.

Finally, it should be emphasised that the most notable feature of employment change was the high percentage of jobs lost in a relatively short period. This pattern reflected the broader experience of UK manufacturing companies for whom job cuts were a central part of their attempts to survive the recessionary economic conditions of the early 1990s. Given the significant level of job losses and some evidence of the maintenance and even expansion of output over the period 1990–94, it seems likely that companies undertook changes in work organisation and production techniques in order to raise the productiveness of the workforce that remained. It is on this question of changes in production organisation that the survey provided particularly useful insights.

Table 8: Composition of the Workforce Survey Sample (1994)

Manufacturing Workforce in East London (1994 estimate)	48,000 (100%)
Manufacturing Workforce covered by Survey Sample by Survey Sample	14,212 (30%)

Table 9: Change in Employment of Workforce Survey Sample 1990–94

	1990	1994	%Change
Total Employed	18,406	14,212	–23%
Men	16,329	12,639	–22%
Women	2,077	1,573	–24%

Table 10: Workforce Survey Sample: Part-Time and Temporary Workers 1990–94

	1990	1994
Part-Time	161 (0.8%)	110 (0.8%)
Temporary	20 (0.12%)	23 (0.12%)

Changes in Production Techniques and Work Organisation

An important objective of the workplace survey was to evaluate the extent to which manufacturing enterprises in East London were undertaking the organisational innovations that have been widely reported as occurring elsewhere. Business and academic publications over the past decade have increasingly focused on the revolution in production techniques and work organisation that have, in particular, taken place in the manufacturing sector. It was useful, therefore, to ascertain the extent to which East London enterprises had been influenced by, and taken part in, this revolution.

Before addressing the specific findings of the survey, it is necessary to briefly sketch the broad characteristics of the transformation in the manufacturing sector that many claim has occurred.[22] The starting point was the early 1980s and the context was the recognition, especially amongst US, UK and other European manufacturing firms, of the competitive advantage enjoyed by Japanese companies, particularly those operating in the automobile industry. Bill Hayden of Ford Europe, for example, returned from a trip to Japan in 1980 expressing concern about the Japanese advantage and immediately initiated an 'After Japan' programme designed to improve productivity and labour flexibility in Ford's European plants. Hayden's concerns reflected the broader situation in the international economy in which Japanese multinationals were increasingly challenging their European and US multinational rivals. The Japanese challenge arose from their role as exporters and from their establishment of local plants in the USA and Europe. Britain was a favoured location for Japanese companies throughout the 1980s and early 1990s with approximately 38 per cent of Japanese European investment taking place in the UK over this period. The success of Japanese plants in the UK sharpened the domestic debates over the causes of Britain's 'productivity problem'.[23] The Japanese model appeared to offer practical strategies aimed at delivering higher productivity.

The precise characteristics of this model was the subject of considerable debate during the 1980s. There was a broad recognition that it primarily involved organisational changes to management structures and production methods and required the development of a highly skilled and committed workforce. In 1990 a very influential study, 'The Machine that Changed the World',[24] was published by Massachusetts Institute of Technology (MIT). It provided a clear exposition of the main features of the Japanese model, which, it claimed was based primarily upon a new form of production organisation called 'lean production'. This new form of organisation could, the study argued, be adopted by manufacturing enterprises across all sectors. Its applicability was not confined to the automobile industry nor was it a product of specifically Japanese conditions. Lean production had several distinctive features. It involved a new approach to the organisation of production. Stocks were minimised and production took place in smaller lots or batches[25] ensuring improved quality and the delivery of the product on a JIT principle. This, in turn, required new approaches to the organisation of the component supply chain and facilitated a process of continuous improvement of production procedures. Associated with these new approaches to production were changes in the organisation of the workforce with the emphasis being placed upon team work and the use of a skilled and well trained labour force. The main advantages of this new production technique were higher capacity utilisation, improved quality and raised productivity.

The MIT study caused considerable debate within European manufacturing companies. Even in the successful and prosperous German manufacturing region of Baden Württemberg enterprises were strongly influenced by the study and proceeded to reorganise production methods and change management styles. Companies like Daimler-Benz, Robert Bosch and Volkswagen bought 'one thousand copies of the book each as a manual for their top management'.[26] In the early 1990s many US and European multinational companies introduced new approaches designed to emulate the Japanese model, incorporating both the reorganisation of production systems and the development of new human resource management techniques (HRM). HRM complemented lean production and was associated with the development of team work, less hierarchical forms of management and the development of a committed and well-trained workforce.[27] Since its publication, the MIT study has been criticised for overstating the uniqueness and success of the lean production approach.[28] Nonetheless, even the more critical academic analyses have acknowledged that amongst managements, who were already concerned by the Japanese threat, the study acted as a catalyst that prompted enterprises to adopt more innovative approaches to production techniques and employee relations.

The purpose here is not to undertake a critical assessment of lean

Table 11: % of Respondents Reporting Changes in Management Organisation, Employee Relations and Production Techniques in the period 1990–94

	% Reporting Changes Adopted
MANAGEMENT ORGANISATION	
Reduced layers of management	76%
Changes in role of supervision	81%
Devolution of financial management	29%
Others	19%
EMPLOYEE RELATIONS	
Human Resource Management (HRM)	62%
Total Quality Management (TQM)	52%
New Performance Measures	81%
Others	10%
PRODUCTION TECHNIQUES	
Just-in-Time (JIT)	19%
Lean Production	52%
Other	33%

production and other new management techniques. The goal is, more modestly, to ascertain the extent to which the wider debate on the new management techniques influenced the strategies and approaches of management in the manufacturing plants that participated in the East London survey. In this context, respondents were asked to identify the types of changes introduced between 1990–94 under three broad headings – Management Organisation, Employee Relations and Production Techniques. The findings are recorded in Table 11.

The survey responses suggest that manufacturing employers in East London have taken an active approach to reforming production organisation, management structures and employee relations. Change in each of these spheres was reported by large and medium sized enterprises and was not confined to the respondents from MNEs. A majority of respondents had reduced layers of management, changed supervisory roles, embraced the HRM approach, developed new performance measures, introduced new quality control procedures and adopted lean production methods. Under the heading 'Other Changes', a minority of respondents indicated that they had introduced continuous improvement programmes, 'professionalised' management organisation and adopted more considered strategies toward customer care and marketing. The survey evidence clearly suggests that managements have implemented a package of organisational innovations in their East London plants. This conclusion is further supported by the responses provided concerning changes to Working Patterns (Table 12). The majority of respondents reported the adoption, or possible adoption in the near future, of team working, multi-skilling and multi-tasking arrangements and one third recorded the increased use of contracting out arrangements. One respondent, making electrical components, reported the transfer of the company's entire manufacturing process to a sub-contractor located in Singapore. Taken together the survey results point to employers adopting a range of innovations that have much in common with central features of the Japanese model.

Such a conclusion, however, requires qualification. The survey approach allowed respondents to define for themselves the meanings attached to the checklist of techniques contained in the survey. There was, therefore, the possibility of different interpretations of what are, in practice, complex sets of changes in production processes and management organisation. Second, it was not possible to ascertain the extent to which the changes reported were undertaken as part of a strategic or more piecemeal management approach. Finally, the survey

Table 12: Working Patterns – number of respondents reporting the adoption of new working patterns in the period 1990–94

	Yes	No	Considering
Contracting out	7	7	–
Flexible working	7	5	1
Team working	13	12	1
Multi-skilling	13	1	–
Multi-tasking	9	1	12

could convey information on the innovations adopted but did not seek to evaluate the consequences of their introduction. Despite these caveats, the survey results indicate a receptive approach, in a sample of East London workplaces, to organisational innovation.

Industrial Relations and Training

The consequences for industrial relations of the adoption of HRM and lean production techniques has been well documented. The emphasis in workplace relations shifts away from the collective and toward individual contractual relations between employers and workers. Often, trade unionism is pushed to the margins of workplace affairs.[29] Approximately half of the survey sample were non-unionised workplaces. Respondents from these workplaces indicated little change to industrial relations procedures in recent years. In unionised plants respondents identified three main trends. First, there had been a move away from national and company wide agreements toward more localised, plant level negotiations. Second, the number of union representatives within plants had fallen and, finally, union influence over work organisation and working practices had diminished in recent years.

Two-thirds of respondents indicated that new training programmes had been adopted in the period 1990–94. The programmes involved a combination of company specific schemes and courses provided by external bodies. Respondents indicated that companies had adopted a variety of approaches to staff development and training incorporating open and distant learning packages as well as encouraging staff to undertake more conventional courses leading to professional qualifications. Training programmes were aimed at all three categories of high, intermediate and unskilled employees, though it was higher level employees who were most likely to obtain access to greater training opportunities. Three respondents commented on the lack of appropriate skills training, offered by external institutions, for intermediate (craft) employees.

Location

Respondents were invited to comment on the reasons for the geographical location of their plant in the East London area. One third of the responses referred to road and rail transport links to routes within the UK as a significant locational advantage and four plants cited proximity to the River Thames as the primary reason for their location in East London. Others offered mainly 'historical' reasons, such as the proximity to the owner's home, for their being cited in East London. In reply to a question specifically designed to elicit attitudes toward the potential value of location along the future East Thames Gateway, one respondent offered a positive view. The attitudes toward geographical location tended to reflect respondents' views of their current, mainly UK, market orientation. Few identified new opportunities arising specifically from the proposed development of new rail and transport links to mainland Europe.

Concluding Comments: Coping with Competition?

Over the past century or more, East London's manufacturing industries have provided a useful barometer by which to measure the condition of the local economy. When manufacturing industries have expanded and developed the East End has obtained a modest level of prosperity and dynamism. When manufacturing has declined many areas have fallen rapidly with it into poverty and decay. In recent decades, the closure of the London Docks and extensive rationalisation in the manufacturing industries have been double blows from which the region is yet to recover. Despite this relatively bleak experience over the last three decades, manufacturing has retained an important role within the region. This chapter has primarily focused upon the manufacturing enterprises that have survived the recent recessions and has attempted, through a survey analysis, to identify recent trends and developments at plant or workplace level.

The survey focused on twenty one manufacturing plants employing a little under one third of the manufacturing workforce of East London. The workplaces taking part in the survey were mainly medium and larger scale employers. The early 1990s was a period in which these enterprises sought to cope with increased competition within the wider context of domestic and international economic recession. The recession particularly affected the performance of UK manufacturers and East London plants that participated in the survey were no exception. The survey revealed several of the measures taken by local workplaces. One in four jobs was lost over the period 1990–94. The reduction of labour costs was a key element in management strategy toward weathering the recession of the early 1990s, just as it had been in the early 1980s. Arguably, what was new about company responses in the 1990s, compared to a decade earlier, was the more considered approach to product markets and organisational innovation.

Survey replies indicated that component suppliers attempted to develop a more responsive approach to customer needs and sought to diversify their customer base and the majority of companies surveyed stressed the importance of changing and improving their product range in anticipation of future market trends. Perhaps the most significant area of change reported by respondents was in relation to management organisation, production techniques, work organisation and employee relations. The performance data supplied suggested that output was sustained and in many cases modestly increased over the period 1990–94. Rising output levels produced by a smaller workforce suggests that improved productivity was achieved mainly as a result of innovations in production techniques and work organisation.[30] Respondents provided evidence of the application of many of the management approaches associated with the Japanese model of lean production. This was revealed in relation to both the organisation of production and in approaches toward employee relations, particularly in the unionised plants. The influence of the new techniques was not confined to those managements in multinational enterprises who were most likely to be aware of the latest fashion in management theory and practice. Several single plant enterprises had adopted the language and policies associated with the new techniques.

Whether 'leaner means fitter' remains to be seen. There was little evidence that companies saw their location in East London and the

East Thames Corridor as providing them with a future competitive advantage in relation to export opportunities to continental Europe. Also innovation was tempered by tradition. The new management techniques were accompanied by more traditional approaches aimed at cutting labour costs and raising labour intensity during a period of economic recession. Indeed, the job cuts may have been a necessary prerequisite for the implementation of the new production techniques and the adoption of HRM policies. Nevertheless, rationalisation was accompanied by a resilience characteristic of the long established manufacturing enterprises of East London. The survey offered firm evidence of manufacturers engaging in organisational innovation designed to keep up with the competition. The evidence suggests, however, that the price of this process of innovation has been paid by the local workforce in the form of job cuts and work intensification.

Acknowledgements

My thanks to the respondents and their companies for providing the detailed information requested in the survey. Thanks also to Jag Pabla of the London East Training and Enterprise Council (LETEC) for his comments and advice at an early stage in the development of the research project.

Notes

[1] London Borough of Newham, *West Ham 1886–1986*, Plaistow Press, Newham 1986.
[2] J. Woodward, *Industrial Organisation: Theory and Practice*, Oxford University Press, Oxford 1965.
[3] London East Training and Enterprise Council, *Labour Market Assessment 1993–94*, LETEC, London 1994.
[4] London Borough of Newham 1986, p52.
[5] *Ibid.*, p53.
[6] G. Poynter, *'Wall Street on the Water?' Employment Patterns in London Docklands*, South East Region TUC, London 1989.
[7] Canning Town Community, *Canning Town's Declining Community Income: The Cost of Industrial Closures 1966–76*, Canning Town Community Publications, London 1979.
[8] London East Training and Enterprise Council 1994, pp6–8.
[9] G. Stedman Jones, *Outcast London: A Study of Relationships Between Classes in Victorian Society*, Penguin, Harmondsworth 1984, Chapters 5 and 8.
[10] M. Boddy, J. Lovering and K. Bassett, *Sunbelt City? A Study of Change in Britain's M4 Growth Corridor*, Clarendon Press, Oxford 1986.
[11] See, for example, J. Womack, D. Jones and D. Roos, *The Machine That*

Changed the World, Harper Row, New York 1991; and T. Elger and C. Smith, *Global Japanisation*, Routledge, London 1994, pp1–24.

[12] Just-in-Time (JIT) techniques relate to the frequency of deliveries to an assembly plant and the organisation of production. Component supplier respondents participating in the survey were referring to their new role in the JIT delivery or supply chain..

[13] See, for example, A. Pollert (ed), *Farewell to Flexibility*, Blackwell, Oxford 1991; N. Gilbert, R. Burrows and A. Pollert, *Fordism and Flexibility, Divisions and Change*, MacMillan, London 1992.

[14] See, for example, M. Carnoy, M. Castells, S. Cohen and F. Cardoso, *The New Global Economy in the Information Age*, Pennsylvania State University, Pennsylvania 1993.

[15] See, for example, J. Henderson, *The Globalisation of High Technology Production*, Routledge, London 1991.

[16] See, for example, M. Piore and C. Sabel, *The New Industrial Divide*, Basic Books, New York 1984; and critics, such as R. Hyman '*Plus ça Change?* The Theory of Production and the Production of Theory', in A. Pollert, *Farewell to Flexibility*, pp259–283.

[17] P. Elias, 'Occupational Change in a Working-Life Perspective: Internal and External Views' in R. Rose, M. Penn and J. Rubery (eds), *Skill and Occupational Change*, Oxford University Press, Oxford 1994, pp77–106.

[18] W. Brown, 'The Changed Political Role of Unions Under a Hostile Government' in B. Pimlott and C. Cook (eds), *Trade Unions in British Politics*, Longman, Harlow 1991, pp274–285.

[19] J. Atkinson, *Flexibility: Planning for an Uncertain Future* in *Manpower Policy and Practice: The IMS Review*, Volume 1, pp26–9 and J. Atkinson, *Flexibility, Uncertainty and Manpower Management*, IMS Report Number 89, Institute for Manpower Studies, University of Sussex, Brighton 1985.

[20] London East Training and Enterprise Council (1994), pp10–11.

[21] *Ibid.*, pp24–25.

[22] See, for example, J. Womack, D. Jones, D. Roos, (1990), and N. Oliver, B. Wilkinson, *The Japanisation of British Industry – New Developments in the 1990s*, Blackwell, Oxford 1992.

[23] D. Metcalf, 'Water Notes Dry Up', London School of Economics, Discussion Paper 314, 1988.

[24] J. Womack, D. Jones and D. Roos (1991).

[25] *Ibid.*, pp161–162.

[26] P. Cooke and K. Morgan, 'Growth Regions under Duress: Renewal Strategies in Baden Württemberg and Emilia-Romagna', in A. Amin and N. Thrift (eds), *Globalisation, Institutions and Regional Development in Europe*, Oxford University Press, Oxford 1994.

[27] See P. Blyton and P. Turnbull (eds), *Reassessing Human Resource Management*, Sage, London 1992.

[28] See, for example, K. Williams *et al*, 'Against Lean Production', *Economy and Society* Volume 21, Number 3, 1992, pp321–354.

[29] See P. Garrahan and P. Stewart, *The Nissan Enigma*, Mansell, London 1992.

[30] There is evidence of this pattern of labour intensification in several other studies of UK manufacturing in the 1990s. See, for example, T. Elger and P. Fairbrother, 'Inflexible Flexibility: A Case Study of Modularisation' in N. Gilbert *et al* (1992) pp89–106.

East London and Europe

Greg Clark

Introduction

In order to place the role of the European Union (EU) in the regeneration of East London in some context it is first necessary to make some points about how the UK regeneration policy has evolved in East London over the past ten years, and how it has been matched with extensive development of the role of the EU over the same period.

A recent report on regeneration programmes in England refers to the 'patchwork quilt' which has built up over the past ten to fifteen years. In East London this has meant a broad range of regeneration and economic development initiatives including:

Task Forces:	Spitalfields, Hackney
City Challenges:	Stratford, Bethnal Green, Dalston
Urban Development Corporations:	London Docklands
Urban Programme:	Newham, Tower Hamlets, Hackney
Housing Action Trusts:	Waltham Forest, Bow
Assisted Areas:	East Thames Corridor, Lea Valley
Business Leadership Teams:	East London Partnership
TECs (Training and Enterprise Councils):	London East TEC, and City and Inner London North TEC
Single Regeneration Budget:	twelve designations

Alongside these major initiatives, there has also been a further tranche of smaller programmes which have orchestrated additional activity in East London. These include Compacts, Education Business Partnerships, Section 11, Ethnic Minority Grants, Enterprise Agencies and Enterprise Zones. Changes in the way that other key agencies are run have also made a contribution to the regeneration of the area; these include the incorporation of further education colleges, and the reorganisation of higher education to create a body of New Universities.

The context of these initiatives is worth describing in some detail. The overall decline in economic performance of East London has been depicted in many ways and some of the figures are well known. The use of urban programme funds by the DoE in East London was testimony to high levels of unemployment, vacant land and sites and a general level of obsolescence in the sub-region. Put together, the commitment from the Government during the mid-1980s, encompassing these urban programme designations along with the London Docklands Development Corporation (still the largest urban regeneration project in Europe) created the beginning of a regeneration triangle that was based on evidence that the populations of Hackney, Tower Hamlets, and Newham were facing some of the most urgent problems in the country. The recession of the early 1990s forced the situation. London's economy, traditionally robust, based on its world city status as a major financial centre, had spawned many new jobs in the business and finance services sectors during the boom of the late 1980s. However, when the recession came, new figures on job losses and unemployment emerged showing that for the first time in history London's aggregate unemployment figures had overtaken the national average. The symbolic impact of this was immense. If London, with its traditional strengths and international role, and its large pockets of wealth and success had overtaken the rest of the country in the unemployment stakes, then something drastic must have happened in its poorest parts. East London, already the poorest sub-region, had lost the single economic factor that had mitigated the industrial decline that had been ongoing for many years previous: jobs in the City and Central London were being lost to East Londoners. The myth that the Central London and City economies could support the employment of East London's unemployed workers was fatally exposed.

Later, in 1994, when the Government published its Index of Local Conditions there was little surprise in the East End that Hackney, Tower Hamlets, and Newham were 'designated' the three poorest boroughs in the country. Earlier in the year, in a survey of local economies published in *The Guardian*, the borough of Barking and Dagenham was identified as the worst place in the country to seek work, with unemployed to vacancy ratios of 150:1 (i.e. 150 unemployed residents for every publicly notified job). The borough of Waltham Forest, with its combination of the features of inner and outer London showed extremely high unemployment at the ward level, especially around Leyton and Walthamstow. Redbridge and Havering, traditionally perceived as 'leafy' suburbia, also showed high scores on key deprivation indexes in certain key wards.

The results of this dramatic recessionary impact on Greater London were highlighted most keenly by the Association of London Authorities (ALA) in 'The Case For London' in the early 1990s. And illustrated vividly in their promotional brochure 'Do You See London Through Rose-tinted Glasses?' which showed, through use of colour-selective plastic specs that the received wisdom, and the true facts about London, were dramatically distinct. This brochure, along with a series of statistical reports, served to support a campaign for greater assistance for London from the EU.

Why was the EU targeted explicitly as a key focus of the campaign about London, and how would East London have stood to benefit? To understand this, an explanation of the role of the EU in the regeneration of urban areas is required.

The European Dimension

Since the origins of the European project in the Treaty of Rome in 1951, a willingness to create European budgets to address specific problems had been evident. The early initiatives, the coal and steel community and the atomic energy programme, had been quickly augmented with the agricultural programmes, eventually leading to the creation of the Common Agricultural Policy. As the European project emerged through the 1960s and 1970s, actions and funding in the fields of industry, technology, environment and trade came onto the agenda, and by the mid-1980s, the EEC was becoming a significant contributor to interventionist strategies in many fields of public life. The wholesale revision of regional policies in the mid-1980s led to the creation of a comprehensive programme of 'structural fund' support for regional development and initiatives to tackle unemployment.

As a consequence of these developments, by the end of the 1980s the EEC was already a major funder of local initiatives with an economic development or regeneration feature across the UK. European regional aid programmes were being used to tackle the key problems that existed in Merseyside, Strathclyde, the North East, Northern Ireland, the Midlands, and other depressed regions, under the industrial regeneration programmes. These programmes were successfully used to complement and enhance the regeneration activities of central Government and local authorities in the regions of the UK. The prime beneficiaries were industrial cities and those communities most harmed by the loss of industrial employment. In most cases, the areas which were benefiting from EEC aid were also those that received support from the Government's 'patchwork quilt' of regeneration programmes.

EEC structural aid had a number of key objectives which were focused on improving economic and social cohesion across the community. It particular, emphasis was placed on assisting those regions suffering from serious underdevelopment and industrial decline and resultant large numbers of young people and adults who were unemployed. The funds themselves were designated on the basis of regional figures on economic performance and measures of deprivation and decline. All regions of the community qualified for support for employment initiatives, but only those regions with significant industrial decline and macro-economic underdevelopment got access to the larger capital budgets.

This meant that whilst London had benefited from employment and training initiatives under the European Social Fund (ESF), it had not secured a share of the much larger capital resources from the European Regional Development Fund (ERDF) for capital reconversion and business development programmes. And whilst other regeneration areas in the UK were benefiting from the EEC support, London was not. Therefore, the ALA, acting for the London Boroughs, was very keen to focus on EEC regional aid, both as a means to bring precious regional aid resources to the boroughs, and to develop a distinctive and more contemporary picture of London's problems and needs. This directly confronted the Government's policy of a low profile approach to London's problems, fearing that it would otherwise 'compromise the dignity of the capital'.

One further feature of London's problem in claiming EEC regional aid was that the strict eligibility for the funds was not related to the mixed indices of deprivation used by the UK government for designating its various urban initiatives, but on much stricter aggregated measures of pure industrial decline or macro-economic underdevelopment. In effect, it was possible for cities with lower overall problems but high industrial collapse to benefit from EEC regional aid whilst some cities, with greater general problems but lower industrial decline were excluded. The distribution patterns of deprivation in the UK had reached the point where parts of London (especially East London) were amongst the poorest in the country but were not based on the right measures of deprivation to receive EEC regional aid (i.e. London's deprivation was not considered to be sufficiently the consequence of industrial decline alone).

This picture was thrown into stark relief by the unemployment figures which emerged in the early 1990s and a debate began about the importance of a more general urban dimension to EEC regional aid as a way of addressing the problems. This lack of an urban dimension to EEC policies, the specific reluctance of the Government to talk up the needs of London, and the general attitude of 'anti-capital city' amongst the industrial cities of northern Europe all conspired to make the task of gaining EEC aid for London (and especially East London) a tall order.

The Campaign for Objective 2 Status

Against this backdrop ALA led a long and difficult campaign to gain Objective 2 (Industrial Regeneration) status for London. The campaign itself focused on achieving a number of distinctive objectives within the general broad aim of making the case for London. The EEC had, in the late 1980s, financed a series of urban pilot projects under the Article 10 of the ERDF. This was a small slice of the regional aid budget offered for the purpose of innovatory projects in the field of regional development. London had won a collaboration project with Marseilles which mounted a small series of demonstration projects in inner city economic development. These Urban Pilot Projects had been supported because there was a general view that the problems of urban areas might well require some distinctive approaches which could improve the general value of structural fund expenditure. This was based on the realisation that a large proportion of all regional aid budgets were actually being spent in urban areas. It was not necessarily indicative of an intention to move towards an EEC urban programme.

The ALA-led campaign therefore had a range of inter-connected goals. These could be simplified as:

* Establish support for a full Urban Competence for the EEC. (i.e. make urban policy an explicit area of EEC activity with budgets and programmes attached).
* Add an additional urban objective to the EEC structural funds. (This would identify urban decline as a key priority alongside industrial decline.)
* Change the criteria for structural support so as to allow for more

flexible designations in urban areas. (i.e. relax some of the strict industrial criteria in order to make areas suffering from industrial decline, but within mixed economies, eligible for support).

* Campaign to ensure that London is supported under any new designations by both UK government and EEC.

The specific results of the campaign can be crudely described as the fulfilment of both the third and fourth of the aims. The first and second goals are now being pursued by the Association of London Government (the newly merged association of all London Boroughs) in collaboration with other cities.

The precise outcome was the establishment of more appropriate criteria through which 'urban communities' could gain access to Objective 2 status. These are enshrined now in the 'Urban Communities' clause within the regulations of the European Regional Development Fund. Alongside this new clause in the regulations a specific Community Initiative for cities known as URBAN was also established in order to build upon the work begun within the Urban Pilot Projects, and the new Article 10 regulations allow for a much greater focus on innovative regeneration activity within urban areas.

In addition, the overall campaign was a success in that it resulted in the designation of a large part of north-east London (East London and the Lea Valley) for Objective 2 (industrial regeneration) support, and the more recent designations of the East End and the Park Royal areas of London for support from the URBAN initiative. This has effectively, and literally, 'put London on the map' and provided for qualification for a broader tranche of EU programmes in the fields of research and technology, business development, innovation, and international co-operation.

The broader campaign around gaining an Urban Competence for the EU continues under ALG leadership within both the Committee of the Regions and the discussions leading up to the Inter-Governmental Conference (IGC) in 1996.

Conclusion

The overall thrust of this introductory section has been to show how East London's position in relation to the major EU policies and programmes has changed in the very recent past, and is gradually expanding. The role of local government, and of the local government associations, has been critical in leading the debates, and the role of partnerships at the regional and sub-regional level has been essential in gaining governmental support for specific designations. East London has become a focus for EU programming within the region because it has attracted the first full structural designation in London and because this has acted a trigger for a large range of other EU-related developments. The next section of this chapter deals with range of EU related developments in East London in some detail.

Analysis of the impact of EU programming in East London has not yet been undertaken and will probably need to wait for completion of the first Objective 2 programme. However, two surveys of EU funded activity in East London have been undertaken, one in 1993, and another in 1995, and these present the best picture so far of the range of activity involved. The surveys, covering six of the seven boroughs identified above (excluding Hackney) were undertaken by London East TEC in order to identify what EU-related activity was already in progress and what remained to be done to which the TEC could contribute.

The 1993 Survey

The main overall findings from the 1993 survey present a fairly clear picture of the aggregated EU related activity which had hitherto been relatively invisible:

* About £10 million of EU funding was being spent each year in East London. The main areas of expenditure were: employment-related training; international education and training; research and technology development.
* Over seventy-five East London-based organisations and agencies were involved in EU-related activity and EU funds from across 14 different organisational sectors. The most active were local authorities, voluntary sector agencies, and the higher and further education institutions. Other sectors included enterprise and business development agencies, careers services and education business partnerships, employers groups and chambers of commerce.
* There was considerable untapped potential, as several EEC funds were not being bid for by agencies with activities which were clearly eligible. There was a general lack of information and awareness about the funds and the technical know-how in putting bids together was concentrated in a small number of agencies.

* Whilst there were a broad range of ad hoc partnership arrangements these tended to be focused on single projects and were short term rather based on agreed objectives with multiple activity.
* Collaboration across East London was identified as a particular problem with many agencies working on European issues either across boroughs or organisational sectors.

The 1995 Survey

The findings of the 1995 survey show that there has been some steady development of EU-related activity at the local level and that many agencies were now poised to make the most of the new investments likely to be available through the Objective 2 and URBAN designations and other related initiatives. In general, the findings can be summarised as follows:

* There has been steady expansion in the level of EU related activity within East London primarily because the name range of agencies have broadened and deepened their programmes. The sixty agencies surveyed showed increases on their activities in 1993. Greater concentration is evident in those agencies which are active.
* About £12 million is now being raised from the EU each year, and this is set to jump up to about £50 million once the Objective 2 and URBAN initiative funding begins to flow and allied funds are attracted. This has effectively meant that East London and the Lea Valley is now receiving about as much EU aid as the rest of the capital in total.
* Much greater levels of collaboration and networking across East London are evident and a much broader range of transnational partnerships can be seen.

Some noteworthy aspects of the detailed findings are as follows:

The agencies

The 1995 survey showed sixty agencies active in EU programming and related activity. This included:

6 local authorities

21 voluntary organisations
9 further education/sixth form colleges
6 training organisations
4 careers services
4 education business partnerships
1 chamber of commerce.
2 enterprise agencies
3 urban regeneration companies
2 universities/higher education institutions
1 training and enterprise council
1 arts centre.

There is, overall, a concentration of the EU funds within those agencies operating within the inner boroughs of Tower Hamlets, Newham, and Waltham Forest. However, EU activity is spread across the whole sub-region with a particular focus on education and training activities in the outer boroughs. An analysis of the range of EU programmes per agency suggests that whilst EU funds are still concentrated in local authorities and higher education institutions, a second tier of agencies is now evolving with the capacity to win and manage a range of EU funds. The voluntary sector is beginning to diversify into a broader range of EU funds, further education and sixth form colleges are doing likewise and partnership organisations like the TEC and regeneration agencies are also making progress with several EU funds at the same time.

The range of EU programmes which the East London agencies are using includes 39 different funds. Interestingly, the most commonly used fund is the European Social Fund (ESF) which provides resources for employment and training projects for the unemployed. There are 87 such projects receiving ESF support in East London. This number will grow with the arrival of Objective 2 and URBAN funds in the East End. Equally, whilst there are no projects currently benefiting from the European Regional Development Fund (ERDF), a large range are now in preparation with the likelihood of 30 to 40 such projects being supported by autumn 1995. The second level of programme usage comes down to single figures with five to ten projects being supported in each of the transnational education and training programmes (such as Petra, Lingua,) which will soon be replaced by the new Leonardo and Socrates initiatives.

The transnational partnerships which have evolved across East London are striking in their range and content. The overview shows that over 160 different bi-lateral partnerships exist between East London agencies and other parts of Europe. For example, there are strong partnerships with France, Germany, Netherlands, Spain, Denmark, and other western/northern European countries. There are also evolving partnerships with Ukraine, Romania, Russia, Czech Republic and Hungary. The partnerships are often used for exchange activities between education and training institutions and collaboration on local development, research, and joint ventures.

Considerable development appears to have happened in the partnership and networking arrangements of the East London agencies within the UK. One problem highlighted by the 1993 survey was the lack of any strong sense of partnership or co-ordination at the local and regional level in London, with any collaboration being basically ad hoc, and horizons therefore being limited by the single agency/single initiative approach. By 1995, most of the sixty agencies report that they are members of both regional European networks (e.g. ALG's European Officers Group, or London Voluntary Sector Training Consortium) and usually part of some more solid local networking, through for example the multi-agency Royals University College partnership which is receiving support from the Sprint programme

Local collaboration was also enhanced by the range of local European events which had sprung up since the first survey in 1993. In all, over fifty events about Europe and EU programmes had taken place in east London over the previous two years, leading to a much greater level of familiarity between the agencies concerned. The establishment of an East London European Forum had been one recommendation of the 1993 survey and this has been taken forward by London East TEC with leadership from the local MEP Carole Tongue and the Chief Executive of Newham, Drew Stevenson.

Future Priorities

An interesting additional question about the future European priorities of the agencies surveyed highlighted some interesting issues about the future of the EU funds in East London and the work that will be undertaken to utilise them well. All answers suggested that East London agencies now see EU funds are potentially a major contributor to their activities and programmes at the local level. Many agencies, for example, which had previously only used one type of EU programme were able to indicate the seven or eight funds to which they intended to bid over the next two years. This suggested a much more thorough level of organisational awareness and planning with regard to EU funds.

Conclusion: East London Poised for the Impact

All in all, 1995 will probably prove to have been the turning point in the role of EU funds and programmes in the regeneration of East London. Not only have the amounts of money likely to be spent more than quadrupled but the level of preparedness of East London agencies has risen markedly. In 1995 the East London European Forum began work on a medium term European strategy for the sub-region and a group of local authorities and the TEC worked together to jointly represent East London at the European networking event, Director, for the first time. East London, as a place, is now widely recognised within the Brussels and Strasbourg EU Institutions as being the 'important' part of London for EU matters.

With the advent of the Single Regeneration Budget (SRB) in Britain, and the development of the regional offices of central government it is likely that a medium term regeneration agenda has been set for London as a whole. One powerful aspect of this is the close link between UK and EU regeneration initiatives in East London and the expectation that they will bring about change over the next five years. Re-integrating the East London economy with the remaining strengths of London, and, at the same time, picking up on new economic flows and opportunities in mainland Europe are the key priorities. A medium term framework is in place within East London and EU funds have been catalytic in bringing it about.

Note

[1] For the purposes of this chapter East London is taken to include the seven London Boroughs: Hackney, Waltham Forest, Tower Hamlets, Newham, Barking and Dagenham, Redbridge, and Havering.

Stratford City Challenge

Rebecca Fearnley and John Pratt

On 1 April 1993, the latest government scheme at that time to promote urban regeneration arrived in the London Borough of Newham. Stratford City Challenge formally started. It was one of thirty-one City Challenges funded by the Department of the Environment. Stratford was in the second round of twenty City Challenges. In 1992, eleven 'pacemaker' authorities had been awarded City Challenge funds.[1] One of these was just down the road in another area of the East End, Bethnal Green. In each City Challenge, the local authority had competitively bid for DoE funds. The successful authorities received an allocation of £37.5 million over five years (£7.5 million per year) to fund an 'Action Plan' for regeneration. It was originally anticipated that there would be several 'rounds' of City Challenge funding. The Government subsequently decided, however, that there would not be any further rounds, and has now replaced all previous funding regimes with the all-encompassing Single Regeneration Budget. The City Challenge concept differed from its predecessors in a number of ways, and presented new challenges to local authorities and the local communities as well as opportunities for regeneration.

The City Challenge Concept

The City Challenge concept was announced in May 1991 by the then Secretary of State for the Environment, Michael Heseltine. Speaking at the annual dinner of the Tyne and Wear Development Corporation, Mr Heseltine set out the philosophy which underpinned the latest government policy for the regeneration of inner cities nationwide.[2] City Challenge initiatives would be aimed at assisting 'communities with limited ability to help themselves'. The Secretary of State and the Government thought that 'people lived in conditions that were unlikely to attract outside assistance or investment except through the public or voluntary sectors'. The problem Mr Heseltine saw with deprived areas, which City Challenge was designed to address, was that they 'lacked the ability to attract, to compete. In any competitive circumstances they would fail. Alone, exposed to the market, they would lose'.

The aims of City Challenge, as later formulated by the DoE,[3] drew on this broadly supportive philosophy, but they embodied also more aggressive elements of the idea of an enterprise culture and implicitly challenged existing local authority management competence. Local authorities, although they would receive public funds, would have to yield some of their independence and conform to strict requirements about the nature of the programme funding and its delivery. They had to form partnerships with 'private, public and voluntary sector bodies and the local community' to compete for resources 'to implement comprehensive economic, social and environmental strategies for the regeneration of keys areas of deprivation'. City Challenge was intended to 'support strategies for a defined area' that would help it 'to attract outside investment, to stimulate wealth creation and widen social provision'. It was intended to 'create a climate of environmental quality and enterprise culture likely to attract people to live and work' in the area. Other aims included the provision of 'added value' to current public and private initiatives in the areas, the promotion of 'effective mechanisms of delivery' of plans, particularly through partnerships between local authorities and other stakeholders in the area, and the development of a capacity in the areas for 'self-sustaining regeneration and self help' which would continue after the period of City Challenge funding.

Thus the City Challenge initiative has several characteristics which set it apart from previous regeneration policies. These have been set out by the DoE[4] in, interestingly, a variety of different forms, but they can be summarised as:

competitive
targeted (on a small area)
comprehensive
partnership-based
output driven
time limited

Despite Mr Heseltine's remark about the inevitability of competitive failure of the target communities of City Challenge, the allocation of City Challenge funds was on a competitive basis. Implicit in the

Heseltine speech and more evident in the guidance given to local authorities was an approach to City Challenge which drew on strategic planning and managerialist approaches. Competition was seen as 'the spur to action and achievement'.[5] Taking a broadly strategic planning approach, familiar in the private sector, local authorities were invited to make their bids on the basis of an 'Action Plan', containing a 'vision' of what the five year programme intended to achieve, identifying 'strategic objectives' and listing the projects to be funded to achieve these objectives.[6] The Action Plan is the basis of DoE decisions about funding in each year of each City Challenge project.

City Challenge is based on the idea of comprehensive small area regeneration. Local authorities had to select a small section – or 'key neighbourhood', as Mr Heseltine phrased it[7] – of their borough and put together an Action Plan upon which their bid would be based and which identified what would be achieved over the five years. The Government indicated that the bids had to be comprehensive, the idea of City Challenge being that it would tackle the multitude of factors which contributed to the deprivation of the area – education, training, housing, crime, inward investment, or lack of. City Challenges would not only equip local people with the ability to work, it should tackle problems of housing and environment of an area as well, and give people an incentive to stay.

This comprehensive approach to small areas is in line with established management and planning norms.[8] But it signified a move away from previous regeneration policies such as UDCs and Enterprise Zones, which, as Michael Rustin points out in the Introduction, sought to remove, or ignore, the 'restrictions' imposed by social and economic planning in an attempt to ensure London in particular retained its status as a world city. Although the Enterprise Zones had some limited success in that firms in the zones seemed to do better than elsewhere, new jobs were created, and there was improvement to the local physical and economic environments, they also often had a detrimental effect on surrounding areas.[9] City Challenge signalled a move away from property-led regeneration as exemplified by the UDCs, as the social costs of this type of expansion are counted in areas such as the Docklands. City Challenge was heralded by the government as a more comprehensive form of regeneration, with its emphasis on social, economic and community issues, as well as physical renewal and attracting inward investment.[10] This perhaps reflects the realisation that if Britain is going to compete and develop on the global stage, there is a need for a supply of semi-skilled service workers as well as a safe environment and a thriving 'cultural ambience' so that, in this case London becomes a pleasant place for global business.

Central to the idea of City Challenge is the concept of partnership and negotiation between three sectors; public, private and community. The Government regards effective partnership as key in developing a sense of 'ownership' amongst local people and in building the 'comprehensive regeneration necessary for lasting change'.[11] City Challenges would be drawing on 'the talent and expertise of local people, the private sector, academic community, statutory agencies and the voluntary sector'.[12] The DoE makes it clear in its guidance notes 'Working Partnerships'[13] that authorities would have to demonstrate the creation of an agency which embodies, amongst other things, the principle of 'full and active partnership involving the private sector and the community', and 'endorsement by the partners of the key decisions'.[14] City Challenge revolves around this idea of key partners within any one area working together towards the successful and sustainable regeneration of the area. Also key is the notion that the initial £37.5 million should generate inward investment, and to this end, all City Challenge projects must demonstrate whether they have generated any private sector 'leverage'. On average, the £37.5 million for each City Challenge is expected to generate some £100 million of private investment.[15] The private sector is therefore a partner not only because of its stake in an area, but also because it is anticipated it will help attract this inward investment which is seen as being so vital for 'lasting change'. It is for this reason that the DoE stress the need to 'involve the private sector thoroughly in managing the programme'.[16] The lead role of local authorities in City Challenge, as well as the position given to local communities sets it apart from previous regeneration initiatives, which have often been nationally guided, and have minimised the role of these two sectors.

This notion of a partnership between these three sectors does seem to represent a change from some recent attempts at regeneration in East London; the LDDC, for example, did not involve local communities at all, but instead quite often up-rooted them, by-passing at the same time local authority planning regulations. Even previous initiatives which have talked about 'partnership' were usually referring to partnership between the private and public sectors alone, or, in the case of Urban Partnerships, between central and local government. Despite these differences in formal policy, however, there are similarities between the speech in which Mr Heseltine announced City

Challenge[17] and the sort of things Peter Shore was talking about when he announced the inner city partnerships in 1977, and many of the themes seem familiar:

> Formally the partnership is between local authorities and central government. But I hope that the concept of partnership will be a pervasive one and will underline the way in which these authorities carry out their programme, and that it will enlist the involvement and enthusiasm of those initially concerned with the creation and sustenance of employment – that is to say, the industrialists, Trades Unionists, voluntary bodies and the community generally.[18]

City Challenge policy incorporates more formally this idea of involving all those with a stake in an area, which was being talked about in not dissimilar terms 15 years previously. The DoE claims to have a genuine interest in hearing the views of the various sectors and in giving them a meaningful role in the decision making process.

City Challenge is described as 'output driven'.[19] The achievements of City Challenge programmes is measured in terms of 'outputs', a list of which has been created by the DoE. Individual City Challenges set targets of 'core outputs' which they expect to achieve and 'milestones' by which time they have to achieve them and they have to monitor what is being produced by projects. The idea of outputs is bound up with the other managerial elements of the City Challenge initiative. As the DoE Guidance puts it: 'City Challenge is particularly rigorous in defining target outputs and establishing systems for their delivery'.[20]

Consistent with this approach, City Challenge policy also introduced the idea of independent evaluation of all City Challenge programmes, which would occur simultaneously with the programme itself, and which evaluates the outcomes and impact of the programme. Evaluators also look at the process, and examine the partnership between the key partners to evaluate how well it is working. In addition the Government set up a national evaluation to look at the progress and impact of all 31 City Challenges taken together, which would perhaps inform future rounds and policy.

The time limitation of City Challenge was also seen as an incentive to effective management. Five year action plans were seen as helping to 'concentrate minds ... motivate people to work together ... achieve timely results and therefore to effect better overall delivery'.[21] The DoE was particularly ambitious here. It insisted that the Action Plan 'should aim to achieve the basis of a lasting regeneration for the area' within the five years of the City Challenge programme: 'The ability to achieve self-sustaining momentum must be maximised.'

Mr Heseltine asserted that City Challenges differed from previous approaches to regeneration which had been criticised for being ad hoc, top-up programmes; City Challenge represents a comprehensive approach to the regeneration of small areas.[22] City Challenge certainly differs substantially from recent initiatives such as UDCs, but some aspects of City Challenge seem to draw on earlier programmes. The concentration on a specific area is not new – in the late 1970s the Urban Partnerships were criticised for concentrating on too small an area and ignoring the wider context and issues surrounding urban problems[23] – and like the Community Development Programmes of the late 1960s and early 1970s, the emphasis is on helping people to help themselves.[24] The idea of City Challenge is to help communities make their areas attractive to outside investment so they can compete in a competitive market. What is different about City Challenge, however, is the more comprehensive approach. The emphasis of the Urban Programme in the early 1980s was on economic regeneration and areas such as Housing and Education got only limited support. More recently, UDCs ignored local concerns in their developments of reclaimed land in an attempt to create areas in which the private sector would thrive. City Challenges are based on a more comprehensive approach to urban regeneration, and on the idea that if you make an area more attractive, with an educated population and workforce who possess desirable skills, not only will people be more likely to want to stay in an area, but private investment and therefore sustainable regeneration will follow. The question is: does it work? and particularly: is it working for Stratford?

Stratford City Challenge

The Stratford City Challenge area runs from Stratford to West Ham along the Lower Lea Valley. It encompasses most of Stratford, and small parts of Canning Town and Plaistow. Six of the borough's 24 electoral wards fall either wholly or partially within the area: Canning Town and Grange, New Town, Park, Plashet, Stratford and West Ham.

The Action Plan which Newham submitted to the DoE sets out the vision for the Stratford City Challenge area as follows: 'Our vision is to put the heart back into East London. We will make Stratford a commercial magnet, looking to Europe and on to the millennium, with a vibrant shopping centre, new secure housing and a wealth of arts, entertainment and culture reflecting the diversity of East London's communities. It will become the focus of East London's regeneration.'[25]

There are four Strategic Objectives outlined in the Action Plan through which this vision will be achieved. These key objectives are:

* Raising the profile of the area as a pre-requisite for securing inward investment on a scale that will achieve Stratford's full potential.
* Access to jobs for local people, in the City Challenge area and beyond.
* Better housing and more choice to encourage people to stay in the area.
* Enabling local people to play a full part in community life and the decisions which affect their lives.

These Strategic Objectives are to be achieved through a number of projects. The Action Plan includes an outline of what the main projects are likely to be, but this is not fixed and it has changed somewhat in the first two years of the programme, with some projects being dropped and others being added as they come up. The overall vision remains the same, however, and new projects must be able to demonstrate that they contribute to this vision and to one or more of the Strategic Objectives. In the first year of the programme there were approximately forty projects, which has increased to around seventy in the second year, and up to eighty are anticipated for year three. The projects are clustered under the Strategic Objective to which they make the most contribution. Projects range in size, cost and ambition from one offering play facilities to young people and receiving a small amount of revenue funding to an investment of millions in the development of a cinema complex.

At the beginning of the five years of the programme a company – Stratford Development Partnership Ltd – was set up to deliver the Action Plan and its objectives.[26] This 'implementing agency' consists of a Board supported by six sub-committees, a staff team headed by a Chief Executive, the local authority, and two organisations set up to represent the business sector and the community – a Business Forum and Community Forum.

The Board of SDP Ltd has twenty one members, who represent the key sectors identified by the DoE as constituting a partnership.[27] Four councillors represent the local authority, there are four representatives from the private sector, four from the Community Forum and nine co-optees. The last are from organisations such as the Metropolitan Police, the local theatre, the local college and other organisations with a substantial interest in the area. Board members have equal voting rights, and with four representatives from each, no one sector dominates. The Board meets monthly, and has ultimate responsibility for the achievements of Stratford City Challenge. SDP Ltd is staffed by a team of nine, including the Chief Executive, and is supplemented by secondees from the local authority, a consultant, and staff from three projects.

The Board is supported by six sub-committees, which relate to different aspects of the programme and report to the Board every month. These sub-committees are:

West Ham Mills
Town Centre
Communications
Employment, Training and Education
Finance
Confidence to Take Part.

Broadly speaking, the sub-committees have similar functions, set out in their general terms of reference. These include monitoring the progress of individual projects, recommending to the Board additions, substitutions and deletions to the original Action Plan, and providing the Board with 'a strategic overview on all matters relating to the lasting regeneration of Stratford'.[28] Each sub-committee also has specific tasks related to its own area of responsibility.

All these sub-committees except the last, Confidence to Take Part, were established in the first year of Stratford City Challenge. Confidence to Take Part was constituted in October 1994, on the recommendation of the Chief Executive. It is led by the Community Forum and its terms of reference cover the fourth Strategic Objective. In addition to the sub-committees, there is also a Housing Task Group, which oversees all housing projects and issues, and whose Chair reports to the Board every month.

The sub-committees are made up of members from the various sectors of the partnership, and there is usually a degree of specialist knowledge of the area covered by the sub-committee among the membership. On each sub-committee there is at least one Board member, usually the Chair, who reports to and makes recommendations to the Board every month.

The Community Forum represents the community sector within the partnership and arranges consultations on City Challenge issues. Its members are 'individuals residing within Stratford, London or with employment (paid or voluntary) or community related activities based in Stratford, London'.[29] Since the first year of City Challenge, the membership of Community Forum has grown from 237 members to 450 in the second year.[30] Members of the Management Committee of Community Forum, elected by its members, represent the community on the Board and sub-committees. In February 1995, the Forum agreed its Memorandum and Articles of Association and is in the process of becoming a company limited by guarantee.

The Business Forum is more informal than the Community Forum. It has no strictly defined membership and no formal constitution. The Forum holds meetings about once every three months, and AGMs, where SDP Board members are elected. When the Forum was first set up, all businesses in Stratford, about 650, were contacted, but subsequently only those who attended previous meetings have been notified, and forthcoming events and meetings are advertised in the local press. Meetings of the Business Forum are also informal, and usually attract about fifty people. They are often used as an opportunity to exchange information and make contacts.

Stratford: Problems and Opportunities

In approving funding for City Challenge areas, The DoE required that the City Challenge companies undertake evaluation of their programme. In January 1993, the Centre for Institutional Studies (CIS) at the University of East London (UEL) was commissioned by the Chief Executive of SDP Ltd to undertake an independent evaluation of Stratford City Challenge.

As the evaluation team, CIS has several tasks, the first of which was to produce a Baseline Study.[31] This presents a picture of the Stratford City Challenge area at the start of the City Challenge programme, and was written in such a way as to make it possible to revisit the issues raised by the Stratford City Challenge Action Plan, to compare and contrast the picture at the start with future development, and to facilitate measurement over the five years of the initiative. The Baseline Study will be updated in years three and five of the programme in an attempt to assess progress and the impact made by the City Challenge initiative.

The Evaluation Team has also analysed the progress made by clusters of projects towards each strategic objective in the first two years of the initiative and twice a year it assesses progress made by the programme as a whole. Because the idea of partnership is central to City Challenge, the Evaluation Team studies the Partnership and evaluates how effectively it is operating. It examines issues such as the involvement of the various partners at various stages of the delivery mechanism, and tries to assess the contribution and involvement of each partner.

The Baseline Study highlights the distinctive characteristics of the Stratford City Challenge area. It reveals that Stratford has suffered from a long period of economic decline and faces many of the problems characteristic of inner city areas. But it also has a distinctive social, economic and cultural profile which could be built on in regeneration.

In the past, the geographical position of Stratford and its locational advantage enabled the area to become the focus for a significant transport infrastructure, manufacturing industry, retail services, as well as being a seat of local government. The decline of the area, however, now so evident, can be traced back to the 1930s and beyond, and attempts made to regenerate the area in the 1970s failed to arrest the decline of local industry and chronic social deprivation.

In the nineteenth century, Stratford, at the north-westernmost point of the parish of West Ham in the county of Essex, consisted of large areas of either marshland or land which was laid down for agriculture. By the turn of the twentieth century West Ham had become the industrial heartland of the south-east of England, and in 1889, West Ham became a county borough enjoying administrative autonomy from the rest of London. Stratford was West Ham's focus for social and retail services, the seat of local government and a major industrial location, strategically located at the centre of a regional transport network. Chemical companies began to settle in the area, and by 1863 there were thirty-four companies in Stratford alone. Amongst the significant industries in the area were two sizeable gasworks at Abbey Marsh, whose by-products sustained the numerous local tar distillers and oil makers.

The area's leading employer in the nineteenth century and major influence on the subsequent development of Stratford was the Eastern Counties (later the Great Eastern) Railway. In 1839 a line was laid from London to Norwich, and within a few years Stratford became the site of an extensive railway depot and locomotive works, which by

1906 employed almost 6,450 people. The company also located its ticket printing works nearby, and houses were built for the railway workers and their families. In 1868, the London, Tilbury and Southend Company line entered West Ham just below Abbey Mills and ran eastward. The company opened a depot and locomotive works by Plaistow station, and what later became the District and Metropolitan line followed the same route in 1902.

Such opportunities for employment drew a workforce to the area, and the population of West Ham expanded at a rapid rate: between 1871 and 1881 it more than doubled to 128,953, and by 1925 it had peaked at 319,500. By the 1930s, however, some of the problems which currently beset the Stratford City Challenge area were already apparent. In 1936 West Ham was advertising itself as 'London's Industrial Centre and Gateway to the World', but it was already slipping into a slow economic decline. The highest unemployment levels in the south-east of England were found in West Ham at the beginning of the decade, with over a quarter of the insured labour force registered unemployed.[32]

The Second World War had a major impact on Stratford. West Ham was a site of industrial importance, and was therefore subject to bombing attacks. Between 1938 and 1941 the population of the area almost halved, although casualties were lighter than expected. Many people were evacuated or left the area by their own efforts never to return, and the population never recovered to more than a peak of 170,993 in 1951. During the war, over a quarter of the 51,000 residential properties (27 per cent) were destroyed, and virtually every other home in the borough suffered some sort of damage.[33] After the war, West Ham was faced with problems of reconstruction, and many homes were declared unfit for human habitation. The tower block, built as part of the inner city housing developments of the 1960s epitomised solutions to these problems, and in 1986 there were still 111 council owned blocks of 8 or more storeys within the former boroughs of West and East Ham. Only a few of these were in Stratford, but some had as many as twenty-two floors.

In 1965, the adjoining county boroughs of West and East Ham were joined together to form the London Borough of Newham. Since then the town hall at East Ham has become the focus for local government in the area, although Stratford is still home to a number of council departments. In the 1970s, the Council instigated a redevelopment strategy for Stratford, and plans were laid for a major new scheme involving the refurbishment of the area's centre. The scheme included a

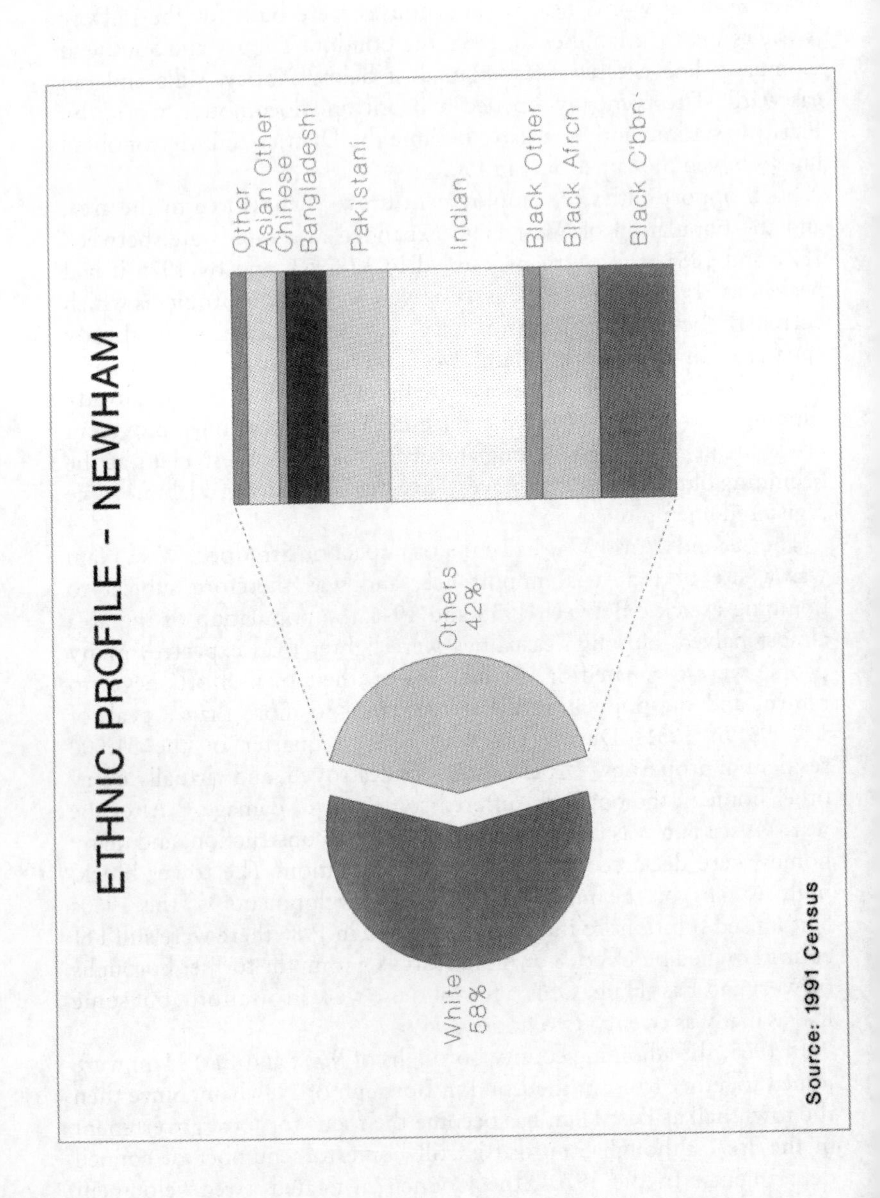
ETHNIC PROFILE - NEWHAM
Other
Asian Other
Chinese
Bangladeshi
Pakistani
Indian
Black Other
Black Afrcn
Black C'bbn
Others 42%
White 58%
Source: 1991 Census

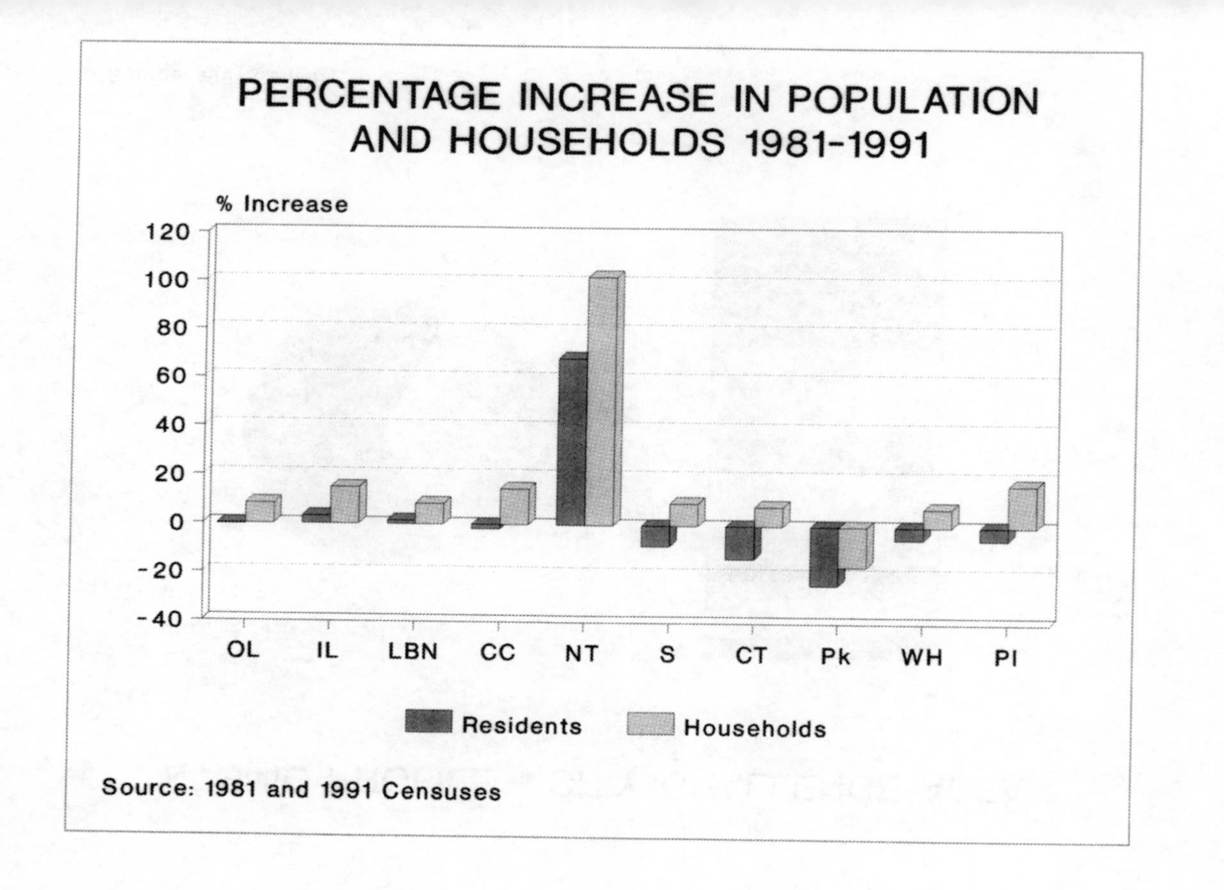
PERCENTAGE INCREASE IN POPULATION
AND HOUSEHOLDS 1981-1991
% Increase
120
100
80
60
40
20
0
-20
-40
OL
IL
LBN
CC
NT
S
CT
Pk
WH
PI
Residents
Households
Source: 1981 and 1991 Censuses

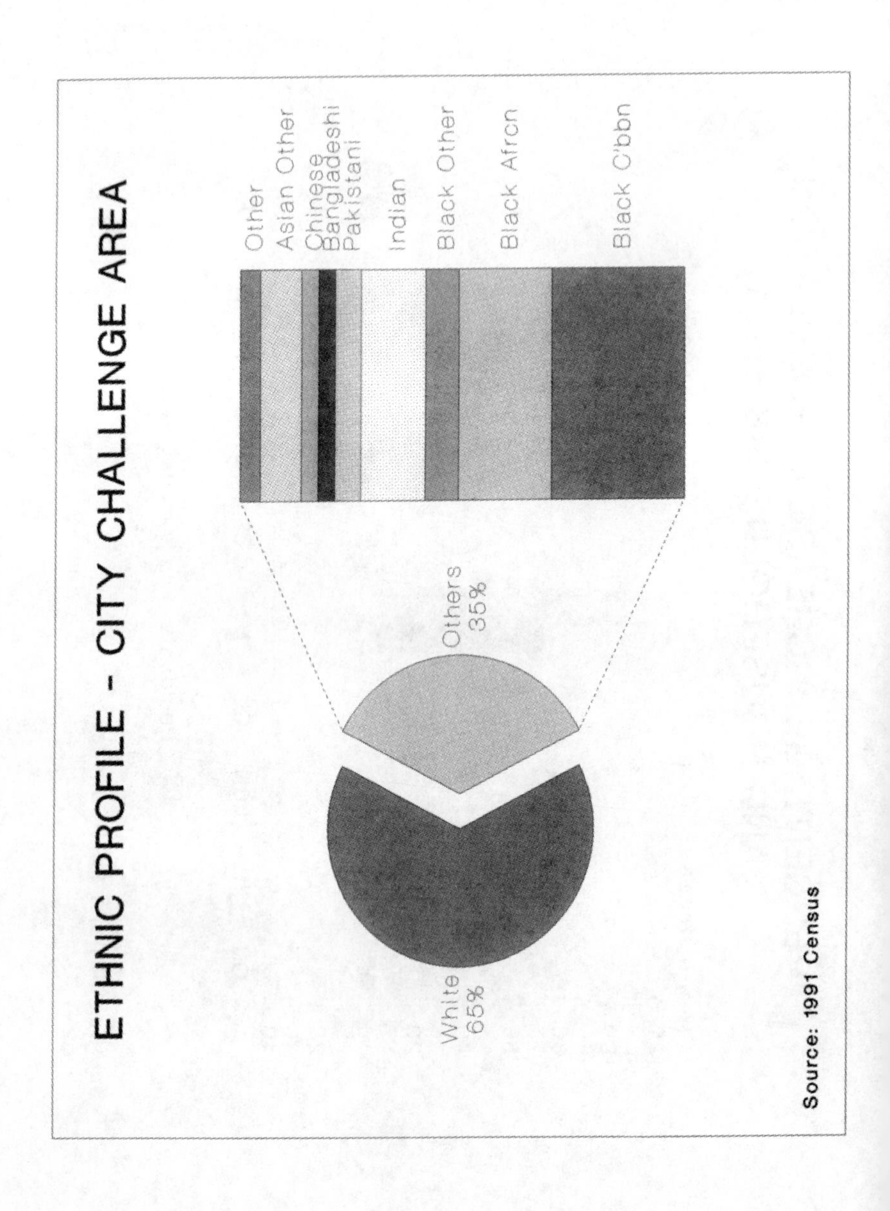
ETHNIC PROFILE - CITY CHALLENGE AREA
White
65%
Others
35%
Other
Asian Other
Chinese
Bangladeshi
Pakistani
Indian
Black Other
Black Afrcn
Black C'bbn
Source: 1991 Census

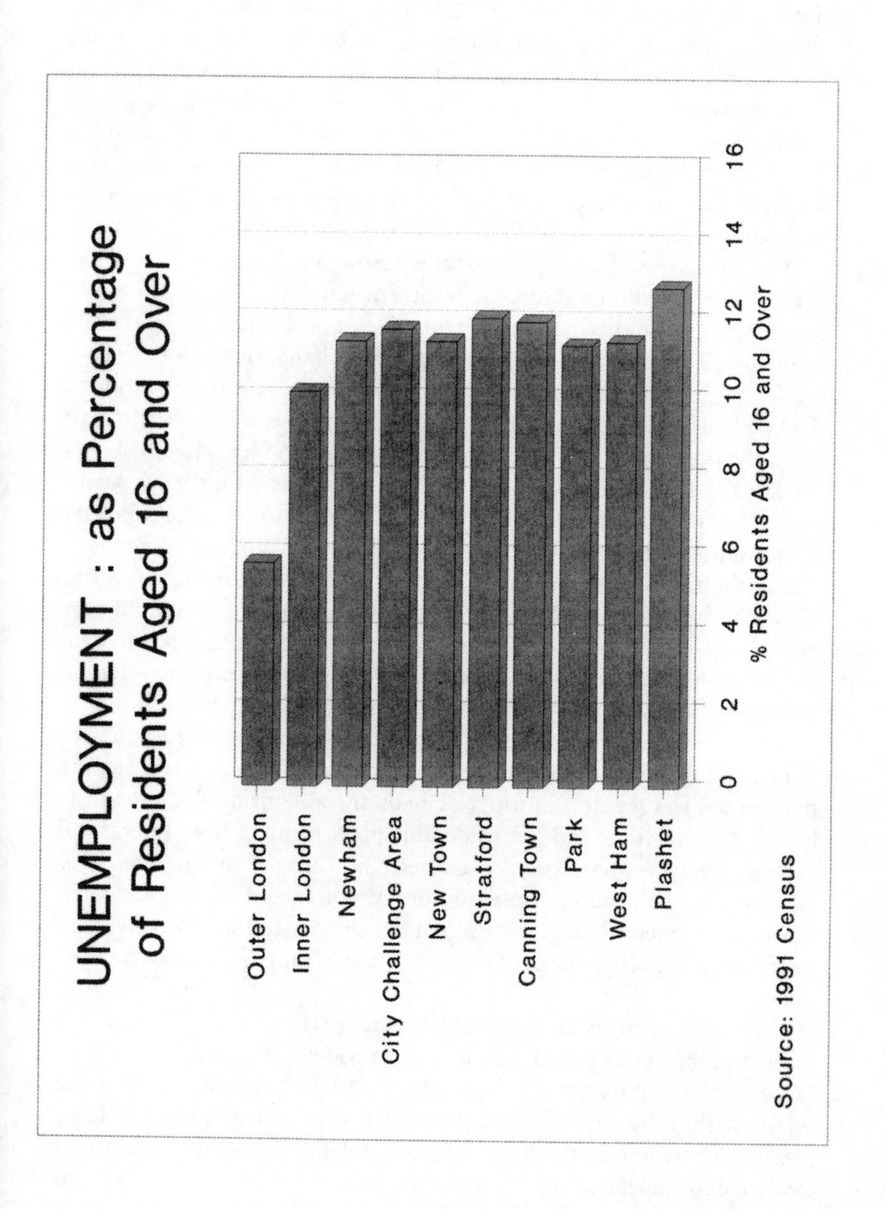
UNEMPLOYMENT : as Percentage of Residents Aged 16 and Over
Outer London
Inner London
Newham
City Challenge Area
New Town
Stratford
Canning Town
Park
West Ham
Plashet
0
2
4
6
8
10
12
14
16
% Residents Aged 16 and Over
Source: 1991 Census

new shopping precinct, multi-storey car parks, a bus station, a new library and a new courthouse. The first phase of the scheme, the shopping centre, was completed in 1976, but the rest of the development failed to materialise. By this time Newham was in serious decline as an industrial centre, and between 1966 and 1974 the borough lost at least 30 per cent of its manufacturing jobs.[34] Today the London Borough of Newham is ranked at the bottom of the socio-economic league both regionally and nationally, according to Deprivation Indicators published by the DoE in 1993.

While it shares some aspects of the borough's demographic profile, there are many things about the Stratford City Challenge area which are distinctive, and which differ from the national average, and from Newham. The City Challenge area has a population of 18,699, which is nearly 9 per cent of the borough's population. The figures show a decline from the census of 1981 of about 5 per cent, which sets it apart from the borough as a whole, where the population has increased over the last ten years (see figure 1). Like the borough of which it is a part, a high proportion of the area's population comes from ethnic minority communities (35 per cent), though less than in the borough as a whole, where the figure is 42 per cent (see figures 2 and 3). In the Stratford City Challenge area the majority of the ethnic minority community are black, whereas in Newham the most prominent ethnic group is Indian. Fewer of the population of the SCC area are pensioners than in Newham, but the area has a higher proportion of lone parent families.

A problem the area faces, highlighted in the Baseline Study, is the poor condition of the housing stock. The area has more houses lacking basic amenities (central heating, or bath/shower/inside WC) than the borough as a whole, and a considerable proportion of both public and private housing has been classified as 'unfit', or 'in need of renovation'. In a public opinion survey conducted by the Council, housing was viewed as an issue of major concern and was perceived by residents as especially poor. Many people said they would like to leave the area.

Unemployment is a significant issue in the area. As figure 4 indicates, the percentage of unemployed residents in the SCC area aged 16 or over is slightly greater than in the borough generally, and in some wards within the City Challenge area it is particularly high. The large number of people in the SCC area dependent on benefits indicates a low earning capacity and a lower than national average propensity to consume. In addition, Figure 5 indicates that the number of children in households with no adult in employment in the SCC area is almost 10

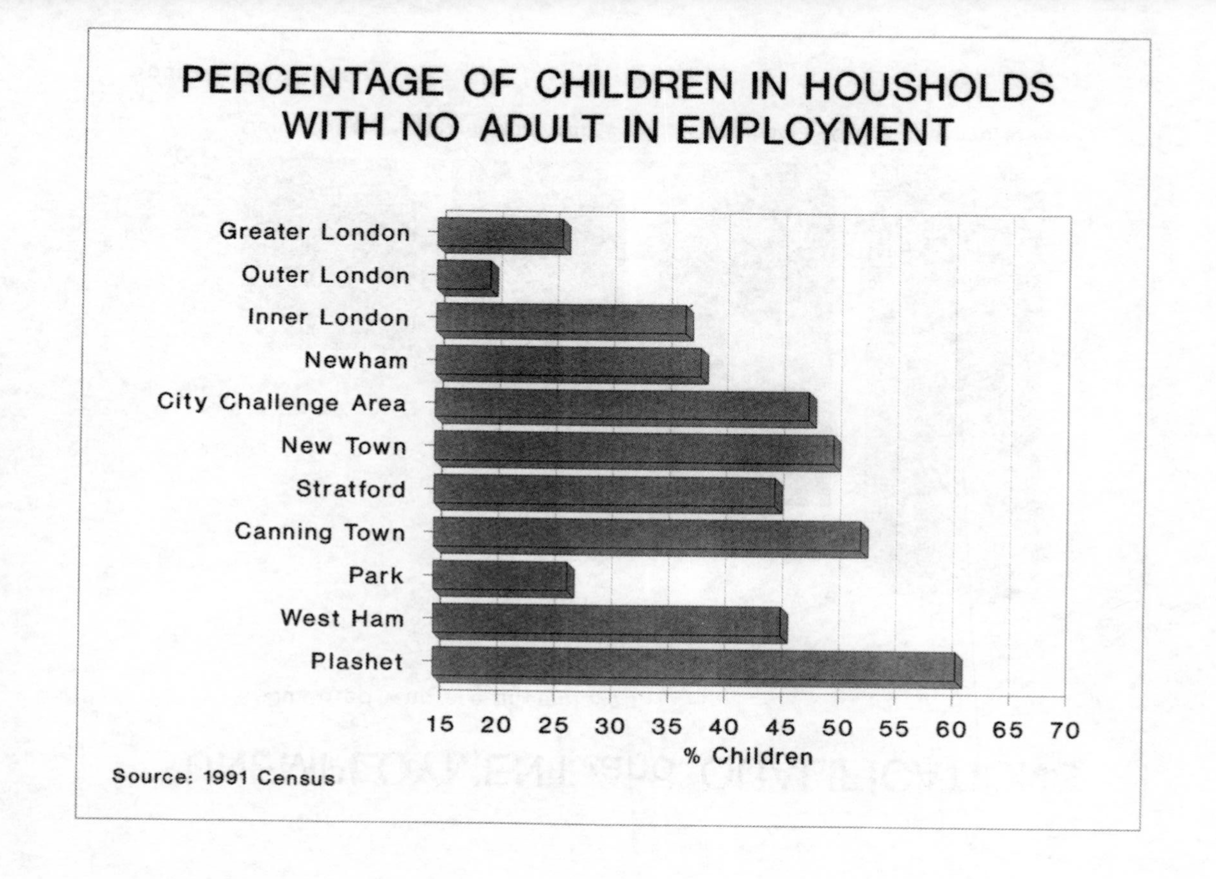
PERCENTAGE OF CHILDREN IN HOUSHOLDS
WITH NO ADULT IN EMPLOYMENT
Greater London
Outer London
Inner London
Newham
City Challenge Area
New Town
Stratford
Canning Town
Park
West Ham
Plashet
15
20
25
30
35
40
45
50
55
60
65
70
% Children
Source: 1991 Census

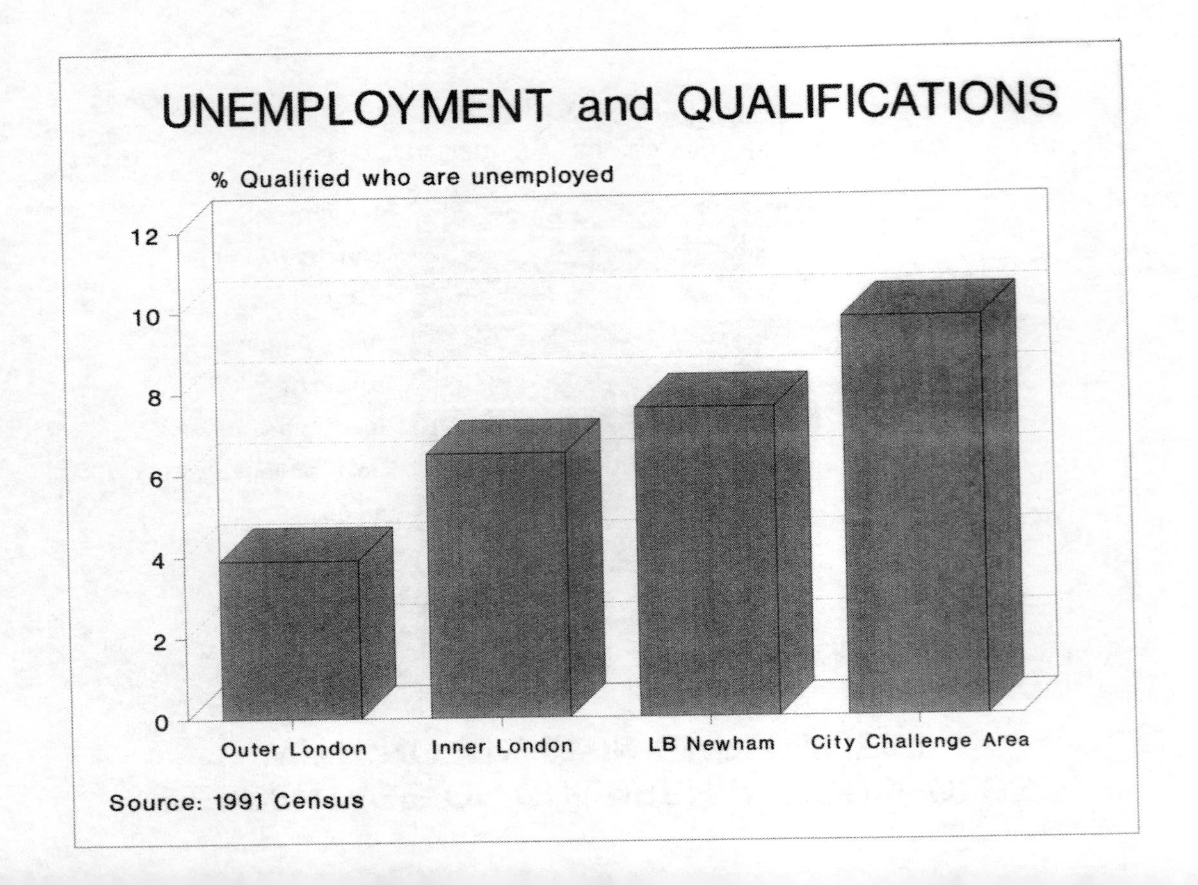
UNEMPLOYMENT and QUALIFICATIONS
% Qualified who are unemployed
12
10
8
6
4
2
0
Outer London
Inner London
LB Newham
City Challenge Area
Source: 1991 Census

per cent greater than for the borough, and 27 per cent greater than in Outer London. This may indicate a situation of poverty and deprivation which is perpetuative in nature.[35]

In terms of unemployment levels, the SCC area is not the worst in the borough, although it was an issue of some concern to residents. However, it was not the groups most likely to be affected who expressed most concern; rather, those who were most worried about this issue were from socio-economic groups A and B, and therefore not the groups most likely to be affected by the change in the structure of employment occurring. Figure 6 suggests that in the Stratford City Challenge area unemployment is not restricted to residents without qualifications.

Despite its industrial legacy, the Stratford City Challenge area has a surprising number of sites which are of considerable environmental importance. Newham itself has two sites which have been identified as being of metropolitan importance, the largest of which is within the City Challenge area; namely, the River Thames and its tidal creeks. The length of river within Newham has been described by the London Ecology Unit as 'of considerable value for birds, as well as being home to a nationally rare snail'.[36] Many of these green sites are inaccessible to residents and are the consequence of disuse; many are none-the-less havens for wildlife and may be lost by proposed developments to the area.

Business opinion towards Stratford seems generally favourable. The evaluation team found that as a business area, Stratford has a number of advantages, particularly in terms of its transport network. This network, and the area's rich natural, cultural and historical features form a good basis on which to build an image and raise the profile of the area.

One of the major barriers to full involvement of local people in the area in which they live is crime and fear of crime, and in the City Challenge area, as elsewhere, there are high levels of both. The Baseline Study highlights that there are, however, some disparities between people's perceptions and the nature of crimes reported. The types of crimes most feared are burglary and assault, but the most common type of crime is car theft. Of particular concern in the area are crimes involving racial harassment, and figures for the SCC area are particularly high, although levels differ considerably within the area.

The distinctive features of the Stratford City Challenge area revealed by the Baseline Study[37] highlighted a number of challenges and opportunities for the project additional to those in the Action Plan.

There were, for example, few projects which specifically address the needs of the high proportion of people from ethnic minority communities. The high number of lone parent families as compared to the borough as a whole means some consideration might need to be given to providing facilities geared towards their needs. Many children in the area are growing up in households without an adult who is in employment, which presents the issue of tackling this characteristic of poverty and deprivation, which, as we mentioned above, may be perpetuative in nature. The expectations of these children may be lower than those of other children, which leads to the probability that such high levels of poverty and deprivation may create a culture which accepts as inevitable the existence of this type of underclass in society.

The Baseline Study also highlighted issues of environmental concern: paradoxically, the wildlife havens are likely to be threatened by proposed developments and ways need to be found of preserving them. In public opinion surveys, however, the environmental issues of most concern to residents were the level of street cleanliness and the lack of communal facilities. The transport network in Stratford was cited by many as one of Stratford's assets which could be built on, both when thinking about developing the cultural and historical features of Stratford, and also in terms of attracting investment and businesses, and generally boosting the economic activity of Stratford. Stratford is perceived as lacking a positive image by residents, and therefore there is a need to create a coherent image for the area with distinctive features.

In terms of training and education in the area, an issue is the low levels of progression onto further and higher education, despite the fact that there are institutions providing both within the City Challenge area. The data suggest a need to publicise the variety of progression routes available to people, and the variety of courses available in both further and higher education, perhaps through the provision of a comprehensive advice service. The problem seems to arise less from a lack of provision than a lack of qualified leavers, and a low rate of progression to post school education. The University of East London already has a high market share of Newham residents qualified for higher education. In the City Challenge area there is a disparity in performance between secondary schools, with one performing less well than the other two. This may suggest the need for special help in the first instance to raise this school to at least the average for the borough.

The health of residents in the Stratford City Challenge area did not feature heavily in the Action Plan. Disaggregated data for the City

Challenge area were not available, but the Baseline study showed that Newham residents have a distinctive health profile. Adult mortality is lower than average, but the health of residents is poor, especially in terms of preventable diseases such as food poisoning, TB and cardiovascular diseases. Rates for mental illness are high, and there are high suicide rates among ethnic minority communities, particularly the Asian community, so supporting voluntary sector projects dealing with mental health might be needed. The data suggested that awareness raising of preventative medicine might be called for, and joint work with the local authority to encourage more use of leisure facilities, which the Baseline Study indicated were often underused. High rates of infant and child mortality suggested that antenatal and postnatal support, perhaps in conjunction with social services or voluntary sector projects, might be appropriate.

Progress

At the time of writing Stratford City Challenge is less than halfway through its life and it is too early to offer a definitive view of its achievements. It is, however, possible to offer some assessment of progress and to identify issues arising from this approach to regeneration.

The first two years have seen changes to the programme in the light of experience. While the 'vision' for Stratford remains constant, the balance of spending between Strategic Objectives has shifted. In the original Action Plan, Strategic Objective Three, Better Housing, More Choice, received the largest proportion of funding at 31 per cent. In part, at least, this reflected the capacity of the local authority to spend on this area in the first year. One of the most compelling the imperatives in all City Challenges is spending the money, particularly during the first year when the planning time has been limited. The evaluation team concluded that the plan for year one was probably rather ambitious.[38] During year two, Strategic Objective One, Raising the Profile, received almost twice as much (31 per cent) as in the first year. This reflected a concern to increase inward investment, and the re-allocation meant resources were now more evenly spread amongst the four Strategic Objectives.[39] However, the re-allocation of resources adversely affected the Strategic Objective for housing, in particular the strategy to improve and build new private sector houses.

In general projects are on target for achieving most of their outputs, although some of these may be achieved later than originally planned.

It is becoming increasingly clear that much of the evidence of progress towards achieving the strategic objectives will be in the long term. In the case of Strategic Objective Two, Access to Jobs, for example, many of the projects involve major building works being carried out to improve schools and colleges and it will be some time before pupils and students can start to use facilities, and therefore to benefit.

Notable achievements in year 1 include an architecturally striking new bus station, new facilities at the local Further Education college, which is producing the majority of the training outputs in the programme, and during the first two years, more than 380 new houses have been completed or improved. Private sector leverage at the end of year two was running at £46.5 million. Although some way short of their estimate of £288 million estimated in the Action Plan (a ratio of 7.7:1), SDP Ltd estimated in their Year Two Annual Review that the bulk of the remaining leverage will be generated from the development sites in the area, and the company is confident of achieving at least £206 million.

Central to the City Challenge concept is the idea of 'partnership'. The inclusion of the community sector in City Challenge partnerships is a new addition, but the extent to which community representatives are included in the decision making processes of the partnership needs to be examined and evaluated. There is, for instance, almost certainly the risk of 'tokenism' if community representatives are given a 'seat at the table' but not the information and knowledge about the way the structure and the other partners operate to fully participate. The DoE outlines three broad levels at which the various functions of a City Challenge implementing agency should operate – these are Representative, Managerial and Implementing. For a partnership to be effective, the DoE suggests that, although they can be organised differently, each City Challenge implementing agency should have a controlling mechanism which operates at least at the first two levels, and that the partnership should be incorporated at all three levels.[40] It is guidelines such as these that are some of the criteria against which the evaluators have to assess the delivery mechanism and process at work in City Challenge.

The reports of the evaluation team have concluded that the partnership which had been created to deliver Stratford City Challenge had a cohesive structure that was strong and flexible, and that all sections of the partnership were represented throughout the structure. The mechanisms of operation and control employed by the partnership were effective and economical. But there were some problems with the operation of this new form of implementing agency. There was a need for the Board to act more as a strategic decision making forum; its decisions were mainly an aggregate of subcommittee recommendations. The role and function of sub-committees needed to be more explicit, as they seemed to perform different tasks within the same structure and general terms of reference. Whilst attendance at meetings by all the partners was generally high, problems were occurring with particular meetings.

Issues

The evaluation of Stratford City Challenge has highlighted some of the dilemmas and contradictions facing policy makers concerned with urban regeneration.

One of the most difficult issues is perhaps the most basic. It is exceedingly difficult to answer the key question: does it work? There are a number of reasons for this. This type of 'small area' regeneration initiative presents substantial problems in assessing its impact. Problems arise from the small area character of City Challenge itself. The area of most City Challenges does not conform to existing administrative boundaries. Thus, even though Census data are disaggregated to the level of enumeration districts (EDs), the Stratford City Challenge area cuts across many of these. It does not conform to wards, police or health districts. All data have therefore to be specially collected. Although, as the City Challenge initiative proceeds, some of the organisations are beginning to work on area-specific data, this is by no means happening everywhere, and the fact that the Census only happens once every ten years presents problems of re-visiting much of the information included in the Baseline Study.

Attributing any change in an indicator directly to City Challenge is also problematical; City Challenge initiatives do not operate in a vacuum, and there are other factors affecting any area. If an indicator in the City Challenge area shows change, it must be looked at in the broader picture, in terms not only of other possible influencing factors, but also in terms of the wider context.

City Challenge initiatives could also cause 'leakage' or 'displacement'; a crime initiative on a City Challenge estate may well push crime levels down, but it could cause the displacement of the problem to an another area outside the city challenge area.

The evaluation of Stratford City Challenge has shown that impacts are likely to take some time to be visible, often beyond the timescale of the project. This means that not only is it difficult to learn from the City Challenge experiment, but it also diverts attention from the longer term, qualitative and potentially more valuable goals. The time-limited and output driven characteristics of City Challenge reinforce this, and tend to focus attention on tangible, measurable outputs. In Stratford City Challenge, individual projects (and the programme as a whole) have sometimes set overambitious targets, driven by these imperatives. It raises the possibility that what gets done by City Challenge is what is possible within the constraints of the programme, not what is needed by the area and its people.

The creation of a new kind of policy-making body driven, in part, by external (ie DoE) agendas creates the potential for conflict with existing bodies and their concerns. The evaluation team of Stratford City Challenge have noted that, at times, the entrepreneurial approach of City Challenge sits uneasily with local authority procedures. It also does not easily accommodate a more time consuming, participative and developmental approach which may be appropriate for the involvement of the wider community. In general in the SDP Board these conflicts have not been significant, but they have been noted by the evaluation team.

Other, potentially more serious, difficulties may arise because of differences between City Challenge and the local authority priorities. City Challenge is concerned with the Stratford area and its residents. The local authority has a wider remit. The issue has arisen in local authority housing allocation policy, which does not permit residents to specify a particular area of choice, jeopardising the City Challenge objective of maintaining the local community. Other similar and obvious problems arise from the legitimate requirements of the local authority in planning procedures, where the timescale sought by City Challenge is difficult to maintain. There is even a possibility that the City Challenge objective to secure local labour agreements may breach EU rules.

One of the main lessons from Stratford City Challenge is that the imposition of new mechanisms for regeneration, however attractive their distinctive characteristics, cannot be done in isolation from the continuing processes of governance of the area. Stratford City Challenge is undoubtedly making a difference in Stratford, but it will be some time before anyone can tell either how much difference or whether it was the right kind of difference, and this is the problem that all thirty-one City Challenges face.

The extent to which other lessons from City Challenge will be learnt is now in doubt. The evaluations of City Challenges being carried out all over the country, as well as at a national level, will certainly help in the judgement of whether any difference has been made and in respect of what. It might also be assumed that the evaluations and the issues they bring to light would be used to inform future urban policy. However, in December 1994, just two and a half years into City Challenge, the government announced the future of urban policy – City Challenge was in the past and the Single Regeneration Budget was born. Several Single Regeneration Budget projects are located in Stratford and its surroundings. The arrival of the SRB and the death of City Challenge mean that lessons from these evaluations cannot be taken on board. The SRB encompasses many characteristics of its predecessor, and many issues arising from the evaluations of City Challenges would be relevant to it, but it came too early for findings from these evaluations to be taken into account and to truly know what were the successes and what were the failures of this type of policy. It remains to be seen whether the SRB will make the same mistakes and encounter the same problems and difficulties as City Challenge.

Notes

[1] Department of Environment, *City Challenge Guidance Note Introduction: Aims and Characteristics*, undated c.1993.
[2] Department of Environment, *Action for Cities News Release*, 23 May 1991.
[3] Department of Environment, *Working Partneerships*, 1992. Department of Environment, *National Evaluation of City Challenge, Annexe A* (project brief), 1994.
[4] *Ibid.*
[5] Department of Environment, *National Evaluation of City Challenge*, Annexe A, 1994.
[6] Department of Environment, *Working Partnerships*, 1992.
[7] Department of Environment, 1991, (*op.cit.*).
[8] J. Friend and A. Hickling, *Planning Under Pressure: the Strategic Choice Approach*, Pergamon Press, Oxford 1987.
[9] P. Lawless, *Britain's inner Cities*, Paul Chapman, London 1989.
[10] Department of Environment, c1993 (*op.cit.*).
[11] Department of Environment, 1991 (*op.cit.*).
[12] *Ibid.*
[13] Department of Environment, 1992 (*op.cit.*).
[14] *Ibid.*
[15] Department of Environment, c.1993, (*op.cit.*).
[16] Department of Environment, 1991, (*op.cit.*).
[17] House of Commons Debate on 'Problems of large towns and cities' (19 July 1977), Hansard Col. 1425, cited in S. Spooner, *The Politics of Partnership*, School of Environment Planning Unit, Polytechnic of Central London, 1980.

[18] *Ibid.*
[19] Department of Environment, 1994 (*op.cit.*).
[20] Department of Environment, c.1993 (*op.cit.*).
[21] Department of Environment, 1994 (*op.cit.*).
[22] Department of Environment, 1991 (*op.cit.*).
[23] Lawless, 1989 (*op.cit.*).
[24] Rob Home, *Inner City Programmes*, Spon, Andover 1982; Lawless, 1989 (*op.cit.*).
[25] Stratford Development Partnership Ltd, *Stratford City Challenge Action Plan*, c. 1992.
[26] *Ibid.*
[27] Department of Environment, 1992 (*op.cit.*).
[28] Stratford Development Partnership Ltd, *Sub-committee Terms of Reference*, 1993a.
[29] Stratford Development Partnership Ltd, *New Articles of Association*, 1993b.
[30] Stratford Community Forum, *Appraisal Form*, 1993.
[31] A. Jiwani, J. Pratt and N. Richards, *Stratford City Challenge Baseline Study*, Centre for Institutional Studies, University of East London, Dagenham 1994.
[32] John Marriot, 'West Ham, London's industrial centre and gateway to the world', *London Journal* 14.
[33] West Ham Borough Council. 'West Ham Development Plan, cited in A. Jiwani *et al.*, 1994 (*op.cit.*).
[34] R. Dennis, 'The Decline of Manufacturing Employment in Greater London 1966–74', *Urban Studies* Vol.15, 1978.
[35] A. Jiwani, *et al.*, 1994 (*op.cit.).*
[36] *London Ecology Unit, Nature Conservation in Newham*, 1991, cited in A. Jiwani *et al.*, 1994 (*op.cit.*).
[37] A. Jiwani, *et al., 1994* (*op.cit.*).
[38] A. Jiwani, R. Fearnley, J. Pratt, G. Gonzalez de Turner and M. Locke, *Stratford City Challenge Evaluation Strategic Objective One, Raising the Profile*, Centre for Institutional Studies, UEL 1995.
[39] R. Fearnley, J. Pratt, G. Gonzalez de Turner and M. Locke, *Stratford City Challenge Evaluation Year Two Six Month Review*, Centre for Institutional Studies, University of East London, Dagenham 1995.
[40] Department of Environment, 1992 (*op.cit.*).

Higher Education and East London: A Case For Social Renewal

David Albury and Carole Snee

A transformed and intellectually innovative higher education can play a vital and pro-active role in social, economic, and personal development in East London, and in the creation of sustainable communities.

The early 1990s have witnessed increasing interest in universities' involvement in urban regeneration and regional economic development. The Committee of Vice-Chancellors and Principals report, *Universities and Communities*,[1] summarised the varying activities of universities and colleges collaboration with local communities and has acted as a powerful stimulus for further development. A number of universities have undertaken local economic impact studies, and each one shows the powerful impact that higher education institutions have on their local labour market and local economy. Nearly every county or region without a higher education institution has plans for a new university or university campus.[2]

The evolving agendas of both higher education and urban regeneration create the ground for new partnerships and possibilities. The recent merger of the Employment Department and the Department for Education bring these agendas closer together, allowing higher education greater involvement with emerging forms of regional government.

The Higher Education Agenda

Higher education is undergoing a process of transformation. A system developed to induct a cultural and occupational elite is, under the pressure of expansion, increasingly stressed and strained. The fundamental structures and practices are breaking down as more and more students are crowded into buildings, with methods of teaching and learning, and regimes of assessment designed for the few rather than the many. Traditional organisational arrangements and forms of accountability are unresponsive to the increasingly varying demands of diverse stakeholders.

Expansion is driven by three interrelated factors. The development of a knowledge-based society is generating demands for a more highly educated workforce and citizenry. The expectations and aspirations of wider sections of the population include participation in higher education. High levels of unemployment encourage individuals and government to use higher and further education as a form of removal from, and possible advantageous entry into, the active labour market.

This expansion has not been accompanied by commensurate increases in state funding. Hence individuals and institutions have sought new, additional sources of support and increasing relevance in the learning and research activities undertaken. Industry and commerce, themselves looking to universities and colleges for skilled employees and assistance in enhancing their knowledge and innovation base, are seen as potential contributors to income and to curricula and research development.

But the expansion is not just a question of more of the same. The nature of the student population has changed radically. In the 1960s the overwhelming majority of students were white, middle class, male 18–21 year-olds with 'A' level qualifications undertaking full-time, undergraduate programmes on a residential basis. Today, ethnic minorities are more heavily represented in higher education than in society generally. The number of students from working-class backgrounds has increased much faster than that for the middle class, though the participation rates are still considerably lower.[3] Almost half of all students are female. Mature students are a large proportion of those in higher education, particularly in inner city universities. Part-time, access and postgraduate programmes have proliferated. And the qualification base has diversified with changes in school and college education and the growth of adult returners.

Many of these developments in the nature of the student population, combined with a decline in the availability and level of student maintenance support, are producing a more regionalised student market. This trend towards the regionalisation of higher education, reinforced by the desire for closer industrial linkages, is promoted further by the increasing importance of funding from the Government's Single Regeneration Budget and European Union programmes allocated on a sub-national, regional basis, both requiring universities to form partnerships with companies, communities, agencies and authorities in their locality.

The commitment of many universities to serving their regions is strengthened by the practical considerations of increasing revenue, enhancing relevance and bolstering recruitment.

The Regeneration Agenda

The changing nature of the economy, the decline and deprivation of inner cities and adjacent areas, and the associated social and cultural tensions and disorders have, over the last two decades, prompted increasing political and academic concern with issues of urban regeneration.

The revitalisation of decaying areas is multi-faceted. The attracting of inward investment, the stimulation of new economic activities, and the rebuilding of public services require the availability of a differently and more highly skilled workforce, a modernised transport and technological infrastructure, and appropriately prepared and serviced development sites.

This range of factors necessitates a partnership approach to urban regeneration. No single government department, company, organisation, agency or authority can implement an effective development programme, though key institutions and enterprises can, through inertia or specific actions, for example to relocate out of an area, block or destabilise plans for regeneration. Regeneration is therefore dependent on the construction of alliances and coalitions between parties with differing agendas and dominant concerns. Successful regeneration requires the development of a unifying vision which articulates the needs and aspirations of the institutions and individuals concerned.

In recent years local authorities, local and regional development agencies, and some government departments have begun to pay attention to the role higher education can play in the regeneration of areas of economic and social decline. The decline of the UK manufacturing base has left many old industrial towns with high unemployment, empty buildings and derelict land. Higher education has been one of the few growth points in the economy, and some of that growth has brought back into use derelict land and buildings.

Universities are major local employers, often among the biggest employers in an area, and significant purchasers of local services. In collaboration with schools, colleges and other education and training providers, they can provide routes and opportunities for skilling and reskilling. Through the transfer of technology and information, they can stimulate innovation. Through the sharing of resources and facilities, they can enhance economic and cultural development. And through their very presence they can symbolise hopes and dreams for the future.

The Specificities of East London

East London is the site of the largest urban development project in western Europe – London Docklands. As several chapters in this book describe, East London is scarred by multiple deprivation. The transfer of dock and port activity to the estuary of the Thames in the 1960s, the relocation of key industries out of the area, and the decline of employment in the car industry have left wastelands and devastation across vast swathes. The resulting high levels of unemployment and corrosion of housing, health and the environment have exacerbated social and racial tensions and fostered the informal economic activities which have characterised the area over many years.

What is to become of East London, what is to be its future, have, for the last twenty years, been key questions for local and national politicians. In the 1970s, when the full impact of deindustrialisation on the area was yet to be realised outside of the area, responses were highly localised. The political left bemoaned the loss of jobs, the break-up of the traditional East End community (a continuing powerful mythology), and the lack of government investment. The right criticised the dependency culture, low achievement in labour controlled schools, and the administration of decline by left councils.

Community activists grew out of redundant trade unions and the plethora of voluntary associations across East London. Community Development Projects, often drawing on the support of staff from the local universities and polytechnics, sponsored and encouraged a range of relatively small-scale employment, housing and environmental initiatives.

Building on some of these initiatives, and fostered by a radical Greater London Council, attempts were made in the late 1970s and early 1980s to generate a 'popular planning' framework for development of, or at least developments in, East London. A mosaic of ideas emerged, centring on the creation of co-operatives which would utilise the redundant skills of the local workforce in forms of organisation which would reflect past and present collectivities – both real and imagined.

This period coincided with a major intensification of racial conflict and racial attacks in East London. It should be noted, however, that the focus of deindustrialisation in East London – the docks and immediately surrounding areas – was different from the site of the murders of and assaults on members of the Asian, predominantly Bangladeshi, community. But in the national consciousness East London was just one place: a place of disorder, increasingly apparent devastation, and the potential for radical dissent.

In 1981, the Conservative government, or more particularly Michael Heseltine, established the London Docklands Development Corporation as an agency of the Department of the Environment. Regulatory, or rather deregulatory, planning and acquisition powers were vested in the LDDC and the representation of local authorities and local people was strictly limited. In opposition to the ideas of small-scale, industrial co-operative development, a new and different vision was promulgated. Local activists organised through the Joint Docklands Action Group and the Docklands Forum and were ranged against the LDDC from which they were both marginalised and excluded themselves.

The Thatcher government's commitment to increasing home ownership, its predilection for services as the engine of economic growth, and its particular fiscal and monetary policies, fuelled and encouraged the property boom of the 1980s. This boom was felt nowhere more acutely than in the City of London itself where constrictions of space and the pressures of explosive growth in financial services produced a property crisis of escalating rents and lack of room for expansion. The dream of London Docklands reborn as 'Wall Street on the Water' began. Investment poured in, particularly to the Isle of Dogs. New homes were built, but many were behind electronically controlled gates and patrolled by private security firms. New jobs appeared in marble monuments but the workers commuted in, clogging up inadequate local roads and transport systems.

The new industries being attracted to Docklands required highly skilled, technology literate labour, and the local populations were largely unskilled or inappropriately skilled. Local unemployment rates continued to be above the London average. Apart from supplying low level clerical and administrative staff, a small number of mainly white, young traders and dealers – with skills honed in the market and informal entrepreneurial cultures of East London, and a limited range of catering, cleaning and support services, the local population was relatively excluded. A new city was to be created in the heart of Docklands, fed by new transport systems, but isolated from the surrounding communities. A developmental dualism was in place: high-tech, skill intensive modern service sector activities mixed with high income refurbished and new housing situated a stone's throw from social and economic deprivation and traditional industrial practices.

Although the legacy of the dream lives on, and Canary Wharf and the gentrification of much riverside accommodation are its testaments, the vision of a new financial district died with the collapse of the property market, taking with it the single largest developer in Docklands – Olympia and York. What has emerged is a more diverse set of developments. Much of Fleet Street, ironically always reliant on East London labour, together with other parts of the new media industries, has relocated there. Some large financial institutions and corporate head offices have moved in. And a range of smaller activities, attracted by the lax planning regulations and significant subsidies and grants, have been set up. Retail, leisure and community services are starting to be established and the network of road and rail developments is making the area more accessible.

The end of the residential property boom exacerbated tensions between the LDDC and local people as those who were homeless or occupying poor quality housing could see an increasing volume of empty new housing. Partly as a response to criticism, partly out of mounting recognition of these tensions, and partly as a result of growing evidence of the importance of social and cultural infrastructural development for economic, commercial and residential regeneration, the local authorities and the LDDC began to work more in partnership.

This brief and condensed history of recent attempts at the regeneration of London Docklands and East London reveals an unhelpful opposition between the preservation of the old skills and traditions – a sort of radical heritage approach – with the risks of lack of viability in a modern economy, and the imposition of the new with the dangers, real and potential, of the exclusion of substantial sections of the existing population.

Education, including higher education, can help fracture this opposition, not just by providing the opportunities for local people to acquire the skills required by the new industries and activities but also by working with them to develop the capacities, individually and collectively, that will enable them to participate in the economic and cultural regeneration of East London. This is the ground on which proposals for a new university campus in London Docklands linked to a Science and Technology Park were forged, but in an area with traditionally low expectations of education, especially of higher education. The assumption often made by teachers and local education authorities that East London working-class children were not capable of benefiting from higher education made its own negative contribution to educational outcomes.

But whilst the Jewish, Chinese and Asian communities saw education as a route out of poverty, the white, male working-class culture was largely focused on employment organised through strong trades unions where education took place essentially 'on the job'. Higher education was frequently inattentive to the cultures and needs of the local population and was unlikely, of itself, to improve radically its members' life chances. We now turn, therefore, to the local demand for higher education before discussing the nature of the higher education that is now needed.

Expectation and Participation

East London has some of the lowest higher education participation rates of any area in the country. In part contributing to this, in part reflecting this, it also has a very low qualification base. But changes are taking place. Developments in local schools and colleges to meet the needs of local children, demographic changes, and shifting patterns of aspiration are combining to increase staying-on rates and improving GCSE, 'A' level, and NVQ/GNVQ results.

East London has a higher percentage of 5–15 year olds and is projected to have a faster rate of growth in its total population than Greater London as a whole. Traditionally there has been a very low take up of post-compulsory education in East London with young men leaving to work in the docks or to be apprenticed in the local motor or engineering industries, and young women going to work in lower skilled service industries or as secretaries. Although the economic base which underpinned these patterns has long since disappeared cultural expectations are slow to change.

A recent report from the Policy Studies Institute found a positive link between ethnicity and staying on rates, and other studies suggest that ethnic minority pupils in inner city areas gain better exam results than their white counterparts. The 1994 GCSE results in Newham seemed to confirm these findings with students from Indian, Pakistani and other Asian backgrounds doing significantly better than the average for the borough. These ethnic minority groups are those most likely for cultural reasons to want their children to go to a local university. In these groups, girls out-perform boys with 39.1 per cent of Indian and 35.1 per cent of Pakistani girls achieving 5 or more A–C grades at GCSE, compared with 27.3 per cent and 22.9 per cent for boys.

National higher education participation rates also suggest greater demand from black and ethnic minority students as in 1993/94 approximately 13 per cent of home undergraduates whose ethnicity was recorded were non-white, whereas black and ethnic minorities represent 8 per cent of the 16-22 year old UK population.

Black and ethnic minority communities are a larger proportion of the population in East London than in most of the rest of London and the UK. Newham has 42.3 per cent, Tower Hamlets 35.6 per cent, and Waltham Forest 25.6 per cent, compared with a Greater London average of 20 per cent. Also the London ethnic minority population shows a different age structure to the white population with a far higher percentage aged under five. Nationally 45 per cent of the Pakistani and Bangladeshi community is aged under fifteen, compared to 19 per cent of the white population.

Not only is demand in East London for higher education places growing, that demand is characterised by being 'local'. Income levels, ethnicity and gender, student grant provision, the need for 'lifelong learning', and local patterns of higher education recruitment, all point to a need for expanded provision within an East London travel to study area.

A New Higher Education

But what sort of higher education?

All higher education institutions are marked by the temporal and geographic conditions of their origins. Those in East London are no exception. Queen Mary and Westfield College's commitment to the locality was rooted in the merger of two colleges: Queen Mary College was built in 1887 as the People's Palace for the education and recreation of East End dwellers, and Westfield College pioneered higher education for women in the late nineteenth century. London Guildhall University, the former City of London Polytechnic, has several main subject areas reflecting the economy of its surroundings, including furniture design, manufacture and restoration, jewellery and silversmith, financial services and law, and, dating back to the polytechnic's beginnings as a nautical college, specialised courses related to transport. City University has a distinctive place in meeting the higher education needs of the professions and enterprises strongly represented in the City of London, including business studies, journalism, and informatics. And the University of East London, formed as a Polytechnic out of a number of regional colleges of technology, developed programmes linked closely to the needs of the engineering and pharmaceutical industries.

Times change, as does the geography of the area. The provision of higher education in East London needs to develop in recognition of the new conditions of its existence.

Skills and employment

As has been indicated above, the sets of skills required for employment in the new and emerging industries and activities in East London are very different from those which have in the past been locally available and utilised. If large sections of the population are not to be marginalised and disenfranchised, if local people are to have access to satisfying and well-paid employment, relevant education and training have to be designed and delivered.

The growth areas for employment are, in the main, in professional, managerial and technical occupations involving higher level skills, and in sectors – media and publishing, financial and business services, IT – which are knowledge-intensive.

Higher education's contribution to the development of the local skills base should have three major components. Firstly, new generations of young adults need to acquire a foundation of competences and capabilities that allow them to gain employment and to acquire new skills and knowledge as organisations and technologies change – learning to learn. Secondly, those currently unemployed, employed in declining sectors, or wishing to return to the labour market, need opportunities for retraining. And, thirdly, linkages with those in work are required to create environments and programmes in which skills and knowledge can be continually updated – lifelong learning.

'Education' and 'training' are frequently seen as in conflict. Employers have labour needs, especially at the non-managerial levels, which lead many of them to press for relatively job-specific, all too often, task-specific training – a reflection of the endemic British disease of 'short-termism'. Such training has the advantage for the trainee of increasing their chances of employment but leaves them 'redundant' when the job or task is restructured or labour market conditions change. On the other hand, 'education' provides a base of skills, competences and knowledge which can, provided the education is of high quality, equip the student with the capability of learning to learn and to transfer skills from one environment to another but at the cost of their being less specifically for any particular job.

Education, as opposed to training, responds to employers' demands for 'flexibility'.

Citizenship and participation

Higher education, however, is much more than vocational education and training. It offers the possibility of individuals developing their understanding of the societies within which they live and work. As is clear from this chapter and many others in this book, East London is undergoing rapid changes, as global forces impact upon the local economy and culture. For students and their communities to understand these contradictory and contested pressures, to be able to participate in the shaping of their region, and to become active citizens, requires critical exploration of the drivers and inhibitors of change.

Good quality vocational education may provide employment possibilities, but, of itself, it will not aid local populations in fashioning their destiny.

Between the task and capability requirements of industrial and commercial enterprises and the engagement in public and political life, lies the important area of public services. For more than a century, East London has been the subject of sometime benign, sometime not, radical social intervention from the outside; indeed, the LDDC could be seen as merely the latest of such interventions. The vast majority of managers of public and social services have been imported; occupational immigrants from more affluent and middle-class areas have moulded the provision for communities rooted in immigration from Eastern Europe, Asia, Africa and the Caribbean and for the communities built around the docks, engineering and other traditional industries.

Higher education can play a key role in the encouragement and formation of a local cadre of health, housing, education and social service professionals. However unless that work is part of a wider regeneration strategy to provide decent housing and quality of life for local people then education may simply become a route out of the ghetto.

Access and accessibility

Much work has already been done, though much remains to do, to improve the access of local people to higher education. Working with other education and training providers, local universities and colleges have created specific and general access programmes, targeted particular communities, and developed mentoring programmes which provide role models and support. A framework of ladders and bridges of educational opportunities, linking progression academically with progression through the labour market – from base skills to PhDs – is slowly emerging whereby students can step into and out of education with a sense of achievement rather than failure.

Opening doors to existing provision is, however, only one element of accessibility. Really to widen access and maintain effectiveness it is necessary to develop provision – to design new curricula and new forms of delivery – which meets the needs of a broader and diverse learner population. Courses and programmes, to be successful, have to develop the expectations and aspirations of the learners and address and build on their real and lived experiences. Marketing what already exists has to be complemented by establishing close linkages with the residential and employer communities to involve them in the shaping and determination of the learning on offer.[4]

Universities and colleges are large and formidable institutions. The structure and buildings create barriers to access, not just for the physically disabled. A step into education through an evening class at a local community centre is far easier than an entry through the intimidating portals of a higher education institution. Outreach and distance education, electronically and personally, can deliver opportunities in settings in which those fearful or anxious can feel more comfortable. Opening up the facilities of the university – including libraries, computers, laboratories, studios, childcare and sports halls – to community use can encourage familiarity and integrate higher education into the social fabric of the area. And co-locating educational and non-educational activities – community health services with faculties of health studies, cinemas and recording studios with media and cultural studies departments, technology arcades with IT courses, start-up business units with schools of engineering – encourages customers to become students, consumers to be trained as producers. Higher education would thus seem no longer something 'out there' beyond people's experience or expectations.

Research
Research activity is an essential component of a vital and vigorous higher education. The economic and cultural redevelopment of a region and its changing national and international position both require and stimulate the need for world-class research activity.

Most areas of research potentially have much to offer to and much to gain from linkage to the region. Social and economic research can elucidate and inform the processes of redevelopment; scientific, engineering and technological research can promote innovation; historical and cultural research can assist in the creation of new identities and services; and business research can assist new enterprises and organisations.

Through the areas of research selected, through the education and training programmes offered, and through the facilities available, higher education plays not just a reactive, responsive role in regeneration, but a pro-active and shaping role. The types of industry attracted to the area, the patterns of inward investment, are influenced by the nature of higher education.

By engagement as full partners in the process of regeneration, higher education institutions can contribute to the personal and intellectual development of individuals and to the determination of what an area is to become. Universities and colleges are local and global institutions, seeking new knowledge from global sources which can enrich and extend the frontiers of their localities.

Making it Happen

The struggle over the direction and objectives of regeneration involve a struggle over the nature and culture of higher education.

By the late 1980s, the LDDC and the local authorities had come to realise the importance of higher education for the development of Docklands and East London. In keeping, however, with the attempt to construct a 'Wall Street on the Water', attention was focused on trying to lure an existing, appropriate high status university or college to relocate – LSE and the London Business School were courted – or to create an MIT-type institution. Had this been successful, it would have reinforced the financial and corporate dominance of the area and, undoubtedly, further excluded and marginalised the local population.

Simultaneously, the University (then Polytechnic) of East London began to consider seriously its relationship with the Docklands developments. An institution with firm roots in its locality but whose industrial and academic base had been eroded over the years, it lacked a distinctive educational mission. The authors of this article, together with others, began to develop a strategy for the Polytechnic's pro-active participation in the regeneration of East London and argue that a new mission could be created through a re-working of the Polytechnic's local and regional commitment – a re-invention of its tradition – in the light of the redevelopment of the area.

To capture a sense of the moment and the possibilities, it is worth quoting at some length from the first document, written in June 1990, to put forward this argument.

> What should a higher education institution do about a development the size and importance of Docklands? How can a Polytechnic contribute to, and benefit from, the 'economic and social regeneration' of its locality?
>
> London Docklands is the largest redevelopment scheme in Western Europe. Millions of square feet of office space are being constructed, hundreds of thousands of jobs are being established, tens of thousands of homes are being built and refurbished and hundreds of social, cultural and educational schemes are being proposed. It is the 'jewel in the crown' of the present government's urban policy.
>
> It is vital to appreciate the scale of this development in order to understand the scale of the proposals which will interest the major organisations involved.
>
> Equally it is necessary to be cautious of the hype which surrounds the marketing and selling of London Docklands. Many of the plans are highly speculative in nature and very dependent on the state of the commercial, retail and residential property markets and hence on the vagaries of the financial system as a whole. In addition many of the schemes face fierce opposition, not only from local communities and some sections of local authorities, but also from rival commercial developments, professional organisations and, indeed, dissident voices within LDDC.
>
> This paper makes a number of major proposals for initiatives which the Polytechnic could undertake and which would benefit the Polytechnic and contribute to the social and economic regeneration of London Docklands and surrounding areas. The proposals have been drawn up in the light of three major inputs: information from, and discussions with, employers, local authorities, members of LDDC, academic analysts, developers and management consultants; interviews with heads of departments in the Polytechnic; the burgeoning research, consultancy and press literature on London Docklands....

> The development of London Docklands has already had a considerable effect on much of East London. The effects in the future may amount to something of a transformation. The industrial and occupational structure, the class, ethnic, age and educational profile of the population, the technological base, the transport infrastructure, in short, the economy and culture of the area surrounding the Polytechnic is undergoing significant change. The Polytechnic will have to adapt to new notions of 'local employers', 'local students' and the needs of the local and regional community. But equally it will need to reinforce its commitment to those currently disadvantaged and the existing residential communities.[5]

These arguments met two major resistances both internally and externally. The dominant vision for Docklands in scale and in nature ran counter to the ethos and principles of the Polytechnic. A Polytechnic recently released from direct local authority control and aspiring to be a national player was fearful of a localism that could easily be seen as parochialism.

As has been discussed above, regeneration is a process shaped by alliances and coalitions, a struggle for competing visions of communities and futures. To achieve such an alliance, the LDDC's and the local authorities' public statements of intent to improve the conditions for the local population were articulated with a more radical view of what higher education could offer. Thus an educational-regeneration alliance was forged around a high quality, community-oriented proposal for a new campus in London Docklands. This alliance included key individuals in the institutions, agencies and authorities, community organisations, leading politicians, academics and educationalists.

A critical moment in the debate on what sort of higher education would be appropriate for Docklands came in 1992 when the LDDC commissioned Coopers & Lybrand to examine the feasibility of establishing a higher education institution in London Docklands. Their report concluded that it was feasible and that there would be significant education and community benefit. Perhaps surprisingly, and in part through the effectiveness of the inputs to the study, Coopers & Lybrand recommended the 'community' rather than the 'high status' option, with the proviso that this should be realised through a consortium of existing local higher education institutions rather than a single institution.

The University of East London initiated the East London Higher Education Consortium drawing in London Guildhall University,

Queen Mary and Westfield College, and City University. Each of the partner institutions has differing strengths ranging from blue sky research excellence, technology transfer expertise, extensive industry links, strong access and guidance, and innovative support structures and programmes for non-traditional higher education entrants.

Academics are used to cross-institutional collaboration at the level of scholarship, but there are few examples of universities working together to jointly deliver new provision, particularly across the old binary divide. From the beginning the inter- and intra-university discussion stressed complementarity not competition with existing provision. Those involved in developing the Consortium recognised that for some staff in the old universities there would be worries about a negative impact on academic reputation and research ratings, whilst for the former polytechnics there would be worries about junior status often engendered by a sense of inferiority. In order for such diverse institutions to work together it was crucial to have a clearly stated agenda and purpose, a clear understanding of each others needs and aspirations, and a mutually agreed vision for the project.

The partners developed proposals for the Royals University College, a new College in London's Royal Docks with a specific mission to contribute to the economic, cultural, and social regeneration of East London and the sub-region by promoting business competitiveness, contributing to wealth creation, and providing a quality teaching, learning and research environment. Its very existence would be a potent symbol of education as a force for regeneration. The curriculum offer would be shaped by the skills needs of existing and newly emerging business sectors, and the education needs of existing and newly developing communities in the region.

The Consortium joined forces with the key regeneration agencies within the area – London Docklands Development Corporation, Newham Council, and London East Training and Enterprise Council – to form the Royals University College Partnership. The Partnership's vision is of an open and accessible higher education, with the university college as the centre of a network of learning activity in homes, offices, schools and community centres. A college which is part of its local community, and physically and electronically accessible to local people and local and regional business, but also part of a global academic community. That vision has won the support of community groups in the area, representatives of the business community, MPs, the London Thames Gateway group of local authorities, and the pan-London group London First. Winning that support has been a time consuming but crucial process. The Royals University College will only succeed if all those with a stake in transforming East London also believe that they have a stake in its newest higher education institution.[6]

Struggles for visions are, however, rarely decisively won or lost. Beliefs remain current that only an elite can benefit from higher education, that only technological and business education is of value, that the economic gains of redevelopment trickle down unaided to the general population, and that higher education should stand aloof from the realities of regeneration.

These forces, both within and without higher education, continue to press and mould the plans for the new college in contest with other visions and other forces. New settlements, new compromises, new alliances are reached.

But the struggle over visions also involve struggles over realisation. Having visions and plans requires finance and support and whilst the higher education and regeneration agendas overlap, they are different agendas. All too easily plans for the university college may be seen only in terms of its contribution to regeneration, or may slip back to traditional conceptions of the content and organisation of academic life. But the sharing of facilities, the construction of a common agenda between public and private sector partners, can provide a platform for larger educational opportunities and a greater return on investment for participating organisations.

To be progressive and to be successful, such plans need to command the support of diverse groups and interests. They need to be consonant with the objectives of chief executives of universities, of companies, of agencies and authorities, and of leaders of communities. And they need to capture, at least in part, the expectations and aspirations of staff in these organisations and of members of these communities.

The model of higher education being proposed for the University College in Docklands is market responsive, not market driven: a twenty-first century version of the nineteenth century concept of 'really useful knowledge' producing the entrepreneurial graduate capable of growing the market, contributing to wealth creation and social progress, but also able to interrogate critically the object of study and the process in which they are engaged.

London Docklands and East London, one of the most challenging areas for regeneration, offers the challenge to higher education to renew itself. It is only a new and different, a genuinely popular and democratic, higher education that can address the needs of the range of social partners involved in the economic and cultural redevelopment of East London.

Notes

[1] John Goddard *et al*, *Universities and Communities*, Committee of Vice-Chancellors and Principals, London 1994.
[2] Including Suffolk, Lincolnshire, south-west England/Cornwall, Swindon/ Wiltshire, the Lake District, and the Highlands and Islands.
[3] John Authers, 'Student Intake Widens', *Financial Times*, 2 May 1995.
[4] For example, fashion design and business courses, and their associated research activities, could be developed to include consideration of the needs, expansion and modernisation of the Asian clothing industries in East London.
[5] David Albury with Sara Bowman, 'Scale and Hype – The Development of London Docklands and the Polytechnic of East London – A Co-ordinated Strategy', June 1990.
[6] It is interesting to note that, of all the proposed developments in London Docklands, the proposal for the Royals University College enjoys the widest cross-party political and community support.

Footnote: Since this chapter was written the proposed Royals University College has received substantial financial backing, which will allow the turning of the vision into reality.

Notes on Contributors

David Albury is a Fellow in Organizational Development with the Office for Public Management. His research and management experience includes issues of higher education and urban regeneration, beginning with a period (1990-92) as Dean of Educational Development at the then Polytechnic of East London.

Andrew Blake teaches Cultural Studies at the University of East London. He is the author of *Reading Victorian Fiction* and *The Music Business* (1992). A saxophonist, he has often performed in East London.

Alice Bloch is a lecturer in the Department of Sociology at the University of East London. Recent publications include: *Refugees and migrants in Newham: access to services* (1994) and *Access to benefits: the information needs of minority ethnic groups* (1993). Her current work is concerned with the employment and training needs of refugees in Newham.

Tim Butler is a Principal Lecturer in Sociology at the University of East London. He is the co-editor of *Social Change and the Middle Classes* (1995) and is the author of a forthcoming book on gentrification, *Gentrification and the Middle Classes*.

Greg Clark has worked as an adviser to the University of East London on European Community funding and is currently a postgraduate student in the United States. Previously he worked for local authorities on European funding initiatives.

Phil Cohen is Senior Research Fellow in the Faculty of Social Sciences where he directs the New Ethnicities Unit. His early work on youth cultures was based on the east end and is included in a forthcoming collection *Rethinking the Youth Question – Education, Labour and Cultural Studies* (1996). He is currently directing an ESRC funded study into young people's perceptions of community safety and racial danger in two areas of docklands.

Notes on Contributors

Rebecca Fearnley is Research Fellow at the Centre for Institutional Studies. Her main work is on the evaluation of Stratford City Challenge, although she also works on other projects including the evaluation of the Single Regeneration Budget programme, New Dimensions for Stratford and Temple Mills.

Martin Hoyles is the author of *The Politics of Childhood* (1989) and *The Story of Gardening* (1991). He has written two studies of gardening books: the first volume, *Gardeners' Delight* came out in 1994 and the second volume, *Bread and Roses*, was published in 1995.

Bruce Jerram works in the Centre of Institutional Studies at the University of East London. He has worked on evaluating the Stratford City Challenge urban regeneration project and has presented a paper to the annual meeting of the British Sociological Association on London Police Stations and the Control of Space. He is currently undertaking a mapping and site survey of the Thames Gateway boroughs for an East London tourism survey.

Deborah Jones is a Research Assistant in the Department of Sociology working with Margaret O'Brien on the study of family and kinship in Barking and Dagenham. Previously she was a PhD student in the Geography Department at Queen Mary and Westfield College.

John Marriot is Senior Lecturer in the Department of Cultural Studies, with research interests in the political culture of East London, particularly during the nineteenth and twentieth centuries. He is the author of *The Culture of Labourism: East London Between the Wars* (1991).

Margaret O'Brien is Principal Lecturer in the Department of Sociology at the University of East London. She is directing the project on family and kinship in Barking and Dagenham which is funded by the University. Forthcoming publications include *Children in Families: Research and Policy* (1996) and, co-edited with Julia Brannen, *Fatherhood, Children and Society* (1996).

Gavin Poynter was a full-time trade union officer before joining the University of East London in 1989. Current research interests include industrial restructuring and change in contemporary workplace relations.

NOTES ON CONTRIBUTORS

John Pratt is Professor of Institutional Studies at the University of East London. As head of the University's Centre for Institutional Studies he has overall responsibility for the Centre's research on urban regeneration in East London including the evaluation of Stratford City Challenge.

Bill Riseboro was a professional architect and town planner for twenty-five years. He now teaches architecture and urban studies at the University of East London. He is the author of *The Story of Western Architecture* (1979), *Modern Architecture and Design: an Alternative History* (1982) and *Fantastic Form: Architecture and Planning Today* (1992).

Vikki Rix is a Research Assistant in the Department of Sociology at the University of East London working on Census data sources on East London. She is the joint author with Prue Chamberlayne and Michael Rustin of a book on European societies to be published in 1996.

Michael Rustin is Professor of Sociology and Dean of the Faculty of Social Sciences at the University of East London. He has been co-ordinating the University's work with LETEC on the economic regeneration of East London. He is one of the founding editors of the new journal *Soundings* and is the author of *The Good Society and the Inner World* (1989).

Greg Smith has lived and worked in the churches and community of Newham for two decades. He is employed as research officer by Aston Charities Community Involvement Unit. His main academic interests are religion, ethnicity, community work, urban poverty, and voluntary sector networks. He is an Honorary Research Fellow in the Department of Sociology at the University of East London.

Carole Snee is Head of the Docklands and Thames Gateway Regeneration Office at the University of East London with responsibility for the university's strategic involvement in the economic and social regeneration of its region. Her previous work experience includes local and community development in the public and not-for-profit sectors.

Richard Wells is Faculty Administrator of the Faculty of Social Sciences at the University of East London and is currently undertaking research into the potential for tourism and leisure development in East London. He has worked as a museum director and co-edited and contributed to *Freud and Art* (1990).

Anna Whyatt has worked in the field of economic and industrial development and in top management in the public sector since 1976. She is currently Senior Research Fellow at both the South Bank University and the University of East London, working with pan-London institutions in the private and public sector on development of the London economy. She was previously Chief Executive of Southwark from 1985 to 1994.

Bibliography

Action for Cities (White Paper), HMSO, London, 1988.

ACUPA – Archbishop's Commission on Urban Priority Areas, *Faith in the City*, Church Information Office, London 1985.

Adult Literacy and Basic Skills Unit, *A Nation's Neglect: Research into the needs of Disordered Times*, London, 1989.

J. Agnew and J.S. Duncan, *The Power of Place*, Unwin Hyman, London 1989.

J. Agyeman, 'The Multicultural City Ecosystem', *Streetwise*, Number 7, Summer 1991.

G. Ahern, 'Cockneys and Clergy Speak', in G. Ahern and G. Davie, *Inner City God*, Hodder & Stoughton, London 1987.

P. Allatt and S. Yeandle, *Youth Unemployment and the Family: Voices of Disordered Times*, Routledge, London 1992.

A. Amherst, (Evelyn Cecil), *London Parks and Gardens*, Archibald Constable, 1907.

A. Amin (ed), *Post-Fordism: A Reader*, Blackwell, Oxford 1994.

A. Amin and N. Thrift (eds), *Globalisation, Institutions and Regional Development in Europe*, Oxford University Press, Oxford 1994.

Annual Abstracts of Statistics, Number 130, HMSO, London 1994.

B. Anderson, *Imagined Communities*, Verso, London 1983.

A. Appadurai, 'Disjuncture and difference in global economy', *Culture and Society* 7, 1987.

J. Archer and I. Yarham, *Nature Conservation in Newham*, London Ecology Unit, London 1991.

J. Ashdown, *Guide to Ethnic Christianity in London*, Zebra Project, London 1993.

A. Atkin, E. Cameron, F. Badger, and H. Evers, 'Asian elders' knowledge and future use of community social and health services', *New Community* 14 (2), April 1989.

J. Atkinson, 'Flexibility:Planning for an Uncertain Future', The IMS Review Volume 1, Institute for Manpower Studies, Brighton 1985.

R. Atkinson and G. Moon, *Urban Policy in Britain*, Macmillan, London 1994.

Audit Commission, *Urban Regeneration and Economic Development:the local government dimension*, HMSO, London 1989.

J. Authers, 'Student Intake Widens', *Financial Times*, 2 May 1995.

L. Back, *New Ethnicities and Urban Cultures*, ULL Press, 1995.

B. Badcock, 'Notwithstanding the exaggerated claims, residential revitalization really is changing the form of some western cities: a response to Bourne', *Urban Studies* 30, 1993.

B. Badcock, 'Adelaide's heart transplant, 1970–88: 3, The deployment of capital in the renovation and redevelopment submarkets', *Environment and Planning A* 24, 1992.

P. Bailey (ed), *Music Hall: the Business of Pleasure*, Open University Press, Buckingham 1989.

BIBLIOGRAPHY

P. Ballard, *An Oasis of Delight, The History of The Birmingham Botanical Gardens*, Duckworth, London 1983.

S. Balloch, *Refugees in the Inner City: A study of refugees and service provision in the London Borough of Lewisham*, Centre for Inner City Studies, Goldsmiths College, University of London, London 1993.

S. Banerji and G. Baumann, 'Bhangra 1984-8', in P. Oliver (ed), *Black Music in Britain*, Open University Press, Buckingham 1990, pp137–152.

J. Barrell, *The Infections of De Quincey*, Yale, Massachusetts 1991.

G. Bataille, *Visions of Excess*, Oxford University Press, Oxford 1989.

Z. Bauman, *Memories of Class*, Routledge, London 1991.

U. Beck, *Risk Society*, Sage Publications, London 1992.

I. Begg and A. Whyatt, *The economic development of London in the context of national policy priorities: conceptual, institutional and practical issues*, on C. Demaziare and P. Wilson (eds), *Le Developpement Economique Local en Europe*, Am Criques, Paris 1995.

J. Bell, *Ugandan Refugees: A study of housing conditions and the circumstances of children*, Community Development Foundation, London 1993.

J. Bell and L. Clinton, *The Unheard Community: A look at housing conditions and needs of refugees from Vietnam living in London*, Refugee Action, Derby 1993.

H. Beynon, *Working For Fords*, Allen Lane, Harmondsworth 1973.

U. Bjornberg (ed), *European Parents in the 1990s: Contradictions and Comparisons*, Transaction, New Brunswick 1992.

A. Blake, 'Re-Placing British Music', in M. Nava and A. O'Shea (eds), *Modern Times: Reflections on the Experience of Modernity in Britain*, Routledge, London 1995.

A. Blake, *The Music Business*, Batsford, London 1992.

A. Bloch, *Refugees and Migrants in Newham: Access to Services*, London Borough of Newham, London 1994, p15.

A. Bloch, 'Improving access to benefits for minority ethnic groups, *Benefits*, Issue 9, January 1994.

A. Bloch, *Access to Benefits: the information needs of minority ethnic groups*, Policy Studies Institute, London 1993.

E. Bloch, *Selected Essays*, Cambridge University Press, Massachusetts 1988.

P. Blyton and P. Turnbull (eds), *Reassessing Human Resource Management*, Sage, London 1992.

M. Boddy, J. Lovering and K. Bassett, *Sunbelt City? A Study of Change in Britain's M4 Growth Corridor*, Clarendon Press, Oxford 1986.

L. Bondi, 'Gender divisions and gentrification: a critique', *Transactions of the Institute of British Geographers*, N.S. 16, 1991, pp190–8.

C. Booth, *Lives and Labour of the People of London*, (seventeen volumes), 1902.

J. Bourke, *Working Class Cultures 1880–1960*, Routledge, London 1994.

L. Bourne, 'Close together and worlds apart: an analysis of changes in the ecology of income in Canadian cities', *Urban Studies* 30, 1993a, pp1293–1317.

L. Bourne, 'The demise of gentrification? A commentary and prospective view', *Urban Geography* 14, 1993, pp95–107.

J. Brannen, K. Dodd, A. Oakley and P. Storey, *Young People, Health and*

Family Life, Open University Press, Buckingham 1994.
J. Bratton (ed), *Music Hall: Performance and Style*, Open University Press, Buckingham 1990.
K. Breault, 'New Evidence on Religious Pluralism, Urbanism and Religious Participation', in *American Sociological Review*, Volume 54, 1989.
P. Brierley, *Prospects for the Nineties: trends and tables from 1989 Census of Churches in England* (especially Volume on Greater London including commentary by Smith G.), MARC Europe, 1991.
P. Brierley and V. Hiscock, *UK Christian Handbook 1994/95* edition, Christian Research Association/Evangelical Alliance, 1993.
D. Buckingham (ed), *Beyond Radical Pedagogy*, Taylor and Francis, London 1996.
T. Bunder, *The Real East End*, Allen and Unwin, London 1953.
J. Bush, *Behind the Lines*, Merlin Press, London 1984.
T. Butler, *People Like Us: Gentrification and the Service Class in Hackney in the 1980s*, Unpublished PhD Thesis, The Open University, Milton Keynes 1992.
T. Butler, 'Gentrification and the urban middle classes', in *Social Change and the Middle Classes*, T. Butler and M. Savage (eds), University College of London Press, London 1995.
T. Butler and M. Savage (eds), *Social Change and the Middle Classes*, University College of London Press, London 1995.
T. Butler and C. Hamnett, 'Gentrification, class and gender: some comments on Warde's "gentrification of consumption" ', *Environment and Planning D: Society and Space* 12, 1994, pp477–493.
B. Campbell, *Goliath – Britain's Dangerous Places*, Methuen, London 1993.
Canning Town Community, *Canning Town's Declining Community Income: The Cost of Industrial Closures 1966–76*, Canning Town Community Publications, London 1979.
M. Carnoy, M. Castells, S. Cohen and F. Cardoso, *The New Global Economy in the Information Age*, Pennsylvania State University Press, Pennsylvania 1993.
M. Castells, *The Informational City*, Blackwell, Oxford 1989.
Central Statistical Office, *Social Trends*, Volume 19, HMSO, London 1989.
Central Statistical Office, *Social Trends*, Number 24, HMSO, London 1989.
G.F. Chadwick, *The Park and the Town*, Architectural Press, London 1966.
E.B. Chancellor, *The Pleasure Haunts of London*, Constable, London 1925.
F. Clark, 'Nineteenth Century Public Parks from 1830', *Garden History*, Volume 1, Number 3, 1973.
S. Clarke, *Jah Music*, Heinemann, London 1980.
P. Close, *Citizenship, Europe and Change*, Macmillan, Basingstoke 1995.
P. Cohen, *Stopping the Wheels*, Macmillan, Basingstoke 1995.
P. Cohen, *Home Rules*, UEL Monograph, 1994.
P. Cohen, 'The other East', *Demos* 16, 1995.
P. Cohen, 'Backbone of the nation, race apart', Docklands Forum 20th Anniversary Lecture Series, 1995.
P. Cohen, *Island Stories*, Runnymede Trust, London 1996.
R. Cohen, *Frontiers of Identity*, Longman, New York 1994.
T. Cole, *Life and Labour on the Isle of Dogs*, Unpub PhD, 1987.

N. Cole, 'The Royal Parks and Gardens of London', *Journal of Horticulture Office*, London 1877.
H. Conway & D. Lambert, *Public Prospects: Historic Urban Parks under Threat*, The Garden History Society and the Victorian Society, 1993.
H. Conway, 'The Manchester/Salford Parks: their design and development', *Journal of Garden History*, Volume 5, Number 3, 1977.
H. Conway, *People's Parks: The Design and Development of Victorian Parks in Britain*, Cambridge University Press, Cambridge 1991.
J. Cornwell, *Hard-Earned Lives: Accounts of Health and Illness from East London*, Tavistock, London 1984.
G. Coster, 'Multicultural Gardening', the *Independent on Sunday*, 26 September 1993.
G. Cranz, 'Women in Urban Parks', in Catharine R. Stimpson *et al, Women and the American City*, University of Chicago Press 1980–1.
M. Cross, 'Race and ethnicity', Chapter 8 in A. Thornley (ed), *The Crisis of London*, Routledge, London 1992.
D. Crouch, and C. Ward, *The Allotment: Its Landscape and Culture*, Faber & Faber 1988; Mushroom edn, Nottingham 1994.
J.S. Curl, 'John Claudius Loudon and the Garden Cemetery Movement' *Garden History*, Volume 11, Number 2, 1983.
R. Currie, A. Gilbert and L. Horsley, *Churches & Church Goers: Patterns of Church Growth in the British Isles since 1700*, Clarendon Press, Oxford 1977.
D. Curson, B. Britton, and M. Game, *Nature Conservation in Barking and Dagenham*, London Ecology Unit, London 1992.
R. Cybriwsky, D. Ley and J. Western, 'The political and social reconstruction of revitalized neighbourhoods: Society Hill, Philadelphia, and False Creek, Vancouver', in *Gentrification of the City*, N. Smith and P. Williams (eds), Allen & Unwin, Boston 1986, pp92–120.
R. Dahrendorf, *Class and Class Conflict in an Industrial Society*, Routledge and Kegan Paul, London 1959.
S. Daniels, *The Paint House*, Penguin, Harmondsworth 1977.
G. Davie, *Religion in Britain since 1945: Believing Without Belonging*, Blackwell, Oxford 1984.
M. Davis, *City of Quartz*, Verso, London 1990.
D. Deacon and P. Golding, *The Information Needs of Voluntary and Community Groups*, University of Leicester, Centre for Mass Communication Research, Leicester 1988.
D. Defoe, *A Tour Through England and Wales*, Everyman Edition, Volume 1, p9, 1927.
R. Dennis, 'The decline in manufacturing employment in Greater London 1966–74', *Urban Studies* 15, 1978, quoted in Jiwani *et al* 1994.
Department of the Environment, *City Challenge Guidance Note Introduction: Aims and Characteristics, c.*1992.
Department of the Environment, *Working Partnerships*, 1992.
Department of the Environment, *National Evaluation of City Challenge*, 1994.
Department of the Environment, *Action for Cities News Release*, 23 May 1991.
Department of Health, *The Patients' Charter*, HMSO, London 1991.

BIBLIOGRAPHY

Docklands Forum, *Once Upon a Time in Docklands*, London 1994.
Docklands Forum, *Race and Housing*, London 1993.
J. Eade, *Local/Global Relations in a London Borough*, Roehampton 1994.
J. Eade, *Politics of Community*, Avebury, Aldershot 1989.
T. Elger and C. Smith (eds), *Global Japanisation*, Routledge, London 1994.
G. Elliott, *Labourism and the English Genius: The Strange Death of Labour England*, Verso, London 1993.
F. Engels, *The Conditions of the Working Class in England*, 1845; Panther edn 1969.
N.D Epstein, 'The Social Explorer as Anthropologist', in H.J. Dyos (ed), *The Victorian City*, Routledge, London 1985.
R.A. Etlin, 'Père Lachaise and the Garden Cemetery', *Journal of Garden History*, Volume 4, Number 3, 1984.
S. Fainstein, I. Gordon and M. Harloe, *Divided Cities: New York and London in the Contemporary World*, Blackwell, Oxford 1992.
R. Fearnley, J. Pratt, G. Gonzalez de Turner, B. Jerram, and M. Locke, *Stratford City Challenge Evaluation, Year Two Six Month Review*, Centre for Institutional Studies, University of East London, 1995.
A. Fein, 'Victoria Park: Its Origins and History', *East London Papers*, Volume V, Number 2, 1962.
D. Feldman and G. Steadman Jones, *Metropolis*, Routledge, London 1991.
M. Fernandez Kelly, 'Towards Triumph: Social and Cultural Capital in the Transition to Adulthood' in *Journal of Urban and Regional Research*, Volume 18, Number 1, 1994, pp88–111.
R. Finke and R. Stark, 'Religious Economies and Sacred Canopies: Religious Mobilisation in American Cities 1906', in *American Sociological Review*, Volume 53, 1988.
W. Fishman, *The Streets of East London*, Gerald Duckworth and Company Limited, London 1979.
K. Fleet, *A Manual for Blind Gardeners*, RNIB 1978.
R. Forrest and D. Gordon, *People and Places: a 1991 census atlas of England*, School of Advanced Urban Studies, Bristol 1993.
J. Foster, *Living with Docklands Redevelopment*, London Journal 17 (2), 1992.
K. Frank, 'A Feminist Approach to Architecture', in Ellen Perry Berkeley, (ed), *Architecture: A Place for Women*, Smithsonian Institution, Washington 1989.
J. Friend and A. Hickling, *Planning Under Pressure – The Strategic Choice Approach*, Permagon Press, Oxford 1987.
P. Fryer, *Staying Power*, Pluto, London 1984.
D. Gale, 'Middle-class resettlement in older urban neighbourhoods: the evidence and implications', *Journal of the American Planning Association* 45, 1979, pp293–304.
J. Gambell, *Welcome to the UK*, NACAB, London 1993.
H. Gammel, A. Ndahiro, N. Nicholas, and J. Windsor, *Refugees (Political Asylum Seekers): Service Provision and Access to the NHS*, College of Health, London 1993.
P. Garrahan and P. Stewart, *The Nissan Enigma*, Mansell, London 1992.
C. Geertz, *Local Knowledge*, Basic, New York 1983.

B.Gilbert, *The Green London Way*, Lawrence and Wishart, London 1991.
N. Gilbert, R. Burrows and A. Pollert (eds), *Fordism and Flexibility, Divisions and Change*, Macmillan, London 1992.
J. Gillespie, 'Poplarism and Proletarianism: Unemployment and Labour Politics in London, 1918–34', in David Feldman and Gareth Stedman Jones (eds), *Metropolis: London Histories and Representations since 1800*, Routledge, London 1989.
S. Gilman, *Degeneration*, Columbia, New York 1985.
P. Gilroy, *The Black Atlantic*, Verso, London 1993.
P. Gilroy, *There Ain't no Black in the Union Jack*, Hutchinson, London 1989.
R. Glass, *Introduction to London: Aspects of Change*, Centre for Urban Studies, London 1963.
J. Goddard *et al*, *Universities and Communities*, Committee of Vice-Chancellors and Principals, London 1994.
D. Goldberg, *Racist Culture*, Blackwell, Oxford 1993.
H. Goldin, *East End My Cradle*, Heinemann, London 1937.
J. Goldthorpe, 'On the service class, its formation and future', in *Social Class and the Division of Labour: Essays in Honour of Ilya Neustadt*, A. Giddens and G. Mackenzie (eds), Cambridge University Press, Cambridge 1982, pp162–184.
A. Goodwin, 'Sample and Hold: Pop Music in the Age of Digital Reproduction', in S. Frith and A. Goodwin (eds), *On Record*, Routledge, London 1990.
P. Graves, *Labour Women: Women in British Working-class Politics, 1918–1939*, Cambridge University Press, Cambridge 1994.
A. Greely, Religion in Britain, Ireland and the USA, in R. Jowell *et al, British Social Attitudes:* the 9th Report, SCPR, London 1982.
L. Green, *Music on Deaf Ears*, Manchester University Press, Manchester 1988.
R. Greenslade, *Goodbye to the Working Class*, Marion Boyars, London 1976.
S. Griffiths, *Poverty on your Doorstep: London Borough of Newham Poverty Profile*, London Borough of Newham, London 1994.
P. Hall, *London 2001*, Unwin Hyman, London 1989.
P. Hall, *The World Cities*, Weidenfeld and Nicolson, London 1966.
S. Hall, 'The local and the global', in A.D. King (ed), *Culture, Globalisation and the World System*, Macmillan, London 1991.
C. Hamnett, 'Social polarization in global cities: theory and evidence', *Urban Studies* 31, 1994.
C. Hamnett, and P. Williams, 'Social change in London: a study of gentrification', *Urban Affairs Quarterly* 15, 1980, pp469–487.
C. Hamnett, 'Gentrification and residential location theory: a review and assessment', in *Geography and the Urban Environment: Progress in Research and Applications* Volume VI, D. Herbert and R. Johnston (eds), Wiley, London 1984, pp283 319.
C. Hamnett and W. Randolph, 'The changing tenure structure of the Greater London housing market 1961–81', *The London Journal* 2, 1983.
C. Hamnett, 'London's Turning', *Marxism Today*, July 1990, pp26–31.
C. Hamnett and W. Randolph, 'Labour market restructuring in Greater London, 1971–81: evidence from the Longitudinal Study', *City University Social Statistics Research Unit Working Paper*, 44, 1986.

P. Harrison, *Inside the Inner City: Life under the Cutting Edge*, Penguin, Harmondsworth 1983.
J. Hart, 'The Religious Life of London 1903', from *EUTP*, PO Box 83, Liverpool L69 8AN, 1988.
D. Harvey, *The Condition of Postmodernity*, Basil Blackwell, Oxford 1989.
D. Harvey, 'Flexible Accumulation through Urbanisation: Reflections on Post-modernism in the American City', in A. Amin, *Post-Fordism: A Reader*, Blackwell 1994.
V. Hausner and B. Robson, *Changing Cities: An Introduction to the Eccnomic and Social Research Council Inner Cities Research Programme*, ESRC, London 1985.
C. Hayes, N. Fonda and J. Hillman, *Learning in the New Millenium*, London National Commission on Education, London 1995.
A. Heath, R. Jowell and J. Curtice (eds), *Labour's Last Chance? The 1992 election and beyond*, Aldershot, Dartmouth 1994.
Healy & Baker, *European Real Estate Monitor*, 1993.
D. Hebdige, *Subculture: the Meaning of Style*, Methuen, Londo, 1979.
D. Hebdige, *Hiding in the Light*, Comedia, London 1988.
D. Hebdige, *Cut'n'Mix: Culture, Identity and Caribbean Music*, Methuen, London 1987.
J. Hein, *States and International Migration: The incorporation of Indochinese Refugees in the United States and France*, Westview Press, Boulder, Colorado 1993.
J. Henderson, *The Globalisation of High Technology Production*, Routledge, London 1991.
C. Hill, *Renewal in the Inner City*, Methodist Home Mission Dept, London 1976.
HMSO, 'Asylum Statistics United Kingdom 1992', *Home Office Statistical Bulletin*, HMSO, London 1993, p7.
HMSO, *The Outdoor Classroom*, Building Bulletin No.71, 1990.
D. Hobbs, *Doing The Business: Entrepreneurship, the Working Class and Detectives in East London*, Oxford University Press, Oxford 1989.
R. Hoggart, *The Uses of Literacy*, Penguin, Harmondsworth 1957.
A. Holme, *Housing and Young Families in East London*, Routledge and Kegan Paul, London 1985.
C. Holmes, *John Bull's Island – Immigration and British Society 1871–1971*, Macmillan, Basingstoke 1988.
R.K. Home, *Inner City Regeneration*, Spon, London 1982.
E. Hostettler, *An Outline History of the Isle of Dogs*, Island History Trust, London 1991.
House of Commons Debate on 'Problems of Large Towns and Cities', cited in S. Spooner, *The Politics of Partnership*, School of Environment Planning Unit, Polytechnic of Central London, 1980.
E. Howes, *The Population of Hackney: Research Note 1*, London Borough of Hackney, London 1980.
E. Howes, *1981 Census for Hackney: Ward Profiles: Research Note 6*, London Borough of Hackney, London 1983.
M. Hoyles, *The Story of Gardening*, Journeyman Pluto, London 1991.
A. Humphries, *Travels in a Poor Man's Country*, CUP, Cambridge 1989.

C. Husbands, 'East End Racism 1900–1980', *London Journal* 8, 1982.
Islington Refugee Working Party, *Refugee Questionnaire Survey*, London 1992.
ICIHI, *Refugees: Dynamics of Displacement*, Zed Books, London 1986, p33.
F. Jameson, *The Cultural Logic of Late Capitalism*, Verso, London 1991.
A. Jiwani, J. Pratt, and N. Richards, *Stratford City Challenge Baseline Study*, Centre for Institutional Studies, University of East London, 1994.
A. Jiwani, R. Fearnley, J. Pratt, G. Conzalez de Turner and M. Locke, *Stratford City Chellenge Evaluation Strategic Objective One, Raising the Profile*, Centre for Institutional Studies, University of East London, 1995.
M.R.D. Johnson, 'Religious Observance in the West Midlands', in *Ethnic and Racial Studies* Volume 8 Number 3, July 1985.
J. Johnston, *Nature Areas for City People*, London Ecology Unit, London 1990.
D. Joly, C. Nettleton, and H. Poulton, *Refugees: Asylum in Europe*, Minority Rights Publications, London 1992.
D. Joly and R. Cohen (eds), *Reluctant Hosts: Europe and its Refugees*, Avebury, Aldershot 1989.
S. Jones, *Black Culture, White Youth*, Macmillan, London 1989.
T. Jones, *Britain s Ethnic Minorities*, Policy Studies Institute, London 1993.
G. Karmi (ed), *Refugees and the National Health Service*, The Health and Ethnicity Programme, North West and North East Thames Regional Health Authority, London 1992.
P. Kasinitz, 'The gentrification of "Boerum Hill": neighbourhood change and conflicts over definitions'. *Qualitative Sociology* 11, 1986, pp161–182.
P.J. Keating, 'Fact and Fiction in the East End', in H.J. Dyos, *The Victorian City*, Routledge, London 1985.
E. Kemp, *The Parks, Gardens, Etc., of London and Its Suburbs*, John Weale 1851.
Key Local Authority Statistics, HMSO, London 1993.
K. Kiernan, *Social backgrounds and post-birth experiences of young parents*, Social Policy Research 80, Joseph Rowntree Foundation, July 1995.
P. Kirkham, *Furnishing the World: the East End Furniture Trade 1830–1980*, Journeyman Press, London 1987.
K. Knott and S. Khoker, *Religious and Ethnic Identity Among Young Women in Bradford*, in New Community 19(4) July 1993.
M. Kohn, *Dope Girls: The Birth of the British Drug Underground*, Lawrence & Wishart, London 1994.
LETEC, *London East Quarterly Labour Market Review*, October 1994.
LPAC Advice Working Papers, *The Economy*, Volume 1, 1994.
LPAC, *Economic Scenarios for Central London*, London 1993.
LPAC, *London: World City*, HMSO, London 1994.
LPAC, *Strategic Planning Guidance to Local Authorities*, HMSO, London 1994.
C. Larkin, (ed), *The Guinness Who's Who of Rap, Dance and Techno*, Guinness Publishing, London 1994.
S. Lasdun, *The English Park: Royal, Private and Public*, Andre Deutsch, London 1991.

A. Lam, *Notes from the Street*, Camerawork, London 1995.
M. Law, *Urban Tourism*, Mansell, London 1994.
P. Lawless, *Britain's Inner Cities*, Paul Chapman, London 1989.
Le Corbusier, trans. Frederick Etchells, *Towards a New Architecture*, Architectural press, London 1946.
L. Lees, 'Gentrification in London and New York: An Atlantic Gap?' *Housing Studies* 9, 1994.
R. Legates, and C. Hartman, 'The anatomy of displacement in the United States', in *Gentrification of the City*, N. Smith and P. Williams (eds), Allen and Unwin, Boston 1986.
D. Ley, 'Gentrification and the politics of the new class', *Environment and Planning D: Society and Space* 12, 1994, pp53–74.
D. Ley, 'Liberal ideology and the postindustrial city', *Annals of the Association of American Geographers* 70, 1980 pp238–258.
G. Lipsitz, *Dangerous Crossroads: Popular Music, Postmodernism and the Poetics of Place*, Verso, London 1994.
G. Loescher, *Beyond Charity: International Co-operation and the Global Refugee Crisis*, Oxford University Press, Oxford 1993.
London Borough of Barking and Dagenham, *Barking and Dagenham Borough Profile*, London Borough of Barking and Dagenham, 1993.
London Borough of Newham, *West Ham 1886–1986*, Plaistow Press, Newham 1986.
London Borough of Hackney, *Borough Profile*, London Borough of Hackney, London 1982.
London Docklands Development Corporation, *Development Frameworks for the Isle of Dogs, Limehouse and Leamouth*, LDDC, London 1994.
London East Training and Enterprise Council, *Labour Market Assessment 1993–4*, LETEC, London 1994.
London Pride Partnership, *The London Pride Prospectus*, London 1994.
London Research Centre, *London Housing Statistics*, London Research Centre, London 1992.
London Research Centre, *Population Change in London 1981–1991*, London Research Centre, London 1993.
London Research Centre, *London Statistics*, HMSO, London 1995.
London School Leavers' Destinations Survey, The Careers Service in London, 1994.
J. Loudon, *On the Laying Out, Planting and Managing of Cemeteries and on the Improvement of Churchyards*, A. Spottiswoode for the Author 1843; Ivelet Books, 1981.
J.C. Loudon, *The Derby Arboretum*, Longman, Orme, Brown, Green and Longmans, 1840.
B. Lucas, 'Strapped for Space', *Managing Schools Today* Volume 3, Number 1, September 1993.
D. Lyon, *The Steeple's Shadow*, Third Way/SPCK books, London 1985.
J. Major, *The Theory and Practice of Landscape Gardening*, Longman, Brown, Green and Longmans, 1852.
C. Marchant, 'Religion', in *A Marsh and a Gas Works; One Hundred Years of Life in West Ham*, W.E.A./Newham Parents Centre Publications, 745 Barking Road London E13 9ER, 1986.

C. Marchant, The Inter-relationship of Church and Society in a London Borough, unpublished PhD. Thesis London School of Economics, 1974.

C. Marchant, *Signs in the City*, Hodder, London 1985.

P. Marcuse, 'Abandonment, gentrification and displacement: the linkages in New York City', in *Gentrification of the City*, N. Smith and P. Williams (eds), Allen and Unwin, Boston, Massachusetts 1986.

P. Marcuse, ' "Dual city': muddy metaphor for a quartered city', *International Journal of Urban and Regional Research* 13, 1989.

J. Marriott, 'Sensation of the abyss – the urban poor and modernity', in M. Nava and A. O'Shea (eds), *Modern Times: The British Experience of Modernity*, Routledge, London 1995.

J. Marriott, 'West Ham, London's Industrial Centre and Gateway to the World' II; Stabilisation and decline 1910–1939, *The London Journal* Volume 14, Number 1, 1989.

P. Marris, *Meaning and Action: Community Planning and Conceptions of Change*, Routledge and Kegan Paul, London 1987.

D. Martin, *A General Theory of Secularisation*, Basil Blackwell, Oxford 1978.

D. Massey, *Space, Place and Gender*, Polity, Cambridge 1994.

D. Massey, *Docklands, a Microcosm of Trends*, Docklands Forum, London 1994.

S. Masters, 'Underworld', *The Lizard*, Summer 1995, pp30–33.

S. Mayo, *Stories from the Island Docklands*, Dyelines, London 1994.

I. McAuley, *Guide to Ethnic London*, Immel Publishing Ltd, London 1993.

H. McCleod, *Class and Religion in the Late Victorian City*, Croom Helm, London 1974.

E. McFarland, M. Dalton, and D. Walsh, 'Ethnic minority needs and service delivery: the barriers to access in a Glasgow inner city area', *New Community*, 15 (3), April 1989.

A. McKenzie, *The Parks, Open Spaces and Thoroughfares of London*, Waterlow and Sons, 1869.

R. McKibbin, *The Evolution of the Labour Party, 1910–24*, Oxford University Press, Oxford 1974.

D. Metcalf, *Water Notes Dry Up, Discussion Paper 314*, London School of Economics, LSE, London 1988.

R. Miles and A. Phizacklea, *Labour and Racism*, Routledge, London 1983.

G. Morgan, 'Local Culture and Politics in Docklands', Environment and Planning D *Society and Space* 11, 1993.

G. Mulgan, and K. Worpole, 'Alien Life in Open Space', *The Guardian*, 17 November 1994.

C.S. Murray, *Crosstown Traffic: Jimi Hendrix and Post-War Pop*, Faber, London 1989.

T. Nairn, 'The nature of the Labour Party', in New Left Review (ed), *Toward Socialism*, Fontana, London 1965.

M. Nava and A. O'Shea (eds), *Modern Times: The British Experience of Modernity*, Routledge, London 1995.

Newham Directory of Religious Groups 2nd Edition (1994) available for £5 from Aston Community Involvement Unit.

Newham History Workshop/Workers Education Association, *A Marsh and A Gasworks: One Hundred Years of Life in West Ham*, Newham Parents

Centre, London 1986.
C. Neveu, 'Espace et Territoire Spitalfield', *Habitations 23*, 1991.
D. Nicholson-Lord, 'The Once-Glorious Municipal Park Languishes on Death Row', the *Independent*, 29 August 1993.
M. O'Brien, 'Changing Conceptions of Fatherhood', In U. Bjornberg (ed), *European Parents in the 1990s: Contradictions and Comparisons*, Transaction Publications, New Brunswick 1992.
J. Obelkvich and P. Catterall, *Understanding Post-War British Society*, Routledge, London 1994.
OECD, *Managing Urban Change: Policies and Finance*, OECD, Paris 1983.
OECD, *Economic Surveys*, United Kingdom, 1994.
M. Oechsle and R. Zoll 'Young People and Their Ideas on Parenthood', in U. Bjornberg (ed), *European Parents in the 1990s: Contradictions and Comparisons*, Transaction Publications, New Brunswick 1992.
J.K. Oliver, Christian Lay learning in an East London Community, unpublished MA dissertation in Youth and Community Work at Faculty of Education and Design, Brunel University, 1992.
P. Oliver (ed), *Black Music in Britain*, Open University Press, Buckingham 1990.
N. Oliver and B. Wilkinson, *The Japanisation of British Industry – New Developments in the 1990s*, Blackwell, Oxford 1992.
OPCs, *1991 Census*, HMSO, Crown Copyright, London.
OPCS, *Classification of Occupations 1980*, HMSO, London 1980.
OPCS, *Census 1981 County Report: London* part 1, HMSO, London 1982a.
OPCS, 'Hackney: Small Area Statistics', *User Guide* 51, Titchfield: OPCS, 1982b.
OPCS, *Census 1981 County Report: London* part 2. HMSO, London 1983.
D. Owen, 'Spatial variations in ethnic minority group populations in Great Britain', *Population Trends* 78, Winter 1994, HMSO, London 1994.
A. Palmer, *The East End*, John Murray, London 1989.
J. Parker, 'Cities', *The Economist*, London 1995.
L. Passerini, *Fascism and Popular Memory*, Cambridge University Press, Cambridge 1987.
R. Penn, M. Rose and M. Rubery, *Skill and Occupational Change*, Oxford University Press, Oxford 1994.
W. Pettigrew, *Municipal Parks*, Journal of Parks Administration, London 1937.
N. Pevsner, *An Outline of European Architecture*, Penguin, Harmondsworth 1943.
C. Pharoah, and E. Redmond, 'Care for ethnic elders', *The Health Service Journal*, 16 May 1992.
B. Pimlott and C. Cook (eds), *Trade Unions in British Politics*, Longman, Harlow 1991.
M. Piore and C. Sabel, *The New Industrial Divide*, Basic Books, New York 1984.
Policy Studies Institute, *Review of Advice Services in Leicester*, Leicester City Council, Leicester 1993.
A. Pollert (ed), *Farewell to Flexibility?*, Blackwell, Oxford 1991.

R. Porter, *A Social History of London*, Hamish Hamilton, London 1994.
G. Poynter, *Wall Street on the Water: Employment Patterns in London Docklands*, South East Region TUC, mimeo, London 1989.
C. Poulsen, *Victoria Park*, Journeyman, London 1976.
S. Pryce, 'Community Action', *Surveyor* 168, 23 July 1987.
J. Ranciere, *Nights of Labour*, Wesleyan, 1991.
A. Rattansi, *On the Western Front*, Polity, London 1994.
A. Rattansi *et al*, *Race, Culture, Difference*, Sage, London 1991.
Refugee Council, 'Careers Guidance – when and where it is needed', *Exile*, November 1992, London.
Refugee Council, 'Santuary on the streets', *Exile*, September 1992, London.
Regional Trends 30, Central Statistical Office, HMSO, London 1995.
T. Renton, 'Refugees: the Responsibilities of the UK Government , Chapter 3 in V. Robinson (ed), *The International Refugee Crisis: British and Canadian Responses*, Macmillan, Basingstoke 1993.
D. Riesman, *The Lonely Crowd*, Heinemann, London 1974.
M. Robbins, *The North London Railway*, The Oakwood Press, London 1953.
W. Robinson, *The Wild Garden*, Century, London 1983.
H. Rolfe, *Careers Guidance and the Employment, Training or Educational Needs of Young Unemployed People in Lambeth*, Policy Studies Institute, London 1993.
N. Rowson, and P.R. Thoday, *Landscape Design for Disabled People in Public Open Space*, University of Bath, 1985.
The Runnymede Trust, *Neither Unique nor Typical*, Runnymede Trust, London 1994.
C. Sadler, 'Women's voices', *Nursing Times*, Volume 88 Number 29, 15 July 1992.
F. Sainsbury (ed), *West Ham 1886–1986*, London Borough of Newham, 1986.
Y. Samad, 'Book Burning and Race Relations: Political Mobilisation of Bradford Muslims', in *New Community* 18 (4) July 1992.
R. Samuel, *East End Underworld*, Routledge, London 1981.
S. Sassen, *The Global City: New York, London, Tokyo*, Princeton University Press, Chichester 1991.
S. Sassen, S.Fainstein and M. Harlow (eds), *Divided Cities: New York and London in the Contemporary World*, Blackwell, Oxford 1992.
S. Sassen, *Cities in a World Economy*, Pine Forge Press, Thousand Oaks, CA. 1994.
M. Savage, J. Barlow, P. Dickens, and A. Fielding, *Property, Bureaucracy and Culture: Middle Class Formation in Contemporary Britain* Routledge, London 1992.
M. Savage and T. Fielding, 'Class formation and regional development: the "service class" in south-east England', *Geoforum* 20, 1989.
M. Savage, 'The missing link? The relationship between spatial mobility and social mobility', *The British Journal of Sociology* 39, 1988.
H.V. Savitch, *Post-Industrial Cities: Politics and Planning in New York, Paris and London*, Princeton University Press, Chichester 1988.
B. Schwarz, 'Where Horses Shit a Hundred Sparrows Feed: Docklands and East London During the Thatcher Years', in J. Harvey and S. Corner (eds), *Enterprise and Heritage*, Routledge, London 1991.

P. Selman and C. Glendinning, 'Teenage Pregnancies: Do Social Policies make a difference?', in J. Brannen and M. O'Brien (eds), *Children and Families: Research and Policy*, The Falmer Press, London 1996.
R. Sennett, *The Conscience of the Eye*, Faber, London 1991.
R. Sennett, *Flesh and Stone*, Faber, London 1994.
R. Sennett, *The Uses of Disorder*, Faber, London 1971.
J. Sexby, *The Municipal Parks, Gardens and Open Spaces of London*, Elliott Stock, 1898.
D. Sheppard, *Built as a City*, Hodder, Sevenoaks 1975.
M. Shoard, *This Land is Our Land*, Paladin, London 1987.
I. Shotter and K. Geiger, *Texts of Identity*, Sage, London 1989.
M. Simo, *London and the Landscape*, Yale University Press, 1988.
A. Sivanandan, *Communities of Resistance: Writings on Black Struggles for Socialism*, Verso, London 1990.
D.N. Smith, *The Railway and its Passengers*, David and Charles, Devon 1988.
S. Smith, *'Race' and the Politics of Residence*, Polity, London 1989.
G. Smith, 'God's in E7', *Evangelical Coalition for Urban Mission*, British Church Growth Association, 1986.
G. Smith, '(Almost) All You Could Ever Want To Know; Newham in the 1991 Census, Implications for Community Work', in *Newham Needs and Responses: CIU Annual for 1994*, Aston Community Involvement Unit, 1994.
G. Smith, *West Ham Parish Survey Report*, Aston Community Involvement Unit, 1992.
G. Smith, 'Evangelicals and Liberation Theology', from *Christian Urban Resource Unit*, University of Bradford, 1989.
G. Smith, *Inner City Christianity; Some Sociological Issues*, MARC monograph series, Number 17, 1988.
G. Smith and D. Driscoll, *Evangelical Coalition for Urban Mission*, West Ham Christians, 1985.
N. Smith, B. Duncan and L. Reid, *Disinvestment, reinvestment and the economic frontier line in gentrifying neighbourhoods*, Paper presented to the Housing Policy and Innovation Conference, Amsterdam, June 1988.
N. Smith, 'Towards a theory of gentrification: a back to the city movement by capital not people', *American Planning Association Journal* 45, 1979.
C. Smith, *Parks and Pleasure Grounds*, Reeve and Co, 1852.
G. Smith and D. Driscoll, *Document submitted to Archbishops Commission*, West Ham Church Life Survey, 1984.
E. Soja, *Postmodern Geographies*, Verso, London 1989.
W. Sollors, *The Invention of Ethnicity*, Oxford University Press, Oxford 1989.
P. Stallybrass and A. White, *The Politics and Poetics of Transgression*, Methuen, London 1986.
G. Stedman Jones, *Outcast London, A Study of Relationships Between Classes in Victorian Society*, Penguin, Harmondsworth 1984.
G. Stedman Jones, *Languages of Trust*, Routledge, London 1989.
B.N. Stein, 'The refugee experience: defining the parameters of a field of study', *International Migration Review*, Volume 15, Number 1, 1981.
On black musics and cultural hybridity, see G. Stephens, 'Interracial Dialogue

in Rap Music', *New Formations*, Spring 1992.
Stratford Development Partnership Ltd, *New Articles of Association*, 1993.
Stratford Development Partnership Ltd, *Sub-committee Terms of Reference*, 1993.
Stratford Development Partnership Ltd, *Stratford City Challenge Action Plan*, *c.*1992.
J. Street, 'Local Differences? Popular Music and the Local State', *Popular Music*, Volume 12, Number 1, 1993.
D. Tanner, *Political Change and the Labour Party, 1900–1918*, Cambridge University Press, Cambridge 1990.
A. Teague, 'Ethnic group: first results from the 1991 Census', *Population Trends*, Summer 72, HMSO, London 1993.
The City Research Project, *London's Contribution to the UK Economy*, 1993.
The Great Eastern Railway Society, *Return to North Woolwich*, PEMT Enterprises Ltd, 1987.
The Thames Gateway Planning Framework, HMSO, London 1994.
W. Thompson, *The Long Death of British Labourism: Interpreting a Political Culture*, Pluto, London 1993.
P. Thompson (ed), *Myths we Live*, Routledge, London 1990.
P. Thompson, *Socialists, Liberals and Labour; the Struggle for London, 1887–1914*, Routledge, London 1967.
P. Thompson, 'Family Myth, Models and Denials in the Shaping of Individual Life Paths', in D. Bertaux and P. Thompson (eds), *Between Generations: Family Models, Myths and Memories*, Oxford University Press, Oxford 1993.
A. Thornley (ed), *The Crisis of London*, Routledge, London 1992.
W. Titman, *Special Places, Special People*, World Wildlife Fund, 1994.
T. Turner, 'John Claudius Loudon and the Inception of the Public Park', *Landscape Design*, November 1982.
W. Turrill, *The Royal Botanic Gardens*, Kew, Herbert Jenkins, 1959.
A. Tweedie, *Hyde Park, Its History and Romance*, Eveleigh Nash, 1908.
J. Urry, *The Tourist Gaze*, Sage, London 1990.
A. Upton and P. Thoday, *A Bibliography of Horticulture and Out-Door Amenities for the Handicapped and Disadvantaged*, Department of Horticulture, University of Bath 1980.
J. Vidal, 'Parks: Who Needs Them?' *The Guardian*, 1 July 1994.
W.T. Vincent, *Records of Woolwich District*, Volume 2, J.S. Virtue and Co. Ltd, London 1890.
G. Vulliamy and E. Lee (eds), *Pop, Rock and Ethnic Music in Schools*, Cambridge University Press, Cambridge 1982.
H. Walker (1896), *East London: Sketches of Christian Work and Workers*, republished in 1987 by Peter Marcan Books, High Wycombe 1987.
J. Walkovitz, *City of Dreadful Delight*, Virago, London 1992.
C. Wallace, *For Richer, For Poorer*, Tavistock, London 1987.
D. Waller, *Town, City and Nation*, Manchester University Press, Manchester 1991.
A. Warde, 'Gentrification as consumption: issues of class and gender', *Environment and Planning D: Society and Space* 9, 1991.

P. Watherston, *A Different Kind of Church: the Mayflower Family Centre Story*, Marshall Pickering, London 1994.
B. Whitaker and K. Browne, *Parks for People*, Winchester Press, 1971.
E. Wickham, *Church and People in an Industrial City*, Lutterworth, 1957.
D. Widgery, *Some Lives: A GP's East End*, Simon & Schuster, London 1991.
K. Williams *et al*, *Against Lean Production*, Economy and Society 21, 3.
P. Williams, 'The role of institutions in the inner London housing market: the case of Islington', *Transactions of the Institute of British Geographers* N.S. 1, 1976.
P. Willmott, *The Evolution of A Community: A Study of Dagenham after Forty Years*, Routledge and Kegan Paul, Hammersmith 1963.
P. Willmott, *Adolescent Boys of East*, Penguin, Harmondsworth 1966.
P. Willmott and M. Young, 'Social Class and Geography', in *London: Urban Patterns, Problems and Policies*, Heinemann, London 1973.
E. Wilson, *The Sphinx in the City*, Virago, London 1991.
Wolfenden, *The Future of Voluntary Organisations*, Croom Helm, 1978.
J. Womack, D. Jones and D. Roos, *The Machine That Changed the World*, Harper, New York 1991.
J. Woodward, *Industrial Organisation, Theory and Practice*, Oxford University Press, Oxford 1965.
P. Wright, *A Journey Through the Ruins: the Last Days of London*, Radius, London 1991.
W. Wroth, *The London Pleasure Gardens of the Eighteenth Century*, Macmillan, London 1896.
M. Young and P. Willmott, *Family and Kinship in East London*, Pelican, London 1962.
K. Young, *Tale Worlds and Story Realities*, Martinus Nyhof, The Hague 1992.
S. Zukin, 'Gentrification: culture and capital in the urban core', *Annual Review of Sociology* 13, 1987.
S. Zukin, *Loft Living: Culture and Capital in Urban Change*, Radius, London 1988.

